Unconventional Methodology in Organization and Management Research

Unconventional Methodology in Organization and Management Research

Edited by

Alan Bryman and David A. Buchanan

OXFORD
UNIVERSITY PRESS

OXFORD

UNIVERSITY PRESS

Great Clarendon Street, Oxford, OX2 6DP,
United Kingdom

Oxford University Press is a department of the University of Oxford.
It furthers the University's objective of excellence in research, scholarship,
and education by publishing worldwide. Oxford is a registered trade mark of
Oxford University Press in the UK and in certain other countries

First Edition published in 2018
Impression: 1

Published in the United States of America by Oxford University Press
198 Madison Avenue, New York, NY 10016, United States of America

British Library Cataloguing in Publication Data
Data available

Library of Congress Control Number: 2017950304

ISBN 978-0-19-879697-8 (hbk.)
      978-0-19-879698-5 (pbk.)

Printed and bound by
CPI Group (UK) Ltd, Croydon, CR0 4YY

Dedicated to the memory of Alan Bryman, 1947—2017

'At present there are strong institutional forces pushing scholars towards publishing safe, conventional papers, which rarely advance methodological thinking or generate major theoretical advances. Unconventional Methodology in Organization and Management Research is a welcome call for pluralism and diversity, which brings together a provocative and stimulating collection of contributions. It should be compulsory reading for students of research methods, but will also provide more experienced scholars with valuable insights and hopefully challenge them to expand their methodological repertoires.'

Professor Bill Harley, James Riady Chair of Asian Business,
The University of Melbourne and Editor of *Journal of Management Studies*

'Most journal editors and readers crave "something different" in topics of inquiry and the design of research. This book shows why conservatism in fact prevails and provides a powerful and comprehensive set of exemplars of alternative unconventional approaches, covering sources of data, methods, and modes of analysis. It will inspire scholars to be more imaginative in their research. Journal editors and their readers will be truly grateful.'

Paul Edwards, Professor of *Employment Relations, University of Birmingham* and former editor-in-chief of *Human Relations*

'Bryman and Buchanan have assembled an interesting and rigorous set of chapters designed to introduce readers to some of the most novel approaches to data collection, research design, and data analysis. Importantly, this assemblage includes ideas sampled from a broad array of disciplines spanning quantitative, qualitative, and mixed methods domains. I strongly recommend this book to any scholar seeking to expand the tools comprising his or her methodological tool chest.'

James M. LeBreton, Professor of Psychology, *Pennsylvania State University*, and Editor of *Organizational Research Methods*

▨ CONTENTS

LIST OF FIGURES   ix
LIST OF TABLES   xi
LIST OF CODES   xiii
CONTRIBUTORS   xv

1 'Not another survey': The value of unconventional methods   1
David A. Buchanan and Alan Bryman

PART 1 **UNCONVENTIONAL SETTINGS AND DATA SOURCES**

2 Desert island data: Using BBC Radio 4's Desert Island Discs
in organization and management research   27
Laurie Cohen and Joanne Duberley

3 Using fiction in organization and management research   45
Robin Holt and Mike Zundel

4 Innovations in unobtrusive methods   64
Andrew P. Knight

5 Research in extreme contexts   84
David A. Buchanan and David Denyer

6 Making the case: A qualitative approach to studying social
media documents   105
Christopher J. Schneider

PART 2 **UNCONVENTIONAL RESEARCH DESIGN AND DATA
COLLECTION METHODS**

7 Netnography: Engaging with the challenges   127
Robert V. Kozinets and Manuela Nocker

8 Institutions under a microscope: Experimental methods
in institutional theory   147
Alex Bitektine, Jeffrey W. Lucas, and Oliver Schilke

9 Beyond one voice: Co-constructed analytic auto-ethnography   168
Steve Kempster and Ken Parry

10 Participant-led video diaries   190
Rebecca Whiting, Helen Roby, Gillian Symon, and Petros Chamakiotis

11 Inter-organizational ethnography: Promises and problems   212
Olivier Berthod, Michael Grothe-Hammer, and Jörg Sydow

PART 3 UNCONVENTIONAL ANALYTIC APPROACHES

12 Unconventional yet consequential: Using a sociomaterial approach
to drive impact in organization studies research   233
Paul R. Carlile and Karl-Emanuel Dionne

13 Path constitution analysis: A methodology for understanding path
dependence and path creation   255
Jörg Sydow, Arnold Windeler, Gordon Müller-Seitz, and Knut Lange

14 Methodology matters   277
David A. Buchanan

INDEX   289

▨ LIST OF FIGURES

1.1 References to "methodolog* innovati*" in article abstracts,
titles, and keywords 1996–2016, based on data from Scopus
abstract and citation database, 9 January 2017   12

9.1 Data from graphic rating scales   180

10.1 Example of participant creativity: the 'silent movie' approach   200

10.2 Example of participant creativity: avoiding filming
colleagues' faces   200

10.3 Ailsa (US) and her digital switch   203

10.4 Simon (SE) undertakes some 'digi-housekeeping'   204

■ LIST OF TABLES

4.1 New unobtrusive measures 69

5.1 Four extreme context studies 94

8.1 Applied and fundamental research logics 151

9.1 Analytic auto-ethnography 178

9.2 Degree of perceptual identification with the auto-ethnographic account 180

10.1 Key methodological stages 197

10.2 Key methodological pros and cons of video diaries 205

12.1 Summary of Barley's observations of patterns of interaction at two hospitals 237

12.2 Total practical CT knowledge among doctors and technologists after nine months 245

13.1 Constitutive features and potential indicators of paths 259

13.2 Empirical evidence for potential indicators of paths 265

LIST OF CODES

Digital Brain Switch project website   211

Work-life boundaries in the digital age   211

Three implications of our digi lives   211

▣ CONTRIBUTORS

Olivier Berthod is Assistant Professor of Organization and Management at the Jacobs University Bremen, Germany. His research focuses on organization theory, networks, the practice of public governance, interpretative approaches to organizational analysis, and case studies. He has published on sensemaking in crisis situations, cooperative management of food-borne disease outbreaks, rationalization of decision-making in public administrations, and high-reliability networks.

Alex Bitektine is Associate Professor of Management at the John Molson School of Business, Concordia University, Montreal, Canada. His research interests include entrepreneurship, institutional theory, social judgements (legitimacy, status, reputation, trust, and others), non-market strategies, sustainable development, as well as application of experimental methods in organizational research. In his research, he seeks to integrate a multi-level approach and findings from microsociology and social psychology into institutional theory and organization studies.

Alan Bryman was Emeritus Professor of Organizational and Social Research at the University of Leicester School of Business, UK. His research interests focused on methodology, leadership, organizational analysis, Disneyization, and theme parks. He published on social and organizational research methods, including two leading textbooks (*Social Research Methods*, and *Business Research Methods*) which have been translated into numerous other languages, and he had a specific interest in leadership in higher education.

David A. Buchanan is Emeritus Professor of Organizational Behaviour at Cranfield University School of Management, UK. His research interests lie with change management and organization politics. He is co-author of a leading text in organizational behaviour, and co-editor with Alan Bryman of *The Sage Handbook of Organizational Research Methods* (2009). Current projects include studies of transformational change in healthcare, post-crisis change implementation, and the implications of technology developments for the role of the human resource management function.

Paul R. Carlile is Professor of Management and Information Systems at the Questrom School of Business at Boston University, USA. His research interests focus on the interfaces that exist among people from different material practices and what can be done to enhance collaboration and innovative outcomes. Paul's work has been published in number of academic outlets and his insights have been applied to the automotive, aerospace, pharmaceutical, software and higher education sectors. He currently serves as the Senior Associate Dean for Innovation at the Questrom School.

Petros Chamakiotis is Lecturer in Information Systems in the Department of Business and Management at the University of Sussex, UK. So far, his research has focused on creativity and leadership in the context of virtual teams, the management of work–life boundaries in the digital age, and the use of video in qualitative research. He has published in relevant journals, such as *New Technology, Work & Employment* and *Information Technology & People*.

Laurie Cohen is Professor of Work and Organization at Nottingham University Business School. Her research interests focus on careers and professional work; gender, work and career-making; and research methods in the study of career, focusing in particular on interpretive approaches and the use of narrative. Her research monograph, *Imagining Women's Careers*, was published by Oxford University Press in 2014. In addition to her Nottingham role, she is Visiting Professor at the Lund University School of Economics and Management.

David Denyer is Professor of Leadership and Organizational Change and Director of Research at Cranfield School of Management, UK. His research interests include leadership, change management, organizational resilience, design science and evidence-based management. He is editor, with Colin Pilbeam, of *Managing Change in Extreme Contexts* (Routledge, 2015). David has also made a substantial contribution and impact outside academia through strategic and advisory roles.

Karl-Emanuel Dionne is a PhD candidate of Management in the research group Mosaic at HEC Montréal, Canada. His research interests focus on the processes of *opening*, *coordinating* and *doing* innovation across different knowledge domains, within and outside organizational boundaries. He currently studies these processes in the emerging field of digital health, with startups, academic hospital organizations and non-profit organizations. He has published some of his work on communities of innovation and collaborative approaches such as *hackathons*.

Joanne Duberley is Professor of Organization Studies at Birmingham Business School, University of Birmingham, UK. Her research interests focus on the lived experience of careers and she has studied this in a variety of contexts including scientific, academic, professional services, military and local government. She is particularly interested in the ways in which organizations can become more inclusive. She has also published on the philosophical underpinnings of research methodologies.

Michael Grothe-Hammer, MA, is a research associate at the Institute of Social Sciences at Helmut Schmidt University, Hamburg, Germany. His research interests include organizational sociology, qualitative research methods, sociological systems theory, and sociology of disasters. His work has appeared in journals such as *Organizational Research Methods, Current Sociology*, and *Journal of Public Administration Research and Theory*.

Robin Holt is Professor in the Department of Management, Philosophy and Politics at Copenhagen Business School, Denmark. In 2017, he published a book on *Judgment and Strategy*, and is writing two further books, one on craft, strategy and technology, and the other on entrepreneurship and desire. He was editor of the journal *Organization Studies* from 2013 to 2017.

Steve Kempster is Professor of Leadership Learning and Development at Lancaster University Management School, UK. His research interests focus on leadership practice and leadership learning. In the process of exploring these areas, Steve has a particular interest in research methods that enable access to inaccessible phenomena associated with tacit learning and practice – notably the development of grounded theory and co-constructed autoethnography. His current work is in the area of responsible leadership and sustainability innovation through collaborative research.

Andrew P. Knight is Associate Professor of Organizational Behavior at the Olin School of Business, Washington University in St Louis, USA. His research interests include group dynamics, affect, and interpersonal relationships. He studies these topics in a range of contexts, but is especially interested in healthcare and entrepreneurship.

Robert V. Kozinets is the Jayne and Hans Hufschmid Professor of Strategic Public Relations and Business Communication at the University of Southern California's Annenberg School for Communication and Journalism, a position he shares with the Marshall School of Business. He is Associate Editor of the *Journal of Consumer Research* and *Journal of Retailing*. His research interests lie in the intersection of technological change, entertainment culture, commercial consumption, and sociality. He is a social media research authority, and has published three books about qualitative methods, including two about netnography. His publications often deal with organizational themes and include early applications of institutional theory to consumer research.

Knut Lange is Senior Lecturer in International Business in the School of Management, Royal Holloway, University of London, UK. His research interests include business models, innovation, networks, comparative country studies, family businesses and family offices. He has published in leading academic journals, such as *Research Policy*, *British Journal of Management*, *International Journal of Human Resource Management*, and *Socio-Economic Review*.

Jeffrey W. Lucas is Professor of Sociology and Associate Dean for Research in the College of Behavioral and Social Sciences at the University of Maryland, USA. He carries out experimental group processes research and has published widely on status, power, influence, and experimental methodology. He is currently leading a large-scale project with personnel at the US military service academies which is funded by the US Army Research Institute to study the roles of leadership and climate in shaping ethical conduct and the reporting of unethical behaviour.

Gordon Müller-Seitz is Professor of Strategy, Innovation and Cooperation at the University of Kaiserslautern, Germany. His research focuses on dealing with risks and uncertainties, innovation management, interorganizational networks and projects, and the digital transformation. His work has been applied at multinational corporations as well as small and medium-sized enterprises, and has appeared in renowned research journals and practitioner outlets.

Manuela Nocker is a Senior Lecturer in Organization and Sustainability at the University of Essex Business School, UK. She holds a PhD in Organizational Psychology from the London School of Economics and a BSc in Work and Organizational Psychology from Padua University. Her research focuses on collaboration in project teams, collective identities, and lived ethics using ethnography and narrative methodology. She is an editor of the *Journal of Organizational Ethnography* and an organizer and co-chair of the Annual Liverpool University Ethnography Symposium.

Ken Parry is Professor of Leadership Studies at Deakin Business School, in Melbourne, Australia. His research interests focus on all methodologies that are associated with the study of leadership. He brought auto-ethnography to management/business studies early in the century. He is co-author, with Brad Jackson, of *A Very Short, Fairly Interesting and Reasonably Cheap Book about Studying Leadership* (Sage Publications). Most of his publications focus on grounded theory and other qualitative methods. He is used widely as a keynote speaker in industry conferences.

Helen Roby is Research Fellow in the Centre for Business in Society at Coventry University, UK. Her research interests focus on the use of novel and innovative methods and interventions to influence consumption practices, particularly in the Smart Cities environment. Much of her work is applied, working with industry and commercial partners. She has published and presented in both academic and practitioner journals and conferences in this area.

Oliver Schilke is Assistant Professor in the Management and Organizations Department and an Assistant Professor (by courtesy) in the School of Sociology at the University of Arizona, USA. He studies institutional practices, as well as trust, organizational capabilities, and market cognition. He has published in leading scholarly outlets, including the *American Sociological Review*, the *Proceedings of the National Academy of Sciences*, and the *Strategic Management Journal*.

Christopher J. Schneider is Associate Professor of Sociology at Brandon University in Manitoba, Canada. His current research and publications focus on information technologies and related changes to police work. His recent book is *Policing and Social Media: Social Control in an Era of New Media*.

Jörg Sydow is Professor of Management and holds the Chair for Inter-firm Cooperation at the School of Business and Economics at Freie Universität Berlin, Germany, and is currently Director of the Research Unit 'Organized Creativity', sponsored by the German Research Foundation (DFG). His research interests focus on the management of interorganizational relations, on which he published a textbook (co-authored with Elke Schüßler and Gordon Müller-Seitz, 2016). He is a member of the editorial review boards of *Organization Studies*, *Academy of Management Journal*, *Academy of Management Review*, *Journal of Management Studies*, and *The Scandinavian Journal of Management*.

Gillian Symon is Professor of Organization Studies in the School of Management, Royal Holloway, University of London, UK. Her research interests lie in the areas of qualitative research practices, implications of digital technologies for working and volunteering practices, and identity work. She has co-edited four books on qualitative methods with Professor Catherine Cassell (published by Sage) and they are co-founders of the journal *Qualitative Research in Organizations and Management*.

Rebecca Whiting is Lecturer in the Department of Organizational Psychology at Birkbeck, University of London, UK. She is interested in a broad range of qualitative research methods, particularly digital and visual approaches, on which she has published a number of articles and book chapters. Her research interests include the implications for contemporary work of digital technologies, and the discursive construction of work identities with a specific focus on age and gender.

Arnold Windeler is Professor of Sociology of Organizations at Technische Universität Berlin, Germany, and is speaker of the Graduate School *Innovation Society Today: The reflexive creation of novelty*, sponsored by the German Research Foundation (DFG). His research interests lie with social, organization, and network theory. He has published on inter-firm networks, competences, and on reflexive innovation.

Mike Zundel is Professor in the Work, Organization and Management Group at the University of Liverpool Management School, UK, where he also acts as associate head, responsible for research. He is interested in processual and media-theoretical aspects of organizing and strategy, and he is a senior editor of *Organization Studies*, consulting editor of the *International Journal of Management Reviews*, and sits on the board of reviewers for the *Academy of Management Review*.

1 'Not another survey'

The value of unconventional methods

David A. Buchanan and Alan Bryman

Source: © ScienceCartoonsPlus.com: reproduced with permission

Aims and readers

Methodology matters: that is one of the main arguments of this book. But most researchers tend to use a limited range of conventional approaches. This is significant, because the research methodology that you use affects what you see, how you see it, and what you do not see. Your methodological perspective also shapes your interpretation of the information that you gather. Different methods, however, can generate different kinds of information, leading to different ways of analysing and interpreting the phenomena that you are investigating. Cornelissen (2017, p.370) thus argues that, 'the nature of our methods, ranging from simulations and experiments to ethnography and case studies, press particular ways, or styles, of theorizing on us. Specifically, methods afford and licence certain ways of thinking and reasoning, and are linked to particular forms of writing and reporting research.' Adhering to convention limits our thinking. *Unconventional* methodology matters.

Research methodology is not neutral. Different designs and methods can generate different insights when applied to the same research questions. The well-known 'two factor theory of work motivation' (Herzberg et al., 1959) was based on critical incident interviews in which respondents were asked to recall events which had made them feel bad about their work, and events which had made them feel good. Stories about job dissatisfaction concerned issues such as pay, supervision, and physical working conditions. Stories about satisfaction focused on achievement, recognition, and the work itself. Herzberg referred to these as hygiene and motivator factors, respectively; the former only reduce dissatisfaction, but motivator factors increase performance. This terminology has entered the language, the theory has face validity, and the job enrichment technique which it inspired has been widely applied. However, researchers who replicated Herzberg's study using different methods came to different conclusions; the critical incident method appears to have stimulated defensive and projective responses (Vroom, 1964; Kaplan et al., 1969). Satisfaction was attributed to personal achievements; dissatisfaction was attributed to factors in the work environment beyond respondents' control. Herzberg's theory thus appears to be method-bound. This may be a historical example, but as journals today are reluctant to publish replication studies (insisting on 'novel contribution'), method-bound results may have become more difficult to detect.

Different designs and methods provide different lenses on the topic of investigation. Researchers as non-participant observers, for example, study social interaction in meetings. With video recording, the interaction can be viewed repeatedly, subtle aspects of verbal and non-verbal behaviour can be observed and analysed more closely, and the recording can be viewed by other researchers who can offer interpretations. Researchers face the trade-off between the rich qualitative information that can be captured from a small number of respondents, and the impressive sample size and quantitative data generated with tick-box questionnaires. Researchers concerned with the 'impact' of their work have to choose between maintaining objectivity in the interests of methodological purity, and engaging participants as co-researchers to increase the probability of producing findings of practical value.

Why should we be concerned with *unconventional* methodology in organization and management research? Social science research methodology in general is a well-established field. If researchers have methodological concerns, these probably relate more to establishing the rigour required to publish in leading journals, and demonstrating the impact on practice that research assessment regimes now require. Concerns with rigour and relevance encourage the use of widely accepted norms, with regard to research design, methods, and analytical procedures, thus putting a premium on risk avoidance, safety, conformity, and conservatism. The unconventional may be risky, undesirable, suspect, and dangerous. But if conservatism becomes the enemy of change, novelty, experimentation, and the development of imaginative new approaches, then we have a problem. If we continue to research using the same approaches, we may keep discovering the same kinds of things. Theory and practice may not be adequately informed. Another problem is that conventional methods become boring, for researchers and for participants: 'not another survey, please', 'no more interviews', 'not another report'. We have encountered some anecdotal accounts of 'survey fatigue' leading to disappointingly small response rates. Participant cooperation and the quality of research activity and outputs may therefore degrade in the absence of interesting methodological innovations.

Unconventional methodology allows us to explore familiar phenomena in new ways. In addition, there are many phenomena in organization and management studies that are difficult or impossible to study using traditional methods, particularly those involving extreme, controversial, rare, or sensitive issues and contexts. Can we use innovative approaches to open up those areas to investigation? Challenges to convention, however, are discouraged by a range of institutional forces, which we will explore shortly. In spite of the benefits, however, we have to recognize that breaking with convention in this field can be risky. Researchers may have limited skill and experience with a new method, with few precedents on which to rely. There may be a degree of uncertainty concerning the nature of the outcomes. Will journal reviewers be able and willing to appraise the method and the findings?

There is a broader case for extending the methodological toolkit. Arguing that '*all* research strategies are *seriously* flawed', McGrath (1981, p.179; emphasis in the original) concludes that it is important to use an array of methods, of different types and classes, to compensate for the weaknesses of each of the approaches being used. Unconventional methods can extend the array. This is not to claim that unconventional methods are necessarily superior to traditional approaches. On the contrary, McGrath's argument that 'no strategy, design or method used alone is worth a damn' still holds. In the face of those known problems, McGrath (1981, p.189; emphasis in the original) observes that:

Methodological discussions should not waste time arguing about which is the right strategy, or the best one; they are *all* lousy! Instead, such discussions might better engage in questions of how best to *combine* multiple strategies (not within one study, but over studies within a problem) by *multiple means that do not share the same weaknesses.*

Our aim therefore is to widen the space for dialogue and experimentation concerning the development of unconventional approaches to organization and management research. This book will be valuable for three groups of readers: first, academic researchers in organization and management studies; second, doctoral candidates on PhD and DBA programmes (and their supervisors); and third, Masters students on, for example, MBA and Masters in Management programmes, who are required to complete research-based dissertations. This third group may be less constrained by institutional norms, and may thus have more freedom to experiment with methodology in their projects.

How do we distinguish 'mainstream' from 'unconventional'? What criteria can we use? How and when does the unconventional become mainstream, and vice versa? These are challenging issues, and our responses are tentative. The chapters in this book are also a guide to the unconventional.

WHAT COUNTS AS MAINSTREAM METHODOLOGY?

What counts as conventional or 'mainstream' is a relatively easy question to answer; in common use, published in leading journals, documented in standard research methods texts. This is particularly the case with regard to research that is positivist in design and quantitative in methods and analysis. Research that is constructivist in design and mainly qualitative in methods and analysis has been 'mainstream' in Europe and the UK for some time, but US journals have only recently begun to recognize that qualitative research has 'come of age' (Bansal and Corley, 2011). Positivist research tends to be methodologically constrained by the hypothetico-deductive framework, with innovative approaches appearing mainly (but not exclusively) in approaches to data analysis. Other recent innovations in methodology appear to derive mainly from qualitative, interpretivist perspectives (Buchanan and Bryman, 2007; Cassell, 2016). However, as our survey of journal editors (summarized below) suggests, this pattern may now be changing.

WHAT COUNTS AS UNCONVENTIONAL?

What is to be considered 'unconventional' is a more difficult question to answer for several reasons. First, responses must by definition be couched in negative terms: 'not that approach'. Second, this is an IKIWISI concept: 'I'll know it [a break with convention] when I see it.' Third, the unconventional for one researcher or research tradition may be mainstream to another (and there are transatlantic differences in this regard). Fourth, ideas which were considered unconventional when first introduced can join the mainstream more or less rapidly over time, as their application becomes more widespread and their value comes to be better understood, and accepted.

Research methodology can be unconventional on several dimensions:

setting   organizations and contexts not previously studied
design   the framework within which data collection and analysis take place
participation   different modes of sampling, participant recruitment, or engagement
methods   ways in which information or data is gathered, including mixed methods
data sources   the use of non-traditional sources of information
data analysis   modes of data reduction, analysis, and interpretation
output   writing style, media, end products

Our aim is not to define the boundaries of the unconventional. Nor is this an attempt to develop a catalogue of unconventional approaches. The boundary between unconventional and mainstream is fluid; a method may be unconventional for a brief period before it becomes accepted as mainstream. Approaches considered to be unconventional may often be an adaptation or extension of an existing method, or the translation of a familiar approach to a novel setting. In addition, approaches once considered mainstream can become unconventional. Two examples illustrate this fluidity.

First, mixed methods research was seen in the 1990s as a promising unconventional approach to social research. This was against a background in which quantitative and qualitative research were seen as incompatible paradigms that could not be blended (Bryman, 2008). However, as several commentators noted, there was in many respects nothing new about mixed methods as there had been a long tradition of researchers combining quantitative and qualitative approaches (Maxwell, 2016; Pelto, 2015). Fetters (2016) argues that these early forays into what we now think of as mixed methods research lacked the systematic integration that is a hallmark of current usage. That may be so, but more importantly mixed methods approaches were in use. Bryman's (1988) book on quantitative and qualitative research included a chapter that examined a selection of studies in articles and books from the early 1950s to the mid-1980s. This identified a number of different ways in which quantitative and qualitative research had been combined. What is striking about these studies is that the mixing of quantitative and qualitative methods was seen as unremarkable by practitioners. Interest in mixed methods research subsequently grew, and came to be viewed as unconventional and exciting. It was given a label, 'mixed methods research', came to be thought of and developed as a 'thing' (Hesse-Biber, 2015), and moved into mainstream social research in the first decade of the current century with its own language and designs (Bryman, 2016).

A second example of the fluid boundary between mainstream and unconventional concerns the use of photography. In the early twentieth century, articles in the *American Journal of Sociology* often included photographs. However, following a drive by the editor in 1907, they disappeared from its pages. His motive was not just related to the perception that photographs were unscientific evidence, but also that they were typically used to depict social reform issues which he did not believe should be the focus of a scientific sociology. Interest in the use of photographs resurfaced in the 1970s and is in danger of being regarded as mainstream once again (Emmison et al., 2012; Bell et al., 2014).

We wish to argue that methodology should be imaginative and inventive, that norms and conventions should be challenged, that standards should be revised, that boundaries should be blurred. Our ultimate aim, of course, is to illustrate this argument with examples from current practice, to inspire and motivate researchers to develop novel methods that are appropriate to their own projects.

Methodological conservatism

Organizational research is a multi-paradigmatic field, with no consensus around theoretical perspectives or practical research approaches (Buchanan and Bryman, 2007). The ontological, epistemological, and methodological pluralism that characterize our field appears to be constrained by the conservatism of researchers, doctoral supervisors, academic referees, and journal editors. In the context of recent debate about the alleged falsification of research findings, and concerns about appropriate procedures not being followed, leading to article retractions (Spoelstra et al., 2016), standardization and conservatism in methodology may be desirable, indeed necessary.

The source of that conservatism lies with the mutually supportive array of institutional forces that discourage innovative approaches, and which generate and reproduce conservatism. These include:

- national 'research excellence' review procedures and expectations;
- journal quality ranking agencies (Association of Business Schools, *Financial Times*);
- peer review processes;
- decision-making structures and processes of funding bodies;
- research ethics committee expectations and requirements;
- the evidence-based management movement which emphasizes perceived credibility and trust in well-known, conventional, risk-averse methodology;
- university research student supervisory arrangements and controls;
- the editorial and publishing policies of academic journals;
- the demands and constraints (explicit and implicit) built into peer review procedures; and
- coverage of a limited range of methods in texts and courses on the subject.

Butler et al. (2017) observe a paradox. These institutional demands and expectations can encourage researchers to *deviate* from the norm, by adopting 'questionable research practices' including 'fabrication, falsification, and pla-giarism' in order to improve their chances of publication.

With regard to the peer review process, and although writing in a geography journal, the observations of Aalbers (2004) apply to social science research and publishing in general. He is concerned with the role of language in the refereeing process, and with the way in which UK and US reviewers force non-native English speakers to cover English language sources: '[T]hrough this Anglo-American hegemony, the UK- and US-based referee's comments often not only force a non-native English-speaking author to rewrite his/her paper, but also increase the "creative destruction" of a paper' (Aalbers, 2004, p.319)—which can weaken the argument and contribution. He claims that referees often 'ride their own hobbyhorse' (p.320), forcing reference to literature that may not be relevant, and allowing no space for competing traditions and contributions. (UK and US scholars, however, are not expected to refer to non-UK and non-US literature, even when those have been published in English.) Anglo-American editors and referees thus serve as gatekeepers and police, disciplining the ideas, interpretations, and modes of communication that are allowed, and rejecting non-conforming work. Those policing and disciplinary functions are also applied to native English-speaking researchers.

As noted above, although mixed methods research was in mainstream use from the beginning of the twentieth century, this approach was seen as questionable by many commentators during the 'paradigm wars' in the 1980s, and mixed methods research has been seen since the 1990s as unconventional. To expose the unconventionality of mixed methods in business and management research, Cameron and Molina-Azorín (2011) examined journals in seven fields: marketing, international business, strategic management, organizational behaviour, operations management, entrepreneurship, and human resource management. They found that quantitative studies dominated in all seven fields, accounting for 76 per cent of the empirical articles. This was followed by mixed methods studies (14 per cent) and qualitative research (10 per cent). They conclude that conservatism is widespread, and 'it would seem that there exists minimal acceptance of mixed methods across these fields' (p.256). When Gardner et al. (2010) compared articles published in the first and second decades (nineties and noughties) of *The Leadership Quarterly*, they found that the percentage of those based on quantitative research increased from 71 per cent to 87 per cent, while those using qualitative research fell from 39 per cent to 24 per cent. Also in the first decade, 64 per cent included a questionnaire as a data source, revealing the high dependence on this single method. (Qualitative research appears also to depend on a single method—the semi-structured interview: Bryman, 2011).

Mingers and Willmott (2013) explore how research is influenced by performance measures, and in particular by journal ranking lists, such as those produced in the UK by the Association of Business Schools and the *Financial Times*. The latter promotes a dominant model of research, implying that North American journals publish the 'best research', which follows a neo-positivist agenda. Journals not listed are seen as having lesser status, and are forced to emulate those which are listed, rather than to develop their own innovative perspectives. Influential articles published in the past ('sleeping beauties') are still cited many years later, but journal impact factors rely on recently published work. Mingers and Willmott (2013, p.1055) thus argue that, 'A perverse effect of ascribing the highest value to "shooting stars" [...] is to incentivise the production of comparatively safe papers that contribute to established or fashionable topics and issues, rather than encouraging innovative scholarship that, potentially, has a longer lasting relevance.' Thus innovation, or heterogeneity, is devalued. Barley (2016) is also critical of how academic incentives and reward systems channel the behaviour of early-career researchers academics in particular, emphasizing 'mainstream' approaches and 'new theory'.

Research that does not adhere to positivist epistemology and methodology is thus likely to be regarded as heterodox, and marginalized. This results in the homogenization of research activity. Citations of research papers are likely to be low if the work addresses non-mainstream topics, or uses unconventional methodologies and perspectives, and appears in 'unlisted' journals. These disadvantages apply in particular to multidisciplinary, interdisciplinary, and transdisciplinary work which often falls outside traditional disciplinary silos, and the journals which cater to those traditional specialisms. A listed journal has become a 'stamp of recognition'. The quality of unlisted journals is therefore suspect; new journals and innovative research are discouraged.

Publications in highly ranked journals affect the perceived status of individual researchers, and also the reputation and funding of their employing organizations. Mingers and Willmott (2013) note that business school deans and directors of research resort to journal rankings when assessing candidates for selection and promotion; why read an unfamiliar article when the journal's ranking can be taken as a proxy quality indicator—a 'halo effect' in other words. National research quality assessment panels in the UK have explicitly said that they do not use journal rankings as quality indicators. However, given the number of articles that these panels have to read and assess in a tight schedule, Mingers and Willmott (2013, p.1059) speculate that panels use these rankings anyway. Journal rankings, they argue, also create an 'authoritative order' which values particular topics, perspectives, and methods, and downgrades research that does not have those characteristics. They describe this as a 'squeeze on heterogeneity', which is reinforced by article citation counts and journal impact factors; diversity is being stifled. Mingers and Willmott (2013, p.1051) conclude that journal lists 'endorse and cultivate a research monoculture in which particular criteria, favoured by a given list, assume the status of a universal benchmark of performance'. These commentators call for a moratorium on the use of journal ranking lists because they narrow and homogenize scholarship, and marginalize innovation and diversity in theoretical perspectives, methods, and writing styles.

Alvesson and Sandberg (2013) offer similar arguments, observing that producing articles for leading journals has replaced the production of useful knowledge as the primary academic goal. They note the shortage of 'high impact' research in organization and management studies, and attribute this to the dominance of 'incremental gap-spotting'. This is paradoxical, they argue, because it is widely known that gap-spotting rarely produces interesting results: 'gap-spotting is more likely to reinforce or moderately revise, rather than challenge, already influential theories' (p.132). Three sets of drivers encourage these trends towards uniformity. First, institutional conditions: quality assessment regimes, publication pressure, and designated journals. Second, professional norms: 'adding to the literature', producing work that fits with and develops popular theories, relating a study to an existing literature, and 'rigour'. Third, researchers' identity constructions: comply with institutional expectations, establish a specialist niche, publish regularly in the 'right' journals. These 'drivers' are interconnected and mutually reinforcing, making them difficult to ignore. However, Alvesson and Sandberg argue that these can and must change.

Some journal editors share the concern for the increasing homogenization of scholarship, which they believe is encouraging formulaic approaches to the conduct and reporting of research. Harley (2015, p.402), for example, observes that in the field of human resource management, 'The dominant stream of research takes the form of reviewing the literature, identifying gaps, collecting data to test hypotheses as a means to fill the gaps, and thus slowly advancing knowledge rather than making any kind of methodological or theoretical leaps.' In an editorial for *Journal of Management Studies* (which appears in the *Financial Times* list), Corbett et al. (2014) report that:

To achieve academic success, management scholars, and particularly those early in their careers, are under pressure to conform to norms concerning the form, the content, the methods, and the type of contribution of their studies. Although this homogenization can have benefits such as providing a common ground for engaging in academic discussion of issues across diverse regions, this move to conformity also has the potential to undermine variety, novelty, and innovation in research   (p.4).

At worst, the research process becomes a templated one, in which the direction, implementation, and communication of the query are all reduced to a set of heuristics common across almost all scholars. Indeed, the voice of the individual in scholarship may become muted to the point where articles in a journal look alike and sound alike, and appear to have been researched and written by the same person   (p.6).

The editors of *JMS* conclude that their status as a high quality 'listed' journal has *encouraged* a standardized approach to research, as reflected in the papers that are submitted to them, thus discouraging research using unconventional or non-mainstream approaches:

Our observation as editors is that as *JMS*'s impact factor has risen and it has become a more desirable outlet for ambitious scholars, the range of the types of papers submitted has narrowed. More and more of the papers we receive are 'standard', 'safe', or 'mainstream' manuscripts. This homogenization leads us to ask whether in the current institutional environment, 'quality' defined as diverse, innovative, and challenging papers is being displaced by 'quality' defined as uniformly designed, high-impact (as measured by citations) papers. The consequence is a marginalization of research that challenges methodological and presentational norms   (pp.9–10).

However, Corbett et al. (2014) also note that, 'research that is seen as riskier or outside the typical norms is often the most influential' (p.8) and that, 'some of the oft-cited and most influential work in management studies has come from research using distinct methodologies and investigations that are outside of the typical "managers in a corporate setting" environment' (p.10). The pressures for standardization are a threat to creativity and innovation, and jeopardize the development of the field.

Researchers wishing to develop the unconventional approaches to methodology advocated in this volume thus face a number of mutually reinforcing constraints, from unsympathetic reviewers, to selection and promotion panels who want to see publications in listed journals. These constraints encourage formulaic work that complies with traditional norms and is therefore seen as safe when submitting papers to those preferred journals. The cost of this conservatism may be counted in stifled creativity. The contributions to knowledge arising from this approach are thus more likely to be minor than significant, incremental than breakthrough, and potentially less interesting (see Alvesson and Gabriel, 2013). Does it matter if research is 'interesting' or not in the context of developing knowledge and understanding? Davis (1971, pp.9–10) certainly thinks so:

It has long been thought that a theorist is considered great because his [sic] theories are true, but this is false. A theorist is considered great, not because his theories are true, but because they are *interesting*. Those who carefully and exhaustively verify trivial theories are soon forgotten; whereas those who cursorily and expediently verify interesting theories are long remembered. [...] Students who follow to the letter all of the injunctions of current textbooks on theory construction, but take into account no other criterion in the construction of their theories, will turn out work which will be found dull indeed.

Davis (1971) was writing about theory development, and not about methodology. However, given that methodology and theory are intertwined and mutually influential (Cornelissen, 2017), the use of unconventional methods may increase the probability of generating interesting findings and theories.

Methodological innovation

Many of the themes in the preceding discussion and in the chapters that follow are addressed in a small but significant body of literature that emerged in the noughties, assessing methodological innovation in the social sciences. Methodological innovation has thus become a subject of research in its own right. Key studies in this area include:

- Forbes (2003). Study of 'cutting-edge research'. Email questionnaire sent to editors of fifty top social science journals and RAE chairs.
- Taylor and Coffey (2008). An overview of forms of methodological innovation in qualitative research and nature of the claims made.
- Travers (2009). An examination of innovation claims in books with a focus on qualitative research and in grant proposals.
- Xenitidou and Gilbert (2012). Desk research examining the nature and forms of methodological innovations outside the UK. Two sets of interviews and email survey of academics and practitioners to identify important methodological innovations and the nature of their innovativeness.
- Wiles et al. (2011). Study of the incidence of methodological innovation claims in qualitative research in social science journals and a narrative review of the nature of those claims.
- Bengry-Howell et al. (2011) and Wiles et al. (2013). Study of the impact of three innovations (netnography, child-led research, and creative research methods). Interviews with key actors involved in development of approach concerning its origins and subsequent development. Diffusion of each innovation in terms of journal citations.

Several of these studies note that claims to methodological innovation are increasingly made by authors of articles and applicants for research funding (e.g. Taylor and Coffey, 2008; Wiles et al. 2011). Figure 1.1 provides some insight into this trend, showing the number of articles including the phrase 'methodolog* innovati*' since 1996. Prior to 1996, citations hovered between zero and three per year, but since the turn of the century there has been a steady rise. The citations include studies claiming to be methodologically innovative, those that investigate the phenomenon of methodological innovation, and a small number which are neither. The data, therefore, are by no means perfect, but provide a sense of the increase in both claims of and interest in methodological innovation.

There is considerable scepticism about how much methodological innovation actually takes place. Forbes (2003, p.276) claims that 'for the bulk of editors and RAE Chairs, less than 25 per cent of research output is cutting edge'. Writing about qualitative research, Wiles et al. (2011) suggest that, due to the pressures on researchers, claims of methodological innovation may be over-stated. Travers (2009) also suggests that innovation claims often cannot

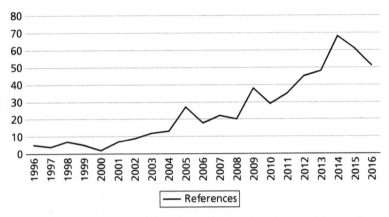

Figure 1.1 References to "methodolog* innovati*" in article abstracts, titles, and keywords 1996–2016, based on data from Scopus abstract and citation database, 9 January 2017

be sustained. The evidence suggests that methodological innovation is rare and most innovations take the form of extensions and adaptations of existing methods and designs. These include:

- the transfer of a method from one discipline to another where it has not previously been used;
- transferring a method from one area within a discipline to another in which it has not previously been used;
- using a new technology to implement an established method (e.g. use of CAQDAS for coding qualitative data; using WWW as a platform for survey questionnaires);
- applying a method to a new population; and
- using a new way of implementing an existing method.

Methodological innovations thus tend to be incremental rather than radical (Conway and Steward, 2009). However, what is and is not an innovation varies considerably between the authors of articles claiming to be innovative. Can even minor adaptations of methods warrant the label 'innovative'? Wiles et al. (2011) mention the use of 'post-it' notes in a focus group study, which some commentators might argue is stretching the claim to being innovative. They also point out that innovation claims are often not substantiated by their authors.

There is disagreement about how to define methodological innovation. As Wiles et al. (2013) observe, for some writers a method needs to have been taken up by the social science community before it can be regarded as an innovation (e.g. Taylor and Coffey, 2008). For others, the key ingredient of innovation is that it has not yet been absorbed into the mainstream (e.g. Xenitidou and Gilbert, 2012; Jewitt et al. 2017). This distinction raises the issue, familiar to students of organization and management studies, of how an innovation becomes diffused into a community of potential users (Rogers, 2003). The comparison of three innovations by Bengry-Howell et al. (2011) shows that diffusion is slow and that the pattern of diffusion varies between methods (see also Hargreaves Heap and Parikh, 2005). There is also the issue of what constitutes diffusion. Bengry-Howell et al. (2011) examined citations of the three methods and found that only netnography had been adopted substantially (in 42 per cent of the articles) and had also been adapted in a further 9 per cent of articles (the corresponding figures for the other two methods were 1 per cent and zero for child-led research, and 8 per cent and zero for creative methods). For child-led and creative research methods, diffusion entailed weaker forms of absorption by the social science community, such as being referred to or referenced in articles (24 per cent and 56 per cent of articles for child-led research, and 11 per cent and 41 per cent for creative research methods, as against 21 per cent and 16 per cent for netnography). However, the time spans involved were short, with all of the citation counts up to 2010. In the case of netnography, the tracking of citations is from the first statement of the method in 1998, but in the case of child-led research it is 2004, and with creative research methods 2006. The last two timeframes are brief and inferences concerning the diffusion of methodological innovation are tentative.

The main conclusions from this foray into the literature on methodological innovation are as follows. First, there is some concern that claims to methodological innovation are sometimes used as part of a rhetoric of persuasion, without the claim being substantiated. Second, completely new innovations are rare, and most cases are adaptations or extensions of existing approaches. Third, what constitutes innovation is not clear, as commentators have different views. Fourth, diffusion is slow and the forms that it assumes are variable. These themes should be borne in mind in relation to the following chapters. But this is a background to what follows, as we have made minimal reference to the concept of innovation in this book, and have not encouraged contributors to use the term. 'Unconventional' may lack the semantic appeal of 'innovative', but its more neutral tone makes it less the subject of exaggeration, while remaining subject to the same critical scrutiny.

Invitations to be unconventional

Given the pressures and trends discussed in the previous sections, several commentators have encouraged researchers to be more bold and imaginative, to challenge the pressures for conservatism and homogenization. Alvesson and Gabriel (2013) advocate 'polymorphic' research, using a wider range of approaches, with more variation and experimentation, including a variety of novel writing styles. Polymorphic methods should be regarded as legitimate because, 'This would increase the chances of more creative, imaginative and readable research being produced and published' (Alvesson and Gabriel, 2013, p.254). They note the increasingly formulaic nature of articles published in organization and management studies journals claiming that it 'assumes standardized forms and expressions, predictable structures and signposts, and even routine content. The result is an increasing uniformity of academic publications and a gradual disappearance of style, imagination, and surprise from academic journals' (p.246).

Alvesson and Gabriel (2013, p.248) are also critical of research that is based on 'find-and-fill-the-gap logic'. Mentioned earlier, this argument is supported in a compelling and humorous manner by Billsberry (2013, p.597) who observes that: 'If no one has studied a particular issue, it is probably because no one is interested in it. Ironically, therefore, justifying a study because there is a gap in the literature is possibly the worst thing a scholar can do because it is akin to saying, "I'm doing this study because no one else is interested in it".'

Alvesson and Sandberg (2013) suggest that the profession itself has encouraged the standardization of research, by exercising 'concertive self-control' in complying with institutional expectations and norms. So, how can interesting and influential research be encouraged? First, change government policy with regard to the way in which 'research excellence' is assessed. Second, revise university and business school policies with regard to hiring, tenure and promotion. Third, rethink professional norms, particularly with regard to the perceived need to respond to all reviewers' comments, redefine 'rigour' in a way that does not work against innovation, and emphasize the need to challenge assumptions. Finally, change professional identity from gap-spotter to 'path-(up)setter':

[G]ap-spotting researchers—at least those who make it into highly ranked journals and therefore 'count'—are not just intelligent, rigorous, diligent, and methodologically and theoretically well trained, but also cautious, instrumental, disciplined, career minded, and strongly specialized. [. . .] But against this, one could put forward more genuine scholarly values and qualities like being intellectually broad-minded, independent, imaginative, willing to take risks, enthusiastic about intellectual adventures, and frequently provocative. This would imply giving priority to discretion and integrity and doing meaningful research that matters rather than prioritizing tenure at a top university, rapid promotion, and publishing in the most prestigious journals (Alvesson and Sandberg, 2013, p.143).

The problem, of course, is that attempts to change government and university policies, and revise professional norms and identity may be extremely difficult, especially in the short term.

Concerned with 'breaking new ground' with regard to theoretical contributions, Cornelissen and Durand (2014) suggest using analogical and counterfactual reasoning to develop new models and alternative explanations. Methodological innovation, however, is required to deliver this agenda. This, they suggest, means the development of more adventurous, interesting, non-mainstream, innovative and polymorphic approaches to research methodology. Critical of the increasingly narrow range of methodological approaches in human resource management research in particular, Harley (2015, p.399) also argues that there is 'room for greater methodological pluralism, and researchers, academic institutions and journals have roles to play in promoting viable alternatives'.

The pressures on researchers to comply with contemporary norms and processes are significant, as are the penalties for non-conformity. However, there are also significant benefits—for individual researchers and for the field of organization and management studies—from more imaginative, innovative, heterodox, polymorphic approaches. Researchers can themselves choose to abandon gap-filling as a research strategy, and to reject formulaic approaches to conducting and reporting research work. Paradoxically, therefore, a return to *traditional* 'scholarly values' (intellectually adventurous, broad-minded, independent, imaginative, willing to take risks, provocative) becomes a driver of the development of *unconventional* methodology.

The view from editors' desks

Journal editors are portrayed in the preceding discussion as villains, stifling creativity by encouraging standardization in research in general, and methodology in particular, in order to maintain their impact factors and ensure their presence on prestige journal lists. But is this stereotype accurate? To find out, we contacted journal editors from March–April 2016 to seek their views on the use of unconventional methodology. Our choice of editors was based on the forty-five journals used (at that time) by the *Financial Times* (FT) newspaper to compile business school research rankings. Journals publishing practitioner-focused articles rather than empirical research were excluded, as were those which did not publish research in organization and management studies. Those exclusions reduced to fifteen the number of journals contacted from the FT list, to which we added a further six journals, giving a total of twenty-one. Contacted by email, editors were asked to respond by email to three questions:

1. Can you give us one or two examples of papers published in your journal—or elsewhere—where the researchers have used unorthodox approaches, with regard to research design, data collection, unusual information sources, or novel ways to analyse data and present findings?

2. In your experience, do researchers tend to be too innovative, or too conservative, in their approach to research methodology? How would you explain your answer?
3. Do the journal's reviewers welcome the use of 'non-mainstream' methodology in work that they are asked to assess, or are they more likely to be sceptical? Why?

We received responses from fifteen editors representing thirteen organization and management research journals—a response rate of approximately three quarters (including two instances of independent replies from two editors of the same journal). These editors said that they found this topic interesting, but they also said that it was difficult to answer questions about unconventional methodology for a number of reasons. First, there is a wide range of methods in use, so it is difficult to determine which are conventional and which are not. Second, what is regarded as 'novel' depends on time and context—with unconventional approaches becoming mainstream as they are more widely applied and accepted, and approaches seen as conventional in one field being regarded as unconventional in another. Third, editorial policy influences these judgements; a journal with a more conservative approach will perhaps more readily reject submissions that are non-mainstream; a journal that explicitly seeks non-traditional submissions may be seeking even more innovative submissions. Important in the context of advice for researchers from this survey, the following two responses illustrate that final point about editorial policy:

We are the primary journal in our area, but we are probably not at the forefront methodologically, and can be regarded as rather conservative in terms of methods.

The journal is seen by some as an outlet for 'non-traditional research'. To ask, then, what is non-traditional in this context is really a tough question.

The survey results as a whole, however, suggest that the stereotype of journal editors in our field as conservative, tradition-bound, and risk-averse is false. Editors equate methodological innovation with providing new lenses, generating fresh perspectives and insights, and expanding the range of issues and questions open to research. Beyond the institutional forces outlined previously, the two main barriers to the development of unconventional methodology appear to lie with two beliefs held by many researchers themselves. First, that it is safer to use traditional methodological perspectives and approaches than it is to depart from convention. Second, that the unconventional will be punished by the inability to publish, which is in turn career-limiting.

This chapter opened with the phrase, 'methodology matters'. Do journal editors agree with this view? Two of the responding editors indicated that, in assessing submissions to their journals, contribution to knowledge was of considerably more importance than methodological concerns:

As a journal, at least under our current editorial team, we are far more focused on the conceptual contribution made by an article (or the lack thereof) than we are on the methods used in the research.

Our main objectives (certainly during the past 6 years) have been on theoretical contributions with the use of rigorous methods, but with an emphasis on parsimony rather than exploring new methodological avenues per se.

Others said:

Methodological sophistication is no substitute for contribution or interest—methods is a 'hygiene factor'; it has to be right but it is not too much of an asset in itself.

At the end of the day, methods is merely a tool and not the contribution per se in our journal.

I tend not to consider methods in isolation, not being interested in methods per se, but in the extent to which they can help to develop our understanding of particular questions or phenomena, or shed new light on them. Methodological novelty and sophistication do not necessarily go hand in hand with 'contribution' at least conceptually; major contributions can be based on pretty standard and straightforward methods.

These were minority views in this sample. However, this indicates disagreement over the status of methodology as a component in the research process, and over the desirability of challenging orthodoxy in this domain. (This does not suggest disagreement over the importance of theoretical contribution, or over using unconventional methods for their own sake.) There is a considerable gulf in perspective between those who regard methodological innovation as 'providing new lenses', 'new ways of seeing the world', and 'giving new insights', and those who see methods as 'uninteresting', 'merely a tool', 'no substitute for contribution', and as a 'hygiene factor'.

Echoing the previous discussion, these editors expressed concern that institutional pressures were 'narrowing the field', and encouraging researchers to use safe, conventional approaches, following prescribed templates. On editor, for example, identified three unwelcome developments:

1. a narrowing of the field in terms of method, notwithstanding the efforts of some journals to attract a wide range of papers;
2. particularly for young scholars there is intense pressure to publish and the best way to publish in 'top' journals is by submitting safe papers;
3. qualitative researchers using 'templates' to mimic positivist approaches—this seems to me to be a dangerous trend in the sense that it undermines precisely what is valuable about qualitative research.

Recognizing these trends and developments, most editors wish to encourage researchers to challenge conventional methodological approaches. However, as in the first point from the editor just quoted, some expressed disappointment that fewer researchers were responding to this invitation, and were continuing to submit standard, safe, mainstream manuscripts. This could be evidence for a vicious circle—researchers do not produce methodologically challenging work in the belief that this will not be well received by editors and referees, but journals continue to publish methodologically conventional articles, thus reinforcing the belief that this is what editors want and expect.

The thirty-six articles cited by editors as displaying unconventional methodology are listed in the appendix to this chapter. In our assessment, twenty of those articles are unconventional on various dimensions: data analysis, research setting, mixed methods, writing style, research design, the translation of theory and evidence from another field, and data sources. Two fifths (fifteen), however, are based on mainstream methods, and those are the 'starred' items in the appendix. (One article—Dul, 2016—is not classifiable in these terms because it is an 'advocacy paper' without underpinning methodology.) Those starred items are interesting and valuable in other ways. For example, the article by Cornelissen and Durand (2014) won the American Academy of Management, Organization and Management Theory Division 'best published paper' award in 2015, even though it was not published in an Academy journal.

We had expected that most if not all of the articles cited by editors would be methodologically unconventional. One explanation for the number of conventional articles cited is that unconventional methodology is comparatively rare. Another explanation is that editors' judgements were influenced by the unusual topics, interesting research questions, excellent writing, and novel findings in the articles that they chose. A further explanation is that our own editorial assessment has been too harsh, and we have tried—perhaps artificially—to separate methodological from theoretical innovation. Readers can of course obtain those articles and reach their own judgements.

We asked editors if they felt that researchers were innovative or conservative in their approach. Most editors felt that researchers were indeed conservative, tending to rely on templates or 'cookbook recipes', exaggerating the risks in deviating from established norms, and believing that journals would not welcome unconventional approaches. As pointed out earlier, this degree of conformity on the part of researchers undermines innovation as much as the institutional forces explored earlier.

Editors also believe that most reviewers are receptive to unconventional approaches, as long as these are clearly explained and justified. However, journals each use a large number of reviewers, and it is therefore difficult to generalize with regard to their individual perspectives. Editors also pointed out that researchers must recognize that it is the job of reviewers to be sceptical, with regard to all aspects of articles that are submitted to their journals, as well as methodology.

Journal editors and researchers operate within the same web of institutional forces, and thus face similar pressures and demands. Editors are understandably concerned with impact factors and article citations. However, editors also know that the 'high impact' research, which turns out to be influential and frequently cited, is often based on work that sits outside traditional methodological norms. Consequently, articles submitted to journals are unlikely to be rejected solely on the grounds that they are unconventional. Researchers who wish to challenge the norms, to break the rules, to expand the envelope, to break with tradition, have editorial permission to do so. We will return to the advice for researchers based on the comments of journal editors in our concluding chapter.

But choose your journals with care; has this journal previously published unconventional work? Explain and justify your approach. Link your work to topical themes. Remember that theoretical contribution remains central.

The structure of this book

Drawing on an international group of leading and inventive researchers, the following twelve chapters illustrate a range of unconventional approaches to methodology in organization and management studies. These chapters are divided into three parts concerning, respectively: unconventional settings and data sources; unconventional research design and data collection methods; and unconventional analytic approaches. This is a 'division of convenience', as individual chapters defy neat categorization by breaking with convention in more than one dimension.

UNCONVENTIONAL SETTINGS AND DATA SOURCES

There are five chapters in this area. Laurie Cohen and Joanne Duberley describe how they used data from the popular radio programme, Desert Island Discs, to inform their study of celebrity scientists' careers. Robin Holt and Mike Zundel explore how fiction and television programmes can be used in organizational ethnography. Andrew P. Knight illustrates innovations in unobtrusive methods, focusing in particular on the uses of new technologies in this respect. Based partly on their own experience, David A. Buchanan and David Denyer assess the benefits and methodological challenges of conducting research in extreme contexts. Christopher J. Schneider explains the sources of research evidence opened up by social media in general and Twitter in particular.

UNCONVENTIONAL RESEARCH DESIGN AND DATA COLLECTION METHODS

There are five chapters in this area. Robert V. Kozinets and Manuela Nocker explain the use of netnography, a method originally developed by Kozinets. Alex Bitektine, Jeffrey W. Lucas, and Oliver Schilke explore the innovative use of experimental methods in developing institutional theory. Steve Kempster and Ken Parry explain how co-constructed autoethnography can open access to issues and topics difficult to research with traditional methods. Rebecca Whiting, Helen Roby, Gillian Symon, and Petros Chamakiotis describe their study of work–life boundary management which was based on participant-led video diaries. Olivier Berthod, Michael Grothe-Hammer, and Jörg Sydow introduce inter-organizational ethnography as a novel methodological perspective.

UNCONVENTIONAL ANALYTIC APPROACHES

There are two chapters in this area. Paul Carlile and Karl-Emanual Dionne consider the methodological implications of a sociomaterial perspective on organizations and management. Finally, Jörg Sydow, Arnold Windeler, Gordon Müller-Seitz, and Knut Lange develop the concepts of path dependence and path creation with the method of path constitution analysis.

▨ APPENDIX: EDITORS' CHOICE OF METHODOLOGICALLY INNOVATIVE ARTICLES (* = MAINSTREAM)

Bernstein, E.S. (2012). 'The transparency paradox: a role for privacy in organizational learning and operational control', *Administrative Science Quarterly*, 57(2): 181–216.

*Carter, N.T., Carter, D.R., and DeChurch, L.A. (2015). 'Implications of observability for the theory and measurement of emergent team phenomena', *Journal of Management*, first published online, 29 October.

Cascio, W.F. and Luthans, F. (2014). 'Reflections on the metamorphosis at Robben Island: the role of institutional work and positive psychological capital', *Journal of Management Inquiry*, 23(1): 51–67.

Chatterji, A.K., Findley, M., Jensen, N.M., Meier, S., and Neilson, D. (2016). 'Field experiments in strategy research', *Strategic Management Journal*, 37(1): 116–32.

Christensen, L.J. and Hammond, S.C. (2015). 'Lost (but not missing) at work: organizational lostness as an employee response to change', *Journal of Management Inquiry*, 24(4): 405–18.

*Cornelissen, J., Mantere, S., and Vaara, E. (2014). 'The contraction of meaning: the combined effect of communication, emotions, and materiality on sensemaking in the Stockwell Shooting', *Journal of Management Studies*, 51(5): 699–736.

*Dagnino, G.B., Levanti, G., and Li Destri, A.M. (2016). 'Structural dynamics and intentional governance in strategic interorganizational network evolution: a multi-level approach', *Organization Studies*, 7(3): 349–73.

Dul, J. (2016). 'Necessary condition analysis (NCA): logic and methodology of "necessary but not sufficient" causality', *Organizational Research Methods*, 19(1): 10–52.

*Edlinger, G. (2015). 'Employer brand management as boundary-work: a grounded theory analysis of employer brand managers' narrative accounts', *Human Resource Management Journal*, 25(4): 443–57.

*Ghumman, S. and Rayan, A.M. (2013). 'Not welcome here: discrimination towards women who wear the Muslim headscarf', *Human Relations*, 66(5): 671–98.

*Goyer, M., Clark, I., and Bhankaraully, S. (2016). 'Necessary and sufficient factors in employee downsizing? A qualitative comparative analysis of lay-offs in France and the UK, 2008–2013', *Human Resource Management Journal*, 26(3): 252–68 (published online, February).

Gylfe, P., Franck, H., Lebaron, C., and Mantere, S. (2016). 'Video methods in strategy research: focusing on embodied cognition', *Strategic Management Journal*, 37(1): 133–48.

Kahl, S.J. and Grodal, S. (2016). 'Discursive strategies and radical technological change: multilevel discourse analysis of the early computer (1947–1958)', *Strategic Management Journal*, 37(1): 149–66.

Kenny, K. (2016). 'Organizations and violence: the child as abject-boundary in Ireland's industrial schools', *Organization Studies*, 37(7): 939–61 (published online, February).

*Knights, D. and McCabe, D. (2015). 'Masters of the universe: demystifying leadership in the context of the 2008 Global Financial Crisis', *British Journal of Management*, 26(2): 197–210.

Kogut, B. and Zander, U. (2000). 'Did socialism fail to innovate?: a natural experiment of the two Zeiss companies', *American Sociological Review*, 65(2): 169–90.

Lee, C.-H., Hoehn-Weiss, M.N., and Karim, S. (2016). 'Grouping interdependent tasks: using spectral graph partitioning to study complex systems', *Strategic Management Journal*, 37(1): 177–91.

Levitt, S.D. and Venkatesh, S.A. (2000). 'An economic analysis of a drug-selling gang's finances', *Quarterly Journal of Economics*, 115(3): 755–89.

Li, M., Ying, L., Huang, S., and Crossland, C. (2016). 'The use of sparse inverse covariance estimation for relationship detection and hypothesis generation in strategic management', *Strategic Management Journal*, 37(1): 86–97.

*Macdonald, S., Steen, J., and Shazi, R. (2016). 'Aiming for excellence: reflections on the advanced institute of management research and its elite', *British Journal of Management*, 27(2): 438–54.

*Munro, I. and Jordan, S. (2013). '"Living Space" at the Edinburgh Festival Fringe: spatial tactics and the politics of smooth space', *Human Relations*, 66(11): 1497–525.

*Oertel, S., Thommes, K., and Walgenbach, P. (2016). 'Organizational failure in the aftermath of radical institutional change', *Organization Studies*, 37(8): 1067–87 (published online, February).

*Ogbonna, E. and Harris, L.C. (2015). 'Subcultural tensions in managing organisational culture: a study of an English Premier League football organisation', *Human Resource Management Journal*, 25(2): 217–32.

Parker, M. (2011). 'Organizing the circus: the engineering of miracles', *Organization Studies*, 32(4): 555–69.

Prasad, A. (2014). 'You can't go home again: and other psychoanalytic lessons from crossing a neo-colonial border', *Human Relations*, 67(2): 233–57.

Quattrone, P. (2015). 'Governing social orders, unfolding rationality, and Jesuit accounting practices: a procedural approach to institutional logics', *Administrative Science Quarterly*, 60(3): 411–55.

*Santacreu-Vasut, E., Shenkar, O., and Shoham, A. (2014). 'Linguistic gender marking and its international business ramifications', *Journal of International Business Studies*, 45(9): 1170–8.

Sgourev, S.V. (2015). 'Brokerage as catalysis: how Diaghilev's *Ballets Russes* escalated modernism', *Organization Studies*, 36(3): 343–61.

*Shortt, H. (2015). 'Liminality, space and the importance of "transitory dwelling places" at work', *Human Relations*, 68(4): 633–58.

Shrivastava, P. and Ivanova, O. (2015). 'Inequality, corporate legitimacy and the Occupy Wall Street movement', *Human Relations*, 68(7): 1209–31.

*Tharenou, P. (2015). 'Researching expatriate types: the quest for rigorous methodological approaches', *Human Resource Management Journal*, 25(2): 149–65.

Timming, A.R. (2015). 'The "reach" of employee participation in decision-making: exploring the Aristotelian roots of workplace democracy', *Human Resource Management Journal*, 25(3): 382–96.

Venaik, S. and Midgley, D.F. (2015). 'Mindscapes across landscapes: archetypes of transnational and subnational culture', *Journal of International Business Studies*, 46(9): 1051–79.

*Wasserman, V. and Frenkel, M. (2015). 'Spatial work in between glass ceilings and glass walls: gender-class intersectionality and organizational aesthetics', *Organization Studies*, 36(11): 1485–505.

Woo, S.E., Chae, M., Jebb, A.T., and Kim, Y. (2016). 'A closer look at the personality-turnover relationship criterion expansion, dark traits, and time', *Journal of Management*, 42(2): 357–85.

Zundel, M., Holt, R., and Cornelissen, J. (2013). 'Institutional work in *The Wire*: an ethological investigation of flexibility in organizational adaptation', *Journal of Management Inquiry*, 22(1): 102–20.

▓ REFERENCES

Aalbers, M.B. (2004). 'Creative destruction through the Anglo-American hegemony: a non-Anglo-American view on publications, referees and language', *Area*, 36(3): 319–22.

Alvesson, M. and Gabriel, Y. (2013). 'Beyond formulaic research: in praise of greater diversity in organizational research and publications', *Academy of Management Learning and Education*, 12(2): 245–63.

Alvesson, M. and Sandberg, J. (2013). 'Has management studies lost its way?: ideas for more imaginative and innovative research', *Journal of Management Studies*, 50(1): 128–52.

Bansal, P. and Corley, K. (2011). 'The coming of age for qualitative research: embracing the diversity of qualitative methods', *Academy of Management Journal*, 54(2): 233–7.

Barley, S.R. (2016). '60th anniversary essay: ruminations on how we became a mystery house and how we might get out', *Administrative Science Quarterly*, 61(1): 1–8.

Bell, E., Warren, S., and Schroeder, J. (eds) (2014). *The Routledge Companion to Visual Organization*. Abingdon, UK and New York: Routledge.

Bengry-Howell, A., Wiles, R., Nind, M., and Crow, G. (2011). 'A review of the academic impact of three methodological innovations: netnography, child-led research and creative research methods', National Centre for Research Methods. <http://eprints.ncrm.ac.uk/1844/>

Billsberry, J. (2013). 'A longitudinal empirical study into the buildup of fluff in my belly button', *Journal of Management Education*, 37(5): 595–600.

Bryman, A. (1988). *Quantity and Quality in Social Research*. London: Unwin Hyman.

Bryman, A. (2008). 'The end of the paradigm wars?'. In P. Alasuutari, L. Bickman, and J. Brannen (eds), *The SAGE Handbook of Social Research Methods*. London: Sage.

Bryman, A. (2011). 'Mission accomplished? Research methods in the first five years of *Leadership*', *Leadership*, 7(1): 73–83.

Bryman, A. (2016). *Social Research Methods*. Fifth edition. Oxford: Oxford University Press .

Buchanan, D.A. and Bryman, A. (2007). 'Contextualizing methods choice in organizational research', *Organizational Research Methods*, 10(3): 483–501.

Butler, N., Delaney, H., and Spoelstra, S. (2017). 'The gray zone: questionable research practices in the business school', *Academy of Management Learning & Education*, 16(1): 94–109.

Cameron, R. and Molina-Azorín, J.F. (2011). 'The acceptance of mixed methods in business and management research', *International Journal of Organizational Analysis*, 19(3): 256–71.

Cassell, C. (2016). 'European qualitative research: a celebration of diversity and a cautionary tale', *European Management Journal*, 34(5): 453–6.

Conway, S. and Steward, F. (2009). *Managing and Shaping Innovation*. Oxford: Oxford University Press.

Corbett, A., Cornelissen, J., Delios, A., and Harley, B. (2014). 'Variety, novelty, and perceptions of scholarship in research on management and organizations: an appeal for ambidextrous scholarship', *Journal of Management Studies*, 51(1): 4–18.

Cornelissen, J. (2017). 'Preserving theoretical divergence in management research: why the explanatory potential of qualitative research should be harnessed rather than suppressed', *Journal of Management Studies*, 54(3): 368–83.

Cornelissen, J. and Durand, R. (2014). 'Moving forward: developing theoretical contributions in management studies', *Journal of Management Studies*, 51(6): 995–1022.

Davis, M.S. (1971). 'That's interesting!: towards a phenomenology of sociology and a sociology of phenomenology', *Philosophy of the Social Sciences*, 1(4): 309–44.

Emmison, M., Smith, P., and Mayall, M. (2012). *Researching the Visual*. Second edition. London: Sage.

Fetters, M. (2016). '"Haven't we always been doing mixed methods research?": lessons learned from the development of the horseless carriage', *Journal of Mixed Methods Research*, 10(1): 3–11.

Forbes, I. (2003). 'Perceptions of cutting edge research in UK social science', *Innovation*, 16(3): 271–91.

Gardner, W.L., Lowe, K.B., Moss, T.W., Mahoney, K.T., and Cogliser, C.C. (2010). 'Scholarly leadership of the study of leadership: a review of *The Leadership Quarterly's* second decade, 2000–2009', *The Leadership Quarterly*, 21(6): 922–58.

Harley, B. (2015). 'The one best way? "Scientific" research on HRM and the threat to critical scholarship', *Human Resource Management Journal*, 25(4): 399–407.

Hargreaves Heap, S.P. and Parikh, A. (2005). 'The diffusion of ideas in the academy: a quantitative illustration from economics', *Research Policy*, 34: 1619–32.

Herzberg, F., Mausner, B., and Snyderman, B.B. (1959). *The Motivation to Work*. New York: John Wiley.

Hesse-Biber, S. (2015). 'Mixed methods research: the "thing-ness" problem', *Qualitative Health Research*, 25(6): 775–88.

Jewitt, C., Xambo, A., and Price, S. (2017). Exploring methodological innovation in the social sciences: the body in digital environments and the arts *International Journal of Social Research Methodology*, 20(1): 105–20.

Kaplan, H.R., Tausky, C.T., and Bolaria, B.S. (1969). 'Job enrichment', *Personnel Journal*, October: 791–8.

McGrath, J.E. (1981). 'Dilemmatics: the study of research choices and dilemmas', *American Behavioral Scientist*, 25(2): 179–210.

Maxwell, J.A. (2016). 'Expanding the history and range of mixed methods research', *Journal of Mixed Methods Research*, 10(1): 12–27.

Mingers, J. and Willmott, H. (2013). 'Taylorising business school research: on the "one best way" performative effects of journal ranking lists', *Human Relations*, 68(8): 1051–73.

Pelto, P.J. (2015). 'What is so new about mixed methods?', *Qualitative Health Research*, 25(6): 734–45.

Rogers, E.M. (2003). *Diffusion of Innovations*. Fifth edition. New York: Free Press.

Spoelstra, S., Butler, N., and Delaney, H. (2016). 'Never let an academic crisis go to waste: leadership studies in the wake of journal retractions', *Leadership*, 12(4): 383–97.

Taylor, C. and Coffey, A. (2008). *Innovation in Qualitative Research Methods: Possibilities and Challenges*. Cardiff: Cardiff School of Social Sciences Working Paper 121. <www.cardiff.ac.uk/socsi/resources/wp121.pdf>

Travers, M. (2009). 'New methods, old problems: a sceptical view of innovation in qualitative research', *Qualitative research*, 9(2): 161–79.

Vroom, V.H. (1964). *Work and Motivation*. New York: John Wiley.

Wiles, R., Crow, C., and Pain, H. (2011). 'Innovation in qualitative research methods: a narrative review' *Qualitative Research*, 11(5): 587–604.

Wiles, R., Bengry-Howell, A., Crow, G., and Nind, M. (2013). 'But is it innovation?: The development of novel methodological approaches in qualitative research', *Methodological Innovations Online*, 8(1): 18–33.

Xenitidou, M. and Gilbert, N. (2012). 'Introduction to the special issue: the process of methodological innovation–narrative accounts and reflections', *Methodological Innovations Online*, 7(1): 1–6.

Part 1
Unconventional Settings and Data Sources

2 Desert island data

Using BBC Radio 4's *Desert Island Discs* in organization and management research

Laurie Cohen and Joanne Duberley

Radio archives: an untapped resource

Each week, for over 70 years, a public figure—be it a scientist, artist, politician, sportsperson, fashion designer or adventurer, is sent to a fictitious desert island. Castaways are allowed to bring eight records, the Bible, the complete works of Shakespeare and one luxury item.

Behind this exile is BBC Radio 4, the UK's best-known spoken word station, and its iconic, weekly programme, *Desert Island Discs*. Since its launch on 29 January 1942, *Desert Island Discs* has never been off the air and has had only four presenters. The founder, Roy Plomley, was host for 45 years, while Kirsty Young, the current presenter, has just celebrated her tenth anniversary. We are writing this on 7 November 2016, and to date 3,092 guests have been sent to Radio 4's fictitious island. Many have been sent twice. Some, like Petula Clark and Terry Wogan, have gone three times, and Arthur Askey and Sir David Attenborough were cast away to that desert island four times (Symons, 2012).

The format of the programme is simple, and has hardly changed over its 70-year history. In each 45-minute slot, castaways are invited to tell their life stories, punctuated by extracts from the eight records they selected. Presenters use these 'desert island discs' as vehicles for castaways to reminisce on the things that are important to them, the choices they have made, the people whose lives they have shared, and the wider worlds in which their lives have unfolded. As they recount their experiences and share their musical choices, they are invited to reflect on the thoughts and feelings that these memories evoke.

For the organization and management researcher, *Desert Island Discs* is a rich, and thus far largely untapped resource. The two of us have been *Desert Island Discs* fans for years: as career researchers, we are fascinated by its use of music in elucidating aspects of experience that are often deeply buried and hard to see using our conventional approaches, and as inveterate interviewers are always keen to see how others do it. When, in 2012, the BBC made the *Desert Island Discs* archive publicly available, as part of its 70-year anniversary festivities, we were able to put our leisure interest to work. The result culminated in our paper, 'Constructing careers through narrative and music: an analysis of *Desert Island Discs*', published in the *Journal of Vocational Behavior* (Cohen and Duberley, 2013).

Our motivations for the *JVB* paper were threefold. The first was our affinity with the programme and interest in the career insights it unwittingly offered. The second was our increasing frustration with our established, talk-based research methods. Semi-structured interviews can certainly be effective in eliciting what happened (e.g. the 'career timeline'), but in our experience they are less useful in tapping into the emotional dimensions of people's experience. Our respondents could tell us the facts and often recounted memories of how they felt at particular moments along the way, but it was much less typical for them to actually feel those things in the cold light of the interview. We were aware that we were often generating rationalized accounts of emotion, rather than emotion itself. In contrast, it seemed that something special happened on *Desert Island Discs* when the music was played, and we wondered how this might add a new dimension to our understanding of career. Our third motivation was practical, about the strictures of doing careers research at times of austerity, the difficulty of securing research grants, and the growing realization that in the world of ubiquitous media, we actually are surrounded by careers data. We just need to recognize it when we see it.

Although our triggers were methodological, the *JVB* paper was empirical: about the construction of scientific identities in the public performance of career. In contrast, in this chapter we are focusing on the methodological issues. We will draw on the *JVB* paper as an example of practice, but our interest here is to reflect on the methodological use and value of this unique programme.

The chapter has four sections. In the first section we detail why we see *Desert Island Discs* as a rich resource for researchers in organization and management, and outline avenues for potential contributions. The second section examines *Desert Island Discs* as public performance. Drawing on Goffmann's (1959) *The Presentation of Self in Everyday Life*, we argue that the three-way conversations between presenters, castaways, and the ubiquitous but invisible audience offer unique insights into the negotiation of identity. In the third section we turn to the music. Finally, in the discussion, we reflect on the benefits, but also the limitations of using this iconic dataset in organization and management research.

Desert Island Discs in organization and management research

Although diverse in a myriad of ways, one feature that many organization and management researchers share is a keen interest in occupations. A cursory glance at the current issues of some of our journals (e.g. *Human Relations, Organization Studies, Journal of Management Studies*) reveals papers on a variety of occupational sectors including media and communication, catering, automobile manufacturing, utilities, chemicals and research. Working from different epistemological and ideological bases, and using a wide spectrum of techniques, we spend huge amounts of time generating and amassing enormous amounts of data which we hope will enable us to better understand how these occupations emerge, develop, succeed and fail; and how people in them experience working life.

The *Desert Island Discs* archive has a great deal to contribute to this common endeavour, extending back to 1942, and easily available online at <http://www.bbc.co.uk/programmes/b006qnmr>

From the home page, a visitor can access every castaway from 1942, searchable by name, musical choices, books and authors, and luxury items. Selection of the 'castaway' tab will lead to further categorization by occupation, presenter, and sex. In an instant we can, for example, access ninety-three interviews with people in the arts, from Tom Webster, sports cartoonist, in April 1942, to singer Michael Bublé in October 2016. We can listen to their stories about how they came to be in those fields, about what life was like there, about the music that evokes important memories of events, people, and feelings, and we can hear how books and their chosen luxury items further contribute to who these people are, and about their relationships with their occupational worlds. On a practical note, interviews are available to listen to as MP3 files, and most can also be accessed as podcasts. In our research we had our selection transcribed to facilitate coding.

In addition to the interviews, the archive includes other interesting information, including information and one-off 'special programmes' about the history of *Desert Island Discs* and the making of the archive; and popular collections, for instance Olympic gold medal winners, museum directors, and repeat castaways. For those of us interested in people's experience of work it is, indeed, a rich and unique resource.

Examined at the level of occupation, the *Desert Island Discs* archive offers vivid insights into how particular sectors are experienced and shaped by *successful* people working within them, highlighting, for instance, the ways in which gender, ethnicity, and class work to constrain and/or enable a person's experience. As we noted above, thus far organization and management researchers have made little use of the opportunities afforded by *Desert Island Discs*. However, in a rare example, McDonald (2014) draws on the transcribed audio files of seventeen highly reputed UK National Health Service doctors, between 1989 and 2012, to examine practices of social closure within the medical profession. Alongside their stories, she examines castaways' musical and literary choices to make an argument about the relationship between cultural capital (in particular Bourdieu's (1984) notion of taste), and occupational status and prestige.

In our case, we used thirty-four interviews with research scientists between 1988 and 2011 to investigate three aspects of career which we argued had been relatively neglected by researchers: the interrelationship of work and the life course; the notion of career as performance, and the role of emotion in the narration of career. We argued that in developing these accounts, scientists identified what they saw as the 'grand career narratives' (Savickas, 2005; Inkson, 2006) within their fields: the scientific career as a product of collective endeavour, triumph over adversity; as a quest for truth and beauty; and as making the world a better place. Through their accounts, they measured their own progress in terms of these socially ratified stories (Cohen and Duberley, 2013).

There are some important similarities, but also some notable differences in McDonald's approach and ours. Like us, McDonald believes that there are important insights to be gained from data generated outside of the conventional researcher-driven interview, in particular offering insights into how aspects of people's experience outside of the immediate occupational setting impact on their working lives. She is also interested in how people present themselves and legitimize who they are and what they do in a public setting. However, while her focus is on how *Desert Island Discs* performances reveal symbolic dimensions of experience and how these connect with their occupational status, we were keen to examine how these performances tapped into emotional aspects of people's lives that are typically subsumed within the overriding rationality of the career narrative, and how these can potentially enrich our understandings of occupational identity.

Although we have thus far been focusing on occupations, the *Desert Island Discs* archive can likewise be cut in other ways: by organization (offering, for example, rich case studies of the National Health Service, the BBC, or Covent Garden); presenter (the impersonal narratives constructed by Roy Plomley, compared to the much more confessional tales generated by Kirsty Young); and social variables like class, ethnicity, national cultural background, sexual orientation, etc. Castaways' choices of music, books, and luxury items offer further avenues for examining their preoccupations, aspirations, and the role of work in the contexts of their unfolding experience (Orbach, 2008).

The long history of *Desert Island Discs* presents yet another fruitful line of enquiry for organization and management researchers. As Bucheli and Wadhwani (2014) observe, scholars are taking an increasing interest in the value of history for our understanding of organizations, echoing trends in the social sciences more generally. 'Surveying these developments', they argue, 'one could fairly conclude that we are in the midst of a "historic turn" in the study of management, organizations and markets' (p.4). Bucheli and Wadhwani (2014, p.4) see historical perspectives as offering new ways of seeing that have the potential to challenge our more conventional approaches:

Unlike the general theory building and hypothesis testing methods valued by most economic, sociological and psychological approaches to organizational studies, historical reasoning emphasizes temporally contextualized explanations of organizations and markets [and we would argue, occupations] and the methodological challenges of assigning significance and meaning to incomplete and temporally distant evidence from the past. The real promise of a historic turn in organization studies, in this regard, lies not in a longitudinal perspective. Rather, it lies in the promise of new perspectives on the nature of organizations.

Bucheli and Wadhwani (2014) identify four key issues that historical perspectives highlight:

1. the notion of people and their actions as 'temporally situated', understood in terms of what came before and after;
2. the centrality of subjectivity and contextualization—how people understand their worlds;
3. an emphasis on 'embedded' rather than universal theory; and
4. the interaction of dimensions of experience over time, rather than the isolation and examination of unique 'variables'.

The nature of *Desert Island Discs* accounts certainly lends itself to such temporally situated perspectives. During the course of their interviews, castaways position themselves within their current contexts: geographical, social, etc. This is vividly illustrated in the following extract from Nobel laureate and astrophysicist Dame Jocelyn Bell Burnell (castaway in 2000), in which she describes her student days:

It was traditional at that time that whenever a woman entered a lecture theatre all the men stamped, thumped the benches, whistled, cat-called, so for my final two years of university, every class I went to I had to face that kind of barrage.

In another episode, geneticist Sir Alec Jeffreys (castaway in 2007) recounts his first experience of chemistry:

It really was my father's fault. He got me at the age of eight a chemistry set. Now if you go to a toy shop now and get a chemistry set it's a very anodyne thing. I mean it's going to do no harm whatsoever. This was the real McCoy chemistry set and I got on very well with the local pharmacist so he would top it up with, I mean, absolutely lethal chemicals.

Castaways speak of current events—of what's happening politically, economically, and culturally. They talk at length about where they have come from, and about where they are headed. Individually these oral histories serve as rich pictures of people in their times. Examined over time, we can observe how certain patterns endure and are reproduced, how others are challenged, and how some are transformed. In another *JVB* paper, Cohen (2006) draws on cultural theorist Raymond Williams' (1977) notions of residual, dominant, and emergent discourses to examine how we make sense of career over time. She argues that, as new meanings emerge, they do not simply erase the old, but rather intersect with them in interesting ways: sometimes to reproduce old patterns, sometimes to transform them, and sometimes to create new kinds of hybrids.

The *Desert Island Disc* archive lends itself to this kind of analysis. We can, for example, examine each of Sir David Attenborough's four appearances on *Desert Island Discs* as a portrait of a man's working life, of the career of a celebrity environmentalist, of society's changing relationship with the nat- ural world, or of working in the BBC. However, if we look at how these themes developed over all four of his appearances, in 1957, 1979, 1998 and 2012, we can observe how, as a new discourse comes to the fore it does not obliterate what came before, but rather intersects with it in a dynamic struggle for visibility, legitimacy, and influence. And we can see how all of these competing meanings are both products and shapers of the contexts in which they emerge.

The Desert Island Discs performance

The centrepiece of *Desert Island Discs* is of course the interview performance. And it is a public performance—broadcast around the world to a huge but largely faceless audience. This intrigues us for a number of reasons. First, a familiar challenge for organization and management researchers is dealing with 'interviewer effects': the manifold ways in which our presence impacts on the research process (Webb et al., 1966; Bryman and Bell, 2015). In the case of *Desert Island Discs*, we are mere onlookers: far from the role of the 'puppeteer' (Watson, 2000) which we more typically play, pulling the strings to ensure that the interview unfolds in a way that enables us to fulfil our goal. In this case, we are part of the faceless crowd to which the castaway is responding, there but not there, impacting but only indirectly and anonymously. On one hand, then, *Desert Island Discs* can be seen as an example of what Webb et al. (1966) describe as unobtrusive, or non-reactive research approaches. How- ever, while the researcher might only be there as a virtual observer, *Desert Island Discs* presenters are central to the performance. Indeed, they generate questions, offer interpretations and act as foils against which the castaways create their narratives.

Second, as researchers we are always mindful of ethical concerns and go to great lengths to ensure the confidentiality and anonymity of our encounters, if this is what our respondents wish. However, the aim of *Desert Island Discs* is to reach millions of listeners. Critics might argue that is the drawback: that *Desert Island Discs* performance is pure and simply entertainment—an opportunity for famous people to tell the public a story that shows them in a favourable light, thus further enhancing their already significant reputations. If this is the case, what possible value could it have as research?

We would argue that for a qualitative researcher, far from being a problem, this 'socially desired' version is actually extremely important. We have long debated this issue, and time and again are asked to defend ourselves against the allegation that our respondents are not being 'truthful', or that they are telling us 'stories that they want us to hear'. Of course they are, and this is precisely what makes them so valuable and so interesting. We can learn a great deal about our current situation from examining these socially ratified versions, and about what it is that makes a particular story so salient right here and right now. In cases where people are positioning themselves in opposition to these versions, these stories reveal the complex interplay of dominant and subordinate meaning systems—how some versions are taken for granted and come to be accepted as natural, while others are obscured, marginalized or dismissed as irrelevant.

Furthermore, we share Schwandt's (2003) concern about a) the ethics of probing into people's innermost thoughts, and of trying to somehow outwit them to get to some kernel of truth, and b) whether this is even possible. Such an intention presupposes a notion of the 'authentic' self that we have some serious doubts about. Instead, we see interviews as local accomplishments (Alvesson, 2003), people's accounts today, in this place. We recognize that each respondent is likely to have different versions of the same thing that they will recount to different audiences in different circumstances. The prescient thing for us is the story they are telling us (or the world) right now and why, in the here and now, we come to accept it. In other words, we see *Desert Island Discs* performances as occasions for establishing legitimacy. This is accomplished through castaways' presentation of self. Here we turn to Erving Goffman's (1959) *The Presentation of Self in Everyday Life* for a framework through which we can analyse these 'performances'.

Goffman, a symbolic interactionist, was interested in how, through their interactions with others, people construct versions of themselves. Others then respond to the individual based on these versions. It is an ongoing, iterative, social process. Using a dramaturgical metaphor, Goffman explains that like members of a cast, people thus work together to shape and re-shape identities. Their performances depend on what they are hoping to achieve. They reveal, conceal aspects of themselves, refuting or confirming others' versions, in order to fulfil these aims.

To any encounter, participants bring particular, prior understandings and idealized versions. These are not 'true' or 'untrue' in any ontological sense, but are shaped by past experiences—of the person, of people like him or her, or of the situation. Based on these prior understandings, or in Goffman's terms 'impressions', we make sense of one another. In the course of the encounter, these impressions are negotiated. Sometimes we accept others' definitions, while at other times we resist them, or present alternatives. This negotiation is at the heart of the *Desert Island Discs* performance.

Each *Desert Island Discs* episode starts with the presenter giving a short introduction to the castaway. In Goffman's sense, the presenter outlines their prior understanding, and asks the castaway to accept or refute it. In the *JVB* paper we cite an example of Sue Lawley's (1995) interview with controversial biologist Richard Dawkins to illustrate this process. We still think it is a powerful example, and so are likewise using it here. In what follows Lawley presents her publicly ratified version, and invites Dawkins to respond:

Lawley: My castaway this week is a biologist. He believes that Darwin's theories of evolution provide the starting point for everything we need to know about our world. He began to develop his ideas as a student at Oxford and later published them in popular books such as *The Selfish Gene* and *The Blind Watchmaker*. Happy to be seen as a bridge between academic science and the general public, he's not frightened of controversy and has frequently found himself in dispute with leading theologians. He is Richard Dawkins. It's not surprising, really, that theologians see you as public enemy number one when you've put God on par with Father Christmas and the Tooth Fairy. But you don't draw those analogies lightly, do you?

Dawkins: No, I think it's a very serious analogy. I think that Father Christmas and the Tooth Fairy are childhood myths...and I think God is very much like that.

This idea of identity as an ongoing negotiation between different versions, some introduced from outside the situation and others generated in the course of the encounter, is at the heart of the *Desert Island Discs* performance.

Key elements of this performance, and of Goffman's framework, are setting and use of space. Given that Goffman's interest is in the processes through which the self is negotiated and constructed in everyday encounters, it is no surprise that his framework attends to the meaning of the social setting. A key element of the *Desert Island Discs* setting is its history and its place in the popular imagination. Each episode acknowledges Roy Plomley, the programme's founder, and avid listeners will know that Eric Coates' 'By the Sleepy Lagoon', the theme tune, has never changed. Indeed, the programme and the tune have come to represent one another.

Desert Island Discs has made appearances in plays, television programmes (Magee, 2012), and even in everyday conversation people share their own 'Desert Island Discs'. Each new episode takes its place in this long history, becoming part of the programme's legacy. Goffman reminds us that prior meanings are not only introduced by actors involved in a particular encounter, but also by the setting itself. In other words, castaways position themselves in relation to the presenter and the meanings they introduce, and at the same time in relation to the programme itself, its 70-year history and its iconic status.

So culturally embedded are these informal rules, that examples of bad behaviour cause something of a stir; for example, in 1958, when soprano Elizabeth Schwarzkopf chose seven of her own recordings, or more recently when Michael Bublé chose a product for which he was a brand ambassador as his luxury item. This is not how castaways are meant to behave! And yet they continue to try their luck with the rules, formal and informal. Only yesterday (we are writing this on 7 November 2016) author Ali Smith asked if along with the Bible she could bring other holy books. Kirstie Young confirmed that this was definitely not possible—that the rules were the rules. Smith said she was going to take the books anyway.

Public responses to these transgressions are interesting because they highlight what Goffman (1959, p.114) conceptualizes as the difference between front and backstage performance spaces. Front stage is where the action happens: where certain meanings are put forward while others are concealed. It is what the audience sees. In Goffman's view, front stage is where acceptable rules of behaviour (what Goffman calls 'decorum') are prescribed and maintained. Some of these rules are explicit. Bringing additional religious books is not allowed, and Ali Smith knows it. Others are informal. Although choosing one's own pieces was not formally prohibited, it was considered discourteous. To do it seven times was a downright affront. By breaking this rule, Schwartzkopf was firmly establishing herself as a rebel.

Indelibly linked to the front stage is it opposite: the back stage. This is where proscribed meanings and versions are revealed. It is a place of subversion. The metaphor often used to described this front/backstage relationship is the restaurant kitchen. Waiters comport themselves beautifully as they serve customers in the front of house, but back in the kitchen can be found eating leftovers off customers' plates, swearing, shouting, and even fighting.

As we explain in the *JVB* paper, we have no first-hand experience of *Desert Island Discs'* back stage spaces. However, in his history of the programme, Magee (2012) provides some insights into how the polished versions we listen to each week come to be. He explains how in the early days Roy Plomley used to write the scripts himself, with little input from the castaways. At alcohol-infused pre-recording lunches at his club, these would be honed and polished in preparation for the final broadcast. These days such boozy lunches have been abandoned, and the groundwork for each programme is carefully prepared by researchers. Presenters do not meet the castaways until the actual show. This difference in back stage activity has a clear bearing on the performance: whereas early examples are staid and formal, rarely if ever straying from what is considered to be 'safe' territory, today's programmes feel alive and spontaneous.

In spite of its longevity and the many aspects of *Desert Island Discs* that have endured, some of the rules of engagement have clearly changed, from the wider range of music that has come to be acceptable, to the intimate, confessional tone of Kirsty Young's interviews. For the organization and management researcher, how *Desert Island Discs'* rules and practices move between front and backstage, and how legitimate public identities are established and re-established in contexts which are at once deeply traditional, and fluid, are rich sites for enquiry.

The music

Of course the thing that makes *Desert Island Discs* stand apart from other celebrity interview formats is the music. It is this aspect of the programme which we feel stimulates responses that are simply unavailable through other means. Guests do not just choose eight pieces of music that they happen to like. Instead, the music serves as a prop, helping them to tell the story of their life. As Kirsty Young comments, in making their choice, guests are reminded that 'it's about pinpointing pieces that cast light on their life's most significant moments—adversities conquered, children born, lovers lost, laughter shared' (Young, 2012, p.vii).

Methodologically, the use of music to elicit discussion from respondents offers a fascinating insight into aspects of an individual's life experience and the ways in which they choose to present themselves. We would argue that this insight is afforded in two key ways. First, the music both evokes and enhances memories of a particular time and place. Second, it gives an insight into the ways individuals construct and present their identity. We suggest that this offers understandings that would not be readily available in a traditional interview format.

EVOKING MEMORY

Taking the first point, music has been shown to be a powerful trigger for particular memories. In his discussion of 70 years of *Desert Island Discs*, Magee (2012, p.xiii) talks of how the music can act as a 'timeshift, bringing an event from years ago right to the front of the castaway's memory'. Work in the field of neuropsychology (see for example Jäncke, 2008) has identified the tremendous role of music in building our autobiographical memories. Scherer and Zentner (2001, p.380) argue that this is because music is a pervasive element of social life and accompanies many highly significant events in an individual's life including, for example, religious ceremonies, marriage, burial rites, dancing, and other festivities. Thus, there are many associations between musical elements and emotionally charged memories. Second, they argue that music, like smell, which also powerfully evokes memories, may be dealt with at levels of the brain that are particularly resistant to modifications by later input, unlike other forms of memory.

Music sociologist Tia DeNora (1999) discusses the different types of memory that music can trigger. First, she argues that particular pieces of music can evoke specific memories—for example, key people or events. Second, she also suggests that music may evoke a more general sense of an era. In both cases, she argues that music is also (re)constituting past experience: 'it is making manifest within memory what may have been latent or even absent the first-time-through and music provides a device of prosthetic biography (Lury, 1998)' (DeNora, 1999, p.48).

This distinction between specific and general memories was clear to see in the *Desert Island Discs* interviews we examined. As discussed in Cohen and Duberley (2013), the scientists, like other castaways, talked about attachments to key people and places in their discussion of their musical choices. All of the respondents talked about how a particular track reminded them of an event. For example, Tom Blundell talks about how the Billy Holliday song 'Strange Fruit' reminds him of a Greyhound bus trip to the Southern States of the United States in 1964. Music was also used as a reminder of a particular person or group of people from the majority of castaways. For example, Mary Archer chose to play an organ voluntary by Walford Davies as her father loved organ music and regularly played it, and Hugh Pennington made the unusual choice of 'The Celtic Clippy' as one of his eight records because it reminded him of the very direct approach he had seen employed by successful women scientists to deal with those around them.

At a more general level, others used their choice of music to reflect on their experiences of working for a time in particular organizations. For example, Baruch Blumberg used the song 'Space Oddity' by David Bowie to talk at length about his experiences working at NASA, and Kay Davies gave a fascinating insight into the feeling of community she experienced at the Institute of Molecular Medicine, talking about how staff listened to 10cc's 'Wall Street Shuffle' whilst 'giggling on the floor'. More generally still, they chose tracks that reminded them of 'being a child of the sixties' (Colin Pillinger), or of growing up in South Africa (Lewis Wolpert). In these instances, music seemed to act as a kind of prop that helped the castaway reflect upon and project a certain version of their pasts. Beyond this it was also evident that the music enabled them to connect emotionally with a particular person or moment from their past. A good example of this recently was when Tom Hanks (interviewed May 2016) broke down in tears as he spoke about the feelings of loneliness that had driven his decision to become involved in theatre: 'What have you done to me?', he said to Kirsty as he began to sob. 'I've put far too much thought into this list.'

In the next section we explore how the music was also used to construct and present a particular self-identity.

CONSTRUCTING IDENTITY

One of the important aspects of the music is that it gives us enhanced insight into how people construct and present their identities. Knox and Macdonald (2015) point to growing research highlighting links between personal music preferences, social identity, and behaviour (see also North and Hargreaves, 2007; North et al., 2000; Tekman and Hortaçsu, 2002). Thus they argue that developing an insight into an individual's music preference can reveal important aspects of personality because music is crucially involved in how we construct, maintain, and negotiate our identities (MacDonald et al., 2002). Our musical tastes and preferences can form an important statement of our values and attitudes and enable us to express our own distinctive views of the world. Nicholas Cook (1998, p.5) puts this succinctly: 'In today's world, deciding what music to listen to is a significant part of deciding and announcing to people not just who you "want to be" but who you are.' In these data, it became apparent that scientists used the music to show their passion for their subject area, to reflect on particular relationships and periods of time and to express their core values. Whilst they differed in the extent to which they appeared to have been strategic in their music choice, as mentioned earlier, it seemed that discussing the music enabled them to touch on more personal and emotional issues and that the music provided an additional means for the listener to identify with the castaway.

On occasions castaways were very clearly attempting to project a particular identity. In these instances they talked about how a piece of music represented a fundamental character trait or belief that they felt explained their career and life decisions. Examples are Colin Blackmore who explained that his choice of Aaron Copland's 'Fanfare for the Common Man' represented the fact that he was both a humanist and a socialist, beliefs which had powerfully shaped his approach to both life and science. Similarly, Harry Kroto used John Lennon's 'Imagine' to talk about the idealism that underpinned his scientific endeavour. Lord May, on the other hand, suggested his choice of John Williamson's 'True Blue' reaffirmed his essential Australian-ness; and Colin Pillinger explained that his choice of 'A little less conversation, a little more action' by Elvis Presley represented an essential orientation to action that had endured throughout his scientific career.

Castaways often used music to talk about the emotional attachment they had to their science. Brian Cox, for example, spoke eloquently about how the song 'Moment in the Sun' represented for him 'the beautiful romantic idea of the regeneration of the universe', which was central to his scientific beliefs, and Joseph Rotblatt discussed how Paul Robeson's 'Ol' Man River' expressed his philosophical beliefs about the evolution of man and majesty of nature. These insights, generated in discussion about the music, arguably would not have been elicited in a more traditional career interview.

In addition, music choices can give the listener an insight into aspects of the castaway's background and experience that the castaways may not themselves have reflected upon. For example, as mentioned earlier, McDonald (2014) in her analysis of episodes of *Desert Island Discs* focusing on doctors, highlights how the music preferences that individuals display give an indicator of their socio-economic background. She argues that an analysis of doctors' music tastes and their mode of acquisition, mainly from their family or at private schools, coupled with the discussion of their cultural capital which takes place in *Desert Island Discs*, serves to highlight the important linkage between class and status in the professions (McDonald, 2014, p.902) as according to Bourdieu, 'nothing more clearly affirms one's 'class', nothing more infallibly classifies, than one's taste in music' (Bourdieu, 1984, p.18).

Discussion

We believe that *Desert Island Discs* is a valuable source of data for organization and management scholars, offering insights beyond the conventional interview approach. Pertinently, in the current funding environment, it is an inexpensive form of data that is freely available. More substantively, though, based on our own experience, what others have done, and considering further possibilities, we summarize the methodological contribution of *Desert Island Discs* as threefold:

1. it breaks the boundaries (e.g. work and non-work, symbolic and material dimensions, emotionality, and rationality) that other approaches often unwittingly reproduce;
2. it highlights the wider social values that underpin the ways in which working lives and careers unfold, and the identities that are constructed in this process; and
3. it captures the ways in which our prescriptions on what constitutes a legitimate (or illegitimate) working life changes over time, and across social groupings.

First, for careers researchers and other scholars interested in people's working lives, *Desert Island Discs'* unique combination of talk and music allows the listener to develop a more complete view of individual career experiences and enables respondents to reflect back on issues that would normally be neglected. Castaways can bring to their career story key individuals or circumstances that could be missed in a traditional researcher-led interview. We suggest that these interviews should be considered a form of life course interview (Elder et al., 2003), as respondents are encouraged to reflect upon key issues and events and the intertwining of the work and non-work aspects of their lives is explored.

A key strength we see in the *Desert Island Discs* data, therefore, is the focus on a whole life rather than merely career in terms of employment. Orbach (2008, p.15) talks of how *Desert Island Discs* has an enduring appeal because of the way in which guests 'conceptualize their whole life, their scientific endeavour, their acting, their writing, their political activity and its relation to the rest of their lives'. The music acts as an accompaniment drawing these different elements of life together, allowing the castaway to express emotion, including passion, sadness, and regret, as well as utilizing the music to convey some core aspect of their self-identity.

Second, as we argued in our *JVB* paper, the insights afforded by *Desert Island Discs* performances extend beyond the individual and their story of working life and career. Researchers can use these interviews to tap into the wider definition of career originally suggested by Everett Hughes in 1937 (pp.409–10) where career is the 'moving perspective in which the person sees his life as a whole and interprets the meaning of his various attributes and actions and the things that happen to him'. We suggest that *Desert Island Discs* also offers participants a public arena for them to make sense of themselves; an opportunity to construct their identity through narrative (Brown, 2004; Patriotta, 2003) in interaction with the interviewer and the wider audience. It is clear that this construction of identity draws from existing stories or myths (Barthes, 1972).

We have shown how by using Goffman's perspective it is possible to identify the ways in which individuals position themselves in relation to existing societal great or meta narratives (Inkson, 2006; Savickas, 2005). Here we see a link between what Alvesson and Karreman (2000) call the micro discourse of individuals' talk about their lives and the macro level discourse represented as an assembly of naturalized and determinative vocabularies that have 'a structuring principle in society, in social relations, modes of thought and individual subjectivity' (Weedon, 1987, p.41, cited in Alvesson and Karreman, 2000, p.1131). Interestingly, whereas researchers usually seek to avoid the impact of 'social desirability' on the answers given to them by respondents, here, by focusing on the public performance of career, as we discussed earlier it is precisely those socially legitimate views of career that come to the fore. Castaways thus negotiate a position for themselves by connecting to 'established cultural accounts' (Meyer and Scott, 1983, p.210) and utilizing what Suddaby and Greenwood (2005) term 'institutional vocabu- laries' to project a particular role identity. This enables the contextualization of an individual's career—not just within their work and economic environment, but also within the social and cultural environment. Such rich and deep contextualization can be difficult to elicit through the typical qualitative inter- view, bound by both convention and the researcher's particular agenda.

Third, given the historical turn in organization and management studies (Bucheli and Wadhwani, 2014), examining the ways in which individuals present themselves and their working lives in shows such as *Desert Island Discs* offers insight into (a) the ways in which the 'great narratives of our times' (Inkson, 2006, p.231; Savickas, 2005) have unfolded over the last 70 years; and (b) how people position themselves within them. Regrettably, in our own work we have not yet done such an analysis. However, given *Desert Island Discs'* long history and the easy accessibility of the archive, it is indeed a fascinating research opportunity.

Clearly there are issues to consider in using these kinds of data. First, as we noted earlier, *Desert Island Discs* could be seen as an unobtrusive or non-reactive method (Webb et al., 1966; Kellehear, 1993), an example of 'found' data, unsullied by the researcher's agenda, which are increasingly available via digital technologies (Lee, 2000; Hine, 2015). However, it is at the same time a public performance, carefully stage managed to ensure a particular effect. And we must remember that *Desert Island Discs* is designed to be entertaining, and all of those involved in its production will presumably be aware of the need to delight the listener. A cynic might for example scoff at our possibly naive acceptance that Tom Hanks—an accomplished actor—really felt such a deep level of emotion as he discussed his decision to enter the theatre. Similarly, we must recognize that the public nature of the interview may inhibit frank discussion of certain issues as presumably respondents think carefully about how their recording might be received by those close to them and their professional communities. Linked to this is the need to be aware that, as a result of an increased public acceptance of 'confessional' shows (Aslama and Pantti, 2006), and the different styles of presenters, the nature of the interviews is likely to have changed over time. On the other hand, as discussed earlier, this could be presented as a strength of the approach, that through analysing these interviews we can track changing institutional vocabularies of careers.

Second, it should also be remembered that the *Desert Island Discs* castaways are those at the very top of their fields. This does not negate the value of their career accounts but it does mean that we cannot assume their accounts are generalizable to others. Furthermore, a Radio 4 analysis of the most requested artists on *Desert Island Discs* over its history identifies the eight most popular choices as Mozart, Beethoven, Bach, Schubert, Verdi, Tchaikovsky, Elgar, and Puccini. The prevalence of classical music might be taken to suggest a largely middle-class group of castaways, or perhaps that castaways make their choice of music with one eye to the perceived tastes of a largely middle-class audience.

Third, our own research has focused on the use of *Desert Island Discs* as a means of understanding how scientists account for their careers. However, we acknowledge that other types of research questions could likewise be explored through these data, and indeed hope that this chapter will encourage other researchers to explore other possibilities. For example, researchers could consider a variety of issues concerning occupation, organization, and the lived experience of work. Importantly, as mentioned earlier, the scale and depth of the *Desert Island Discs* archive would allow consideration of how these issues evolved over time.

Through this chapter, we have discussed the unique nature of *Desert Island Discs* and the importance of the music as an autobiographical prop, arguing that it offers insights which are less available through more conventional research interviews. However, we also recognize the abundance of other potential sources of data from radio and television programmes. For example, Radio 4 has an archive of film interviews featuring discussions with people from all aspects of film making from a variety of different programmes (*Woman's Hour, The Film Programme*, and *Front Row*). Our own interest in scientific careers could perhaps be furthered through an examination of Jim Al-Khalili's *The Life Scientific*. Gendered aspects of organizational and domestic life could be examined through an analysis of programmes such as *Woman's Hour*. In fact the BBC (2007) has produced a fascinating book charting 60 years of *Woman's Hour* with summaries of key interviews and a commentary on the main social issues covered in each decade. Other radio stations likewise provide rich offerings. Television is also a huge potential resource, as discussed by Robin Holt and Mike Zundel in this volume, with many reality-based shows and 'fly-on-the-wall' documentaries giving insight into organizational life. We encourage creative thinking around such potential sources of data, particularly at a time when funding to undertake new empirical data collection is so hard to obtain.

Clearly the use of secondary data such as these has its frustrations—as a researcher you are not in charge and you can't take an interview in the direction you would like. However, the plus side of this is that it does open you up to unexpected delights and associations that you may never have considered.

■ REFERENCES

Alvesson, M. (2003). 'Beyond neopositivists, romantics, and localists: a reflexive approach to interviews', *Academy of Management Review*, 28 (1): 13–33.

Alvesson, M. and Karreman, D. (2000). 'Varieties of discourse: on the study of organizations through discourse analysis', *Human Relations*, 53 (9): 1125–49.

Aslama, M. and Pantti, M. (2006). 'Talking alone reality TV, emotions and authenticity', *European Journal of Cultural Studies*, 9 (2): 167–84.

Barthes, R. (1972). *Mythologies*. London: Paladin.

BBC (2007). *Woman's Hour: From Joyce Grenfell to Sharon Osbourne: Celebrating Sixty Years of Women's Lives*. London: John Murray.

Bourdieu, P. (1984). *Distinction: A Social Critique of the Judgement of Taste*. London: Routledge.

Brown, A. (2004). 'Authoritative sense making in a public inquiry report', *Organization Studies*, 25 (1): 95–112.

Bryman, A. and Bell, E. (2015). *Business Research Methods*, Fourth edition. Oxford: Oxford University Press.

Bucheli, M. and Wadhwani, R.D. (eds) (2014). *Organizations in Time*. Oxford: Oxford University Press.

Cohen, L. (2006). 'Remembrance of things past: cultural process and practice in the analysis of career stories', *Journal of Vocational Behavior*, 69: 89–201.

Cohen, L. and Duberley, J. (2013). 'Constructing careers through narrative and music: an analysis of *Desert Island Discs*', *Journal of Vocational Behavior*, 82: 165–75.

Cook, N. (1998). *Music: A Very Short Introduction*. Oxford: Oxford University Press.

DeNora, T. (1999). 'Music as a technology of the self', *Poetics*, 27 (1): 31–56.

Elder, G., Johnson, M., and Crosnoe, R. (2003). 'The emergence and development of life course theory.' In J. Mortimer and M. Shanahan (eds) *Handbook of the life course*, pp.3–19. New York: Kleuwer Academic.

Goffman, E. (1959). *The Presentation of Self in Everyday Life*. New York: Doubleday, Doran and Co Ltd.

Hine, C. (2015). *Ethnography for the Internet: Embedded, Embodied and Everyday*. London: Bloomsbury.

Hughes, E.C. (1937). 'Institutional office and the person', *American Journal of Sociology*, 43(3): 404–13.

Inkson, K. (2006). *Understanding Careers. The Metaphors of Working Lives*. London: Sage.

Jäncke, L. (2008). 'Music, memory and emotion', *Journal of Biology*, 7(6): 1–5.

Kellehear, A. (1993). *The Unobtrusive Researcher: A Guide to Methods*. St Leonards, NSW: Allen and Unwin.

Knox, D. and Macdonald, R. (2015). 'The Role of Technology in Music Listening For Health and Wellbeing', *Journal of Biomusical Engineering*, 3(1): 1–3.

Lee, R.M. (2000). *Unobtrusive Methods in Social Research*. Buckingham, UK: Open University Press.

Lury, C. (1998). *Prosthetic culture*. London: Routledge.

McDonald, R. (2014). ' "Bourdieu", medical elites and "social class": A qualitative study of "desert island" doctors', *Sociology of Health & Illness*, 36(6): 902–16.

MacDonald, R.A., Hargreaves, D.J., and Miell, D. (2002). *Musical identities*. Oxford: Oxford University Press.

Magee, S. (2012). *Desert Island Discs. 70 Years of Castaways*. London: Bantam Press.

Meyer, J.W. and Scott, W.R. (1983). 'Centralization and the legitimacy problems of the local government.' In J.W. Meyer and W.R. Scott (eds) *Organizational Environments: Ritual and Rationality*, pp.199–215. Beverly Hills, CA: Sage.

North, A.C. and Hargreaves, D.J. (2007). 'Lifestyle correlates of musical preference: 2. Media, leisure time and music', Psychology of Music, 35(12): 179–200.

North, A.C., Hargreaves D., and O'Neil, S. (2000). 'The importance of music to adolescents', *British Journal of Educational Psychology*, 70: 255–72.

Orbach, S. (2008). 'Work is where we live: emotional literacy and the psychological dimensions of the various relationships there', *Emotion, Space & Society*, 1: 14–17.

Patriotta, G. (2003). 'Sensemaking on the shopfloor: narratives of knowledge in organizations', *Journal of Management Studies*, 40(2): 349–75.

Savickas, M. (2005). 'The theory and practice of career construction.' In S.D. Brown and R.W. Lent (eds) *Career Development and Counselling: Putting Theory and Practice to Work*, pp.42–70. Hoboken, NJ: Wiley.

Scherer, K.R. and Zentner, M.R. (2001). 'Emotional effects of music: production rules.' In P.N. Juslin and J.A. Sloboda (eds) *Music and Emotion. Theory and Research,* pp.361–92. Oxford: Oxford University Press.

Schwandt, R. (2003). 'Three epistemological stances for qualitative inquiry: interpretivism, hermeneutics and social constructionism.' In N.K. Denzin and Y. Lincoln (eds) *The Landscape of Qualitative Research.* Second edition. London: Sage, pp.292–331

Suddaby, R. and Greenwood, R. (2005). 'Rhetorical strategies of legitimacy', *Administrative Science Quarterly*, 50(1): 35–67.

Symons, M. (2012). *Desert Island Discs. Flotsam and Jetsam.* London: Bantam Press.

Tekman, H.G. and Hortaçsu, N. (2002). 'Music and social identity: stylistic identification as a response to musical style', *International Journal of Psychology*, 37(5): 277–85.

Watson, T. (2000). 'Making sense of managerial work and organizational research processes with Caroline and Terry', *Organization*, 7(3): 489–510.

Webb, E.J., Campbell, D.T., Schwartz, R.T. and Sechrest, L. (1966). *Nonreactive Measures in the Social Sciences.* Second edition. Dallas, TX: Houghton Mifflin.

Weedon, C. (1987). *Feminist Practice and Poststructuralist Theory.* Oxford: Basil Blackwell.

Williams, R. (1977). *Marxism and Literature.* Oxford: Oxford University Press.

Young, K. (2012). Foreword in Magee, S. *Desert Island Discs. 70 Years of Castaways.* London: Bantam Press.

3 Using fiction in organization and management research

Robin Holt and Mike Zundel

Why fiction?

Following the inauguration of a new president in 2017, the United States struggled to come to terms with the flurry of 'fake news' and 'alternative facts' that accompanied the electoral process, and which then started to shape the executive orders signed by Donald Trump during his first days in office. So unsettling were these events that George Orwell's novel *1984* shot into the bestseller lists (de Freytas-Tamura, 2017). Bereft of reliable referents to the 'real', the world turned to fiction, which made more sense than fact, and indeed was being used to make sense of fact, as it has always been.

But what is fiction and how does it differ from scientific accounts? A fictional story, John Searle (1975, p.328) says, is 'a pretended representation of a state of affairs'. A provisional and simplistic answer, then, would have scientific accounts representing what is real, and so aspiring to truth, whilst fictions would make no such verifiable claims. This division has deep roots, reaching back to René Descartes. To know what was certain, it was insufficient to trust our senses. To prove his point, he examined a burning candle, noting how it altered with heat. Had it changed its nature? The only way of telling was to 'strip the wax of its clothes and mentally perceive it naked', in its basic elements (Russell, 1946; Rorty, 1989). Only the rationally trained mind can ascertain what is real, and under its categorising analysis fictitious appearances melt away, revealing facts in a manner that secure the agreement of any other rational inquirer (MacIntyre, 2009). Those writing fiction would relate to and recount a candle differently, playing with the effects of candlelight, for example, how it would stir memory, or cast the familiar in strange hues. They would not, though, be doing science.

However, as soon as the ontological difference between fiction and fact is claimed, counter-claims emerge. First, rather than being 'mere' literature, many stories began as factual accounts. Ancient sagas, Hesiod's *Theogony* or the *Book of Genesis*, for example, all purported in some way to touch on the realities of the human condition and were believed as such, and this continues to be the case for some (Eagleton, 1996). There are also fiction authors who draw on social scientific methods to source their materials: Sebald's historical analyses; Pynchon's studies of techno-historical complexities; Bolaño's scholarly literature criticism; or the ethnographic field study by Ed Burns and Dave Simon for the fictional TV series *The Wire*. And novelists such as Virginia Woolf (1984, pp.160–1) are so committed to revealing the nature of everyday life that they refuse to leave it, not for one second:

Examine for a moment an ordinary mind on an ordinary day. The mind receives myriad impressions—trivial, fantastic, evanescent, or engraved with the sharpness of steel. From all sides they come, an incessant shower of innumerable atoms; and as they fall, as they shape themselves into the life of Monday or Tuesday, the accent falls differently from of old; the moment of importance came not here but there; so that if a writer were a free man and not a slave, if he could write what he chose, not what he must, if he could base his work upon his own feeling and not upon convention, there would be no plot, no comedy, no tragedy, no love interest or catastrophe in the accepted style, and perhaps not a single button sewn on as the Bond Street tailors would have it. Life is not a series of gig lamps symmetrically arranged; life is a luminous halo, a semi-transparent envelope surrounding us from the beginning of consciousness to the end. Is it not the task of the novelist to convey this varying, this unknown and un-circumscribed spirit, whatever aberration or complexity it may display, with as little mixture of the alien and external as possible?

All such writing reflects a commitment to empirical experience that is no less trenchant than that of scientists.

Second, the fiction/fact distinction also looks shaky from the other side, when we look at the scientific production of fact. Take Latour and Woolgar's (1986, p.255) description of the work of a lab technician in their book *Laboratory Life*:

The observer had his protocol book and an empty data sheet in front of him. He seized the jumping frogs, beheaded, and flayed them, and finally immersed thin sections of skin into the beakers. He placed each of the beakers over a source of light and took readings from the reflectometer, which he then wrote down. By the end of the day, he had accumulated a small stack of figures which could be fed into the computer. After this he was left only with standard deviations, levels of significance, and means in the computer listing. On the basis of these he drew a curve and, taking it into his boss's office, argued about the slight differences and or similarities in the curve in order to make a point.

Latour and Woolgar notice that what may appear like a hard science—fact-establishing method—includes several more or less arbitrary choices: only a few pieces of skin were taken from the frog's complex organism; a premium was placed on effects which were recordable; data were cleaned up to improve contrast; and the whole affair was merely the basis of an effort to persuade others. The accounts so produced are fictitious—not, Latour and Woolgar (1986, p.261) argue, in any specific step, but in terms of understanding the entire fact-production process. They conclude that the assumed difference between the hard natural and soft social sciences bleeds into insignificance.

This is seen in all research experience. Throw yourself into interview talk, or into the detail of a survey, and as data is amassed, so are questions of its veracity, of its structuring and its guiding our attention and memory, of its reliance on existing facts without which the study is meaningless. How, for example, is a researcher to discern whether the way people project themselves in the world—their identity—is consistent across an ethnic group or social class? Is identity conscious or unconscious, and how does one access the latter? Will it change with time and how then to explore identity longitudinally? How is identity deliberately altered depending on the context of performance, or how instinctual is it? How to get at the background conditions by which such presentations make sense? Evidently by using already existing categories like ethnicity and class, but who authorizes these? All analyses proceed with an existing assembly of concepts and generalities pre-reflexively present in researchers' and subjects' minds (Arendt, 1998/1958, p.267). Things are not experienced in the raw, but as objects associated with patterns that Korzybski (1933, p.383) calls 'extended macroscopic events'. These patterns are abstracted from the chaotic detail of life, and are used as groundings from which to jump into the everyday experience of event, sensation, contradiction, and exception, in order to clean it up by posing new patterns; theory permits analysis as well as validating it.

The third reason to doubt the fiction/fact distinction comes with the paucity of results generated if only strictly scientific methods are followed in social science. What can social scientific studies tell us about what it is like to live or work in, say, the US city of Baltimore? We might begin by taking in the decline of industrial production in the West, and with it the disappearance of unionized, stable, and well-paid jobs, along with a growing disparity in wealth and a reduction in government support for education, health, and infrastructure development. We might also adduce patterns of migration and immigration, race relations, urban flight, and generationally inherited dependence on welfare and/or crime. We might then set all this in wider contexts of global trade, the movement of capital, and the ongoing mechanization of work processes— and then we get a glimpse of the complex tapestry of current and historic interdependencies that mark the affairs of institutions, organizations, and individuals in many post-industrial cities in the West.

Let us view these political, social, civic, and economic patterns following the standard disciplinary terms of social science. Economists may plot curves, or calculate ratios for trade and production, detailing the decline of a city, region, or country through coefficients. Sociologists may study changing demographics and household incomes, and set these in relation to crime rates, mortality, and substance addiction figures that reveal the human cost of economic and social decline. Political scientists may theorize the rise of populism fuelled by anger about declining living standards. Institutional theorists may study competing logics of professionalism and managerialism in the provision of government services. Finally, organizational scholars may arrive to study strategy documents or planning meetings to understand how firms enact strategic renewal, leaner processes, and cost cutting. And, with luck, someone will investigate how the environment of precarious work, looming unemployment, and the disappearance of homes may affect workers' lives. Life is dissected by scientific method; hygienically separated and prepared. But just as Latour and Woolgar's (1986) graphs say little about the life of the frog, the results of the various branches of social science are only ever partial, leaving an unguided audience to piece together the accounts and to struggle with the differences, contradictions, and gaps these present.

All these studies produce knowledge with the methodological apparatus developed and legitimized in a paradigmatically sealed community of scholars, thus arriving at specific facts and causal relations set within the tightly defined parameters whose mastery signifies the almost tribal belonging of the researcher to the scholarly clan. What is missing in these accounts is a sense for the connections between these different disciplinary strands: what it is like to live and work somewhere is related to all this and a whole lot more; why isolate income level, or class, or education? And so, as every study needs to abstract a limited number of factors to populate its models, theories or narratives, how can we know that the data researchers chose to emphasize are more important or representative than those they neglected? There are many methodological devices to 'compensate' for these problems of verification and reliability. But then who is to say the many voices of, say, triangulation, are more compelling than the solitary insight of a prescient informant? This averaging of data, most noticeably in statistical analysis, begs the question whether the common denominator opinion or condition is the most insightful one to adopt. The average is, after all, nobody and nothing in particular.

Finally, what is the role of shifting media in the generation of knowledge claims? The progress of science has been fuelled by changes in technology and communication. At one point knowledge was transferred through the façades and stained-glass windows of churches, palaces, and public buildings (Ernst, 2013, p.38); then came books and with them the acceptance of the word as an authoritative source of fact; and we are now rushing into an era where newspapers and books are superseded by Twitter feeds, blogs, videos, multicoloured neuro-scientific imagery, and so on. What is the wider story of scientific development and what roles do we play in its unfolding?

Uses of fiction in organization and management research

Rejecting the binary fiction and fact relationship between science and fiction opens up questions about the uses of fiction in organization and management studies. We discuss four ways in which the relationship between organization and management studies, and fiction can be conceived. First, fiction can play a role in the development of scientific accounts, without losing the characteristics of non-truthfulness. This may go unacknowledged, as in what we term *fictional research*, where research is itself fictionalized, or draws upon fictional elements. Second, this role can be explicit, in what we call *fiction as inspiration*; instances where fictionalized accounts provide ideas and legitimacy for organizational theorizing. Third, examples of *fiction as a source of data* treat fictions as sites of empirical research. Fourth, treating *fiction as research* means attributing science-like qualities to fiction.

FICTIONAL RESEARCH

Where Latour and Woolgar (1986) dealt with real frogs, real scalpels, and real death as the starting point for the scientific process, the matter is not always as solid. Take Taylor's (1911) famous analysis of workers loading pig iron onto wooden gondola rail carriages at the Bethlehem Iron Works from 1899–1900. He and his assistants took a group of the company's best workers, measured how many tonnes they loaded in a day, deducted 40 per cent of the total to account for breaks and delays, and established this as a standard performance level attracting piece rate pay (incentive pay) considerably higher than their current levels on day rate. For those accepting the optional piece rate system productivity soared. This is the story. Wrege and Hodgetts (2000), however, went back to the original documents used by Taylor's team, and these tell a different story. The planks and blocks used to help stack the pigs were varied and complicated to arrange, depending on which part of the gondola one was on, and at what level one was working. In certain positions, more time was spent on arranging planks and blocks than actually loading pigs. The weather also made a difference: wood is slippery when wet. The way the pigs were stacked ready for loading made a difference to the loaders; some were uneven and took longer to sort. Finally, the workers grew tired and had to opt out of the piece rate system to recover, either temporarily, or for good. The upshot? Taylor's incentive scheme actually cost the company money (Wrege and Hodgetts, 2000, p.288).

Why do organization scholars continue to accept the veracity of Taylor's account? Because, in the *Principles of Scientific Management*, he tells a coherent story of economizing that extends to his being economic with the 'truth'. He selects anecdotal data that work with the narrative, and omits contradictions, like the company's own figures, which showed the costs of his new loading method in red, not black. In reading a compelling story of success, readers want to believe him—and this was a tendency he was happy to exploit. Industrialists, politicians, architects, and artists were enamoured of his alluring blend of industrial productivity, scientific methods, and commitment to fairness for workers; everyone seemed to win. Why ruin a good story? Most management texts repeat the story, without bothering to check, as do many academics when creating their own narratives in which Taylor, as a founding figure of the discipline, finds his rightful place. Even those attacking Taylorism, the self-styled critical management scholars, have often not bothered to look at the original evidence debunking Taylor as a fabricator, for they too need the stature of Taylor to remain 'high' so that rather than get stuck with the empirical detail of everyday life, they can challenge his eponymous ideology which, surely, is a far more serious and worthy target.

FICTION AS INSPIRATION

Research frequently takes inspiration from fiction. One example is Weick's (2001) story of Hungarian soldiers getting lost in the Alps and finding the impetus to keep going, with a map which turns out to be of the Pyrenees. Is the story based in reality or fiction? Basbøll (2006) traces the incident to a poem written by Mirsolav Holub in 1977 entitled 'Brief thoughts on maps'—so it did not happen as Weick makes us believe. Instead, what is important is the moral of the story—a parable that Weick deploys with rhetorical success in his idiosyncratic form of theorizing. His approach involves disciplined imagination, an emphasis on style from which theory emerges as a form of persuasive orientation using techniques of repetition and amplification to create allegorical effect (Weick, 1996).

Weick's (1993) theory of organizational resilience emerges from another story, that of a real disaster fictionalized by Norman Maclean (1992). A group of firefighters in Montana parachuted into a forested gulch that was ablaze. From above, the fire looked containable, a '10 o'clock' fire, indicating the time it would be under control the next day. The fire was not so predictable; the wind was erratic, the undergrowth dry, and the firefighters were caught by their own complacency; all but three died. Weick takes Maclean's account (based on interviews and secondary data) and rereads it. In Weick's reading, the firefighters objectified their response to the fire, relying too easily on their categorization of a '10 o'clock' fire. This put them at ease, and they felt safe, so when the fire unexpectedly leapt across the valley bottom and came at them rapidly up the slope they were descending, they were in utter confusion. Dodge, their leader, recognized the danger and told them to drop their firefighting equipment and run. Dodge himself lit an escape fire and crouched in the centre, as the flames passed around. The others were not so lucky and died, save two who found a rocky niche in which to crouch. Weick reads this as a 'cosmology episode', the moment when all one's habits, skills and sense of being are overwhelmed by events: there is no organization to be had any more.

What can be learned from this story about how organization can be sustained in such uncertainty? Weick's answer is a theory of resilience: to persist, organizations must be attentive to their capacity to improvise (Dodge's escape fire); to practise dealing with emergencies; to be aware that distance from events gives a general picture at the expense of nuanced sensitivity; and encourage face-to-face interactions, as in collective engagement there is deep practical potential. Weick's use of fiction is interesting, mainly for his essay-istic style, and its ending—not a series of hypotheses, or a definitive interpret-ation, nor exploring the many questions that the story leaves open and that make the message so compelling (Van Maanen, 1995). This link between sense, organization, and fabrication is the ground that Weick places before us, and we are taken in: it must be like this.

And yet the differences between Weick and Maclean's accounts are start-ling. Weick constructs a compelling narrative of disintegrating order carrying didactic messages for better organization. Maclean writes of human decency and frailty, and of indifferent and capricious nature. Maclean's account says little about the framing and categories by which the firefighters were lulled into a false sense of security, so why does Weick not acknowledge this different telling (Basbøll, 2010)? The enthusiastic uptake of Weick's work in the organ-ization and management literature means that in referring to him, we refer to a series of fictions. The soldiers are fictional objects; they are referred to by Holub under the pretence that they exist—but we who take leave from this genesis of fictional characters 'really' refer to them when talking about maps and organizations. We can refer to these fictional people without pretending at all; the utterances are real, with real effects.

FICTION AS DATA SOURCE

Commenting on the work of George Orwell, the American philosopher Richard Rorty (1989) suggests how, in creating the character of O'Brien in his novel *1984*, Orwell was imaginatively condensing and making visible to us a hitherto inchoate capacity for intellectually guided cruelty. Orwell shows us the possibility of what happens when free speech is taken away and the inner self withers; it tests and finds compelling the idea of an intimate connection between language and autonomy. The same might be said of John Steinbeck's portrayal of the immiserated people of the American mid-west in the 1930s, or Edith Wharton's evocation of the relentless and unhinging pressure of upholding bourgeois niceties along the upper reaches of the US eastern seaboard. We might argue with Crump et al. (2007), De Cock, and O'Doherty (2017), and Phillips (1995) that fiction resonates not only because its central concern is the cultural, moral, economic, and social detail of contemporary lives, but that it makes such concerns more heightened and visible than they might otherwise be. Orwell revealed the impoverished and cruel idea of freedom informing the drive for equality amongst planned economies of eastern Europe with an intensity that no factual rendition could achieve.

We have argued (Holt and Zundel, 2014; Zundel et al., 2013) that *The Wire* is a 'novel for television', opening up experiences of living in the urban tide lines of a fast-receding commonwealth. The fiction emphasizes the marginalization of people facing the task of self-production under the impress of remote and fickle institutional forces. The TV series details the lived experiences of different individuals, energized by habits, hopes, and projections. The realism is one of frayed, partial human projects expressed within unacknowledged institutional settings. The filming, acting, scenes, editing, gestures, and dialogue are all rooted in observation and are orchestrated to evoke a sense of unfolding involvement with real life. Very little is explained, or contextualized, or wrapped up into consumable packages. The series and the research behind it capture the institutionalized setting that ascribes roles and routines, and the conventionalized patterns of behaviour of those involved in 'the game' of drug trafficking. This institutional backdrop coupled with the scale, depth, and ambition of the story-lines in *The Wire* exposes the playing out of organizational affairs with astonishing clarity and accuracy.

This intensity engenders a different relationship with the viewer/reader of whom it requires an immediate and ongoing engagement. This is unlike many other fictional TV dramas, and is also unlike the fictional products of scientific research. While the storylines in *The Wire* have no direct representation—the people are as fictional as the events—the characters are represented with acuity. This specific individual never existed, but somebody like them surely has. While this event may have never happened, similar ones occur daily.

The Wire is an ethnographically dense work of realist fiction that makes viewers aware of the ever-morphing nature of meaning as it sways from the revealed (breakdown in expectations, explicit organizational aims, hopes) to the concealed (habit, unspoken traditions, organizational memory). Viewers, characters, and writers have to work at what makes sense. Meaning emerges through ongoing engagement of characters, actors, writers, and audiences. For example, the serial manipulation of crime statistics is met with an admixture of shock, bemusement, and indifference by different characters, or even the same character over time.

FICTION AS RESEARCH

Do 'data' from fiction such as *The Wire* create a crystallized and abstracted understanding different from the abstractions of theoretical conceptualization? Let's take the character Howard 'Bunny' Colvin. He is a Major and police commander in the Western District of Baltimore. Colvin has become disgruntled with the institutional culture surrounding police work, with time and resources spent on policing addicts, on arresting low-level dealers ('street rips'), and on the 'creative' composition of crime figures. There is little time for 'real' police work and efforts to bring lasting change to the city's communities are undermined. Every other district commander has started to 'juke the stats' under pressure from the Police Commissioner and politicians. Colvin refuses to do this, and his stats honestly reflect a 2 per cent rise in felonies. He is berated for this and his command is threatened. Colvin wonders if there is a way for drugs to be safely and freely traded, making it easily managed. Meeting the District's church deacon (*The Wire*, season 3, episode 2, minute 52:30), he elaborates his frustration with the lack of positive lasting change achieved by police work; mostly, Colvin says, we focus on the 'absence of a negative'.

Colvin uses the next staff meeting with the officers in his district to outline his intention to change policing practices:

Somewheres, back in the dawn of time, this district had itself a civic dilemma of epic proportion. The city council had just passed a law that forbid alcoholic consumption in public places, on the streets and on the corners.

But the corner is, and it was, and it always will be the poor man's lounge. It's where a man wants to be on a hot summer's night. It's cheaper than a bar, catch a nice breeze, you watch the girls go by.

But the law is the law. And the Western cops rolling by, what were they gonna do? If they arrested every dude out there for tipping back a High Life, there'd be no other time for any other kind of police work. And if they looked the other way? They'd open themselves to all kinds of flaunting, all kinds of disrespect.

Now, this is before my time when it happened, but somewhere back in the Fifties or Sixties, there was a small moment of goddamn genius by some nameless smokehound who comes out the Cut Rate one day, and on his way to the corner, he slips that just-bought pint of Elderberry into a paper bag. A great moment of civic compromise. That small wrinkled-ass paper bag allowed the corner boys to have their drink in peace, and it gave us permission to go and do police work.

The kind of police work that's actually worth the effort. That's worth actually taking a bullet for. [Officer] Dozerman, he got shot last night trying to buy three [drug] vials. Three! There's never been a paper bag for drugs, until now.

Colvin talks of creating 'free zones'—derelict areas where addicts and dealers would be allowed to conduct business under police supervision but without interference. This would clean up the corners and invigorate community life. In the next address to his senior officers, he explains his initiative:

COLVIN: The new strategic plan for the district is to move all street-level trafficking to these three areas. We want to push it.

POLICE OFFICER: Push it, boss?

COLVIN: If they don't go easy, then they go hard. But we let these knuckleheads know that if they move to these areas, away from the residential streets, away from commercial areas, away from schools, if they take that shit down the road they can go about their business without any interference from us. It's going to be hands-off in the Western District for the foreseeable future.

POLICE OFFICER: Bullshit, man. No fucking way.

POLICE OFFICER: Wait. You want us to give them a free pass? How are we going to look them in the eye? They'll shit all over us, tell their kids to shit all over us.

LIEUTENANT: The Major wasn't finished.

COLVIN: You got to take the long view here. Once they're all comfortable, once they're all rounded up, once they've been down there a bit and they're used to putting their feet up and playing with the remote, then we move. Then we go back and we do police work. Look at it this way, gentlemen. Would you rather shoot at fish in the ocean, or would you rather gather them up in a few small barrels and start emptying your clips then?

Colvin succeeds in setting up the 'free trade' areas that, colloquially termed 'Hamsterdam', lead to an immediate drop in crime, turning Colvin into a cause célèbre—until the press discover that in effect the police commander has legalized the drugs trade. Colvin loses his job and pension.

The portrayal of Colvin's motives and rhetoric resonate with much that we know about ethics, entrepreneurship, and strategic leadership. The cunning is straight from Clausewitz's 'fog of war', the reactions of his officers straight from tales of change management, and the refusal of the politicians to admit to the pragmatic necessity of his policy straight from the field of institutional theory. What the TV series gives, and these theories do not, is the sense of this being lived out and the messy, rough, and incredibly partial sense of all this. The fictional format allows the viewer to witness Colvin's growing antipathy towards a system rendered dysfunctional by a twofold ideological stupidity: the framing of the drugs problem as a 'war', and the governance of organizational actions through metrics. Gone are the days of police on the beat building relations, replaced by violent raids on low-level drug dealers whenever incarceration figures are low or when a high-profile murder of a 'civilian' requires a show of strength. These restless, merging, and opaque norms deflate as much as excite Colvin, a seasoned cop schooled in proper police work, his despair multiplying with each generation of new officers indoctrinated in the new ethos of mass arrests, intimidation and distrust.

The Wire shows how Colvin's character defines his fate. Colvin resents the police, but not good policing. He breaks the law to uphold the law, but without the sovereignty to sustain such a state of exception. He loses his pension a few months from retirement, and yet he is not stupid. He manages to set up Hamsterdam because he is crafty and knows the system; because he is wise to the chains of command; and because his brilliant rhetoric and negotiation skills give him a sense of possibility. He knows that police brass only look at pie charts and not at the streets. So he gets away with things until he is grassed up by one of his own officers, not for being morally wrong, but because the officer feels cheated of his police role—the identity of someone who can exact physical violence on others with impunity. Colvin knows these risks and that he cannot ultimately succeed. Yet he persists.

Despite the complexity of events and emotions, despite the paradoxical relations, and despite the non-rationality of his behaviour, we understand why he does what he does. We understand the frustrations without having to isolate the institutional logics at play. We do not need to resort to the figure of an institutional entrepreneur to account for Colvin's actions against the legal forces at play, because we witness the humiliation and bullying by police commissioners, and we feel the mix of anger and despair at the futility of their actions and the sacrifices they are forced to make for no reason. And we do not need the figure of the calculative strategist as we bear witness, while watching *The Wire*, to the 'thin simplifications' (Scott, 1998, p.309) offered by statements such as the US Government's policy of 'war on drugs'. In short, we do not need theoretical concepts at all.

Benefits and drawbacks of using fiction

FICTIONAL RESEARCH

In Taylor's case, we can see the utility of the fiction for the proliferation of scientific management principles. That the 'fabrication' was deliberate is shown by the narrative structure of his arguments, using the prevailing tendencies of his socio-cultural context, including: commercial norms associated with elimination of waste; the resilience of pioneering (white) Americans; the growing influence of systems thinking; the rhetoric of 'betterment' that became known as 'The American Dream'. Readers feel comfortable with the message. As Banta (1993, p.124) notes when analysing Taylor's testimony to a congressional hearing, even though we might hear a 'sliding away from the bedrock of scientific inquiry that he [Taylor] insists validates the truth of everything he says', he is still believed, because his narrative is consistent with wider expectations. As Latour and Woolgar (1986) have shown, even natural sciences rely on a degree of narration, to move projects along, and in final reports. Fictions of this kind form the fabric of much organizational life. They appear in narratives and formal models, in business school case studies, and in myths that lionize or pillory leaders (March, 2010). They also operate in closed systems, from modern physics producing theories that invalidate the very materials used in their production (Cetina, 1994, p.15), to firm–accountant combinations such as Enron–Arthur Andersen.

How are we to assess the benefits and dangers of fictional research accounts? Take leadership, where the heroism of the individual as the helms (wo)man of an enterprise is sung in countless biographies and self-help books. This can be innocent, if egregious, when confined to a throwaway read in an airport lounge, but becomes dangerous when it finds its way into management theories and education. Taylor's scientific management had an immense impact, such that the scientific basis of the work was increasingly veiled behind the ideological exchanges between supporters of this classless, meritocratic, functional ideal and its principled, critical, and equally dogmatic objectors (Monin et al., 2003). Neither side had an interest in the empirics of the case.

Is there a place for research? Van Maanen (1979) elaborates on these thickets of inquiry, teasing out a narrative line by which a researcher, in his case an ethnographer, might still be acknowledged as such, rather than a reporter, or commentator, or opinion monger. For Van Maanen, researchers must struggle to acknowledge who is talking and acting, and whether these are facts in themselves or the facts are being spoken for, and whether patterns cohere or diverge, and how this might matter to the different constituents without falling in with one or another inadvertently. They must also consider how their own practice—their impatience, lack of skill, limited perspective or evaluative leanings—colours the emergence of fact and theory. Theory can only ever be tentative, suggestive rather than assertive, open to re-working as life too opens itself anew, thus softening the impact of fictional elements, as any abstract theoretical statement is looked at with suspicion from the start.

FICTION AS INSPIRATION

The question of benefit and drawback is simpler when considering authors who draw on existing fiction to enliven, exemplify, or give shape to the phenomena under investigation. This approach relates to a wider trope of 'metaphor' studies in business and management (De Cock and Land, 2005). Here the use of fiction is intriguing, because it allows for the transmission of morals, epiphanies, and related insights, working as allegories or parables. In Weick's case, Holub's poem of the lost soldiers is eloquent, tucked away and brief, and it is with hesitation that Weick acknowledges the origins of this story. Weick's readers are left to guess whether this actually happened—it is, after all, an unlikely but plausible series of events. The sparkle of the story is Weick's (1989) bait to others to engage in theory construction as a process of imagination; organizational scholars eagerly took the bite.

Here fiction is less representing the world than shaping it. There is a long tradition supporting this role, exemplified by the Russian poet Vladimir Mayakovsky. He argued that art—especially his poetic art, enabled and ennobled by Bolshevik revolutionary fervour—was not a mirror to reflect reality, but a hammer to shape it. Writers and photographers created posters exhorting viewers to further heights of revolutionary intensity, dramatists wrote plays encouraging peasants and workers to produce more than they were already, and novelists and artists wrote children's books using new, formal language untainted by bourgeois values. 'Art', wrote Mayakovsky, 'must not be concentrated in dead shrines called museums. It must be spread everywhere—on the streets, in the trams, factories, workshops, and in the workers' homes' (Mayakovsky, 1918/1987, p.15). Fiction, along with wider literary and artistic practice, became integral to the creation of a new society in which all organization was a legitimate subject of cultural concern and all art was judged by its capacity to construct new social forms.

So does it matter that the soldiers never got lost in the Alps, or that the story told by Andersen's auditors had little basis in Enron's 'real' finances? The former uses non-serious assertions that invoke different language games and conventions for the ways in which literal meanings are constructed (Searle, 1975). The latter is a serious assertion and thus, by failing to invoke a fictional frame, becomes a lie: the utterance of a falsehood with the intention to deceive (Eagleton, 2012). Eagleton (1996, p.183) notes that discourses— film, television, the languages of the natural sciences—'produce effects, shape forms of consciousness and unconsciousness, which are closely related to the maintenance and transformation of our existing systems of power.' The question is not whether these stories correspond to reality, but what the authors want to achieve.

FICTION AS DATA SOURCE

Realist fiction allows the researcher to theorize differently, to examine experience as it unfolds, with limited awareness of how things will turn out, putting the researcher in a similar position to the characters. The researcher can thus exploit what Shotter and Tsoukas (2007) call the prospective account of living within situations in which 'what happens' and 'what is the case' are always emerging, in forms as subtle as glances, or as monumental as death. This is how we experience organizational life. In analysis, however, we typically get retrospective accounts (Dimov, 2011) in which the status of events has already been accepted, resulting in retrospective sense-making, rather than an understanding of what has been lived. Booth (1961, p.3) argues that, 'One of the most obviously artificial devices of the storyteller is the trick of going beneath the surface of the action to obtain a reliable view of a character's mind and heart.' Artifice is unmistakably present whenever the author tells us what no one in real life could possibly know. In life we never know anyone but ourselves, and most of us achieve a partial view at that. *The Wire*, and other 'novels', refuse to collapse their narratives into such an episodic, conceptualized neatness, but follow the tracery of lives as they are lived, admitting the inconsistencies that plague and puzzle human lives.

Watching *The Wire*, we were struck by its breadth and depth, and its intellectual, social, and emotional appeal. We felt we could trust these 'data' because they felt right, and when inquiring into how the series was written, we found further evidence to support this feeling. The writers' biographical details as journalist and police officer; their ethnographic books on the police and life on 'the corners'; the number of sociological studies commenting on *The Wire*; enthusiastic commentaries in the cultural press. So when Ed Burns, one of the writers, argues there is a strong 'organizational ethos' to the commercial drugs trade in Baltimore, we trusted the veracity of this claim (Alverez, 2009, p.12). We were also aware of Simon's and Burns' social and political agenda. Simon became a public figure with regular media appearances and a blog, passionately attacking the neo-liberal agendas he felt were eating the soul from American rust belt cities. This motivational transparency kept us on our toes when, seduced by the characters and plots, touched by the lives being portrayed, we fell in line with these sentiments. This remains open for other researchers. The data are available on streaming services and DVD. Unlike interviews or observations or surveys, with these data verifiability is an issue of public record. Our analysis can be re-examined or audited by others, assessing the overall dependability as readily as other methodological techniques. Go watch, and see if you care in similar ways, or remain neutral, objective, and disinterested in what is being shown.

RESEARCH AS FICTION

Seeing fictions as outputs of research requires suspension of disbelief. The power of fiction stems from its self-referential character. Unconstrained by the pressures of 'the real', fiction establishes an internal reality that does not exist without its performance, through which it establishes its own realities (Eagleton, 2012). But herein lies a paradox, because fiction sits within the wider socio-historical milieu in the form of genres, language, and norms, without which any text would be unintelligible. Fictitious worlds may differ in content to what really is assumed to be the case, but they share features of form with the realities in which they are set. They chart possible ways of being, what people could be like under transformed social, historical, and political circumstances (Beyes, 2009). Eagleton (2012, pp.145 and 156) calls this the 'negative truth of everyday discourse' whereby fiction can reveal the 'truth of things'—albeit not in its content but rather by pointing to the 'criteria for determining what kind of things there are and how we can speak of them'.

Consider Charles Dickens' novel *Barnaby Rudge*, a story of industrial unrest brutally suppressed by a sovereign state willing to declare a state of exception and suspend already fragile legal procedure. This is also a story of mental, gender, and class differences set in city and countryside, and full of pathos, tragedy, comedy, and reportage. Dickens wrote the novel as entertainment for the everyday reader, as well as commenting on historical events, and thus as a prompt for social reform. Nowhere in this story is there a character with a singular perspective save the omniscient narrator, nor is there a single narrative thread. Instead, we have the to-and-fro of personal and collective lives being lived in and out of focus, and in and out of joy, without definitive conclusion. Numerous themes abound: the destructiveness of economic production; how persisting codes of hospitality wash through the impotency of law; setting the idiocy and cruelty of the state against the practical intelligence of those deemed idiotic. None dominate, none are complete, none demur completely.

For Levine (2015), commenting on another Charles Dickens' novel *Bleak House*, this is how fiction can teach us about what shapes our social and personal lives, how novelists can acknowledge what she calls the rhythms, wholes, hierarchies, and networks that organize all human life. The legal rhythm identified by Dickens is one of emptying slowness, contrasted with the sporadic rapidity of military intervention. The country folk and city dwellers live at different speeds, and criminals live in more darker, sealed off spaces than peasants, but similar to the corridors walked by government officials. This novel offers what Levine calls a theorizing of the social by affording readers a way into the plenitude of forms vying with one another through different times and spaces. Fiction allows the reader not just to feel with the characters, but to do so knowing that the characters, places, and plots are not real but written by someone with a certain end in mind. In reading fiction, we can keep our own reflective powers intact and not only get inside a fictional character but also grasp something about the meaning of that character's fate—emotively and intellectually.

Most characters in *The Wire* are not singularly graspable. Drug dealers are not merely defined by their habit but have lives that unfold through highs and lows with the raft of human experiences from friendship to love, from hope to despair. Police officers can be 'by the book' as well as corrupt; sometimes both at the same time when caught between paradoxical policies and directives; and they have lives outside the force which pulsate in the rhythm of shifts and drunken escapades and which collapse in numbing regularity as do the careers and bodies of those in uniform. The only creeds being depicted with stereotypical rigidity are those pragmatic ones of politicians; even those coming into politics pure at heart are drawn into the dark. This shows the potential and also the limits of fiction. Its potential lies in broadening the abstractions from 'extended macroscopic events' (Korzybski, 1933, p.383), such as identities or routines that are the elements that characterize a person or event with enduring or recurring regularity, towards holistic, multifaceted, and complex depictions of human and organizational affairs. Its limits come in the form of authorial choices. Simon and Burns have more than one axe to grind; their characterization of politicians reveals their agenda.

Fiction invents and accentuates, implicating the author in the real. Yet it places demands on readers, to use their own imagination and to absorb their suspicion at contrivance. In particular, fiction brings into focus those relations that make social life work. Because there may be no actually existing characters or events, readers cannot feed their senses with real objects. Instead, they have to piece together these phenomena through the author's references. Fiction has to be plausible, to resonate, in a way that appears not to be fictional. This means that we are open to those possibilities afforded, but often not exploited, when fiction pulls vast spaces and time frames into communion—the connection between consumption and deforestation, for example, or historically constituted colonial borders and contemporary moments of genocidal murder. Fiction can thus be used as a provocative disturbance to orthodox ways of understanding management practice in a mutual but also risky 'dialogue between the literary and the organizational' (Beyes, 2009, p.433). Putting apparently inappropriate figures into habituated patterns of activity brings these into view, an explicit rendering of what otherwise lies implicit. Proximity and distance are enacted, as are intimacy and hostility—and telling or showing this *as fiction* and not *as theory* resists the subordination of the literary to the organizational (De Cock and Land, 2005).

Conclusion

So what use does fiction have in organization and management studies? One answer concerns an expansive view of a subject area. Surely few organizational scholars would think that their subject area is merely a matter of academic research, but rather the very matter of history, of literature, of plays, and thus also of fiction. As literature, fiction itself is a historical phenomenon, allowing us to gain deeper and richer views on an area of interest (Eagleton, 1996). Blaise Pascal noted that accumulating more facts, even supposing it were an additive process with our knowledge expanding into the unknown, simply widens and lengthens the borderline at which we touch ignorance. The more we know, the more we realize we know very little: in knowing more we touch on much more of what we do not know. By engaging with fiction, we can expand our understanding of organizations and those working within them in ways that go beyond the truncated formulas that tend to dominate scientific discourse. Fiction can illuminate phenomena that are hard to capture, measure, or relate to theoretical ideas. They can do so across the full spectrum of human affairs, tying together emotions, hopes, fears, connecting spatio-temporally dispersed affairs, and do so without concern for the limits of specialist silos. Levine (2015) argues that fiction, especially novels, enable us to appreciate our social condition in complex and subtle ways because they, like life, refuse to be easily distilled into simple elements and chains of cause and effect.

Consider how existing categories and concepts skew what researchers investigate. Studies are inevitably based on the language that they use, pushed this way then that according to the meaning residing in the theoretical approach. Examine entrepreneurial opportunity, or an emerging market, and immediately the world is scripted as a space amenable to the appearance of such things. They are presumed to exist, despite it being difficult to define them, or even to point to them. Where to point? And why is pointing as a gesture an indication of something being present anyhow? Well, because we as a species have collectively scripted it into our bodies over time. It was made up as a way of indicating phenomena of interest, and categories and concepts are more sophisticated indications by which parts of the world are isolated and held up, leaving far more that is concealed.

Or consider conducting an interview and the structured and restricted perspective imposed on what is 'found'. Interviewees must stick to the phenomena of interest to the interviewer; they are expected to articulate their responses in words, not gestures; and they are expected to use memory and anticipation to mediate and filter what has and may happen, and to be accountable for what they say, while remaining consistent and truthful. All this before categories and concepts are used, and there is nothing innocent about the use of categories and concepts, which present a prefabricated world into which inquiry seeks to slot findings. Fictions throw these structures and restrictions into critical relief: when we use fiction as inspiration or a source of data, we continually have to remind ourselves of these fabrications and thus liberate ourselves from 'methods' which can no longer establish a truth for us.

At the end of *Les Mots et Les Chose* (*The Order of Things*), Foucault (1966) talks of the emergence of literature, the manner in which through modernism we give up on absolutes and instead consider our role as investigators. Literature is what takes us back from concepts and the order of grammar and toward the open force of language, the scenes of ordinary life, the untamed and imperious presence of words without end.

◾ REFERENCES

Alvarez, R. (2009). *The Wire: Truth Be Told* (revised edn). Edinburgh: Canongate.
Arendt, H. (1998/1958). *The Human Condition*. Chicago, IL: Chicago University Press.
Banta, M. (1993). *Taylored Lives: Narrative Productions in the Age of Taylor, Veblen, and Ford*. Chicago, IL: University of Chicago Press.
Basbøll, T. (2006). 'Substitutes for Strategy Research', *Ephemera*, 6(2): 194–205.
Basbøll, T. (2010). 'Softly constrained imagination: plagiarism and misprision in the theory of organizational sensemaking', *Culture and Organization*, 16(2): 163–78.

Beyes, T. (2009). 'An aesthetics of displacement: Thomas Pynchon's symptomatology of organizations', *Journal of Organizational Change Management*, 22(4): 421–36.

Booth, W.C. (1961). *The Rhetoric of Fiction*. London and Chicago, IL: University of Chicago Press.

Cetina, K. (1994). 'Primitive classification and postmodernity: towards a sociological notion of fiction', *Theory, Culture & Society*, 11(3): 1–22.

Crump, N., Amiridis, K., and Costea, B. (2007). 'A historical-cultural approach to the study of business ethics using the modern novel: an illustration', *Management and Organizational History*, 2(3): 237–54.

De Cock, C. and Land, C. (2005). 'Organization/literature: exploring the seam', Organization Studies, 27(4): 517–35.

De Cock, C. and O'Doherty, D. (2017). 'Ruin and organization studies', *Organization Studies*, 38(1): 129–50.

de Freytas-Tamura, K. (2017). 'George Orwell's 1984 is suddenly a best-seller', *The New York Times*, 25 January: <https://www.nytimes.com/2017/01/25/books/1984-george-orwell-donald-trump.html?_r=2> (accessed 30 April 2017).

Dimov, D. (2011). 'Grappling with the unbearable elusiveness of entrepreneurial opportunities', *Entrepreneurship: Theory and Practice*, 35(1): 57–81.

Eagleton, T. (1996). *Literary Theory: An Introduction*. Second edition. Malden, MA and Oxford: Blackwell Publishing.

Eagleton, T. (2012). *The Event of Literature*. New Haven, CT and London: Yale University Press.

Ernst, W. (2013). *Digital Memory and the Archive*. Minneapolis, MN and London: University of Minnesota Press.

Foucault, M. (1966). *The Order of Things: An Archaeology of the Human Sciences* (*Les Mots et les Choses*). Paris: Ēdition Gallimard.

Holt, R. and Zundel, M. (2014). 'Understanding management, trade and society through fiction: lessons from *The Wire*', *Academy of Management Review*, 39: 576–85.

Korzybski, A. (1933). *Science and Sanity*. Fort Worth, TX: IGS.

Latour, B. and Woolgar, S. (1986). *Laboratory Life. The Construction of Scientific Facts*. Princeton, NJ: Princeton University Press.

Levine, C. (2015). *Forms: Whole, Rhythm, Hierarchy, Network*. Princeton, NJ: Princeton University Press.

MacIntyre, A. (2009). *God, Philosophy, Universities*. London: Continuum.

Maclean, N. (1992). *Young Men and Fire*. Chicago, IL: University of Chicago Press.

March, J. (2010). *The Ambiguities of Experience*. Ithaca, NY: Cornell University Press.

Mayakovsky, V. (1918/1987). 'Shrine or Factory?' In Mikhail Anikst et al. (eds.) *Soviet Commercial Design of the Twenties*. Translated by Mikhail Anikst. New York: Abbeville Press.

Monin, N. Berry, D., and Monin, D. (2003). 'Toggling with Taylor: a different approach to reading a management text', *Journal of Management Studies*, 40(2): 377–403.

Phillips, N. (1995). 'Telling organizational tales: on the role of narrative fiction in the study of organizations', *Organization Studies*, 16(4): 625–49.

Rorty, R. (1989). *Contingency, Irony, and Solidarity*. Cambridge: Cambridge University Press.

Russell, B. (1946). *History of Western Philosophy*. London: George Allen and Unwin.

Scott, J.C. (1998). *Seeing Like a State*. New Haven, CT and London: Yale University Press.

Searle, J. (1975). 'The logical status of fictional discourse', *New Literary History*, 6(2): 319–32.

Shotter, J. and Tsoukas, H. (2007). 'Theory as therapy: towards reflective theorizing in organization studies.' Paper submitted to The Third Organization Studies Summer Workshop: 'Organization Studies as Applied Science: The Generation and Use of Academic Knowledge about Organizations', 7–9 June 2007, Crete, Greece.

Taylor, F.W. (1911). *Principles of Scientific Management*. New York: Harper.

Van Maanen, J. (1979). 'The fact of fiction in organizational ethnography', *Administrative Science Quarterly*, 24(4): 539–50.

Van Maanen, J. (1995). 'Style as theory', *Organization Science* 6(1): 133–43.

Weick, K.E. (1989). 'Theory construction as disciplined imagination', *Academy of Management Review*, 14(4): 516–31.

Weick, K.E. (1993). 'The collapse of sensemaking in organizations: the Mann Gulch disaster', *Administrative Science Quarterly*, 38(4): 628–52.

Weick, K.E. (1996). 'Drop your tools: an allegory for organizational studies', *Administrative Science Quarterly*, 41(2): 301–13.

Weick, K.E. (2001). *Making sense of the organization*. Oxford: Blackwell.

Woolf, V. (1984). 'Modern Fiction.' In Andrew McNeillie (ed.) *The Essays of Virginia Woolf Volume 4: 1925–1928*. London: The Hogarth Press, pp.157–65.

Wrege, C. and Hodgetts, D. (2000). 'Frederick W. Taylor's pig iron observations: examining fact, fiction, and the lessons for the new millennium', *Academy of Management Journal*, 43(6): 1283–91.

Zundel, M., Holt, R., and Cornelissen, J. (2013). 'Institutional work in *The Wire*: an ethological investigation of flexibility in organizational adaptation', *Journal of Management Inquiry*, 22(1): 102–20.

4 Innovations in unobtrusive methods

Andrew P. Knight

Introduction

Twenty years ago, engineer and computer scientist Rosalind Picard (1997, p.228) imagined a future in which 'a financial analyst might combine his cell phone, pager, online stock reports, analysis software, and personal email agent into one computer that fits in a belt, watch and shirt pocket'. Clearly the future is now. An estimated 1.4 billion people owned a smartphone in 2013—more than one fifth of the global population (Heggestuen, 2013). By 2020, that proportion is expected to rise to approximately 70 per cent (Ericsson, 2015). And smartphones are just the tip of the iceberg, as a proliferation of internet-connected devices expands the linkages among humans, computers, and networks. Consider just a few of the devices released recently. Glasses developed by companies like Google and Snap enable users to capture and share multimedia content in real-time; wristbands like those developed by Fitbit, Apple, and Samsung facilitate fitness tracking, payments, and more.

The ubiquity of connected devices (Swan, 2012)—and the metrics that they unobtrusively capture—has led data to become increasingly central to the global economy. Companies have integrated novel unobtrusive data streams into their business models and operations (e.g. Walker, 2012; Wilson, 2013). These data streams can elucidate consumer preferences and responses to advertising, enhance human resource practices, and improve collaboration networks—to name just a few publicized applications.

Much like new data streams have enriched contemporary businesses, innovative unobtrusive methods hold great promise for researchers who study organizational functioning (Tonidandel et al., 2016). The idea that researchers can benefit from using unobtrusive methods is certainly not new. More than half a century ago, Webb and colleagues (1966) implored researchers in their classic book *Unobtrusive Measures* to use a more diverse set of data streams in their work, noting that, 'Today the dominant mass of social science research is based upon interviews and questionnaires. We lament this overdependence upon a single fallible method' (pp.1–2). Notwithstanding a steady drumbeat of pleas over the years for researchers to use unobtrusive methods (e.g. Hill et al., 2014; Webb and Weick, 1979), survey methods continue to dominate the literature, especially in organizational behaviour, and researchers still often rely on a single data source (Podsakoff et al., 2012; Scandura and Williams, 2000).

The purpose of this chapter is to describe a new suite of unobtrusive methods, such as the traces that people leave throughout the digital world as they search the Internet, post content on social media, and navigate an increasingly digitally connected physical world. These methods, which did not exist when Webb and colleagues published their book, make it easier and cheaper for researchers to use unobtrusive methods than ever before. As a result, we social science researchers have fewer and fewer excuses for relying on a single source of data, obtrusively acquired, in empirical studies.

I begin by discussing three ways that new unobtrusive methods can enrich organizational research. Then, I explain why now is a propitious time for these methods to become ubiquitous. After discussing these broader issues, I detail five new unobtrusive methods and describe how researchers have used them in recent work. I conclude by offering some caveats and cautions, as well as a few recommendations, for using new unobtrusive methods.

The value of new unobtrusive methods

As with learning any new method or statistical approach, learning a new unobtrusive method will require an investment of time and energy. Why might one make this investment and adopt one of the methods described in this chapter? The unobtrusive methods described below can add value to almost any research programme in several ways.

First, several of these methods sidestep reactance effects—alterations in participants' cognitions, attitudes, or behaviours as a result of their awareness that someone is studying them. Survey methods are particularly vulnerable to reactance effects. Consider, for example, Schwarz's (1999) commentary on how subtle survey elements, such as introductory prompts or terminology, can alter participants' responses. The new unobtrusive methods are not completely immune to reactance effects; participants might alter their behaviour in substantive ways if they know that computer programmes or wearable sensors are recording what they do. However, these methods are not vulnerable to reactance effects in the same way as survey methods. Accordingly, data collected through the methods described in this chapter can help to triangulate on valid effects.

Second, researchers can benefit from using these methods to examine dynamics—how and why phenomena change over time. Several commentators have noted the dearth of research in organizational behaviour that examines and models patterns of change (e.g. Cronin et al., 2011). One reason underlying the lack of research on dynamics is that the dominant approach for data collection—the self-report survey—is not amenable to frequent administration. Because unobtrusive methods do not require a participant to consciously respond to a question, they can be particularly useful for recording a continuous stream of data over time (e.g. Kozlowski et al., 2016). To use an analogy, the measurement approaches frequently used in organizational research today provide static photographs of behaviour; novel unobtrusive methods, in contrast, can provide dynamic movies that enable researchers to analyse phenomena in motion.

Third, novel unobtrusive methods help researchers expand the scale of their investigations. Several of these methods passively record phenomena using technology that is already widely disseminated (e.g. web browser, smartphone). The cost of repurposing technologies that are already in people's hands for research is relatively low and affords the opportunity to expand the scale of an investigation with respect to context and to time. Expanding the scale of research with respect to context—collecting data across larger and more diverse sets of groups, organizations, industries, and cultures—is useful for addressing calls for research that accounts for the role of context (Cappelli and Sherer, 1991; House et al., 1995; Johns, 2006). Expanding the scale of research with respect to time—collecting data across longer time horizons—is useful for addressing fundamental questions of change, such as how organizations grow and develop, or wither and die, over time.

A propitious time for unobtrusive methods

The time is ripe for researchers to reap the benefits of unobtrusive methods. Much has changed in the fifty years since Webb et al. published their influential book. The methods that they proposed in the 1960s were costly, requiring major investments of time and resources in data collection and analysis. Consider how time intensive it would be to manually track the wear on carpet tiles at a museum to understand consumer preferences. The cumbersome nature of unobtrusive methods in the past limited their feasibility.

Several technological developments have made unobtrusive methods more accessible than they were fifty years ago. First, there has been a steady march of miniaturization in computer-driven devices. Around the time Webb and colleagues published their book, Intel co-founder Gordon Moore (1965) predicted that there would be exponential growth in the number of transistors that could be squeezed onto each square inch of an integrated circuit, with the number doubling every year. This prediction—'Moore's Law'—largely came to fruition over the subsequent decade, and a steady march of increasing computing power has continued ever since. One by-product of Moore's Law has been the miniaturization of computing devices. The room-sized computers of the 1950s became the desktop computers of the 1980s and 1990s; the desktop computers of the 1990s became the pocket computers of the 2000s. We have gone from having a single computer for an entire business, to a computer on everyone's desk, to a computer in every pocket and, increasingly, a computer on every wrist. This proliferation of devices provides a means for capturing behaviour in new unobtrusive ways.

A second development, supported by miniaturization, is enhanced precision and affordability of a variety of sensors, contributing to the widespread deployment of sensors throughout society. As an example of this growth in the deployment of sensors, consider the technological trajectory of the Samsung Galaxy S smartphone from its debut in 2010 through the Galaxy S6 model released in 2015 (Fitchard, 2016). Embedded in the original Galaxy S were about a dozen sensors, such as an accelerometer, proximity sensor, and magnetometer. The number of sensors nearly doubled over the next five years, with the Galaxy S6 adding a pedometer, barometer, gyroscope, and heart rate monitor. The inclusion of such sensors in devices carried by millions of people provides researchers with the ability to unobtrusively measure behaviour in new ways. The Galaxy smartphone is just one illustration of the diffusion of sensors throughout society. From networked thermostats to connected office lights, sensors are everywhere, capturing and storing data that could be of use to researchers (Swan, 2012). This trend continues to grow; it has been estimated that a self-driving car will generate 100 gigabytes of data a second (*The Economist*, 2017).

A third development is the ubiquity of networked computers. Over the past two decades the Internet has become interwoven with business and society. Beyond just laptop computers and smartphones, we increasingly live in a world that is the Internet of Things, in which devices communicate regularly not just with us but with other devices. Concordant with interconnectivity is regular logging of activity on computing networks, resulting in a staggering volume of information being stored about the everyday environment that surrounds us. Consider a contemporary office. As workers arrive and swipe magnetic cards to enter elevators and offices, their movements are tracked. Wireless network beacons in the ceiling record pings as their smartphones request access to the network. Networked cameras unobtrusively capture video streams of parking lots, entry ways, and stairwells. The exponential growth in connected devices—and the consequent growing reliance on connectivity to accomplish daily tasks—makes available to researchers a wealth of unobtrusively collected data.

A fourth development is the increasing standardization of protocols and methods for providing data access to third parties. Standardization is essential to manage the scale of data currently collected and stored in organizations. Further, standardization is essential to enable computers to communicate with one another and facilitate the growth in interconnectivity described above. The value of standardization is evident in the proliferation of application programming interfaces (APIs)—pathways for third parties to interact with an application—in many software applications. As one example, the technology company Garmin has an API for its fitness tracking application. Through the API, and with the user's consent, other applications can access and display a user's stream of fitness activities. Standardization of database structures and methods for accessing data, like this one, can also enable researchers to more easily use data.

A fifth development is the increasing availability of computational resources— hardware and software—to process the large datasets created by these technologies. Compared to limited access in the 1960s, researchers today have at their fingers the computational horsepower needed to process and analyse large datasets. Computing power has grown exponentially since the 1960s, increasing roughly by a factor of a trillion. The computing power that many people today carry around in their pockets equals or exceeds the supercomputers used in the 1980s. And in addition to hardware advances, researchers have easy access to algorithms to process large data sets. The R project (R Core Team, 2015) is one example of how the open source software movement, along with the dissemination of tutorials and guidance through online forums and courses, has given researchers the tools needed to make sense of large-scale data streams.

Webb et al. (1966) were ahead of their time. But in the years since their plea for researchers to complement surveys with unobtrusive methods, the technological landscape has changed. Together, the five factors described above reduce the costs of using unobtrusive methods and make now a propitious time for the diffusion of these methods.

New unobtrusive methods

Webb and colleagues described five categories of unobtrusive methods, giving examples of and ideas for how these methods could be used in research. Using their categories as a starting point, I describe a suite of new unobtrusive methods that are amenable for use by researchers today. Table 4.1 gives an overview of these methods. Although these methods are presented within discrete categories, these are in reality not mutually exclusive. A given method can (and often does) fit multiple categories, stemming from the interdependence of the physical and digital worlds today, as well as the fact that data are central to the functioning of most contemporary organizations.

Table 4.1 New unobtrusive measures

type	classic measures (Webb et al., 1966)	new measures	background and example articles
trace data	datasets created using traces left in the physical world through the erosion or accretion of physical material	datasets created using traces left in the digital world by people's navigation of their physical and digital environments	Dai et al. (2014); Kosinski et al. (2015); Park et al. (2015); Wang et al. (2016)
public archival data	datasets compiled using information routinely collected and made public by, generally, government entities	datasets compiled by the government and made widely-available and easily-accessed via the public Internet	Barnes et al. (2015); Bianchi (2016); Harrington and Gelfand (2014)
private archival data	datasets compiled using information routinely collected, but held privately, by entities like for-profit corporations	datasets created using information routinely collected, but held privately, by private entities' information-technology systems	Jackman and Kanerva (2016); Kleinbaum et al. (2013); Pierce et al. (2015); Saavedra et al. (2011); Staats et al. (2016)
simple observation	datasets created by systematically and manually coding people's public and observable behaviour	datasets created by recording attributes of people's affect and behaviour using wearable sensors and devices	Chaffin et al. (2017); Ingram and Morris (2007); Kim et al. (2012); Knight and Baer (2014); Swan (2012)
contrived observation	datasets created by systematically and manually coding video or audio recordings of people's behaviour in structured situations	datasets created by automatically coding, using computers, video or audio recordings of people's behaviour or textual content	Barsade et al. (2015); Kosinski et al. (2016); Li et al. (2015); Woolley et al. (2016)

TRACES: FROM PHYSICAL TO DIGITAL

The physical traces that people leave throughout the world are evidence of their behaviour. In addition to these traces—like wearing down carpet tiles in a museum—people today leave traces throughout the digital world. Digital traces reflect the data streams that result from the logging of people's behaviour—in both the physical and digital worlds—in digital data streams.

To appreciate the potential of digital trace data, imagine some of the moments that can now be unobtrusively captured in a slice of a typical day. Your day might begin with a smartphone buzzing to awaken you. As you move to silence the alarm, the device records what time you begin your day. It is possible that the device has been tracking your sleep, marking when you are in deep sleep and when you are restless, throughout the night. Fast forward to your arrival at your workplace. To enter your building you hold your identification badge, which has an embedded radio frequency identifier (RFID) tag, up to a reader. The networked reader logs your entry and opens the door.

Minutes later, when you sign into your computer, your presence at your desk is recorded and logged. Meanwhile, your smartphone has been pinging wireless beacons in the ceiling, leaving the footprints of your smartphone in the network's logs.

As this illustrates, many behaviours leave traces throughout the digital world, enabling researchers to measure time usage, physical location, and more. Researchers have recently begun to leverage the power of digital trace data to understand a wide range of phenomena. For example, Dai et al. (2014) used digital trace data to study how temporal landmarks prompt individuals to engage in aspirational behaviour. Partnering with a university, the authors gained access to records of how frequently students used the university's fitness centre. Attendance was unobtrusively tracked as students swiped magnetic identification cards to enter the centre. Focusing on a delimited time period, this yielded data on fitness behaviour for nearly 12,000 people for more than 400 days—a dataset with more than 5 million observations. Because the central question of the investigation was how temporal landmarks induce changes in aspirational behaviour, having a continuous record of behaviour over time was essential. Findings showed that individuals do engage in more aspirational goal-directed behaviour when they encounter temporal landmarks such as New Year's Day.

A second example concerns the study of handwashing behaviour in hospitals by Staats et al. (2016). The researchers partnered with a supplier of technology that monitors handwashing behaviour to understand how the implementation of a monitoring system influences caregivers' compliance with handwashing standards. The monitoring system used RFID tags—one worn by caregivers and a second attached to handwashing stations—to record valid opportunities for handwashing (i.e. times when providers should wash their hands because, for example, they are entering a patient's room) and actual handwashing behaviour (i.e. times when providers washed their hands in a way compliant with standards). Staats et al. (2016) examined a rich dataset tracking handwashing behaviour across time in a set of hospitals that had implemented the technology. In total, the multilevel dataset contained records for more than 5,000 caregivers working in 71 units of 42 hospitals for two and a half years. Because handwashing opportunities were timestamped, there were more than 19 million observations in the dataset. Illustrating the value of this data stream, Staats et al. (2016) examined the effect of having the system activated (i.e. compliance would be tracked and monitored by management) and the effect of having the system deactivated (i.e. compliance would be tracked, but not monitored by management). The record of behaviour over time enabled the researchers to answer questions about how workers' behaviour changed in response to a monitoring system; monitoring increased compliance, but continued compliance was dependent on sustained management attention.

Both Dai et al. (2014) and Staats et al. (2016) illustrate the power of using digital trace data to understand organizational phenomena. In particular, these studies show the utility of digital trace data for unpacking phenomena over theoretically meaningful time horizons and at a scale that would be difficult to accomplish using more traditional research methods.

PUBLIC ARCHIVES: FROM CUMBERSOME TO CLICKABLE

Researchers have long benefited from archival data collected by government entities. Webb et al. recognized the value of this type of archival data, highlighting it as an unobtrusive data stream that could complement survey data. One benefit of public archival data is that the government bears the cost of collection and maintenance. But a major hurdle to using such data in the past was the transaction cost of data access. However, the rise of the Internet—and a push for transparency in some societies—has now made many valuable public archival datasets easily accessible. Rather than mailing a request for a dataset and waiting months to receive disks, researchers can now access data easily using government websites. In the United States, for example, researchers can access datasets regularly collected by—to name a few—the Bureau of Labor Statistics, the Census Bureau, and the Social Security Administration. Many agency websites provide links to download databases, along with data dictionaries and guidance.

Bianchi's (2016) investigation of the connection between the state of the economy and individualism provides several examples of using publicly available and easily accessed data via the Internet. First, she used data on the state of the economy, operationalized as the annual unemployment rate, provided by the United States Bureau of Labor Statistics via the Internet. Bianchi (2016) linked unemployment data with several other publicly available datasets, which she used to measure individualism in different ways and over long time horizons. In one study, she used data on baby names between 1948 and 2014 provided by the United States Social Security Administration. Bianchi (2016) operationalized individualism as the use of relatively unusual, compared to more commonplace, baby names. Linking name data with unemployment rates enabled Bianchi to show—using a dataset comprising more than a quarter of a billion observations—that American parents selected unique names for their babies more frequently during economically prosperous years.

In a second study, Bianchi (2016) analysed the lyrical content of American popular music over nearly 35 years. She accessed the lyrics of songs on the Internet and used the Linguistic Inquiry Word Count software (Pennebaker et al., 2007) to measure the proportion of lyric words that were first-person singular (indicating higher individualism) versus first-person plural (indicating lower individualism). First-person singular words are, for example, 'I' and 'Me'; first-person plural words include, for example, 'We' and 'Us'. Bianchi (2016) examined covariation between pronoun usage and the state of the economy over time, finding that in prosperous years song lyrics were more individualistic.

These studies illustrate a key benefit of publicly available archival data (aside from the fact that the government bears the cost of collecting and maintaining the data). Many public archival datasets track the same metric over a large scale (i.e. across a large number of people) and over a long time horizon (e.g. across decades). Each of these properties is useful for understanding how more macro contextual trends might influence behaviour.

PRIVATE ARCHIVES: FROM PERSONNEL TO INFORMATION TECHNOLOGY

Webb et al. distinguished between archival datasets held by the government and archival datasets compiled and maintained by private entities, such as personnel data on turnover or absenteeism within a private corporation. In the years since their book, the nature of private archival data has changed dramatically. Whereas in the past private archival data were limited in scope and in scale, many organizations today collect and store vast amounts of data in their daily operations. Also driven by the developments described above, the locus of work in many organizations has shifted from face to face and physical to virtual and digital. This trend is evident if you consider how researchers work today. Whereas accessing an article in the past required a trip to the library, researchers can now log into their library through a web browser and download an article at their own desk. Whereas editing a manuscript with a colleague in the past required mailing and marking up a physical copy, researchers today can collaborate on a digital file in the cloud. And whereas the journal review process in the past required printing and mailing hard copies, researchers today can upload digital files to Internet-based applications that coordinate the review process. All of these activities are tracked and stored in digital private archives that could be used in research.

For example, Saavedra et al. (2011) partnered with a stock trading firm focused on day trading. Partially due to regulations requiring the firm to capture trading behaviour and traders' communications, the firm's information technology systems offered the potential to examine how patterns of communications might influence the pattern of decision making across traders. The researchers examined the emergence of synchronous trading and the performance implications of making a trade either before or after the synchronous trading of most other people. Further, the researchers also examined how communication patterns among traders relate to the emergence of synchrony. Saavedra et al. (2011) gained access to two data archives, focused on sixty-six employees over roughly a year and a half. The first data source comprised more than a million live trades, captured on a second-by-second basis. The second data source contained 2 million messages sent via an instant messaging system. Because, like trading activity, messages were timestamped, the researchers could examine second-by-second communication and trading behaviour. Their results revealed several fascinating aspects of synchronous behaviour in a real-world setting. This study illustrates how the data that private corporations routinely collect and store through information technology systems can help understand dynamic interpersonal phenomena.

Also illustrating the value of private archival data, Pierce et al. (2015) partnered with a vendor of a point of sale (POS) system used by staff in restaurants to, among other tasks, enter customers' orders and send them to the kitchen, prepare customers' bills, and process customers' payments. The POS system captured a running record of activities that the restaurants used in their operations (e.g. for inventory, marketing). The research centred on how the activation of a theft-monitoring module in the POS influenced employees' behaviour. Using a proprietary algorithm, this module flagged actions by employees that likely constituted theft. The researchers identified a sample of nearly 400 restaurant locations that had, at some point in a two-year window, activated the theft-monitoring module. Importantly, the module could be applied to historical data even if it had not been activated at the time the data were initially captured; so, the authors could examine how the implementation of the monitoring module influenced employees' behaviour and outcomes, such as losses, revenue, and tips. Exemplifying the power of novel unobtrusive methods, the data were multilevel and permitted a fine-grained analysis. The researchers examined revenue and tips at the employee-week level of analysis (i.e. average revenue and tips for each worker on a weekly basis) and also at higher levels of analysis, such as the restaurant level over time. The dataset contained data on the behaviour of more than 22,000 employees, yielding a dataset with more than 400,000 weekly observations. Results showed that how a monitoring system changes workers' behaviour is complex, possibly leading workers to invest additional effort in productive activities to secure higher tips from customers.

Private archival data offers researchers many of the same benefits as public archival data. Working with private entities may also offer the advantage of customizing an unobtrusive method to focus on or capture something of particular interest to a researcher. Both of the examples above show the importance of close collaborations with private entities—collaborations enhanced when researchers study problems of interest to the private entities.

SIMPLE OBSERVATION: FROM PEN AND PAPER
TO WEARABLE SENSORS

The kind of simple observation that Webb et al. described—watching and recording notes or measurements of behaviour over time—is costly to implement. Because capturing data in this way requires researchers to spend time directly observing others, the time required to collect data is a multiple of the number of observations and the amount of time subjects are watched. Given these costs, simple observation has been used relatively sparingly in organizational research. The technological developments described above, however, have facilitated a new form of 'observation', in which the observer is not a researcher, but a wearable device comprising sensors. Devices with sensors are ubiquitous, exemplified by the smartphones that more than a billion people now own. In addition to devices designed and manufactured for consumers, engineers and researchers have developed devices specifically for research. For example, one multidisciplinary team has developed a wearable sensor platform to continuously assess team dynamics, such as the development of cohesion over time (e.g. Kozlowski, 2015). A second team (Kim et al., 2012) has developed a device with a set of sensors (e.g. microphones, Bluetooth, infrared) to map social networks.

In one early application of this technology, Ingram and Morris (2007) used a wearable sensor to study interpersonal dynamics during professional 'mixers'—events organized to facilitate relationship formation. The authors were specifically interested in the degree to which mixers fulfil their stated purpose of sparking relationships between previously unfamiliar people. In the study, ninety-two members of an executive MBA program wore devices around their necks during a roughly 90-minute networking event. The devices used infrared sensors to record when two devices were facing one another, as would happen during a face-to-face conversation. The authors operationalized a meaningful conversation between two people as an instance when the infrared sensors of two badges detected one another continuously for one minute. Wearable sensors enabled Ingram and Morris (2007) to address questions that a traditional survey-based approach cannot answer. For example, having a continuous record of interactions enabled the authors to examine the temporal dynamics of homophily. They found that homophily effects are strongest early in a networking event, but that heterophily becomes more common as the event progresses. Addressing such a question using a survey would require participants to document their conversations throughout the evening—a task that would interfere with their networking.

As a second example, Knight and Baer (2014) used a wearable sensor to study how physical space influences group dynamics, proposing that groups produce more creative ideas when working in a non-sedentary space, which induces them to stand, than when working seated around a conference room table. Standing, they argued, leads to elevated levels of group arousal and lower levels of territorial behaviour—expressions of possessiveness over contributions to the group. Together, activation and territoriality influence the creativity of the group by shaping how much people collaboratively build upon one another's ideas. To measure arousal, participants wore a wrist-based device that measured electrodermal activity. The devices that Knight and Baer (2014) used (see Poh et al., 2010) recorded individuals' physiological arousal eight times per second. This example illustrates two benefits of wearable sensors. First, the use of a wearable device allows researchers to track information that may not be accessible to participants. Second, a sensor can provide continuous measurement over time.

Wearable devices range in how unobtrusive they are—something that is in the eye of the beholder. The devices described above are on the more obtrusive side of the continuum, given that they were specifically deployed for the purposes of the investigation. In thinking about how obtrusive a given device is, it is important to consider the degree to which wearing the device is a routine for research participants. The more that wearing the device is a part of daily life—such as an activity tracker that one regularly wears or a smartphone carried in a pocket—the less obtrusive the research is likely to be.

CONTRIVED OBSERVATION: FROM MANUAL TO COMPUTER-ASSISTED CODING OF RECORDINGS

Webb et al. described a second kind of observation—involving the use of video and audio recordings—which they referred to as contrived observation. The use of recording devices can reduce the costs of data collection, since multiple devices can be used to collect data over time and across situations. However, the use of recording devices introduces the additional challenge of making sense of what has been recorded. Traditionally, researchers have employed teams of trained coders to transform recorded material into standardized measures of constructs. Accordingly, the costs of observation shift; rather than observing behaviour in real-time, researchers must observe behaviour on recordings. Several recent innovations, however, have enabled researchers to more efficiently make sense of data in the form of audio and video recordings. Through the application of machine learning, computer scientists and researchers have developed algorithms that can score audio, video, and text data automatically. Although improvements in microphones and video cameras have enhanced the precision of the raw inputs, software—developments in machine learning—is the underlying engine of these new methods.

The study of the dynamics of emotional contagion by Barsade et al. (2015) provides one illustration of the use of computer-assisted coding. The researchers sought to test predictions regarding how the emotional expressions of in-group and out-group members might differentially influence people. The authors postulated that congruent contagion—in which one person's expressions mirror another person's—would occur from exposure to an in-group member, but counter contagion—when one person's expressions are opposite another person's—would occur from exposure to an out-group member. This study used computer-facilitated coding of research participants' facial expressions to precisely track the timing of individuals' facial expressions in response to an experimentally manipulated stimulus. Using software called *Noldus FaceReader 5*, the authors captured participants' emotional expressions in real-time using a camera mounted on top of the computer that the participants used to view video-based stimuli. *FaceReader* detects changes in several hundred points on the face. Using this facial mapping, the software classifies individuals' facial expressions into a set of standard emotions, such as happiness, sadness, surprise, fear, and disgust. This study illustrates how new technology can ease the burden of converting video recordings into usable data to answer theoretically grounded research questions.

The study of competition, group composition, and collective intelligence by Woolley et al. (2016) offers a second example of this new form of contrived observation. The researchers' laboratory study examined how competition among group members influences collective intelligence in different ways, depending on the group's gender composition. The researchers used group members' conversations to measure competition, operationalized as the frequency with which members interrupted one another. Each group member wore a headset with a microphone, which recorded each person's contributions to the group. Illustrating the utility of computer-assisted coding, the authors used algorithms to transform the digitized audio stream into a time series dataset with a binary indicator of whether a given group member was speaking at a given point in time. This time series dataset was then used to construct measures of speaking patterns within the group, including times when one person interrupted another's speech. This study shows the value of using computer algorithms to efficiently process audio recordings of interpersonal interactions.

Similar computer-assisted approaches are also increasingly used to reduce the costs of coding textual data, and processing data from digital traces of behaviour, shown in the aforementioned Bianchi (2016) study. As an additional example, Kosinski et al. (2015, 2016) illustrate how algorithms can help code data captured through new unobtrusive methods. To date, their work has focused principally on the use of textual digital trace data and traces left on websites like Facebook. In one study, Kosinski et al. (2013) showed that personal characteristics—demographic attributes, political orientation, and sexual orientation—can be inferred from an individual's behavioural ratings of content on Facebook (i.e. 'likes'). Similarly, Park et al. (2015) used computer-assisted coding of the text of individuals' social media posts to measure personality according to The Big 5 taxonomy. The authors demonstrated the reliability and validity of the computer-coded approach, connecting this language-based measure to scores produced through a traditional survey-based approach. This stream of work highlights how computer-assisted coding can streamline methods that were onerous and time-consuming in the past.

Caveats, cautions, and recommendations for using new unobtrusive methods

New unobtrusive methods clearly present many opportunities for researchers. Yet, because of the novelty of these methods, several caveats are necessary. Before embarking on using a new unobtrusive method, researchers should consider issues of requisite expertise, measurement validity, and research ethics.

ACQUIRING REQUISITE EXPERTISE

Researchers using a new unobtrusive method must carefully consider whether they possess the knowledge, skills, and expertise needed to use the method effectively and efficiently. Several approaches, involving sensors and computer-assisted coding, for example, require specialized expertise. To use these methods effectively a researcher would benefit from having deep knowledge of specifically how the technology interacts with the human body, or with external signals of interpersonal behaviour. For example, understanding how a Bluetooth sensor measures interpersonal interactions (i.e. through the strength of the signal connecting two devices) can help in understanding why interactions may seem under- or over-detected in different environments. For some methods, the necessary expertise transcends the technology itself. Because these methods often capture considerable volumes of data over time, benefiting from a new unobtrusive method likely requires a set of skills that are not as critical when using smaller-scale datasets. With large-scale datasets, tasks like database maintenance and data manipulation are impossible if a researcher is not a skilled computer programmer. Programming skills are essential for efficiency and to minimize error.

Given the depth of expertise required for some of these methods, researchers interested in using a new unobtrusive method would benefit from collaborations with domain experts. Multidisciplinary teams can help organizational researchers (and technologists) climb the steep learning curve of a new method. Indeed, a number of the exemplar papers described above resulted from the work of multidisciplinary teams of social scientists, computer scientists, and engineers.

ADDRESSING MEASUREMENT VALIDITY

Because these methods are relatively new, it is imperative that researchers adopt a healthy scepticism regarding measurement validity; reviewers certainly will. Scholars (e.g. Daft, 1995) have noted that lack of evidence for measurement validity—even for established measures—is a common reason that papers are rejected by management journals. When a measure is new and without a track record of use, demonstrating validity is paramount. To provide confidence in the validity of a new unobtrusive measure, researchers should follow the same process used to validate any measure (e.g. Edwards, 2003). At a high level, it is important to connect clearly the conceptual definition of the construct with the operationalization of that construct. To do so, it helps to map the causal model that connects a latent construct with a concrete indicator (Borsboom et al., 2004; Edwards and Bagozzi, 2000). Further, and especially for new measures, evidence of convergent and divergent validity can build confidence that the measure assesses what it is intended to assess. Existing measures, such as surveys, can be useful in this process. However, one must remain open to the idea that an unobtrusive measure may show a weak link with an obtrusive one. This does not necessarily mean that the new measure is flawed; indeed, it could be that the new measure reveals the flaws or idiosyncrasies of established approaches. Social network researchers, for example, have shown that there are differences between email-based network measures and survey-based network measures. These differences do not necessarily invalidate an email-based method. It is incumbent on the researcher, however, to explain why email is the right measure given the interpersonal interactions being studied.

Validating a new measure is especially important when using new technologies. Illustrating the importance of in-depth and systematic validation of a new unobtrusive method, Chaffin et al. (2017) examined the measurement properties of one type of wearable device designed to track interpersonal interactions (Kim et al., 2012). Chaffin et al. (2017) used several carefully controlled studies to examine the measurement properties of a subset of the sensors in the device. For example, they attached devices to easels and manipulated the distance separating the easels, comparing the physical distance to the output of the device. Their findings raised concerns about the reliability and validity of the sensors for assessing interpersonal interactions. Given that these tests were conducted under controlled conditions, these problems could be exacerbated in field applications.

Findings such as those generated by Chaffin et al. (2017) underscore the fact that exciting new technologies do not sidestep old standards of measure validation. When considering a new unobtrusive method, it is imperative to question how well the measurement properties of the method have been tested, what might be required to instil confidence in the validity of the measure, and—of course—how closely the measure fits with the phenomenon under examination. If systematic validation of an archival data source is not possible, it is advisable to use several different measures to triangulate on the phenomenon of interest. This is precisely the approach used in several studies described above, such as Bianchi (2016) who used baby names, song lyrics, and more to measure individualism. Any one indicator is insufficient. By packaging them together, however, Bianchi (2016) builds confidence that her conclusions are not due to measurement artefacts.

CONTENDING WITH AMBIGUOUS ETHICAL STANDARDS

A third issue requiring special consideration when using a new unobtrusive method is research ethics. Researchers should, of course, always consider the ethics of their design and measurement approaches. New methods require special attention, however. Compared to established methods for which researchers and Institutional Review Boards (IRBs) have decades of experience, formal policies, and established norms, new methods break new ethical ground. For unobtrusive methods, this is often with respect to issues of informed consent and privacy. Many of the methods described above—and especially the use of digital trace and archival data—are riddled with ethical grey areas.

Consider a recent examination of contagion using data from Facebook (Kramer et al., 2014). The authors partnered with Facebook specifically to study how exposure to posts with different affective tones influences users' behaviour. The design involved manipulating the prevalence with which a subset of Facebook users viewed relatively positive or relatively negative information. Although the users did not provide informed consent for this research study, they had agreed to Facebook's terms of use, which allow Facebook to shape information feeds. This kind of manipulation of content (and design) is ubiquitous in web and mobile applications. Does the fact that Facebook regularly manipulates content eliminate the need for researchers to seek informed consent? In this case, the authors' IRB determined that because the researchers were working with Facebook, the study did not fall under its purview.

Nevertheless, the study generated considerable controversy and led several commentators to argue that it violated research ethics. The editor of the *Proceedings of the National Academy of Sciences* issued a formal expression of concern, 'that the collection of the data by Facebook may have involved practices that were not fully consistent with the principles of obtaining informed consent and allowing participants to opt out' (Verma, 2014, p.10779). A primary source of ambiguity is the fact that for-profit corporations are not subject to federal research ethics standards because they do not receive federal funding. Clearly this presents researchers using new unobtrusive methods—and, in particular, those using private archival data—with an unmapped ethical landscape. Sparked by reactions to the study, Facebook's

Jackman and Kanerva (2016) recently called for greater attention by for-profit entities to ethical standards for research, detailing the steps that Facebook has taken. As this example illustrates, it behoves the researcher using new unobtrusive methods to seek counsel and guidance from multiple perspectives, thoughtfully vetting any project with respect to issues of consent and privacy.

Conclusion

Did you download this chapter from a digital repository? If so, you have left a trace in the digital landscape—one that some enterprising researcher might use. The world has changed dramatically in the decades since Webb and colleagues' plea for researchers to complement survey and interview methods with unobtrusive methods. Unobtrusive methods are now more accessible and cheaper to use than they were even just 20 years ago. Using digital trace data, large-scale archival data, wearable sensors, and computer-assisted coding, researchers can gain new insights into organizational phenomena.

■ **REFERENCES**

Barnes, C.M., Dang, C.T., Leavitt, K., Guarana, C.L., and Uhlmann, E.L. (2015). 'Archival data in micro-organizational research: a toolkit for moving to a broader set of topics', *Journal of Management*, XX(X): 1–26.

Barsade, S.G., Smith-Crowe, K., and Potter, J.M.I. (2015). 'Emotional contagion or not? The role of in-groups and out-groups.' Paper presented at the 30th Annual Conference of the *Society for Industrial and Organizational Psychology*, Philadelphia, PA.

Bianchi, E.C. (2016). 'American individualism rises and falls with the economy: cross-temporal evidence that individualism declines when the economy falters.' *Journal of Personality and Social Psychology*, 111(4): 567–84.

Borsboom, D., Mellenbergh, G.J., and van Heerden, J. (2004). 'The concept of validity', *Psychological Review*, 111(4): 1061–71.

Cappelli, P. and Sherer, P.D. (1991). 'The missing role of context in OB: the need for a meso-level approach', *Research in Organizational Behaviour*, 13: 55–110.

Chaffin, D., Heidl, R., Hollenbeck, J.R., Howe, M., Yu, A., Voorhees, C., and Calantone, R. (2017). 'The promise and perils of wearable sensors in organizational research', *Organizational Research Methods*, 20(1): 3–31.

Cronin, M.A., Weingart, L.R., and Todorova, G. (2011). 'Dynamics in groups: are we there yet?', *The Academy of Management Annals*, 5: 571–612.

Daft, R.L. (1995). 'Why I recommended that your manuscript be rejected, and what you can do about it.' In L.L. Cummings and P.J. Frost (eds.), *Publishing in the organizational sciences*. Thousand Oaks, CA: Sage, pp.164–82.

Dai, H., Milkman, K.L., and Riis, J. (2014). 'The fresh start effect: temporal landmarks motivate aspirational behaviour', *Management Science*, 60(10): 2563–82.

Edwards, J.R. (2003). 'Construct validation in organizational behaviour research.' In J. Greenberg (ed.), *Organizational behaviour: The State of the Science.* Second edition. Mahwah, NJ: Erlbaum, pp.327–71.

Edwards, J.R. and Bagozzi, R.P. (2000). 'On the nature and direction of relationships between constructs and measures', *Psychological Methods*, 5(2): 155–74.

Ericsson (2015). *Ericsson Mobility Report: On the Pulse of the Networked Society.* Stockholm, Sweden.

Fitchard, K. (2016). 'Sensing Samsung: the evolution of sensors in the Galaxy S series.' Retrieved January 12, 2016, from <https://opensignal.com/blog/2016/02/19/sensing-samsung-the-evolution-of-sensors-in-the-galaxy-s-series/>

Harrington, J.R. and Gelfand, M.J. (2014). 'Tightness-looseness across the 50 united states.' *Proceedings of the National Academy of Sciences of the United States of America*, 2014(22): 7990–5.

Heggestuen, J. (2013). 'One in every 5 people in the world own a smartphone, one in every 17 own a tablet.' <http://uk.businessinsider.com/smartphone-and-tablet-penetration-2013-10>

Hill, A.D., White, M.A., and Wallace, J.C. (2014). 'Unobtrusive measurement of psychological constructs in organizational research', *Organizational Psychology Review*, 4(2): 148–74.

House, R.J., Rousseau, D.M., and Thomas-Hunt, M. (1995). 'The meso paradigm: a framework for the integration of micro and macro organizational behaviour', *Research in Organizational Behaviour*, 17: 71–114.

Ingram, P. and Morris, M.W. (2007). 'Do people mix at mixers? Structure, homophily, and the "Life of the Party".' *Administrative Science Quarterly*, 52: 558–85.

Jackman, M. and Kanerva, L. (2016). 'Evolving the IRB: building robust review for industry research', *Washington and Lee Law Review*, 72(3): 442–57.

Johns, G. (2006). 'The essential impact of context on organizational behaviour', *Academy of Management Review*, 31: 386–408.

Kim, T., Mcfee, E., Olguin, D.O., Waber, B., and Pentland, A.S. (2012). 'Sociometric badges: using sensor technology to capture new forms of collaboration', *Journal of Organizational Behaviour*, 427: 412–27.

Kleinbaum, A.M., Stuart, T.E., and Tushman, M.L. (2013). 'Discretion within constraint: homophily and structure in a formal organization', *Organization Science*, 24(5): 1316–57.

Knight, A.P., and Baer, M. (2014). 'Get up, stand up: the effects of a non-sedentary workspace on information elaboration and group performance', *Social Psychological and Personality Science*, 5(8): 910–17.

Kosinski, M., Stillwell, D., and Graepel, T. (2013). 'Private traits and attributes are predictable from digital records of human behaviour', *Proceedings of the National Academy of Sciences of the United States of America*, 110(15): 5802–5.

Kosinski, M., Matz, S.C., and Gosling, S.D. (2015). 'Facebook as a research tool for the social sciences', *American Psychologist*, 70(6): 543–56. <http://doi.org/10.1037/a0039210>

Kosinski, M., Wang, Y., Lakkaraju, H., and Leskovec, J. (2016). 'Mining big data to extract patterns and predict real-life outcomes', *Psychological Methods*. <http://dx.doi.org/10.1037/met0000105>

Kozlowski, S.W.J. (2015). 'Advancing research on team process dynamics: theoretical, methodological, and measurement considerations', *Organizational Psychology Review*, 5: 270–99.

Kozlowski, S.W.J., Chao, G.T., Chang, C.H., and Fernandez, R. (2016). 'Team dynamics: using 'big data' to advance the science of team effectiveness.' In S. Tonidandel, E.B. King, and J. Cortina (eds.), *Big data at work: the data science revolution and organizational psychology*, pp.272–309. New York: Routledge Academic.

Kramer, A.D.I., Guillory, J.E., and Hancock, J.T. (2014). 'Experimental evidence of massive-scale emotional contagion through social networks', *Proceedings of the National Academy of Sciences*, 111(29): 8788–90.

Li, R., Curhan, J., and Hoque, M.E. (2015). 'Predicting video-conferencing conversation outcomes based on modeling facial expression synchronization', *11th IEEE International Conference and Workshops on Automatic Face and Gesture Recognition, FG 2015*, 1–6.

Moore, G.E. (1965). 'Cramming more components onto integrated circuits', *Electronics*, 38, 1–4.

Park, G., Schwartz, H.A., Eichstaedt, J.C., Kern, M.L., Kosinski, M., Stillwell, D.J., Seligman, M.E.P. (2015). 'Automatic personality assessment through social media language', *Journal of Personality and Social Psychology*, 108(6): 934–52.

Pennebaker, J.W., Booth, R.J., and Francis, M.E. (2007). *Linguistic inquiry and word count: LIWC*. Austin, TX.

Picard, R. W. (1997). *Affective computing*. Cambridge, MA: MIT Press.

Pierce, L., Snow, D.C., and McAfee, A. (2015). 'Cleaning house: the impact of information technology monitoring on employee theft and productivity', *Management Science*, 61(10): 2299–319.

Podsakoff, P.M., MacKenzie, S.B., and Podsakoff, N.P. (2012). 'Sources of method bias in social science research and recommendations on how to control it', *Annual Review of Psychology*, 63: 539–69.

Poh, N., Swenson, N.C., and Picard, R.W. (2010). 'A wearable sensor for unobtrusive, long-term assessment of electrodermal activity', *IEEE Transactions on Bio-Medical Engineering*, 57(5): 1243–52.

R Core Team (2015). 'R: A language and environment for statistical computing.' Vienna, Austria: R Foundation for Statistical Computing.

Saavedra, S., Hagerty, K., and Uzzi, B. (2011). 'Synchronicity, instant messaging, and performance among financial traders', *Proceedings of the National Academy of Sciences*, 108(13): 5296–301.

Scandura, T.A. and Williams, E.A. (2000). 'Research methodology in management: current practices, trends, and implications for research', *Academy of Management Journal*, 43: 1248–64.

Schwarz, N. (1999). 'Self-reports: how the questions shape the answers.' *American Psychologist*, 54(2): 93–105.

Staats, B.R., Dai, H., Hofmann, D., and Milkman, K.L. (2016). 'Motivating process compliance through individual electronic monitoring: an empirical examination of hand hygiene in healthcare', *Management Science*, mnsc.2015.2400.

Swan, M. (2012). 'Sensor Mania! The Internet of Things, Wearable Computing, Objective Metrics, and the Quantified Self 2.0', *Journal of Sensor and Actuator Networks*, 1(3): 217–53.

The Economist (2017). 'The world's most valuable resource', 6 May, p.9.

Tonidandel, S., King, E.B., and Cortina, J.M. (2016). 'Big data methods: leveraging modern data analytic techniques to build organizational science', *Organizational Research Methods*. DOI: <https://doi.org/10.1177/1094428116677299>

Verma (2014). 'Editorial expression of concern: experimental evidence of massive-scale emotional contagion through social networks', *Proceedings of the National Academy of Sciences*, 111(29): 10779.

Walker, J. (2012, September 20). 'Meet the new boss: big data.' *Wall Street Journal*. Retrieved from <https://www.wsj.com/articles/SB1000087239639044389030457806252019616768>

Wang, W., Hernandez, I., Newman, D.A., He, J., and Bian, J. (2016). 'Twitter analysis: studying US weekly trends in work stress and emotion', *Applied Psychology*, 65(2): 355–78.

Webb, E.J. and Weick, K.E. (1979). 'Unobtrusive measures in organizational theory: a reminder', *Administrative Science Quarterly*, 24: 650–9.

Webb, E.J., Campbell, D.T., Schwartz, R.D., and Sechrest, L. (1966). *Unobtrusive Measures: Onreactive Research in the Social Sciences*. Chicago, IL: Rand McNally.

Wilson, H.J. (2013, October 20). 'Wearable gadgets transform how companies do business.' *Wall Street Journal*.

Woolley, A.W., Chow, R.M., Mayo, A., and Chang, J.W. (2016). 'Competition and collective intelligence: do women always make groups smarter?' In *Academy of Management Meeting*. Anaheim, CA.

5 Research in extreme contexts

David A. Buchanan and David Denyer

What's the problem?

Corporate crises, property and forest fires, mountaineering and polar expeditions, an army base in a combat zone, space shuttle losses, the global financial crisis, a blow-out on an oil rig, a toxic chemical spill, the mistaken shooting of a suspected terrorist, a militarized border crossing, hospital operating theatres, nuclear reprocessing. These settings have little in common beyond the fact that they all involve degrees of threat and risk, and can thus be described as 'extreme' in some respect. Contexts can be or become extreme in different ways. High-altitude mountaineering, space exploration, and firefighting are intrinsically hazardous. Operating theatres are extreme contexts for hospital patients, not for theatre staff. Any organizational context, however, can become extreme; consider a shopping centre, when a fire breaks out or a marauding terrorist attack occurs. Hannah and Parry (2014, p.614) argue that, 'organizational contexts in general are becoming more volatile and dynamic, and thus the study of extreme contexts might provide findings that can generalize to less extreme yet still turbulent contexts'. Extreme context research may not be as specialized as the 'extreme' label suggests.

Research interest in extreme contexts has been prompted by three related factors. First, issues such as leadership, decision-making, motivation, resilience, and teamwork, become more critical than they are in 'normal' settings. Inappropriate leadership behaviours and ineffective teamwork can, in some extreme contexts, cost the lives of those directly and indirectly involved (e.g. Kayes, 2004; Hannah et al., 2010; Fraher, 2011; Cornelissen et al., 2014). Second, given the heightened significance of those issues, the potential for generating fresh insights may also be greater than in routine settings. Eisenhardt (1989) and Pettigrew (1990) advise that, in selecting research sites, it is valuable to go for extreme situations, 'mavericks', and outliers. In our experience, many researchers (not just junior academics) still consider it too risky to follow that advice. Third, for those concerned with research relevance and impact, this is one area where improved understanding can make a major difference.

Extreme context research faces several problems. Many extreme contexts arise from accidents and failures, which can occur suddenly and unexpectedly, and are difficult to study in real time. James et al. (2011, p.481) thus note that 'it is unlikely that researchers can capture firsthand information from organizational leaders in the midst of a crisis'. Passive or participant observation is rarely an option. Proximity may expose researchers to danger. Corporate crises raise sensitive legal and reputational concerns. Research access is often denied. Approaching those who may have been traumatized by involvement in a crisis raises ethical issues. Longitudinal studies are especially challenging.

Nevertheless, there is now a rich literature addressing all of the contexts mentioned in our opening paragraph, and many others. Buchanan and Denyer (2013) argue that researchers have overcome those methodological problems by adopting a range of unconventional approaches. The aim of this chapter, therefore, is to explore the nature of extreme context research, and to encourage others to experiment with this approach in their own work. The structure of this chapter is as follows. First, we describe extreme context research that relies mainly on organizational documents and sources in the public domain. Second, we consider studies conducted by researchers who were themselves directly involved with or embedded in the extreme contexts that they were investigating. Third, we look at the growing use of film and television as sources of research evidence concerning extreme contexts. Fourth, we report examples of extreme context research from our own experience. We conclude with an assessment of the benefits and drawbacks of extreme context research, and offer advice for others wishing to advance their own research in this manner.

Researcher, historian, detective

Many researchers have used secondary sources to study the extreme contexts that interest them. 'High profile' incidents in particular generate large amounts of analysis and commentary. Some of these sources, however, have not traditionally been regarded as valid empirical evidence. This includes literary non-fiction, newspaper and magazine articles, phone call records, television documentaries, and sensitive internal organization documents. However, reporters and camera crews do not first have to satisfy research ethics committees before they can start work, and they can access extreme contexts more easily and rapidly than can academic researchers. Journalistic accounts can thus be valuable, as evidence in their own right, and because they influence public perceptions of and organizational responses to extreme contexts, thus becoming part of the narrative under investigation.

Another feature of extreme context research is the use of single cases, which is unavoidable, given the idiosyncratic nature of extreme contexts. Case study designs, however, are not seen as 'mainstream' (Eisenhardt and

Graebner, 2007; Barends et al., 2014), a point which is addressed shortly. Here we consider four cases illustrating combinations of unconventional and conventional sources.

Weick's (1993) seminal study of sensemaking was based on an analysis of the Mann Gulch disaster in Montana in 1949, in which 13 firefighters were killed. Weick relied on a book written twenty years after the disaster by a firefighter who had witnessed the incident (Maclean, 1972). Maclean based his account on direct observation and personal experience, interviews, trace evidence, archival records, mathematical modelling of how fires spread, and a report in *Life* magazine. Perrow's (1999) studies of 'normal accidents' caused by high-risk technologies also relied on published sources. For example, his analysis of the partial meltdown at the Three Mile Island nuclear power plant in 1979 was based on the report of the formal inquiry into the accident, articles in the *New York Times, Science*, the *Washington Post*, the *Bulletin of the Atomic Scientist*, and other specialist journals, transcripts of press conferences held by an engineering sub-contractor who was blamed for the accident, and books written by others about the incident. Perrow (1992, 1999) also describes how his involvement with this situation arose from a chance invitation to provide a social science contribution to what would have been a wholly engineering oriented investigation—an invitation that he initially rejected.

Snook (2000) analysed a friendly fire incident in which two US Air Force F15 fighter jets shot down two US Army Black Hawk helicopters over northern Iraq in 1994, killing all 26 passengers and crew. For this analysis, he used an extraordinary combination of sources:

[O]fficial government documents, archival records, interviews, physical artefacts, gun target footage, videotapes, audio tapes, training records, maintenance records, technical reports, trial transcripts, AWACS data tapes, internal Department of Defense (DOD) memoranda, press releases, newspaper clippings, congressional hearings, criminal investigations, conference briefings, flight records, mishap reports, personnel records, military flight plans, oil analyses, medical evaluations, psychological evaluations, human factors reports, optics reports, crash site analyses, equipment tear-downs, weather observations, accident site photographs, witness statements, regulations, directives, maps, communications logs, intelligence briefings, task force airspace control orders, pre-mission briefs, flight logs, lists of corrective actions taken, and DOD fact sheets (Snook, 2000, pp.15–16).

Snook (a lieutenant-colonel in the US Army) also obtained two commercial videos, from an Iraqi news team and from ABC news *Prime Time Live*. He obtained a copy of the F-15 gun-sight video footage of the shootdown, with an audio record from the cockpit of the trail F-15, and a copy of the video taken by a camcorder inside the AWACS. In other words, Snook combined a vast array of conventional and unconventional sources to explain an incident that lasted eight minutes.

Jean Charles de Menezes, a Brazilian, was working as an electrician in London when he was shot dead in 2005 by police who believed, mistakenly, that he was a terrorist involved in recent bomb attacks. Cornelissen et al. (2014) analysed the collective sensemaking and escalation of commitment that led to this incident, known as 'The Stockwell Shooting' after the London underground station in which it occurred. Their analysis relied on transcripts of the evidence from seventy-three witnesses (police, forensic examiners, anti-terrorism experts) presented to the inquest into the event, on recollections of officers involved in the shooting, and on material evidence stored in over 1,000 separate files which included photos, logged accounts, police documents, and records of telephone conversations on the day of the incident. This evidence allowed the researchers to construct a detailed account of the sequence of events leading up to the shooting, and to identify the combination of factors that led to the 'contraction of meaning' and to the officers' commitment to a mistaken course of action.

Typical of this style of extreme context research, these case studies demonstrate the contribution of unconventional data sources in building explanations for the sequences of events and outcomes of interest. The researchers in these cases were cast in the roles of historian and detective, reconstructing event sequences from the available evidence, from different sources, assessing the relative value of that information, and drawing it into a coherent account (Buchanan and Denyer, 2013).

What is the value of these single cases, from which convention says we cannot generalize? This criticism is traditionally based on the concept of *statistical* generalization, from findings based on a representative sample to the wider population. But this mode of generalization is not appropriate for studies of the kind summarized here. How could we generate representative samples of firefighter fatalities in Montana, of nuclear power plant meltdowns, of friendly fire incidents with F15 jets and helicopters in Iraq, of shootings by London police officers of civilians mistaken for terrorists?

Fortunately, there are four other modes in which case study findings can be generalized (see Buchanan, 2012, pp.364–6). First, Williams (2000, p.138; Payne and Williams, 2005) coined the term *moderatum generalization* to refer to 'an intermediate type of limited generalization' involving modest speculative associations. Eisenhardt (1989) and Langley (1999) argue that it is possible to identify low-level patterns and develop moderate generalizations with eight to ten cases (or fewer: see Perrow, 1999 and Whiteman and Cooper, 2011). Second, Stake (1994, p.240) argues that with case accounts, 'The reader comes to know some things told, as if he or she had experienced them. Enduring meanings come from encounter, and are modified and reinforced by repeated encounter.' He calls the process through which we learn from case studies *naturalistic generalization*. Third, several commentators argue that case study findings generalize from observation to theory (e.g. Tsang, 2014).

Tsoukas (2009) refers to this process as *analytical refinement*, where the case, as an example of the phenomenon under investigation, widens our understanding with fresh observations. Fourth, Toft and Reynolds (2005) note that the same lessons from otherwise unique accidents and disasters keep recurring; technical problems are usually outweighed by organizational and managerial factors. They argue, therefore, that lessons from one setting can be applied to different settings with similar properties through the process of *isomorphic learning*, informing practice rather than theory.

These four modes of generalization are not mutually exclusive. Isomorphic learning is a form of naturalistic generalization. Analytical refinement and naturalistic generalization both apply to most case studies. The point is that these modes of generalization are more appropriate and more powerful than statistical generalization, with regard to theory development, and contribution to practice. With regard to understanding behaviour in extreme contexts, Weick developed the concept of sensemaking; Perrow, the implications of interactive complexity; Snook, the phenomenon of practical drift; Cornelissen et al., the notion of contraction of meaning. The 'problem' of generalizing these findings does not arise; is the concept of sensemaking applicable only in the context of forest fires in Montana? It is with their contributions to theory and practice that the value of such cases lies.

The embedded researcher

Some researchers have studied aspects of organizational behaviour in extreme settings where they were personally involved or embedded. For example, Roberts' (1998) pioneering work on high reliability organizations was facilitated by Admiral Thomas Mercer, captain of the nuclear-powered aircraft carrier, *USS Carl Vinson*. Their relationship helped to overcome issues of access, including an Act of Congress that prohibited female assignments to naval duty. Roberts explains how, 'a navy officer suggested I persist. I did and spent some part of the next four years at sea with the Navy' (Roberts 1998, p.225). Roberts and Rousseau (1989) offer valuable advice on research in extreme contexts, with regard to access, problem identification, data collection and interpretation, and relationships with organization members.

For his study of urban poverty, Venkatesh (2008) befriended a leader of the Black Kings, a criminal gang selling crack cocaine in Chicago. The gang leader, JT, allowed Venkatesh to 'hang out' with him over six years. Often in danger, and at risk of being arrested himself, Venkatesh was able to explore the gang's organization structure, leadership style, working conditions for 'foot soldiers', management practices, community links, relationships with the police, and details of the gang's revenues and expenses (Levitt and Venkatesh, 2000).

Venkatesh adopted this embedded ethnographic approach when, at the start of the fieldwork for his sociology degree, he discovered that interviews and questionnaires were going to be of little use. This is from his first encounter with JT:

He looked at a few more pages of the questionnaire. 'You ain't going to learn shit with this thing.' He kept shaking his head and then glanced towards some of the older men standing about, checking to see if they shared his disbelief. Then he leaned in to me and spoke quietly. 'How'd you get to do this if you don't even know who we are, what we're about?' His tone wasn't accusatory as much as disappointed, and perhaps a bit bewildered [....] Then, as I began gathering up my bag and clipboard, he talked to me about the proper way to study people. 'You shouldn't go around asking them silly-ass questions', he said. 'With people like us, you should hang out, get to know what they do, how they do it. No one is going to answer questions like that. You need to understand how young people live on the streets.'   (Venkatesh, 2008, pp.16 and 21)

So, 'hang out' was exactly what Venkatesh did, with fascinating results.

Goffman (2014) spent six years living in one of America's most disadvantaged neighbourhoods in Philadelphia, studying the lives of young African American men, mostly small-time drug dealers, and their interactions with the police, courts, prison, and the wider community. Her access was based on chance encounters which developed into personal relationships—especially with 'Mike' who treated her as his adopted sister. Like Venkatesh, Goffman was part 'fly on the wall', and part participant observer—a young blonde white woman in a male-dominated Black community, who was herself often exposed to danger, and the possibility of arrest and imprisonment. Goffman's methodological appendix offers insights into the nature and value of this prolonged immersion and involvement:

I learned how to sleep on cue and in short intervals, and amid the clamor of others; to distinguish between gun shots and other loud bangs; to run and hide when the police were coming; to identify the car modes, haircuts and body language of undercover cops in plain clothes. I learned how to get through a stop without placing myself or anyone else at greater risk, and how to remain silent during an interrogation so as not to give up any information. I learned how to be a woman closely linked to a man on the run, to go through his hunt and capture and court dates and confinement and release.
(pp.242–3)

This intense experience had a profound effect on Goffman who, when resuming her graduate research studies at Princeton, reports that:

The first day, I found myself casing the classrooms in the Sociology Department, making a mental note of the TVs and computers I could steal if I ever needed cash in a hurry. I got pulled over for making a U-turn, and then got another ticket for parking a few inches outside some designated dotted line on the street that I hadn't even noticed.   (p.247)

Judging Goffman's work to be a classic ethnography, Van Maanen and de Rond (2017) present a balanced assessment of the criticisms levelled at her work, and its many strengths.

Whiteman and Cooper (2011) describe a study of ecological sensemaking, which they compare with Weick's (1993) analysis of the Mann Gulch disaster. Their study, however, is set in subarctic Canada where, at the start of the study of the management practices of Cree hunters in this harsh environment, Whiteman slipped down a rock face above some rapids, and nearly died. Whiteman was herself 'ecologically embedded' in the system which she was studying, spending 18 months as a participant observer at two villages and a trapline in James Bay. She also visited other villages and camps (by snow-mobile), conducting hundreds of informal interviews, and thirty-one in-depth interviews with Cree trappers, elders, youths, teachers, Band Council members, and representatives from Cree regional organizations. Their study shows how those who live in this context use spatial and temporal cues from topography and ecological processes, which affect their resilience and survival.

Prasad (2014) gives a compelling autoethnographic account of his first-hand experience of Qalandiya, a militarized border crossing point between Jerusalem and the West Bank cities of Ramallah and al-Bireh. Prasad's aim in this account is to assess the impact which the fieldwork had on him. His information sources include voice recordings, email exchanges, telephone conversations, personal introspective diary entries, and memory. Autoethnography, he argues, is a lens through which a range of organizational phenomena can be observed and explored. Prasad (2014, p.252) also observes that, in advancing knowledge, 'we often negate, or otherwise wholly erase, the impact that the field has on us, and vice versa.' That oversight, he argues, represents missed opportunities.

Given the opportunity to 'embed' with a team of combat surgeons in Afghanistan in 2011, de Rond (2012; de Rond and Lok, 2016) went through eighteen months of interaction and negotiation, and six weeks of predeployment training, before spending six weeks in the military base at Camp Bastion (now Camp Shorabak). The aim was to explore how cultural, professional, and organizational contexts affect the experience and psychological costs of war from the standpoint of soldier, combat surgeon, ethnographer, and photojournalist. Evidence for this ethnographic account included observation (de Rond had unrestricted and unsupervised access to all areas of the camp hospital), field notes, the personal reflections of participants (including their poetry), two post-tour reports by surgical team members, hospital admissions and triage data, data from weekly morbidity and mortality meetings, and over 1,000 photographs taken by de Rond himself (some of which appear in de Rond and Lok, 2016). Many of these photographs were used in photo-elicitation interviews, to prompt further information. The informal socialization (involving alcohol) during predeployment training is also described as providing 'a particularly rich source of insight' (de Rond and Lok, 2016, p.1970).

Discussing the emotional impact that this experience had on him personally, de Rond (2012, p.259) says that, 'I genuinely tried to do important work yet remained acutely aware that, even at the best of times, my academic output compares poorly to the most mundane of medical interventions. The headwork was exhausting. I returned home intolerant to bullshit.' He continues:

What has remained are a lingering impatience with all things trivial and a confusion about what matters and why. At no prior moment have I felt so disillusioned with what often feels like a publishing game of our own devising. If we took stock of the problems we've solved to date, and their consequences for humanity, would we have reason to be proud? Are there diminishing returns to methodological sophistication? Where are the real problems that should guide our research?   (de Rond, 2012, p.260)

Research opportunities such as these may not be commonplace, and many researchers may be unable or unwilling to exploit such opportunities should they become available. The benefits, in terms of generating interesting research findings and novel insights, however, are likely to be significant.

Extreme contexts in social science fiction

One solution to the problem of research access is to observe behaviour in extreme contexts on film, and in television series. How can fictional accounts constitute empirical evidence? Phillips (1995) observes that film narratives are typically produced to be unique and idiosyncratic, to illustrate extremes, mavericks, and the extraordinary. He argues that fictional sources can generate insights that theoretical discussion and empirical data cannot provide. Advocating the use of novels, short stories, plays, songs, poems, and films as legitimate approaches to the study of organization and management, Phillips (1995, p.636) concludes that:

[F]ictional sources can provide insight into important aspects of organization in a way that no amount of theoretical discussion of empirical data can provide. Narrative fiction can examine organization as a way of life and explore the impact of various organizational dysfunctions on individuals. We do not have to find an actual occurrence of what we wish to talk about, we can instead draw on the library of situations already constructed by talented storytellers, or, if we are very brave, we can make up stories ourselves. In effect, we are lying to tell the truth; we are constructing (or using pre-constructed) situations that never actually happened, but that exemplify issues that occur in actual organizations.

Hassard and Buchanan (2009) also argue that films can be viewed as theoretical narratives, case studies, and proxy documentaries. For example, Buchanan and Huczynski (2004) explore the film *Thirteen Days* (2000, director Roger Donaldson), based on the Cuban missile crisis of 1962, which almost led to nuclear war. They use this film to develop a processual-contextual theory of strategic decision making in an exceptionally extreme context. Penfold-Mounce et al. (2011) illustrate the value of social science fiction in their analysis of the cult HBO television crime drama series *The Wire*. Set in the drugs trade in Baltimore, they explain how *The Wire* sheds light on the challenges of urban life and inequality, with morally complex characters, exploring the working of drug-dealing gangs, the police, the legal system, the dockworkers' union, public schools, print media, and local political institutions. The series also illustrates how individual decisions and actions are shaped and constrained by social, political, and economic factors beyond their control. Asking if this is 'better sociology' than sociologists produce, they note that parts of the action encourage viewers to conduct their own 'thought experiments'; to explore and test ideas, possibilities, consequences, and the repercussions of particular decisions and actions.

In their analysis of *The Wire*, Holt and Zundel (2014, p.576) observe that, 'With ethnographic depth, it shows the unintended consequences of apparently minor managerial decisions and how these spin out and merge with other equally "innocent" decisions to sustain the very institutional conditions being decided against' (p.576). They also note (p.578) that, 'What is powerful about *The Wire* is the manner in which these conditions are investigated and expressed using fiction, especially the opportunity to show passion (conviction), to evoke the world from within (expressive power), and to remind us of what is particularly human in the unfolding of events (tragedy).' (See also Holt and Zundel, Chapter 6, this volume, and Zundel et al., 2013).

To plan for extreme situations, the security establishment has also turned to fiction for inspiration. Cordesman (2001), Professor of Strategy at the Center for Strategic and International Studies in Washington, argues that planning for the future use of biological weapons, by state and non-state adversaries, can be informed by the TV series *Buffy the Vampire Slayer*. Buffy has to deal with a constant stream of novel threats from vampires and demons. 'The Buffy Paradigm' describes the contemporary global security situation, characterized by uncertainty, unpredictability, and changing transborder threats. Features of this paradigm include: 'The attackers have no firm or predictable alliances, cooperate in nearly random ways, and can suddenly change method of attack and willingness to take risks'; 'All efforts at planning a coherent strategy collapse in the face of tactical necessity and the need to deal with unexpected facts on the ground'; 'No success, no matter how important at the time, ever eliminates the risk of future problems' (Cordesman, 2001, p.4). The Buffy Paradigm thus contributes to our understanding of global security, despite its unconventional source.

Buus (2009) also observes that security scholars and policy-makers have turned to contemporary fiction following the 'failure of imagination' that led to the 9/11 attacks on The World Trade Center in New York. She argues that, 'popular fiction may be better equipped to evoke Rumsfeld's "unknown unknowns", flesh out possible actors and envision potential actions than other more traditional and recognized forms of disaster and crisis scenario planning' (Buus, 2009, p.401). Fey et al. (2016) use the 'naturalistic science fiction' TV series *Battlestar Galactica* to explore controversies including the use of torture, detainee policy, occupation practices, civil–military relations, and religion, in addition to the 'taboo' concerning the deployment of nuclear weapons. *Battlestar Galactica*, they argue, can be regarded as an allegory with regard to the post-9/11 'war on terror'. They conclude that fiction can thus be used to reflect on and critique mainstream contemporary conditions and policies, challenge taken-for-granted concepts and the status quo, and suggest alternative meanings and scenarios. Considering an iconic extreme context, a zombie apocalypse, Reed and Penfold-Mounce (2015) use the TV series *The Walking Dead* to examine issues such as consumerism, interpersonal cooperation and conflict, and gender and race relations. Locatelli (2016, p.3) interprets *The Walking Dead* as 'speculative fiction' exploring aspects of leadership, conflict and war, arguing that the most intriguing aspect of the series concerns 'how the survivors shape their own relations, both individually and as a group'.

Social science fiction on film and television allows us to explore new ways of seeing and thinking, to experiment with ideas, challenge assumptions, assess responses, generate fresh evidence, explore and build arguments, and to test and develop theory. These sources can be analysed in their own right, but if that is seen as too unconventional and risky, can be used to complement conventional methods.

Our own extreme context experience

Our own extreme context research has included the four cases summarized in Table 5.1. Those studies explored the causes of the incidents that had taken place, and the fate of the post-crisis change agenda. In these cases, the organizations had experienced extreme events which caused considerable shock and disruption: serious patient safety incidents, accidental release of radioactive waste, gas leak and explosion resulting in injuries, serious injuries to a firefighter. These studies were triggered by observation of a recurring pattern: an extreme event occurs, an investigation is held, recommendations are developed to prevent a recurrence—and those recommendations are either partially implemented, or not at all. One might expect post-crisis change to be welcome and rapid, but that is not always the case, and the research aim was to find out why. Full reports of these studies can be found in:

- Magill Hospital: Buchanan and Moore (2016);
- THORP Sellafield: Denyer (2015b);
- Centrica Storage: Denyer and Sibbick (2015); and
- Richley Fire and Rescue: Denyer (2015a).

Table 5.1 Four extreme context studies

Context	information sources
Magill Hospital*	14 interviews with staff
Acute hospital in England. In 2011, four serious 'never events' in operating theatres—unprecedented given the hospital's reputation for patient safety; staff were shocked.	four investigation reports
	report of a hospital 'listening exercise' which asked staff about 'life in theatres'
	'compliance review' by a regulatory body
	independent external review of theatre practice
	review by the hospital's commissioners
	workshop conducted by researchers for 11 theatres staff to explore the causes of and responses to these events
THORP Sellafield	22 semi-structured interviews
Thermal Oxide Reprocessing Plant (THORP) Sellafield in Cumbria. In 2005, radioactive waste was discovered to have leaked from a crack in a pipe. The leak comprised 83,000 litres of nitric acid containing liquefied uranium, plutonium, and fission products. No injuries or environmental contamination. Leak had gone unnoticed for eight months; how? Plant closed for two years, Board of Inquiry, and investigation by the Nuclear Installations Inspectorate. Firm fined £500,000 for safety breaches; lost revenues around £1 million a day.	documentary evidence including investigation reports and other docs relating to the event
	presentations and reports
	planning documents
	project plans, models, diagrams
	organization charts
	20 focus groups with 400 middle managers
Centrica Storage	17 interviews, 6 identified by a key collaborator, and those 6 identified a further 11
Offshore oil and gas storage facility in the North Sea. In 2006, massive gas release, explosion and fire, two people injured, no fatalities. Major disaster, shock to the company and to the industry. Post-incident change sought to develop a 'high reliability organization'.	company documents and consultancy reports
	Health and Safety Executive investigation
	project proposals and presentations, models and diagrams
	film made by the company to capture the event, and eyewitness accounts
Richley Fire and Rescue*	18 interviews with fire service staff involved in the incident and in subsequent change process
Fire in a high-risk building; two firefighters with breathing apparatus went in, the fire developed rapidly, leading to an explosion seriously injuring one of the crew. Major incident, but investigation produced recommendations which were not implemented.	investigation report (no external inquiries or reviews—all handled internally)
	fire service documents
	fire service DVD 'learning the lessons'

* pseudonyms

A full report of the healthcare research project of which the Magill study was part can be found in Buchanan et al. (2013). The other three cases are detailed, along with further extreme context research exploring post-crisis change, in Denyer and Pilbeam (2015).

Table 5.1 summarizes the research settings and information sources. As those sources are similar in scope and diversity to those in cases described earlier, we will not explore these further. We will focus instead on two other key aspects of extreme context research—obtaining access, and relationships with participants. These issues are rarely discussed in published accounts (but see Roberts and Rousseau, 1989). In what follows, Buchanan is DB, and Denyer is DD.

MAGILL HOSPITAL

Permission to carry out research at Magill was brokered by a colleague who was advising the hospital board, and who introduced us to the chief executive. Our funding allowed us to appoint a management fellow, seconded full time from her hospital operations management role for eight months, and attached to the project part time over two years. She helped to design and conduct a successful change initiative, and co-authored the report of that project (Moore and Buchanan, 2013). She also brokered access to the investigation reports into four 'never events' that occurred in the hospital operating theatres during the fieldwork, along with reports of internal and external reviews of those incidents, and arranged a workshop with the theatres staff. 'Never events' are serious patient safety incidents that should not happen if preventive measures are in place. The events included retained object after surgery, wrong site surgery, patient misidentification, and wrong implant.

Having a colleague known personally to the chief executive enabled us to establish access more quickly than perhaps would have been possible through a 'cold call'. The chief executive in turn nominated a senior colleague to act as our lead contact, who was supportive, and facilitated the search for candidates for our fellowship. While DB managed the fellowship arrangement, DD established a relationship with the hospital's director of risk, whose first response was 'I'm not giving you access to these documents'. However, as the relationship developed, he changed that view, gave DD access to sensitive information, and invited him to attend board meetings where findings of the investigations into the never events were presented and discussed.

These relationships involved a degree of reciprocity, with the research team providing ideas and advice to hospital staff not always involved in the research. DB conducted a role review, and ran a management skills workshop, for the senior nurses group. DD and DB, jointly with our management fellow, facilitated the workshop in which operating theatres staff explored the causes of the recent never events and appropriate responses. DD was asked to attend a patient safety strategy away day as an external adviser. When the chief executive left and was replaced, our web of relationships meant that confirming continuing access with the new chief executive was straightforward.

THORP SELLAFIELD

DD obtained access to the nuclear reprocessing plant at Sellafield while working there on a Cranfield School of Management executive development programme on safety leadership. Senior management at Sellafield wanted this programme to be co-delivered with their senior staff, and DD worked with the heads of nuclear safety and human performance. They in turn brokered access to staff who had been involved in the THORP incident, including the manager of the facility.

CENTRICA STORAGE

DD's wife worked as an associate for a management consultancy which was running a leadership development programme for Centrica Storage. They were interested in the concept of high reliability, and had been approached by another consultancy with expertise in the operational issues, but not with the cultural and behavioural aspects. DD's wife suggested that they should speak to him, and brokered a meeting with the company board. The director of operations for the platform where the explosion had occurred was at another location, and was involved in this meeting through a video conference link. Following an introductory conversation with the board, the operations director came on the video link. DD explained who he was and what he did. The operations director replied, 'What the fuck do you think you can tell me about running my operation?' In the conversation that followed, DD talked about his work at Sellafield and elsewhere, and about some of the latest thinking on organizational failures. Towards the end of the meeting, the operations director said, 'You've got to come over here and spend a day with me and we'll continue this conversation.' Later, the operations director explained that his initial negative reaction at the video conference stemmed from his frustration that everyone else to whom he had spoken had focused on systems and processes. In contrast, DD was discussing culture and behaviour, which he had seen as being the major factors behind their incident. And that was how access to study the incident was established; the operations director co-authored the research publication.

RICHLEY FIRE AND RESCUE

The chief fire officer at Richley was a neighbour and friend of another academic colleague, who brokered the introduction which led to research access being granted. The aim was to study the changes that had been introduced following serious incidents. The chief fire officer suggested that we look at a case where he felt that the post-incident change process had been particularly well-managed: two firefighters had entered a high-risk building, and one had been seriously injured. This would illustrate the successful management of post-incident change.

The investigation of this incident, however, had been managed badly. This was the worst incident in the history of this part of the fire service, and they chose an investigator who had no experience of investigation work, was overloaded, did not know what he was doing, and had low credibility with his team and lacked their respect. DD interviewed the two firefighters soon after the event, and again nine months later. They asked, 'So what was the outcome of the investigation?' They had not been briefed, and had not seen the report. The service had made a DVD about 'learning the lessons', but the copies were sitting under one of the officer's desks in the fire station because he did not like the manner in which he had been portrayed in the film. The lessons were not shared with the rest of the service, and there was a very similar incident involving a fire in an identical building in another area.

This was not the case study that was anticipated, but the research was valuable nevertheless. It was published anonymously due to the criticism of how the aftermath of the incident was managed.

Our experience points to four issues affecting access and relationships in extreme context research.

1. Follow the Opportunities

Access to these contexts and cases was not planned, but was opportunistic. Colleagues and family members were particularly helpful. In each case we had a contact who brokered the first meeting with a gatekeeper, who was then key to opening access to the site. But surely, site selection for the purposes of case research should be systematic and rigorous and not dependent on chance? With regard to extreme context research, we would disagree with that traditional perspective. It may be possible to plan access in some circumstances, but extreme contexts and events are not often waiting to be selected for study at a time and in a location convenient for the researcher. Where possible, these opportunities need to be grasped as and when they arise. We have also seen at Richley an example where permission led to a case study different from that which had been anticipated, but which was nevertheless interesting and valuable.

2. Establish Rapport

The issues that arise in extreme contexts can be sensitive for the individuals and organizations involved. Initially, requests for access are likely to be met with scepticism and defensiveness. The first conversation with a gatekeeper, and the first part of that conversation, are therefore critical. In our experience, two factors are significant. The first concerns demonstrating to the gatekeeper that the research will offer a new perspective, a fresh angle, something which they had not thought of. It can also be helpful to indicate that their situation is not unique, that you have seen this before, that other organizations face similar issues. The second concerns leading them to believe that, 'I can work with this person.' These relationships have often been personal as well as professional. For example, although the research discussed here was completed some time ago, we still exchange documents and ideas with our contacts at Magill and Centrica.

3. Build and Maintain a Network

The studies described here each unfolded over several months; we worked with Magill Hospital for three years. These timescales mean that the original gatekeepers through whom access was granted can move to new roles and other organizations. It can then be difficult to gain the consent of their replacements who are new to the project. That first critical conversation has to take place all over again. However, if through the research a web of relationships across the organization has been built—as at Magill—the members of that network can exert their influence to ensure that the study continues.

4. Recognize the Reciprocity

When we first began work in this area, we assumed that it would be difficult to get people to talk to us about their extreme context experiences. In one case, for example, we were unable to speak to a nurse who had witnessed a patient commit suicide by jumping from a seventh-floor window in a hospital wing. She believed at the time that the patient was going to take her with him. Traumatized by this event, she was understandably unwilling to talk about it, least of all to a researcher. But this was a rare example. We have found that people in extreme contexts are generally willing to be interviewed, and to be open about events and their involvement, including errors and mistakes. Sharing a difficult experience can be cathartic, and this casts the researcher in the role of coach or counsellor—a position for which many researchers may not feel prepared. A senior leader at Sellafield stood for an emotional two-hour interview, with his back to DD, staring at the THORP plant on the other side of the road, saying, 'I've broken it. That was the flagship plant and I've broken it.'

Conclusion

This excursion through the varied territory of extreme context research suggests four sets of conclusions. These concern the possibilities and benefits of this research approach, the drawbacks and limitations, the need to ignore methodological convention, and the consequent advice that other researchers may find helpful in developing their own work.

POSSIBILITIES AND BENEFITS

As indicated earlier, extreme contexts often display issues in a form more amplified and intense than in routine settings. This can lead research participants to share experiences and feelings that perhaps they would not reveal in other settings. This explains why some commentators prioritize the selection of outlier and maverick cases over average and representative settings, and also why extreme context research can increase the probability of generating fresh insights.

The study of extreme contexts and crisis events forces the researcher to think differently, in terms of research design and methods. To develop understanding, it is necessary to consider how events unfold over extended timeframes, to explore phenomena from multiple levels of analysis and from different theoretical perspectives. Organization and management research, conventionally, means exploring relatively mundane issues through the lens of the researcher's favourite theory, level of analysis, and methods. Is that approach conducive to making novel contributions to knowledge? Extreme context research encourages different approaches and ways of thinking.

Researchers who feel that studies of extreme contexts are impossible, or too difficult, challenging and risky, should reconsider. Numerous studies have been successful in understanding the nature and implications of extreme contexts, despite the alleged methodological hurdles. This success applies to a range of settings; from bushfires to hospital operating theatres, from an explosion at an oil and gas storage facility to the accidental shooting of a suspected terrorist, from a military combat zone to a city's drugs trade. This research has generated concepts, such as interactive complexity and practical drift, which apply to other extreme contexts, and also to what would be considered normal settings.

DRAWBACKS AND LIMITATIONS

We have to acknowledge at least four problems with extreme context research.

First, some researchers may find work in an extreme context uncomfortable, particularly if this involves observing others facing hazards, pressure, and stress, and perhaps in some settings also exposing the researcher to harm. This is not, therefore, a route for all researchers, or for all topics.

Second, although some studies rely on documents in the public domain, negotiating direct access to extreme contexts is not always problematic.

We have to admit, however, that some researchers were simply lucky. They knew the right people, or were in the right place at the right time, and gained access to an extreme context by chance. As argued earlier, luck is not a good reason for rejecting offers of research access. On the contrary, identifying and exploiting such opportunities is part of the research 'mindset'. How long should one wait, however, for such an opportunity to arise?

Third, the adoption of unconventional methods to study extreme (and other) contexts is not widely accepted. Films and television programmes are still likely to be dismissed by many (but not all) doctoral research supervisors, journal editors, and reviewers as valid evidence. The belief that one cannot generalize from single cases is widespread, and although we have argued that this belief is unfounded, the issue is still disputed. Researchers using social science fiction, or developing single cases or small-n studies in extreme contexts will often have to defend their methods against criticism.

Finally, it is possible, as in our experience, that access to an extreme context is granted, and that permission to publish is subsequently withheld. That is a risk facing all field researchers, but given the sensitivity of the issues, this may occur more often in extreme settings. Extreme context research is not risk and problem free; researchers have to be able to use their local knowledge and informed judgement before deciding whether or not to proceed with this approach.

IGNORE CONVENTION

The methodological problems in studying extreme contexts have been overcome by researchers ignoring convention. In addition to the reliance on single cases, this has meant making imaginative use of information traditionally regarded as biased or trivial. Piecing together information from a range of sources, each with different degrees of provenance and credibility, puts the researcher in the position of historian and detective, as mentioned earlier. Extreme context studies also encourage researchers to develop relationships with participants that surpass the role of the objective, neutral observer, to become partners, participants, co-producers, friends. This can happen in any research setting, but seems more likely, and more central to the research process, in extreme contexts.

ADVICE

We have four pieces of advice to offer to other researchers embarking on extreme context research, or considering this as a potentially valuable approach:

1. Go for it. As this chapter has shown, the methodological challenges in extreme context research are not insurmountable, and are not always as

severe as they may appear. Do not, therefore, dismiss the possibilities and opportunities prematurely. Follow the suggestion that you are more likely to generate interesting research and findings by choosing maverick, outlier, extreme cases, instead of representative examples (Davis, 1971; Pettigrew, 1990).

2. Use your personal relationships to gain access to extreme contexts for the purposes of research. Your mature students may also be able to broker access to some settings, and may be interested in supporting research work which can in turn contribute to their own dissertation or thesis requirements. In our experience, arranging a secondment from an organization to the research team can be time-consuming, but immensely valuable.

3. Adopt an open and receptive approach to data collection. Any information relating to the subject of your investigation is potentially valuable, however suspect, trivial, biased, partial, or dated it may seem. Your task is to piece all of that information together into a coherent narrative, developing an explanation which does not necessarily rely on any one particular source or item. The weight given to those various sources is a matter of judgement. Even obviously self-serving or biased sources can be valuable evidence, in their own right, and because they may have influenced the perceptions and actions of others in that context.

4. Remember that you are often your own data. This is especially true for researchers who are embedded in the extreme context being studied. But given the nature of extreme contexts, it may be difficult to avoid being affected by circumstances and events even through temporary exposure and observation. The effects of an extreme context on you, therefore, may contribute to our understanding of the implications of that context for others.

We finally confess that we find it far more interesting to be involved with and to study extreme contexts than it is to research 'routine' organizational settings and problems. The links between research and teaching are blurred when working in extreme contexts, as our experiences at Magill and Sellafield in particular illustrate. The concepts and theories underpinning the research can be tested in staff and management development settings and briefings, with those who are involved in the context concerned. Teaching and research thus inform each other in a virtuous circle. If as a researcher your interest lies with understanding significant organizational problems, with making a difference, and with influencing practice, then consider taking your work into an extreme context. You will find no shortage of opportunities, through personal involvement, through the use of social science fiction sources such as films and television programmes, through published sources—and through other unconventional approaches still to be uncovered and developed.

■ REFERENCES

Barends, E., Janssen, B., ten Have, W. and ten Have, S. (2014). 'Effects of change interventions: what kind of evidence do we really have?', *Journal of Applied Behavioral Science*, 50(1): 5–27.

Buchanan, D.A. (2012). 'Case studies in organizational research.' In Gillian Symon and Catherine Cassell (eds), *The Practice of Qualitative Organizational Research: Core Methods and Current Challenges*. London: Sage, pp.373–92.

Buchanan, D.A. and Denyer, D. (2013). 'Researching tomorrow's crisis: methodological innovations and wider implications', *International Journal of Management Reviews*, 15(2): 205–24.

Buchanan, D.A., Denyer, D., Jaina, J., Kelliher, C., Moore, C., Emma, P. and Pilbeam, C. (2013). 'How do they manage?: a qualitative study of the realities of middle and front-line management work in healthcare', *Health Services and Delivery Research*, 1(4).

Buchanan, D.A. and Huczynski, A. (2004). 'Images of influence: Twelve Angry Men and Thirteen Days', *Journal of Management Inquiry*, 13(4): 312–23.

Buchanan, D.A. and Moore, C. (2016). 'Never say never again: post-incident change and the investigation trap', *Journal of Change Management*, 16(3): 159–83.

Buus, S. (2009). 'Hell on earth: threats, citizens and the state from Buffy to Beck', *Cooperation and Conflict*, 44(6): 400–19.

Cordesman, A.H. (2001). *Biological Warfare and the 'Buffy Paradigm*. Washington DC: Center for Strategic and International Studies.

Cornelissen, J., Mantere, S., and Vaara, E. (2014). 'The contraction of meaning: the combined effect of communication, emotions, and materiality on sensemaking in the Stockwell Shooting', *Journal of Management Studies*, 51(5): 699–736.

Davis, M.S. (1971). 'That's interesting!: towards a phenomenology of sociology and a sociology of phenomenology', *Philosophy of the Social Sciences*, 1(4): 309–44.

Denyer, D. (2015a). 'A firefighter is a firefighter is a firefighter.' In David Denyer and Colin Pilbeam (eds), *Managing Change in Extreme Contexts*. London and New York: Routledge, pp.83–103.

Denyer, D. (2015b). 'THORP: leading change in extreme contexts.' In David Denyer and Colin Pilbeam (eds), *Managing Change in Extreme Contexts*. London and New York: Routledge, pp.199–225.

Denyer, D. and Sibbick, G. (2015). 'Towards a high reliability organization at CSL.' In David Denyer and Colin Pilbeam (eds), *Managing Change in Extreme Contexts*. London and New York: Routledge, pp.227–49.

Denyer, D. and Pilbeam, C. (eds) (2015). Managing Change in Extreme Contexts. London: Routledge.

de Rond, M. (2012). 'Soldier, surgeon, photographer, fly: fieldwork beyond the comfort zone', *Strategic Organization*, 10(3): 256–62.

de Rond, M. and Lok, J. (2016). 'Some things can never be unseen: the role of context in psychological injury at war', *Academy of Management Journal*, 59(6): 1965–93.

Eisenhardt, K.M. (1989). 'Building theories from case study research', *Academy of Management Review*, 14(4): 532–50.

Eisenhardt, K.M. and Graebner, M.E. (2007). 'Theory building from cases: opportunities and challenges', *Academy of Management Journal*, 50(1): 25–32.

Fey, M., Poppe, A.E., and Rauch, C. (2016). 'The nuclear taboo, *Battlestar Galactica*, and the real world: illustrations from a science-fiction universe', *Security Dialogue*, 47(4): 348–65.

Fraher, A.L. (2011). *Thinking Through Crisis: Improving Teamwork and Leadership in High-Risk Fields*. Cambridge: Cambridge University Press.

Goffman, A. (2014). *On the Run: Fugitive Life in an American City*. Chicago, IL and London: University of Chicago Press.

Hannah, S.T. and Parry, K.W. (2014). 'Leadership in extreme contexts.' In David V. Day (ed.) *The Oxford Handbook of Leadership and Organizations*. Oxford: Oxford University Press, pp.613–37.

Hannah, S.T., Campbell, D.J., and Matthews, M.D. (2010). 'Advancing a research agenda for leadership in dangerous contexts', *Military Psychology*, 22(1): 157–89.

Hassard, J.S. and Buchanan, D.A. (2009). 'From *Modern Times* to *Syriana*: feature films as research data.' In David A. Buchanan and Alan Bryman (eds) *The Sage Handbook of Organizational Research Methods*. London: Sage, pp.620–35.

Holt, R. and Zundel, M. (2014). 'Understanding management, trade, and society through fiction: lessons from *The Wire*', *Academy of Management Review*, 39(4): 576–85.

James, E.H., Wooten, L.P., and Dushek, K. (2011). 'Crisis management: informing a new leadership research agenda', *The Academy of Management Annals*, 5(1): 455–93.

Kayes, D.C. (2004). 'The 1996 Mount Everest climbing disaster: the breakdown of learning in teams', *Human Relations*, 57(10): 1263–84.

Langley, A. (1999). 'Strategies for theorizing from process data', *Academy of Management Review*, 24(4): 691–710.

Levitt, S.D. and Venkatesh, S.A. (2000). 'An economic analysis of a drug-selling gang's finances', *Quarterly Journal of Economics*, 115(3): 755–89.

Locatelli, A. (2016). 'No peace after the zombie apocalypse: the representation of war in the TV series *The Walking Dead*', *Annual Conference of the Standing Group on International Relations—Societa' Italiana di Scienza Politica*, Trento, Italy, 23 June.

Maclean, N. (1972). *Young Men and Fire*. Chicago, IL: Chicago University Press.

Moore, C. and Buchanan, D.A. (2013). 'Sweat the small stuff: a case study of small scale change processes and consequences in acute care', Health Services Management Research, 26(1): 9–17.

Payne, G. and Williams, M. (2005). 'Generalization in qualitative research', *Sociology*, 39(2): 295–314.

Penfold-Mounce, R., Beer, D., and Burrows, R. (2011). '*The Wire* as social-science fiction?', *Sociology*, 45(1): 152–67.

Perrow, C. (1992). 'An almost random career.' In A.G. Bedeian (ed.) *Management Laureates, Volume 2*. Greenwich, CT: JAI Press.

Perrow, C. (1999). *Normal Accidents: Living with High-Risk Technologies*. Princeton, NJ: Princeton University Press.

Pettigrew, A.M. (1990). 'Longitudinal field research on change: theory and practice', *Organization Science*, 1(3): 267–92.

Phillips, N. (1995). 'Telling organizational tales: on the role of narrative fiction in the study of organization', *Organization Studies*, 16(4): 625.

Prasad, A. (2014). 'You can't go home again: and other psychoanalytic lessons from crossing a neo-colonial border', *Human Relations*, 67(2): 233–57.

Reed, D. and Penfold-Mounce, R. (2015). 'Zombies and the sociological imagination: The Walking Dead as social-science fiction', in L. Hubner, M. Leaning and P. Manning (eds), *The Zombie Renaissance in Popular Culture*. Houndmills, Basingstoke: Palgrave, pp.124–38.

Roberts, K.H. (1998). 'Having the bubble.' In A. Bedeian (ed.) *Management Laureates: A Collection of Autobiographical Essays*. Greenwich, CT: JAI Press.

Roberts, K.H. and Rousseau, D.M. (1989). 'Research in nearly failure-free, high-reliability organizations: having the bubble', *IEEE Transactions on Engineering Management*, 36(2): 132–9.

Snook, S.A. (2000). *Friendly Fire: The Accidental Shootdown of US Black Hawks Over Northern Iraq*. Princeton, NJ and Oxford: Princeton University Press.

Stake, R.E. (1994). 'Case studies.' In Norman K. Denzin and Yvonna S. Lincoln (eds), *Handbook of Qualitative Research*. Thousand Oaks, CA: Sage, pp.236–47.

Toft, B. and Reynolds, S. (2005). Learning from Disasters: A Management Approach. Third edition. Basingstoke: Palgrave Macmillan.

Tsang, E.W.K. (2014). 'Generalizing from research findings: the merits of case studies', *International Journal of Management Reviews*, 16(4): 369–83.

Tsoukas, H. (2009). 'Craving for generality and small-N studies: A Wittgensteinian approach towards the epistemology of the particular in organization and management studies.' In David A. Buchanan and Alan Bryman (eds) *The Sage Handbook of Organizational Research Methods*. London: Sage, pp.285–301.

Van Maanen, J. and de Rond, M. (2017). 'The making of a classic ethnography: notes on Alice Goffman's *On the Run*', *Academy of Management Review*, 42(2): 396–406.

Venkatesh, S. (2008). *Gang Leader for a Day: A Rogue Sociologist Crosses the Line*. London and New York: Penguin Books.

Weick, K.E. (1993). 'The collapse of sensemaking in organizations: the Mann Gulch disaster', *Administrative Science Quarterly*, 38(4): 628–52.

Whiteman, G. and Cooper, W.H. (2011). 'Ecological sensemaking', *Academy of Management Journal*, 54(5): 889–911.

Williams, M. (2000). 'Interpretivism and generalization', *Sociology*, 34(2): 209–24.

Zundel, M., Holt, R., and Cornelissen, J. (2013). 'Institutional work in *The Wire*: an ethological investigation of flexibility in organizational adaptation', *Journal of Management Inquiry*, 22(1): 102–20.

6 Making the case

A qualitative approach to studying social media documents

Christopher J. Schneider

Introduction

An officer tweets on an official police service Twitter account, 'That awkward moment in a Tim Hortons [coffee shop] line-up, in uniform, ordering a coffee with all those sweet, chocolatey donuts staring at me.' A few months later another officer tweets, 'Don't eat donuts. Refuse to be a stereotype.' Eight months after the first of these donut themed posts another officer tweets, 'We all love our donuts.' These represent a few of numerous similar examples. How are we to collect, examine, and make sense of such tweets and what insights might this process provide into organizations?

In this chapter, I discuss Qualitative Media Analysis (QMA) as one such approach for dealing with social media artefacts, and outline how I have drawn from social media platforms as useful data sources to gain insight on organizations. I focus exclusively on police, an organization that is typically restricted to outsiders. Scholars and researchers looking to make use of an unorthodox methodology in the organization and management field may find some parallels with key points made in this chapter. Much of what follows draws from published research on document analysis (Altheide and Schneider, 2013) and social media and policing (Schneider, 2018, 2016a; 2016b; 2015a; 2015b; Schneider and Trottier, 2012; 2013). These latter works investigate public aspects of the management, use, and control of social media by police agencies.

Recent developments in social media have dramatically changed how police and publics are repositioned in relation to one another (Schneider, 2016a; Trottier, 2012). Social movements like *Black Lives Matter* that have gained momentum on Twitter are evidence of some of these historical changes. For this reason, as outlined below, it is important to consider further some of these social media data in specific relation to policing issues. These data help to provide additional insight, albeit indirectly, into recent organizational shifts in policing and police work (Schneider, 2016a). In exploring these developments, this chapter provides an occasion to illustrate the step-by-step process of Qualitative Media Analysis (Altheide and Schneider, 2013). I outline my own use of QMA as a methodological approach in dealing with data materials gathered from social media platforms as a 'how-to reference guide' for those in the management field seeking to engage in similar forms of document analysis in their own research projects.

Conceptual issues

Social media goes by many names such as social networking and new media. As such, there is also no one universally agreed upon definition or accepted classification of these media. I have suggested elsewhere (Schneider, 2016a) that conceptual ambiguity emerges from the constantly evolving and changing nature of social media. Dozens of social media definitions exist among numerous self-proclaimed 'social media experts' (e.g. Cohen, 2011) and conceptual concerns among professional groups often suggests little about how social media are defined and understood even by groups that use these media forms in the course of their professional work (Schneider, 2014).

The point is not necessarily to define these media precisely; rather, the concern is to identify basic characteristics of these media. Social media and the host of monikers these media forms go by can all be said to constitute a hybrid of social interaction and media. As such, these media forms allow creation, rely on audience participation relative to the production of content, and involve user engagement (see Mandiberg, 2012). The most important characteristic, for our purposes here, is that no matter what we may call these platforms, all forms of social media result in the production of documents.

QUALITATIVE MEDIA ANALYSIS

The study and analysis of documents is significant because documents, understood as symbolic representations retrievable for analysis, capture and reflect social meanings and context (Altheide and Schneider, 2013). 'A *document* can be defined as any symbolic representation that can be recorded or retrieved for analysis' (Altheide and Schneider, 2013, p.5; emphasis in original). A tweet, Facebook post, or YouTube video, are all examples of types of documents. Documents can provide insight into institutional contexts, and, therefore, document analysis can serve as a fruitful approach when seeking to gain understandings into organizational and structural relations. Changes in the media landscape have contributed to a growing interest in qualitative approaches to studying social media documents.

QMA is a specific type of document analysis that utilizes an approach toward defining, organizing and examining documents. Since the first edition of *Qualitative Media Analysis* (Altheide, 1996) numerous peer-reviewed articles, book chapters, PhD dissertations and theses have used this method (see the appendix of Altheide and Schneider, 2013, pp.133–7, for a sample of these works). The first social networking site launched a year later in 1997 (boyd and Ellison, 2007). The further development of QMA and new methodological approaches alongside existing research methods are necessary if we are to deal adequately with social media data and the new challenges that these 'big data' provide to researchers. Big data gained wider use in 2008 and refers to unstructured large data sets (Boellstorff, 2013). The use of conventional methods in processing big data is often inadequate. According to Lupton (2015, p.3):

big data also include 'user-generated content', or information that has been intentionally uploaded to social media platforms by users as a part of their participation in these sites: their tweets, status updates, blog posts and comments, photographs and videos and so on.

Contemporary methodological principles have emerged to aid with the challenges of working with issues associated with big data sets (e.g. Tinati et al., 2014). Many of these contemporary approaches focus on meta-level types of analysis. In so doing, qualitative nuances are often lost in the quest for meanings contained in forms of user-generated data. The use of QMA addresses many of these concerns, as the primary task of this methodology is to identify meaningful patterns and place meaning in context.

QMA can be outlined in the following twelve specific steps (Altheide and Schneider, 2013):

1. identify a specific topic;
2. become familiar with the information source and review any existing literature on the topic;
3. become familiar with about a half a dozen or so examples of relevant documents, note the format of these selected documents, and identify the unit of analysis (tweets, Facebook posts, news articles, etc.);
4. list several categories (i.e. variables) on a data collection sheet or protocol;
5. test the protocol by gathering data from various documents;
6. update and revise the protocol to reflect additional cases;
7. employ sampling rationale and strategy (e.g. theoretical sampling, outlined below)
8. collect descriptive examples (i.e. data) using preset codes, add additional categories to protocol if necessary and complete data collection;
9. conduct data analysis;
10. compare and contrast extremes and significant differences in each category and write summaries;

11. combine summaries with typical examples of the key differences (i.e. extremes); and

12. integrate these materials with your findings and interpretations in another draft in what will become your manuscript.

In what follows, I briefly sketch these steps as basic points of reference in relation to the examples provided in the two vignettes below. A much more detailed discussion of these steps can be found in Altheide and Schneider (2013, pp.39–73). The first three steps involve the research question and unit of analysis. Step one is to identify the research problem or topic, i.e. police and social media. A few basic questions may include: How do police use social media? What kinds of platforms are used? What is said on these platforms? A cursory review of the research literature (step 2) indicates that police use social media, that these platforms are used for the purposes of circulating crime and traffic-related information, and that Twitter appears to be a choice platform. We could modify our last question to the following: What else are police saying on social media (aside from crime and traffic related information)? One key feature of QMA rests with its reflexive research design and interactive researcher involvement in the process that allows for the modification of questions during the research.

Next, the researcher should develop a familiarity with the information source. This may include perusing a few police service Twitter accounts as determined pertinent by the researcher. Step three involves becoming familiar with examples of relevant documents from the platform source. Social media site Twitter, for instance, operates primarily as a text-based micro blogging platform, whereas Instagram is a photo-based medium, and a site such as YouTube is oriented to video media. In these circumstances, units of analysis may include individual tweets in the form of 140-character text messages (Twitter), photographs (Instagram), and videos (YouTube).

Steps 4–6 concern the construction of a data collection instrument, or protocol. The protocol design emerges from categories that are identified during step 3. For instance, during the research process the researcher might notice the use of specific words across the units of analysis (i.e. tweets). The word 'crime' may be used in the context of other words like 'prevention'. These terms and relevant phrases would then be added to the protocol. Themes and frames that emerge during the research process should also be added as protocol categories. Frames and themes are overlapping concepts. Frames provide the *context* for what will be discussed; themes concern *how a story is told* or those general meanings within a frame. As an example that we give in QMA, consider illegal drug use framed in news media as a 'public health issue', rather than a 'criminal justice issue', and how these two frames would entail a specific way in which each story would be told.

Step 5 involves testing the instrument against the collection of more data, and then, step 6, revising the protocol by including several additional categories. Throughout the development of the protocol the researcher gains an intimate familiarity with the topic at hand and is able to ascertain when the protocol instrument is completed so that one can proceed to sampling the data, or step 7. Familiarity with the topic influences how and where the researcher chooses to look for data. The goal of QMA is not to generalize findings to an entire population, but rather, the concern is with the search for meanings and definitions in documents, and for this principal reason, much of this approach utilizes a theoretical sampling procedure. While the aim is not to generalize findings, sampling procedures can be incorporated to accommodate this consideration (see Altheide and Schneider, 2013, pp.60–2). Data materials are purposively selected in accordance with progressive theoretical sampling. As Altheide and Schneider (2013, p.56) note:

This refers to the selection of materials based on emerging understanding of the topic under investigation. The idea is to select materials for conceptually and theoretically relevant reasons. For example, a researcher might want to include materials that are similar or different on a particular dimension.

Sampling in this manner ensures that the full range of situations present in the data are included in the analysis. Theoretical sampling also confirms frames and themes that emerge during the researcher's interaction with the data. Frames are the focus of an event and themes are recurring typical statements consistent across examined documents:

The significance of frames, themes, and discourse for document analysis cannot be overemphasized. Theoretically, frames and themes are crucial in defining situations and provide much of the rationale for document analysis. These are the most powerful features of public information, and the study of their origins, how they change over time, and their taken-for-granted use in everyday life is essential to understanding the relevance of communication media for our lives.   (Altheide and Schneider, 2013, p.53)

Step 8 is to collect the data. Unlike more conventional methodological approaches, the researcher need not necessarily rely exclusively on coding or counting data materials:

Qualitative data analysis is not about coding or counting, although these activities can be useful in some parts of fulfilling the goals of the quest for meaning and theoretical integration. The goal is to understand the process, to see the process in the types and meanings of the documents under investigation, and to be able to associate the documents with conceptual and theoretical issues. This occurs as the researcher interacts with the document. [Therefore] it is best to rely on the more straightforward 'search-find-replace' options on most word processing programs.

(Altheide and Schneider, 2013, p.70)

In illuminating the process and meanings in documents the researcher is better able to connect selected documents with identified conceptual and theoretical matters. Data are collected by utilizing the protocol instrument that emerges from interaction with the data as outlined in the examples below (see Altheide and Schneider, 2013, for numerous additional examples).

After data have been collected, the next stage (step 9) is to analyse these data. Analysis allows the researcher to begin to understand the particular characteristics and organizational elements of identified documents as social products. Other methodological approaches like various quantitative techniques do not have the same flexibility that allows for an interactive space for the researcher in the research process. In some ways, the use of various qualitative software programs (e.g. NVivo, MaxQDA, etc.) can place similar restrictions on the research process. Other programs, including data scrubbing software used for collecting big data materials, cannot decide for the researcher the best way to conceptually integrate data materials. That is to say, these programs do not deal directly with symbolic meanings. Software programs can restrict researcher reflexivity.

Step 10 is to identify the ends of the range or 'extremes' in the collected data. Short summaries that note some of the key differences should be included in the protocol instrument under the 'Notes' section (see below). Concepts and categories will emerge by drawing comparisons, key words, terms, and phrases. This process should be repeated, and the protocol continually amended, until no new terms, categories, etc., emerge from interaction with the data, i.e. the point of saturation is reached (Glaser and Strauss, 1967). Step 11 is to bring together in early manuscript form the short summaries included in the 'Notes' section of the protocol and include examples of the typical and the extreme. The final stage, step 12, is to merge the findings with the researcher interpretations from the brief summaries into a more cohesive narrative. This narrative will serve as the basis of an early draft of what will later become your final manuscript.

Before turning to a short overview of police and media, which informs my approach and sampling criteria, beyond what is discussed above, a word on citation style and research ethics is worth a mention. While citation standards are not uniform and differ on the particular citation style, a general rule when working with social media materials is to provide the date and time following a quote from a social media post. The particular platform need not necessarily be referenced, as the platform should be noted elsewhere in the manuscript. These materials also do not need to appear in the references section of your manuscript. Another query becomes: What about the name of the user? The answer to this question depends, and has us more directly confront the matter of research ethics.

As a general rule, if social media materials are publicly available then you need not necessarily acquire ethics approval, and in this circumstance can provide the name of the social media user. If, however, the platform in question is restricted in any way (e.g. privacy settings) you will likely require ethics approval. If the former, the preference to include the name is up to the researcher. I tend to avoid using names of private citizens, as this information is often not germane. I usually will include the user name if the person is a public official, such as a police officer. Social media has in some ways provided unique access, like never before, to persons who have been historically inaccessible to researchers, including government officials like heads of state. As such, social media have allowed researchers to redirect their gaze 'upward' that helps provide new insights into meanings of control and authority (Nadar, 1969; see also Aguiar and Schneider, 2012). Further, providing user names of authority figures situates accounts 'according to the statuses of the interactants' (Scott and Lyman, 1968, p.46). Some social groups and organizations are much less accessible than others, including police. Consider celebrities as another example, an elite and usually impenetrable group where the use of QMA can help provide new insight (Schneider, 2012). Increased documentation on social media of celebrities, police, and other restricted organizations and groups allows new opportunities for researchers to collect, analyse, and locate meanings providing vantage points that reveal previously unavailable empirical changes.

Police and media: a 'new visibility'

In this section, I turn my attention to a short overview of the relevant literature in police studies. My task here is not to provide a robust literature review. Instead, I wish to briefly show the relationship between police and media, on the one hand, and highlight the limited amount of research that addresses the development of this relationship on social media, on the other hand. Work in this area is rapidly growing. For a nuanced discussion of this body of literature see Schneider (2016a); see also Lee and McGovern (2014, pp.113–40). The literature in this area informs my research questions, and, subsequently, my use of qualitative media analysis. Moreover, having a familiarity with the topic at hand helps answer important methodological questions about the topic of study, timeline, and the selection of social media data, as outlined in the sections that follow.

For organization and management researchers, it is useful to familiarize yourself with an institution's mandate as one point of entrée. All organizations outline tasks that serve to justify the existence of an organization, or mandate. The police mandate consists of two components (Manning, 1978): public order (maintaining the peace), and upholding criminal law (making arrests). Much of what police work involves, however, concerns the former of these and, in maintaining the peace in conjunction with their mandate, police usually do not uphold the law, and therefore very rarely make arrests (Bayley, 1994). In other words, above all else, police work entails norm enforcement and defining social situations. One element of this definitional process is conditioning the public to believe that 'crime work' is in fact what constitutes police work. In line with this perspective, police work then is largely 'image work' (Ericson, 1982, p.10), which is central to the legitimation process of the institution itself (Mawby, 2002). How police present themselves to the public is symbolic (Manning, 1978), and often occurs through direct promotion in news media (Ericson et al., 1987; Fishman, 1980; Schneider, 2015a).

Legitimacy, and hence police authority, stems, in large part, from citizens' deference to symbolic meanings presented to the public (Manning, 1997). Widespread citizen deference is primarily acquired from police 'presentational strategies' (Manning, 1978), particularly those presented in media. For this reason, police have modified their institutional activities to incorporate oligopolistic media as a routine form of police work. Consider the carefully scripted presentation of information (e.g. media releases provided by press officers) to news media as an example (Fishman, 1980).

Police now routinely use social media for the purpose of image work (Schneider, 2016a, 2016b; O'Connor, 2015). However, while research in this area is quickly growing, police issues associated with social media continue to remain relatively under-explored (Schneider, 2016a). Research in Canada suggests a decline in public confidence in police because of scrutiny on social media (Brown, 2015; Campeau, 2015; Council of Canadian Academies, 2014). This public scrutiny of police is attributed to a 'new visibility' of the police organization (Thompson, 2005). This is the idea that:

making visible of actions and events is not just the outcome of leakage in systems of communication and information flow that are increasingly difficult to control; it is also an explicit strategy of individuals who know very well that mediated visibility can be a weapon in the struggles they wage in their day-to-day lives. (Thompson, 2005, p.31)

The concept of new visibility has been applied to policing because this visibility is 'a critical component of how [the police] *appear to the public*' (Goldsmith, 2010, p.914; emphasis in original). The new visibility has added contemporary challenges to police image work and online order maintenance in general (Bullock, 2016). Some of these challenges have led police to use social media to counter growing concerns over 'corporate reputation' (Council of Canadian Academies, 2014; Lee and McGovern, 2013). Research also shows that police use social media to reduce authoritarian roles associated with police (Schneider, 2016a).

Policing scholar Peter Manning (2015, p.273) notes that, 'the problems presented by the use of new data from social media, emails, videos, "instant observations", and data from ephemeral events that may be policed are yet to be faced. These new problems can be understood in relation to three interrelated "rationalities that underlie modes of media and public engagement by police": publics, police image, and police legitimacy' (Lee and McGovern, 2014, p.38).

I now turn my attention to two vignettes that speak in various ways to each of these three rationalities that collectively illustrate social media platforms as important qualitative data sources that help provide insight into police as an organization while also demonstrating the usefulness of QMA in dealing with big data materials.

Vignette 1: Police use of Twitter

I direct my focus toward police *use of* social media. A basic question is: How are police using social media? This is a very broad research question. More specifically, we might then ask, in what ways are police using social media for organizational and strategic purposes? To be certain, it would be an impossible task to examine every single police agency on every social media platform. There are billions of possible units of analysis to select. This has created opportunities and challenges. The sheer amount of data helps qualitative researchers develop more in-depth understandings of the research questions, and may steer research to future unforeseen topics. New challenges, however, emerge in a growing confusion in what data to include, how to include these data, and, importantly, when to stop data collection.

The first edition of *Qualitative Media Analysis* in 1996 was written as an attempt to answer questions from students, researchers, and colleagues regarding various techniques for conducting document analysis and the search for meanings in documents. The advent and rapid expansion of social media and communication and information technologies have reintroduced and exacerbated many of these initial concerns. While we address many of these concerns in the second edition of QMA, I outline a few of these below.

I have provided numerous workshops across North America on QMA and social media since the publication of the second edition of our book. I continue to regularly get asked the 'how' and 'when' questions, i.e. how to conduct analysis using social media, and, given the infinite amount of documents, when to stop data collection. Conducting document analysis online can be akin to drinking water from a fire hose. It can be daunting to think about a research project using data materials gathered from social media. My short response to these sorts of concerns is always the same: *just make a case*.

To make a case, when approaching our question above (i.e. How are police using social media?), we need to decide what social media site(s) to investigate, a time frame, and what materials to include from the millions of possible text posts, images, videos, memes, etc. Relevant information emerges during the early stages of the research process. For instance, a quick scan of the literature (some noted above) indicates that Canadian police have adopted and incorporated social media ahead of many other police agencies, including police departments in the United States (Robertson, 2014; Schneider, 2016a). With this observation in mind, it makes some sense when seeking to understand police management and use of social media to direct our attention toward a police service in Canada. A quick Google search indicates that the Toronto Police Service (TPS), with more than 5,000 sworn members, is the largest municipal police agency in Canada, and one of the largest police forces in North America. Upon further review, one discovers that the TPS hired the first 'social media officer' in Canada in April 2010. The next year the TPS launched their 'social media strategy'—the first of its kind in North America. Selecting the TPS for analysis makes good sense.

All TPS accounts are listed here: <http://www.torontopolice.on.ca/socialmedia/> where it is also noted: 'service members can be seen regularly tweeting and posting to Facebook and YouTube.' As of 2016, 193 official social media accounts are listed, up from 164 in 2015 (Schneider, 2016a), and 119 in 2014 (Schneider, 2016b). The TPS lists the most active social media accounts under a single police service in Canada. A cursory review shows that Twitter is by and large the most used platform. All 193 accounts are represented on Twitter with the exception of just a single account (TPS 41 Division is presently only on Facebook). Twitter was modelled after police dispatch technologies and evidence suggests that police were drawn to this platform because the format and logic was one that is already familiar to police (Schneider, 2016a).

Thus far, we have made a good case for the selection of a specific police service (TPS) and a social media platform (Twitter). We must now decide what time frame to include, and what types of data materials, such as text, images, videos, etc., to include for analysis. The answers to these questions, that is, what to focus on, emerges as the research process develops according to the steps outlined above. A cursory review of the TPS Twitter profiles provides a rather extreme range of user activity. There are some prolific officers such as Constable Scott Mills with more than 49,000 tweets, to much less active officers like Superintendent Hugh Ferguson with just 341 tweets, and everywhere between.

After surveying the range of officer activity across the possible data we can direct our attention toward data collection. There are a few ways to acquire data from Twitter and other social media sites. A quick Google search returns a growing supply of web-scraping tools to extract online data. This is one option. Another way of acquiring data is to scroll through each account and open the contents of the feed and then save these data as a single PDF file. While a bit more arduous, I prefer this latter process as it allows for a simultaneous albeit cursory review of the data that aids in the development of a protocol instrument (steps 4–6). Scrolling back through less active Twitter accounts is often quick and provides data usually to the first tweet made during officer training at the Toronto Police College. This discovery helps establish a timeline of analysis. Access to data from more active accounts is limited. At the time of the collection of these data, Twitter only allowed access to the most recent 3,200 tweets. There are numerous tools that one may employ to access these data. One free and easy tool is <www.allmytweets.net>.

Tweets from all active TPS accounts were collected from the launch of the TPS social media strategy. Each account was saved as a PDF document for analysis. PDFs were collapsed into a single document using Adobe Acrobat Pro. A total of 105,801 tweets were collected and combined into a searchable single 7,498-page PDF dataset.

We have now narrowed down a police service, a platform, a range of users and tweets (units of analysis), and an approximate timeline (from the launch of the TPS social media strategy to the present). Now we turn to the matter of what types of data to include. In this regard, how documents are organized to fit the logic of each platform is worth further consideration. To be certain, texts, images, and videos—each serving as possible units of analysis—can be posted and shared on nearly every social media site. Each platform, however, is oriented to a specific type of media as noted previously. Since Twitter is oriented to text, we can elect to direct our attention to tweets as text documents.

There are many computer programs for qualitative documents analysis. Reliance on software is primarily geared to aiding with data coding and is not always necessarily useful for analysis. At the center of the quest for meaning is researcher interaction with the document. Principally for this reason, my focus and attention is on interacting directly with the PDF data file. Key terms and phrases consistent with knowledge and familiarity with the research topic at hand provides the researcher with an entry point into the data (terms emerge from a review of the relevant literature in the subject and also from the data collection process, i.e. scrolling through Twitter profiles). Specific words that the researcher should be familiar with can be entered into the search box of the PDF document. Beginning in this manner is an initial way to review the dataset beyond, say, the cursory review during initial data collection for emergent themes. We might first reconsider that popular understandings of police work are consistent with crime work.

Entering the word 'crime' into the 7,498-page PDF file returns 6,631 tweets where the word appears. It is not surprising to discover crime as a basic theme of police tweets, which is why I started with crime. A quick review of these data reveals that 'crime' usually appears in specific contexts; examples include 'solving crime', 'crime tips', 'crime scene', 'report a crime', 'crime prevention', 'crime stoppers' (a crime prevention organization), 'crime victims' and an officer Twitter handle ('23 Crime Prevention'). We also see that the word 'crime' is associated with specific acts like 'fraud' and 'cybercrime'. Upon a more nuanced examination of these data, prevention emerges as a key theme. After a review of these initial relevant tweets a protocol should be developed. Constructing a protocol is an inductive process. The protocol instrument—a data collection sheet—aids the researcher in providing the data that will answer the research question.

The first step in the protocol process is to list several items or categories to guide data collection. Once these initial variables have been identified, the researcher can test the protocol instrument by acquiring additional data. The researcher should then revise the instrument by selecting additional items for further refinement. In other words, the protocol emerges from researcher interaction with the data, i.e. by entering terms into our searchable PDF dataset as noted above. For example, consider a sample protocol as an adapted version from Altheide and Schneider (2013, p.110):

Initial Twitter Sample Protocol
Event: Toronto Police Service (TPS) 'Social Media Strategy'.
Date/time frame: August 2011 to present (May 13, 2013: the time these data were initially collected).
Social media platform: Twitter.
Topic/focus: Crime.
Number of tweets collected: 105,801 across 119 TPS Twitter accounts.
Search term(s):   'crime'.
Type(s) of crime/activities: 'fraud', 'cybercrime', 'solving crime', 'crime tips', 'crime scene', 'report a crime', 'crime prevention', 'crime stoppers', 'crime victims'.
File format: 7,498-page PDF file.
Data/unit of analysis: Text postings in the form of 140-character tweets.
Supplementary data: n/a.
Frame: Public safety.
Theme(s):   Crime maintenance (e.g., prevention and proactive responses), safety.
Language: Criminal justice discourse.
Perspective/view: Crime as negative (undesirable), victimization.
Sources: TPS police officers (first-person accounts, i.e. tweets and second-hand accounts, retweets), Police services (e.g. Peel Regional Police), community crime watch organizations (e.g. CrimeStoppers), Toronto Police Service media releases.
Notes: A reflexive summary of the searches performed (words, phrases) and data retrieved should be noted in the protocol. Note what stood apart from most tweets (this will help you locate, identify, and retrieve the range between extremes). Include several tweets that best summarize key findings by copying and pasting or taking screen shots. Why did you select these tweets? A response in the form of a paragraph or two should follow in your notes.

Performing an 'Advanced Search' in Adobe Acrobat Pro will search and sort these data. After a review of these data, we learn that the word 'crime', however, does not necessarily need to appear in crime-themed tweets. We might add the following search terms to an amended protocol and enter these into the interactive PDF dataset: 'safety' (3,604), 'prevention' (4,094), '#prevention' (22), 'CrimeStoppers' (297) 'Crime Stoppers' (428), and '#crimes-toppers' (139). Hashtags (i.e. '#') allow authors of tweets to contextualize their messages across Twitter. These data can be saved as aggregated PDF files for further analysis. To do so save the search results in the Advanced Search box.

Reviewing these additional aggregated data leads to the emergence of other terms. For instance, one tweet by retired TPS Staff Sergeant Michael Matic, in part read: 'Be a good neighbour, report suspicious persons knocking on your door #Prevention' (January 5, 2013, 1:41pm). While '#prevention' returned just 22 results it is worth exploring these data in an effort to locate the range in the examined data (e.g. 'prevention' appears 4,094 times whereas '#prevention' appears 22 times). This observation should be noted and the protocol continually revised to reflect these discoveries in the data. An answer to one of our research questions begins to emerge: In what ways are police using social media for organizational and strategic purposes? The police use social media, Twitter in particular, largely as a strategy to initiate calls to the public. This argument is more fully articulated elsewhere (Schneider, 2016a). The point of this chapter is to outline the methodological process of using social media to shed light on an organization like the police. Examples that illustrate this finding should be sampled from the dataset and included in the manuscript as it develops.

Vignette 2: Police response to YouTube video

I build on a few of the techniques outlined above and turn my attention to another popular social media site, YouTube. I wish to show here that while very similar techniques can be employed when acquiring and working with social media data, questions and themes that emerge from these data can redirect our focus to other data materials that augment our social media data.

YouTube launched to the public in December 2005 (Ratcliff, 2006). The site is a popular video-sharing platform where users upload videos and audiences engage with other users (Burgess and Green, 2009; Schneider, 2016c). YouTube is one of the most popular destinations online. A lot has changed in the last decade or so. In 2005, online videos were a novelty. An important feature of YouTube, as with all social media, is the population of the site with user-generated content. Users upload dozens of hours of video each passing minute and tens of thousands of clips are added to the site each day. These videos span from the mundane to the extraordinary. Consider police use of force. A search for 'police brutality' on YouTube returns millions of hits (see Brown, 2013). One question becomes: What exactly constitutes police brutality and how is it determined?

More specifically, we might ask: In what ways have videos on YouTube affected police definitional claims? The literature, briefly outlined above, provides some context for us to ask this question. Sometimes the questions we ask cannot be wholly answered by social media data alone and must be augmented by other data sources. Considerations then must also be given to other types of documents. Technological developments have contributed greatly to document analysis. When a question cannot, at first, be answered by social media data, a good place to turn is LexisNexis, an online information base. The service has access to billions of documents for researchers from over 45,000 sources. These data can easily be searched and can help bring our attention to recorded instances, in this case of police violence that, in turn, can help direct our attention to very specific and relevant police videos. The very first reported video documentation as discussed in news media reports of police abuse—and hence to challenge police definitional claims—was uploaded to YouTube toward the end of 2006 (Schneider, 2015a). Searching LexisNexis for this information helps to establish some search parameters when a specific timeline may not be immediately available.

Recordings that document police violence are certainly nothing new. Arguably one of the most infamous (prior to the circulation of videos in social media—see Schneider, 2018 and Schneider, 2016a for further discussion) was the 1991 citizen-recorded beating of Rodney King in Los Angeles, California. The video and subsequent acquittal of the police officers that were involved served as a catalyst to some of the worst rioting in United States history. The King video, 'seen everywhere in the world', was a watershed moment in media exposure of police violence (Skolnick and Fyfe, 1993). Williams (2007, p.6) noted that the King beating 'was unusual only because it was videotaped'. Social media have greatly expanded the concept of 'secondary visibility' (Goldsmith, 2010), the idea that police activity, and subsequent public interpretations, appears in its representation, rather than face-to-face interaction and beyond the control of police. Video representations are especially salient.

Some evidence suggests that online users tend to believe video recordings of untoward conduct as the most complete, accurate, and truthful depiction of an event in question (Schneider, 2015c). Meanings of misconduct that might include police use of force as justified or not (e.g. authorized force versus police brutality) can circulate online in direct response to documentation (e.g. YouTube videos) as an interactive meaning-making process that may affect police definitional claims. To address the above research question, I first searched LexisNexis to locate reports of user-generated videos to which police agencies have provided official (i.e. authorized) institutional responses. One of the first of these videos (in Canada) was a 5:23 minute recording of a protest in the afternoon of August 20, 2007 at the Montebello Summit held at the Chateau resort in Quebec (Schneider, 2015a). It was the uploading of the video on YouTube that led to the police acknowledgment of the use of undercover officers at a protest after days of denial. Critics accused police of using undercover agents to incite violence among protestors and police officially denied these accusations. This video is unique as it was the first of its kind in Canada that initiated a police response in defence of police behaviour.

My preliminary searches on LexisNexis helped me to determine an approximate timeline allowing for the discovery of a YouTube video and a specific location (in the form of a web address). When working with social media data gathered from YouTube there are circumstances of multiple videos that depict a particular event in question or in other cases users that repost the same video. All of these circumstances can serve as data sources. However, it is not necessary to collect all of these data to understand how police actually responded to the video: it only matters that they responded to it. The issue then becomes how (process) police responded (meanings) and what this may tell us about an organization like the police. I turn my attention to making a case for social media data collection from YouTube, briefly discuss my analysis, and then draw a few conclusions.

Searches of LexisNexis started with 'police' and 'YouTube'. I narrowed my searches to between 2005–2007. This led to the discovery of the Montebello summit video. I re-entered terms 'Montebello', 'police', and 'YouTube'. I learned that the YouTube video was shot and uploaded to YouTube by filmmaker and activist Paul Manly. I entered the aforementioned terms along with 'Paul Manly' into the YouTube search engine. This quickly led to the discovery of the video in question. A video is an example of a single document. The study of single documents that focus on depth is an approach not consistent with QMA. So, while YouTube is a video-based medium, text posts as documents (i.e. multiple units of analysis) offered by users in response to the video serve as more appropriate units of analysis.

Over a period of five years, four months and twenty-six days, 2,866 comments were made to the original Manly video. These comments were accessed by clicking on 'show more' at the bottom of the page until posts were viewable and retrievable. These YouTube user data were saved and downloaded as a 204-page PDF document. Initial search words entered into the PDF data included 'police', 'admit', 'admitted', and 'admission'. National news stories made extensive use of these terms as discovered in my preliminary LexisNexis searches. Additional search terms included 'agents provocateurs', as this expression was used in the official police acknowledgement in response to the video. An examination of the social media data indicated no evidence to suggest police responded on YouTube (these searches also included other YouTube videos of the Montebello summit protest). In my analysis of the

PDF dataset, I learned that many users were initially reluctant to believe that the video in question even depicted undercover police officers at all, let alone officers engaging in untoward conduct, that is until police acknowledgment occurred in the days following the uploading of the video to YouTube. According to one thematic user post, 'if police did not admit that these guys were cops everyone would still be saying it's just a "conspiracy theory".' In fact, it was the police admission, in news media documents, that contributed to how the problem was discussed and framed by users on YouTube. I used these discoveries to develop and construct my protocol:

Initial YouTube sample protocol
Event: Montebello Summit Protest.
Date/time frame: 20 August, 2007.
Social media platform: YouTube.
Topic/focus: Undercover police tactics.
Number of posts collected: 2,866.
Search term(s): 'police', 'admit', 'admitted', 'admission', and 'agents provocateurs'.
File format: 204-page PDF file.
Data/unit of analysis: Individual posts.
Supplementary data: News articles in the form of links posted by users.
Frame: Undercover police tactics.
Theme(s): Misconduct.
Language: Accusatory/conspiracy theory rhetoric.
Perspective/view: Pro-police (protester as bad)/anti-police (protesters as good/recognizing the rights of people to lawfully assemble in Montebello).
Sources: Strictly news media sources: national news CBC News, *Globe and Mail, National Post*; and regional news *Toronto Star* and *Montreal Gazette*.
Notes: As with the previous protocol, reflexive summary of the searches performed (words, phrases) and data retrieved should be noted in the protocol. What stood out in these data was the strict reliance on news media as legitimate sources of information (the video on YouTube was not immediately accepted as legitimate by online users). This discovery led me back to news reports to in search of police statements to answer the research question.

Videos uploaded to YouTube can provide unforeseen user-driven challenges to police definitions. An analysis of the collected YouTube data suggests that police sometimes provide official statements to news media in response to select materials on social media (not all videos labelled by users as 'police brutality' receive an official police response). What emerged from an analysis of these social media data is that how police control the definition of the situation continues to occur through news media; however, data collected from YouTube also reveal that the police definitional process is actually reinforced by social media users who cite news media reports on YouTube, i.e. information provided by police to news media and cited by users to verify the legitimacy of the video in question.

Conclusion

One of the challenges for organization and management researchers is to investigate how formats like social media platforms mediate social life. Qualitative Media Analysis is just one of many methodological approaches when working with social media data materials. As a reflexive method, QMA offers a unique approach that is attentive to subtle nuance; however, unlike other qualitative approaches, it retains openness to emerging discoveries throughout. This continuous openness allows for a wealth of insights, dynamic research questions, and innovative research findings. Social media data are useful insofar that they can provide some insight into organizations such as the police. However, when working qualitatively with any data materials there are always limitations.

First and foremost, police agencies are public organizations (Bayley, 1990). A limitation of document analysis when seeking to understand the policing apparatus is that this approach can only provide insight into the public aspects of the use, management, and control of social media by police. In this regard, much less is actually known about the internal use of social media by police agencies for the purposes of investigation, evidence, etc. Much work remains. Another limitation is that we are usually unable to generalize research findings, although accommodations can be made as noted above.

I have shown through the above two vignettes a few of the ways that social media data can be collected, organized, examined, and augmented to gain some insight on an organization such as the police. The hope is that readers can locate parallels with their own research projects in some of the key points discussed in this chapter. Regarding police institutional activity, what we can ascertain from the above vignettes and related work in this area is a few of the ways that social media have altered institutional police practices, including how police now manage their institutional image (Schneider, 2016a). What an examination of these data also reveals is how attempts to make sense of events become more media-focused. Following news media, social media platforms operate as increasingly important sites that augment police visibility, on the one hand, stressing police legitimacy concerns, on the other hand.

■ **REFERENCES**

Aguiar, L.M. and Schneider, C.J. (2012). *Researching Amongst Elites: Challenges and Opportunities in Studying Up*. Farnham: Ashgate.

Altheide, D.L. (1996). *Qualitative Media Analysis*. Thousand Oaks, CA: Sage.

Altheide, D.L. and Schneider, C.J. (2013). *Qualitative Media Analysis*. Second edition. Thousand Oaks, CA: Sage.

Bayley, D.H. (1990). *Patters of Policing: A Comparative International Analysis*. New Brunswick, NJ: Rutgers University Press.

Bayley, D.H. (1994). *Policing for the Future*. New York: Oxford University Press.

Boellstorff, T. (2013). 'Making big data, in theory', *First Monday*, 18(10). (http://firstmonday.org/ojs/index.php/fm/article/view/4869/3750) (last accessed 6 October 2016).

boyd, d.m. and Ellison, N.B. (2007). 'Social network sites: definition, history, and scholarship', *Journal of Computer-Mediated Communication* 13(1): 210–30.

Brown, G.R. (2013). 'The blue line on thin ice: police use of force in the era of cameraphones, "Citizen Journalism", and YouTube.' MA thesis, Carleton University, Ottawa. https://curve.carleton.ca/system/files/theses/27515.pdf.

Brown, G.R. (2015). 'The blue line on thin ice: police use of force modifications in the era of cameraphones and Youtube.' *British Journal of Criminology*. doi:10.1093/bjc/azv052.

Bullock, K.A. (2016). '(Re)presenting "order" online: the construction of police presentational strategies on social media.' *Policing and Society: An International Journal of Research and Policy*. http://epubs.surrey.ac.uk/810451/

Burgess, J. and Green, J. (2009). *YouTube: Online Video and Participatory Culture*. Malden, MA: Polity Press.

Campeau, H. (2015). '"Police culture" at work: making sense of police oversight.' *British Journal of Criminology*, doi:10.1093/bjc/azu093.

Cohen, H. (2011). '30 social media definitions.' Heidi Cohen: Actionable Marketing Guide (blog), 9 May. http://heidicohen.com/social-media-definition/.

Council of Canadian Academies (2014). *Policing Canada in the 21st Century: New Policing for New Challenges*. Ottawa, ON: The Expert Panel on the Future of Canadian Policing Models, Council of Canadian Academies.

Ericson, R.V. (1982). *Reproducing Order: A Study of Police Patrol Work*. Toronto: University of Toronto Press.

Ericson, R.V., Baranek, P.M., and Chan, J.B.L. (1987). *Visualizing Deviance: A Study of News Organization*. Toronto: University of Toronto Press.

Fishman, M. (1980). *Manufacturing the News*. Austin, TX: University of Texas Press.

Glaser, B.G. and Strauss, A.L. (1967). *Discovery of Grounded Theory: Strategies for Qualitative Research*. Chicago, IL: Aldine de Gruyter.

Goldsmith, A. (2010). 'Policing's new visibility', *British Journal of Criminology*, 50: 914–34.

Lee, M. and McGovern, A. (2013). 'Force to sell: policing the image and manufacturing in public confidence', *Policing and Society*, 23(2): 103–24.

Lee, M. and McGovern, A. (2014). *Policing and Media: Public Relations, Simulations, and Communication*. New York: Routledge.

Lupton, D. (2015). *Digital Sociology*. Routledge.

Mandiberg, M. (2012). *The Social Media Reader*. New York: New York University Press.

Manning, P.K. (1978). 'The police: mandate, strategies and appearances.' In P.K. Manning and J. van Maanen (eds) *Policing: A View from the Street*. Santa Monica, CA: Goodyear, pp.97–125.

Manning, P.K. (1997). *Police Work: The Social Organization of Policing*. 2nd ed. Prospect Heights, IL: Waveland Press.

Manning, P.K. (2015). 'Researching policing using qualitative methods.' In Heith Copes and J.M. Miller (eds) *The Routledge Handbook of Qualitative Criminology*. New York: Routledge, pp.265–82.

Mawby, R. (2002). *Policing Images: Policing, Communications and Legitimacy*. Cullompton, UK: Willan.

Nader, L. (1969). 'Up the Anthropologist: Perspectives Gained from studying up', pp. 284–311 in D. Hymes (ed) *Reinventing Anthropology*. New York: Random House.

O'Connor, C.D. (2015). 'The police on Twitter: image management, community building, and implications for Canada.' *Policing and Society*, doi: 10.1080/ 10439463.2015.1120731

Ratcliff, B. (2006). 'A new trove of music video in the webs' wild world.' *New York Times*, 3 February.

Robertson, I. (2014). 'Toronto police increasing social media use', *Toronto Sun*. 12 January. <http://www.torontosun.com/2014/01/12/toronto-police-increasing-social-media-use> (last accessed 10 September 2016).

Schneider, C.J. (2012). 'Examining elites using qualitative media analysis: celebrity news coverage and TMZ' (pp.103–19). In L. Aguiar and C.J. Schneider (eds) *Researching Amongst Elites: Challenges and Opportunities in Studying Up*. Farnham: Ashgate.

Schneider, C.J. (2014). 'Social media and e-public sociology.' In *The Public Sociology Debate: Ethics and Engagement*, edited by A. Hanemaayer and C.J. Schneider, pp. 205–24. Vancouver: University of British Columbia Press.

Schneider, C.J. (2015a). 'Police image work in an era of social media: YouTube and the 2007 Montebello Summit Protest.' In D. Trottier and C. Fuchs (eds) *Social Media, Politics and the State: Protests, Revolutions, Riots, Crime and Policing in an Age of Facebook, Twitter and YouTube*. New York: Routledge, pp.227–46.

Schneider, C.J. (2015b). 'Public criminology and the 2011 Vancouver Riot: public perceptions of crime and justice in the 21st century', *Radical Criminology*, 5: 21–46.

Schneider, C.J. (2015c). 'Meaning making online: Vancouver's 2011 Stanley Cup Riot.' In M. Dellwing, S. Grills, and H. Bude (eds) *Kleine geheimnisse: Alltagssoziologische einsichten (Little secrets: Everyday sociological insights)*. Wiesbaden: Springer, pp.81–102.

Schneider, C.J. (2016a). *Policing and Social Media: Social Control in an Era of New Media*. Lanham, MD: Lexington Books | Rowman & Littlefield.

Schneider, C.J. (2016b). 'Police presentational strategies on Twitter in Canada.' *Policing & Society: An International Journal of Research and Policy*, 26(2): 129–47.

Schneider, C.J. (2016c). 'Music videos on YouTube: exploring participatory culture on social media', *Studies in Symbolic Interaction*, 47: 97–117.

Schneider, C.J. (2018). 'Police deviance and new media: the death of Eric Garner.' In O. Sefiha and S. Brown (eds) *Handbook on Deviance*. Routledge, pp.337–47.

Schneider, C.J. and D. Trottier. (2012). 'The 2011 Vancouver Riot and the role of Facebook in crowd-sourced policing', *BC Studies* 175 (Autumn): 93–109.

Schneider, C.J. and D. Trottier. (2013). 'Social media and the 2011 Vancouver Riot', *Studies in Symbolic Interaction*, 40: 335–62.

Scott, M.B. and Lyman, S. (1968). 'Accounts', *American Sociological Review*, 33(1): 46–62.

Skolnick, J., and J. Fyfe. (1993). *Above the Law: Police and the Excessive Use of Force.* New York: Free Press.

Thompson, J.B. (2005). 'The new visibility', *Theory, Culture & Society*, 22(6): 31–51.

Tinati, R., Halford, S., Carr, L., and Pope, C. (2014). 'Big data: methodological challenges and approaches for sociological analysis', *Sociology*, 48(4): 663–81.

Trottier, D. (2012a). 'Policing social media.' *Canadian Review of Sociology*, 49(4): 411–25.

Williams, K. (2007). *Our Enemies in Blue: Police and Power in America*. Cambridge, MA: South End Press.

Part 2

Unconventional Research Design and Data Collection Methods

7 Netnography

Engaging with the challenges

Robert V. Kozinets and Manuela Nocker

Introduction

In their influential article, Buchanan and Bryman (2007, p.483) assert that organizational researchers' choice of methods is 'influenced by organizational, historical, political, ethical, evidential, and personal factors'. Organizational researchers routinely find themselves face-to-face with the same rapidly changing world that confronts investigators in other fields: a world where technology increasingly impacts communications and information exchanges, and where the fabric of sociality is constantly being unravelled and rewoven. This never-ending flux of novel technological affordances and assemblages creates a panoply of challenges and opportunities that directly impact our quest for understanding and open the door to unconventional approaches to method.

Ethnographic research plays a crucial role in organization and management studies in terms of understanding in depth the contexts of phenomena such as group cultures and practices, and everyday lived experience. The scholars behind today's organizational ethnographies engage closely with broader shifts in the social sciences, reflecting and critiquing theoretical positions consistent with disciplinary thinking. Researchers also continue to explore ethnographic possibilities that venture into new territories. Our work engages with this latter group.

During an ethnographic study on the institutional implications of *Star Trek* communities in 1995–1996, Kozinets (2001) collected rich cultural data from online forums, fan web pages, and corporate pages. He created a 'Star Trek Research' website which offered fans a research-oriented look at the *Star Trek* phenomenon, and invited them to get involved in his research. From contacts made through the web page, he supplemented the project's observational data collection with ongoing email correspondence interviews with sixty-five community members from twelve different countries. Throughout, as part of his overall ethnography, he kept detailed field notes on his online explorations, experiences, and participation. He found that this dataset offered challenges and opportunities that were distinct from the face-to-face ethnographic component of his work and were, at the time, undocumented and under-developed. As a result, he developed the approach of netnography, a specific set of ethnographic research procedures adapted to the study of online communications, interactions, and experiences. Since its introduction in 1996, netnography has become established within the fields of marketing, consumer research, business research, and tourism. In many other fields, it is still novel. Yet its applications are spreading through the social sciences (Bengry-Howell et al., 2011), with recent uptake in sociology, education, library and information studies, nursing—and organizational and management research, as we will discuss shortly. Netnography is a dynamic cultural approach to online research, constantly transformed by encountering new fields of inquiry and sources of insight.

Three tension-laden disjunctures seem especially relevant to current ethnographic efforts and are taken here as points of departure from which to explore the special vantage points afforded by netnography. First, ethnography has evolved over the decades, yet a strong foundational tradition stemming from anthropology still encourages a focus on the study of groups and their cultures as communities 'located' in a particular time and place. Although originally noted by Marcus (1995), only recently has attention been dedicated to the complexities of multi-site ethnography across several locations (see Chapter 11, this volume). Such ethnographic research is often simultaneously inter-organizational (Zilber, 2014) as well as 'multi-event' in nature (Aguilar Delgado and Cruz, 2014). Leaving aside the difficulties of conducting such ethnographies, we use our introduction of netnography to organization and management studies to encourage a rethinking of 'situatedness' and its notions of cultural and communal sites, co-presence, location, and place.

Second, ethnography emphasizes reaching the traditional point of 'data saturation', and completing fieldwork as intended at the outset of the investigation. A netnographic viewpoint challenges this. Completion may never be achieved in netnography, at least not in the same terms as it has been conventionally cast. We may have to think more of the temporariness of project work and the often abrupt and forced 'terminations' of fieldwork (Nocker, 2009; Nocker et al., 2013). Beyond this, the ontological question of the role of participants' memory and open-endedness of identities online are ubiquitous issues in a digital age. Hence, we suggest that it is important to follow different 'lines of flight' in netnographic studies.

Third, we call attention to the 'time issue' in ethnography. The ideal of prolonged engagement and immersion with and within a particular social group may no longer be viable for various reasons, such as reduced funding. Moreover, face-to-face ethnographic incursions might not even be needed, as there are an increasing number of organizational groups who rarely meet face-to-face, such as virtual global teams. So, rather than emphasizing a regular pace and immersion, investigation of these sites may become more about 'dotting' periods of intense immersion, sometimes becoming a 'rapid ethnography' (Millen, 2000; Isaacs, 2012)—which may be controversial for those who maintain conventional views of ethnography.

In this chapter, an organizational ethnographer and the founder of the method team up to discuss the technique of netnography and its potential employment by organization and management scholars. After outlining the approach and its underlying principles and practices, we discuss the applicability of netnography to contemporary theory building. We explore how the understanding of key and emergent problematics, constructs, and research areas in organizational and management studies fields might be linked to some of netnography's methodological strengths. Consistent with the purpose of this volume, we consider netnography's unconventional nature. We explore the possibility that netnography can complement ethnographic research as it addresses 'head on' the three problem areas in theory and practice described above. Multisitedness, the vagaries of immersion, and the acceleration of the research process, seem to be fundamental characteristics of contemporary social communications and life in the 'digital age' and in netnographic practice. They also typify organizational and managerial existence. We close by discussing how netnography might benefit from the closer involvement of the many innovative scholars in organization and management studies.

The basis of netnography

There are now several technologically infused variants of ethnography designed to adapt ethnographic principles to a digital age. The field of digital anthropology casts the widest net. Following Coleman's (2010) classification, ethnographies of 'digital media' cover a range of technologies and their effects on cultural politics, vernacular cultures, and prosaics. According to Miller and Horst (2012), digital anthropologies can include investigations of software programmers' occupational culture, and technology use in the home, as well as the materiality of digital content.

In terms of specific techniques, Hine's (2000) 'virtual ethnography' focuses on the role of physical presence in the online experience, attending to digital technology's multiple ruptures in accepted boundaries between place, artefact, setting, and production. Like virtual ethnography, netnography is a specific type of online ethnography: 'Netnography is participant-observational research based in online hanging out, download, reflection, and connection' (Kozinets, 2015, p.67).

In management studies, netnography has been employed to understand the conversations, languages, online behaviours, and symbolic repertoires of different groups of interest. In line with the 'practice turn' (Gherardi, 2009) in organization and management studies, netnography has been used together with activity theory by Hemetsberger and Reinhardt (2009) to study online collaboration in open-source projects. Madsen (2016) used a netnographic approach to study how workers at a large Danish bank use internal social media to contribute to the construction of organizational identity. Other suitable netnographic subjects that might interest organization and management researchers include employees, managers, shareholders, publics, regulators, companies, non-profit organizations, and institutions.

Using the term netnography implies the use of a common understanding and set of standards for the conduct of online ethnography: this is the *sine qua non* of a netnography. A netnography is 'a *specific* set of related data collection, analysis, ethical and representation research practices' (Kozinets, 2015, p.79). But this important notion is still not recognized, as 'some studies purporting to be netnographic neither follow nor adequately report on netnographic processes' (Costello et al., 2017, p.1). Employing the established standards of netnography confers upon future studies a consistency and dependability they would not otherwise yield. However, as with ethnography, the netnographic approach is fixed in some ways, yet immensely flexible—indeed, as a technique netnography must continually stretch to accommodate almost continuous technological and technical change.

Compared to other approaches, netnography is digitally native. Its observational elements offer a less intrusive research experience than ethnography because they use unprompted data. If people are talking about a particular topic online, then it can be studied using a netnography. If they are not talking about it, then there is no observational data to collect. It can thus be argued that netnography is more naturalistic in its pursuit of online conversations and topics than a study using methods such as personal interviews, focus groups, surveys, and experiments. Questions of ethics and consent thus arise, because netnography uses information that may not have been provided explicitly for the purpose of particular research projects. Netnography is often used to research sensitive topics, making a cautious stance towards ethics questions more urgent. Netnography tends to be less costly and timelier than other methods because it leverages online archives and existing technologies to rapidly gather potentially relevant data. However, netnographers must also cope with the inconsistencies and mixed blessings of over-abundant data. Reading, understanding, sorting, classifying, and making sense of vast amounts of information can prove challenging. These are some of the key contours, advantages, and deficiencies of the method.

To established practices of participant observation and fieldnote-taking, netnography adds new dimensions. These include procedures for locating online field sites to pursue particular research questions and topics of interest, dealing with issues relating to large digital datasets, navigating challenging and constantly shifting online ethical arenas, and dealing with the public aspects of the researcher's participation.

Netnography's purpose lies in asserting the pre-eminence of meaning making and its understanding, providing a cultural approach to studying the social interaction transpiring through interactive communications media. For the purpose of netnography, a cultural insight involves an understanding of cultural elements such as language use, rituals, roles, identities, values, stories, myths and, centrally, meanings. For example, netnography is fascinated by commonalities in symbol use such as emojis. Recent netnographies have used emoticons and other graphic images as linguistic data to shed light on hidden meanings and cultural connections in social media communication. For example, Fujita et al. (2017) study how students and staff use a university Facebook page to co-create a complex cultural experience, which both inter-relates with as well as extends the university's physical sites of community. 'The netnographic analysis unpacked locally relevant indicators of content strategy, student engagement and co-creation by interpreting the meanings of the social acts in text, image and video content, comments and replies, including "emoji" text' (Fujita et al., 2017, p.154). Researchers are thus giving more attention to the use of visual images in social media. Also, as the work of Hsu et al. (2009) attests, the value of shared narratives in social media inter-actions cannot be overstated in netnographic research. Hsu et al. (2009) bind together the use of narratives by tourists telling stories about their travels with netnographers telling stories about their research participation. The result is an intriguing juxtaposition of netnography and storytelling. Although not as critical of the phenomenon as they might have been (a flaw shared by most business research, compared with ethnographic work in anthropology and cultural studies), Hsu et al. (2009) break new ground in developing these narrative–netnographic linkages.

Guba and Lincoln (1994) first pointed out the importance of epistemology, ontology and methodology. However, Heron and Reason (1997) added axiology as a further paradigm for participatory inquiry. Axiology encompasses both ethics and aesthetics, as a practical knowing about the world. It asks, what is inherently valuable about a purpose and the ways in which purposes are achieved? In the research context, axiology is about the purpose and intent of research. Knowledge is never neutral; it always has ambitions—so what does the research seek to achieve? Knowledge is always powerful; who does it seek to empower? Netnography's axiological orientation is humanist, artful, crit-ical, and moral. An explicit axiological perspective suggests that we do not eschew ethical questions and that we do not shy from engaging in the constant redefinition of spheres of action and ethnographic selves. Explicitly being aware of the moral, power- and value-ladenness of the research enterprise draws us to emphasize the emergent and ongoing need to attend to a lived 'ethics of sharing' using wisdom, not just knowledge, to foster collaboration (Nocker, 2017). We return to notions of netnographic axiology in our conclusions.

Netnography's epistemology—the way it knows things, its knowledge base—values a human-level interpretation, recognizing the layers of humanity operating behind and thought-forms represented within the technology. There is also an art to netnography, as with interviewing and observational work. Like an ethnographer, the netnographer is there to study a phenomenon, and must become a part of that phenomenon. Entrenched in the reality of an issue that matters to a people, the ethnography often assumes a moral stand with the public good in mind. When a netnographer is absorbed into a set of communications that present moral quandaries, or opportunities to speak to issues of social and self-betterment, this presents a choice. Netnography, like ethnography, offers multiple opportunities to question, to empathize, to understand, and to produce a stronger sense of personal morality, and professional opinion on particular matters, taking a stand about the rightness, wrongness, and all of the shades of moral in-between existing in the digital world and beyond.

In practice, online and embodied social interactions are often intermingled. Online images increasingly intermix with the carnal in contemporary realignments of technologies, bodies, and identified senses of social being. This sense of self being created and transmitted through devices such as mobile phones, tablet devices, wearable technologies, AI intelligence helpers, and surveillance regimes is a suitable jurisdiction for netnography. Indeed, selfie taking has been a recent fascination of netnographies, with one concluding that, 'Selfie taking, after all, is not merely a manifestation of the mirrored self questing for its own sense of identity. It is also a social act, a call for connection, a response to competition, and an act of mimicry' (Kozinets et al., 2017, p.10). Despite the many overlaps between the physical reality and its imagistic depiction in the contemporary world, there are still enough fundamental differences between life on and off screen to necessitate lucid adaptations of ethnographic practices into those of netnography. So we might ask: 'How is netnography different from ethnography?'

Five differences between ethnography and netnography

Here, we build upon and expand longstanding work charting the difference between online ethnographic work in a netnographic vein, and the traditions of in-person ethnography. In particular, the work was intended to delineate a course for the pragmatic alterations of practice. Sections related to these have been presented numerous times, are constantly changing, and were inspired by Kozinets (2010 and 2015), yet contain much that is novel for this chapter. There are five key aspects to the social world that have transformed, in relation to management, corporations, governments, and organizations, and in a general sense for groups, communities, and individuals. These are termed alteration, access, archiving, analysis, and accommodation.

ALTERATION

Social worlds are altered. Technology changes communications; communications change cultures; cultures change communications; and communications change technology. Change itself changes to suit the technological medium. Language compresses into 140-character bombs. YouTube is TV for everybody. Communication connects and exposes, revealing fears and hate, but also love and desire. How can an ethnography of this rapidly changing reality account for these transformations?

Every photo that sits on an employee's desk, every corporate acronym and joke shared on a corporate site, every meme of a boss, every nuance of the organizational communicators' world is a social event suspended within, connected to, and endlessly re-spinning a web of cultural meanings that deeply affects our understanding of contemporary organizational life. LinkedIn profiles and their stalking, informal employee videos, long rambling Reddit conversations between former employees, staff private Instagrams, corporate sponsored Snaps, and Facebook page updates, every Whatsapp conversation, every email: all of this might be included and understood in an investigation of an organizational culture. The goal of a netnography is to capture a slice in time. A key question is, 'How do we understand this new form of sociality and set of new meanings in human and organizational social life?' How can we approach the faithful translation of this strange new world that has so many different forms of communication within it? The answer is ethnographic participation. How? The answer to this is access.

ACCESS

Social worlds are accessible. Technology provides a radically different experience of social access from traditional ethnography. People with particular needs or interests can find each other much more easily, regardless of physical or geographic barriers—and increasingly, linguistic and cultural barriers that might stand in their way. If you want to find out what Starbucks employees are saying about working at Starbucks, candidly, you can do this easily online. For example, Kozinets' (2002) investigation of online coffee connoisseur culture incidentally includes assessments of Starbucks as an employer and arguments between past and present Starbucks' employees. In a netnography, you reach out, start to communicate with other people who might share widely different interests from you, contact them and familiarize yourself with them, their beliefs, their activities, as part of the netnography. You are recording it, you are taking notes. You are disclosing your work and your identity, keeping nothing secret. Social moments can happen closer together, one after another.

Accessibility cuts both ways. Managers who are not as technologically literate may be locked out of key communication channels, excluded from important business conversations because the communications links are broken. In a process described with some alarm by Turkle (2012), online interactions can gain prominence over physical ones. Does avoiding technology alter one's standing within a company? Does it alter access to employment, advancement, social activities, and other important resources? There is a safe, almost utilitarian aspect to the private technological communications of social media, almost a promise. The questions here are, 'What sort of new access do social media and other online interactions and experience grant us as researchers of organizations, cultures, and human social life? What is excluded?' The answers are highly contextualized—and important to every netnographic investigation.

ARCHIVING

In these social worlds, the camera and microphone are always on. In the online world, conversations are easily and automatically recorded and archived. All online social communications are automatically stored in various ways and places—some we have access to, others not. In an ethnography, unless a camera or a microphone is turned on, a personal, face-to-face interaction leaves only wispy memories which we scramble to field note, because they evaporate as soon as they occur. In organizational settings, these sensitive conversations can be precarious. People's jobs might be at stake when they reveal hidden events, their true feelings, the ways that they believe they are being oppressed or made to oppress. Online, we can anonymize and offer confidentiality. Or we can simply overhear existing conversations—the proverbial fly on the wall. This explains why netnography scholars seeking to study clandestine and stigmatized activities like drug use, underage drinking, and marital infidelity have found netnography useful. In organizational and managerial settings, these activities extend to criticizing management and the company, whistleblowing, and other urgent matters.

Netnographies deal with traces that are automatically archived, easily shared, and create permanent records. Online, people organically conduct conversations that matter to them. The microphone is on. The interactions are archived. In netnography, with programs to capture moments and events, an online system that records and allow us to code online social interactions is simple to arrange. How do we record faithfully the events in our investigation? The answer concerns technique and tools.

ANALYSIS

The way we approach our understanding of these social worlds is similar, but also very different. How do we collect and analyse this different type of social interaction and experience? How do we create insight and understanding? This, too, is different. To over-emphasize the term 'data' as part of a netnography is to legitimize the practice, and to begin sliding down a slippery slope that ends with meaningful anthropological interpretation reduced to mere context analysis. We use the term because it has gained meaning as that which we collect online, but we prefer not to reduce the anthropological venture to mere data collection and analysis. Instead, we might think about data collection in netnography as being like mushroom hunting in the forest. Sometimes, for some fungi, it is easy, enjoyable work. Sometimes, there is only poison and no food. At other times, you come home empty handed. Data collection is not something like scraping, mining, and capturing using bots and software driftnets to grab words and phrases and things inexplicably recognized by AI engines as significant. It is about handpicking the 'good stuff', and leaving everything else behind.

If we can analogize big data analysis as a robotic information factory where algorithms inexpensively weave descriptive cloths from many digital strands, netnography is haute couture. Netnography is high-end research that is handmade from start to finish, made from the most choice, high-quality, rare, expensive to collect, and often unusual informational fabric and assembled into intelligence and insight with extreme attention to detail, finished by the most experienced and capable researchers, using a variety of time-consuming, customized techniques. Every netnography is customized, each designed to answer different questions, at different points in time, by different investigators, with different people, for different reasons, in different contexts. Because it is hand-crafted and high quality, it is of considerably more interest to scholars than to most organization managers whose concerns are generally more about immediate needs, ease of use, and economies of scale.

Analysis of the traces that we collect as netnographic data is more like putting together the pieces of a complicated puzzle, or finding the clue that solves a crime than it is about using ever-more-sophisticated software programs to automatically categorize and analyse the mass of textual, visual, audio, and audiovisual social information. Throughout a netnography, we are not summarizing so much as clue gathering, following a process of induction, developing 'a causal model built by someone like a forensic pathologist, a detective or an historian, using a progression of inferential analyses to run an evidential trace out to its end point' (Huberman and Miles, 1983, p.329). In this sense, we advocate proceeding as 'wayfinding' (Ingold, 2000, p.155) or 'feeling your way' when 'moving around' in the multiple and layered spaces and times of netnographic exploration. (For a similar view of researcher as detective, see Buchanan and Denyer, Chapter 5, this volume.)

Even though there are various new technologies that provide multitudinous ways to analyse and visualize data, these are so remote from the experience of netnography, that they divert attention from the reality of the cultural experience. Cayla and Arnould (2013, p.12) note how organizational theorists have revealed the impact of organizational storytelling on sense-making. They extrapolate this point to explore the value of ethnography in all forms of understanding business and management—a point which is easily extrapolated to the storytelling potential of netnography. That is why the person doing the analysis needs to think not only like an anthropologist, but also like a storyteller and a graphic designer, like someone who, at the end, needs to turn their research into a compelling narrative and a visual presentation. With more and more tidbits and tastes of interaction flowing through digital streams, the coding and decoding of traces into information, and interpretation, and into a narrative, is more important now than ever before.

ACCOMMODATION

These social worlds are intertwined with commercial enterprises in an unprecedented manner. 'Your cell phone provider tracks your location and knows who's with you. Your online and in-store purchasing patterns are recorded, and reveal if you're unemployed, sick, or pregnant. Your emails and texts expose your intimate and casual friends. Google saves your private searches. Facebook knows your sexual orientation without you ever mentioning it' (Schneier 2015, np). Public access to people's postings and personal information, which forms the basis of netnography, raises novel ethical, legal, and social questions that society has not addressed. Online social spaces are owned by and aligned with large corporate and organizational interests.

As with everything ethnographic, defamiliarization is critical. A key question that a netnography must ask concerns how the commercial medium inflects the social expression. How is commercialism accommodated, in the interaction and in the netnography itself? The good social scientist raises alarm when need be. Netnographers of institutions and organizations must not only collect data but theorize within these spaces related to social, economic, business, and government strategies. Practical matters abound. Who owns this information? Can you use it legally for research purposes? Is it monitored and governed by fair use doctrines? Our legal and moral systems are gasping in the face of rapid technology change like a fish out of water.

The fact that we are being watched, that stock portfolios are built on the labour of amateurs, that managers are spying on their workers, and so much else, have unprecedented implications not only for how you make your research decisions, but also how we decide what we stand for as human beings, as scholars, and as members of society—not citizens of any one nation, but citizens of multinational corporations, incorporations of computational financial forges. What are the netnographer's ethical standards? Will your organizational netnography also talk about companies, brands, executive celebrities, and celebrity executives? Are you going to talk about inequitable situations? About class and jobs? About the role of religion, belief, and its own powerful brandings? About impending environmental and social disasters?

These five elements chart a methodological path from ethnography's past to its future. This section contains provocations for those who wish to include a study of a social world that has altered, and continues to transform management, corporations, governments, and organizations. The five aspects map the alteration of the way social worlds are enacted, the dramatic changes in access to these social worlds, their automatic archiving, the different routes that exist to analysis, and the need to acknowledge and theorize their accommodation by powerful corporate and institutional interests. With this background in place, we can consider specific ways in which netnography suggests a break from conventional anthropology.

On the liquidity of sites

Ethnography as an anthropological practice generally requires in-person fieldwork, which requires, of course, a field. Traditionally, fieldwork involves gaining membership of particular social groups and observing and participating in them. However, in netnography, this conception is complicated. Any topic, even one that does not exist discretely in the physical world—crowdfunding or fashion blogging—is a fair choice for netnographic investigation. Does this investigation need to focus on particular online places, people, or other bounded concepts? That question intrigues us.

Here we will continue the anthropological project of interrogating and destabilizing the ethnographic notion of a site. The early netnographies of media fandom were conducted across multiple online and in-person sites, sampling widely the phenomenon (Kozinets 1997; 1998; 2001). Some early work (Kozinets, 2002; Nelsen and Otnes, 2005; Muniz and Schau, 2005) kept their investigations close to single sites, because these were either the focus of the study, or because single sites were such rich sources of insight that no additional sources were required. So it has been established from the beginning of the conduct of netnography that a focus on a single site is unnecessary.

The ethnography site is disrupted in netnography, where the concept of having a stable field site liquefies as soon as a website is taken down, messages are retracted, or conversations erased. In an ongoing investigation, particular topics can constitute sites, and people can constitute topics. The netnography can follow a hashtag across multiple sites, rather than a single site, as Moreillon (2015) did in her study of a school librarian's self-organized chat group. Personal brands can also be the subject of a topic search; see Kretz and de Valck's (2010) netnography of fashion bloggers. Groups or individuals (such as fashion and luxury bloggers or vloggers, or other media 'influential'), can constitute sites as their content moves through multiple communication channels. Netnographers track the traces; thus, the bounded physical site is no more. However, some of the practices used to engage within those sites remain surprisingly salient.

A particular online community can still be the focus of a netnography. One example is a corporate LinkedIn group dedicated to workplace rumours and complaints. Or the topic could be more widely dispersed among different locations, such as using social media to cope with the challenges of being a Muslim manager in a Western company, or a female entrepreneur in a male-dominated industry. Investigating such topics could mean a tight focus on the online interactions of particular individuals. Or it also could involve paying attention to discussions of these issues across many sites.

The best netnographers are masterful in their use of ordinary search engines. What we might term, colloquially and fannishly, 'Jedi Googlers'. Topics do not slip through their legs, good hashtags fail to escape them. Their Jedi wisdom manifests through a subset of app sites, platforms, and sites accessed from multiple locations and through many different devices. In the search stage of netnography, researchers invest themselves fully into the process. A netnography is never merely a portrait of a particular place in time, although it always is this as well. Reading through netnographies that are only a decade old, such as Sandlin (2007) with its massive magazine subscription numbers, is already a trip down technological memory lane. That impression reflects a foundation of what a netnography certainly is: an analytical document in its time, but also a type of chronicle, a snapshot of a particular set of online phenomena, embedded in and wedded to its time, with the ethnographer at its focal point—the centre of the circle of sites which are assembled, or accreted, in a process as much random and affected by the world as it is intentional, objective, and focused.

Who are the people of interest? What are the things of interests? Where are the places of interest? Netnography is not some rote set of steps, but a toolkit of evolving practices enacted every time the researcher steps into the pilot's seat and begins a new search. Netnography is not meant to stand in one place, and it never has. Netnographies follow concepts across sites, creating fields from scraps of conversation, pictures and videos, roaming far and wide in their often intuitively guided quest, crossing media and also moving into personal interactions and interviews. Sites can be created to become 'research web pages' in netnography, deployed to create a controlled interactional space, something easy to enact on Facebook or Reddit. Apps can be designed to gather data, to enact mobile ethnographies where employees speak to us about their day during lunch breaks. We can form online research communities and panels. Bloggers or vloggers can be paid to co-develop, promote, and publicize your research message. Every site that the netnographer touches becomes part of the network of the netnography. Any site is now possible—commercial, grassroots, single, multiple, past, present, global, local. The idea behind a netnography is not to set up boundaries, but to follow the path of meaning. As we follow it, the network should be analysed in as many ways possible, to emphasize the disruption of the site and the meaninglessness of pre-specifying a site to gather knowledge before we have completed our journey, before we may know fully what it is we seek.

On the open-endedness of participation

As with many qualitative techniques, netnographies are subject to rules of 'saturation', such that the collection of data should stop once new insights on the topics of interest seem no longer to be generated by the engagement. Some netnographers will closely track the amount of text collected, reporting it quantitatively, and accounting for the number of participants. Often, this enumeration serves to placate reviewers who feel that reporting the collection of large amounts of data, like large sample sizes, somehow ensure the conduct of high-quality research. This sort of accounting can also satisfy researchers who wish to understand the composition or extent of the dataset.

However, accounting for when a netnography stops is even more ambiguous than determining when an ethnography ceases. Netnographic participation is a matter of debate. Given the fluidity of notions such as culture, community, and membership in the online social context (see Kozinets 2015, pp.9–13), participation can run from starting a web page, posting on a blog, and commenting, to reading a post, tagging an article, or liking something on a social networking site. If one is studying a topic that is already of interest, such as contemporary academic workplace culture, then despite the netnography having a discrete beginning and end point, can we ever truly say that we stop researching? All netnographies take on this native aspect, as we are all now digitally native to some extent. All netnographies are, in this same sense, auto-ethnographic: we reflect upon our own digital reflections, even as we cast those images out in the digital void. In netnography, researchers must negotiate the same spectrum of inside and outside the culture that has haunted ethnography since its inception, except that now the culture blurs with communications and information technologies.

In anthropology, it is commonplace for researchers to return repeatedly to their field sites over the length of their careers, always deepening their cultural understanding with new layers of personal and professional involvement. The reading of netnography's multiple accounts and communication trails sits uneasily with the 'realist tales' of a detached observer-researcher (Van Maanen, 1988). Instead, the researcher is much more like an actor within a dispersed social and technological network, an element of a vast social assemblage becoming aware of its own territorialization.

Lest this seem too dehumanizing, netnography seeks cultural engagement on a human level. This requires meaningful engagement in online practices, which is participation in context. Any engagement of this kind raises the question when to stop data collection. Buchanan et al. (1998, p.64) pointed out how 'the leap' out of the field may be experienced as 'awkward' by researchers. Indeed, we may wish to go back to the field and gather 'some more data'. Saturation, in a complex, dynamic, and transformative world, might never be reached. This aspect of netnography—that it is never truly finished—might simply point us back to the reality of the anthropologist, who bears the culture of the field within them, and thus can never fully leave it. In this sense, the open-endedness of our research is a shared opportunity and a challenge that moves beyond netnography.

On the issue of time

The notion of time invested in an ethnography or netnography is related to participation. Traditionally, ethnographic work was painstaking and time-consuming. The researcher was tasked with travelling, joining a distant culture, learning their ways, returning, then engaging in complex acts of translation and theory building. Imported into business, the ethnography has become a part of the 'managerial toolkit', with occupational and marketing ethnographies conducted over two or three months. In netnographies, time can be more compressed, some taking six to eight weeks, or less.

In such a world, what happens to the anthropological ideal of prolonged immersion? Is this still necessary? Are there requisite tradeoffs that accompany these shorter time spans? The simple fact is that netnography can effectively study online phenomena. For example, Quinton and Wilson (2015) use netnography to understand how business networks are changing due to the increasing use of occupational social networks such as LinkedIn. Their findings show that 'Trust is still incremental in the social media network environment, but membership of a professional social media network acts as a trust-worthiness heuristic and in addition, the compression of time within the digital environment has reduced the period of establishing trust and the "warming-up" of relationships' (Quinton and Wilson, 2015, p.22). The phenomenon they study is perfectly suited to netnography, revealing the same time compression that the digital environment has on the conduct of ethnography. Obviously, a team which meets globally, or the very phenomenon of virtual meetings, are important topics whose understanding can be advanced through the application of netnography.

The field of marketing developed an early taste, and also an ambivalence, for rapid ethnographic work. According to Belk (2014, p.387), anthropologist John 'Sherry's [field] journal entries often warned of the dangers of "blitzkrieg ethnography" in which too little time was spent at each site to truly understand the local culture'. The term was coined during a foundational time in marketing ethnography, when twenty consumer researchers journeyed forth 'in a recreational vehicle and [went] across the country in the summer of 1986, looking at consumption in a way that it had really never been looked at before' (Belk, 2014, p.397). These ethnographers moved rapidly between sites, developing comparisons about consumption relating to the different places they visited. Another option is to 'dip in and out' of field sites. With a mobile phone, this is easy. One can stay in contact with a field site for weeks or even years, learning and communicating. Although traditionalists might dismiss this as a dilettante's approach to ethnography, as long as the researcher has a purpose, and keeps reflective field notes on the process, this is a viable way to conduct netnography.

Responsibilities and horizons

We have explained the netnographic method and its underlying principles and practices, and offered suggestions about how the method can be used by organization and management researchers. We also explored the key differences between netnography and ethnography. We also exposed three disruptive disjunctures which netnography highlights. First, single field sites versus the dispersed nature of online sociality. Second, prolonged field immersion which is less meaningful with netnographic investigations. Third, the increased pace of research that is encouraged and permitted by the pace of internet technology development.

Finally, there are several thought-provoking issues that would benefit from engagement by researchers in organization and management studies, and related fields. The first is axiological. As noted earlier, axiology encompasses research ethics and aesthetics. An axiological orientation asks about the research purpose, about what the research wishes to achieve. Ethnography and netnography are not value-neutral in their orientation. In the organization and management field, there are obvious tensions between the requirement to be critical of the institutions being researched, and the fact that these institutions often pay the bills. That tension is external, as corporations and governments expect research to be applicable, rather than idealistic and critical.

This implies doing research that helps companies to increase their efficiency, global footprint, legitimacy, and profitability. The critical and the practical thus coexist in an uneasy tension, which can sometimes be productive and illuminating.

The axiology of netnography is more critical than applied. However, that is not to say that it cannot be used for practical matters. Netnography offers researchers a powerful view on how various constituencies are connecting and disconnecting using technology. Yet, at its heart, netnography draws more from cultural studies and critical anthropology than it does from case analysis. In its purpose, it seeks to confront, challenge, and seek solutions to address the often soul-crushing problems of inequity and environmental devastation wrought by contemporary organizations.

Part of the problem may be our distance from ourselves and each other—as well as our disregard for and distance from the natural world. Increasingly, our 'life online' is conducted on 24/7 mobile devices. The 'Internet of Things' challenges our understanding of materiality and immateriality. There is conspicuous polarization of views. Researchers position themselves in terms of believing in texts having material effects, or not. On one side, the idea of an immaterial world may be hard to maintain. Social practices and knowledge are often being objectified (Law, 2002). Even the view of projects can be objectified through dominant discourses and practices of project management (Nocker, 2006). Can we claim the existence of immateriality in a digital world? In the view outlined earlier, it would not be possible to believe in the immaterial, or at least not entirely. Netnographers will probably be pushed to take stances. Believing in materiality may have a 'tangible effect' in society in terms of resource use and redistribution (Miller and Horst, 2012).

We think, however, that a holistic view of netnography should not fall into the trap of polarisation, as it tends to render invisible other dimensions—psychological and spiritual—in the lives of participants and researchers. For netnography, it should be of interest that the 'immaterial' exists in the 'psychological space', the unconscious or imaginary that are largely sidestepped in much management literature. Not everything may be classified in the material realm, after all. Not everything that cannot be counted, does not count.

Speaking of numbers and counts, the shift towards data science is a harbinger of new developments in organizational research, not all of them welcome. In 2015, the University of Manchester organized a workshop in the School of Social Sciences called 'Big data from the bottom up' to discuss the use of ethnography in data analytics. The organizers invited papers exploring how ethnographic practices may inform big data. The original interest in the use of ethnography in data analytics was about providing companies with data. Yet some scholars stress that research now is about discovering data together: ethnographers and data scientists have much in common (Ford, 2014). Netnography incorporates these big data approaches, but does so warily (Kozinets, 2015). Based on researcher participation, reflexivity, immersion, and a human-centric cultural understanding, netnography has little in common with methods that collect, store, and code vast amounts of data with little or no researcher participation in the interactions that are studied.

We have outlined a range of concerns which react to the evanescence of the online experience, noting its disruptive effects on the ethnographic notions of field sites, immersion, participation, and engagement. This ever-partial approach to online ethnography has much in common with the virtual ethnography approach of Hine (2000). However, even though it may be partial, it remains paramount for us to maintain that the question of ethics will remain a 'constant companion' in netnography. Taking a view of a researcher's lived experience, ethics cannot be deemed as finally resolved with any participant consent, even if confirmed in writing. It is thus paramount to remain alert to and engage with emerging ethical dilemmas in the field and beyond (e.g. Ferdinand et al, 2007). Indeed, what is a conventional choice of method and what is an unconventional one is, as Buchanan and Bryman (2007) argue, dependent on the context of that choice.

We invite readers to reflect on the importance of human presence and engagement in netnographic studies. We have a responsibility as cultural researchers—to our field, to our peers, to our readers, to ourselves, to our time, and to our humanity. We thus agree with a recent review of netnography that there would be the danger of 'missed opportunities' to 'reap rich benefits' without the active engagement of the participative stance (Costello et al., 2017, p.1). But the participant's stance is a risky and unsteady one, as unconventional in research as it ever has been. To be a participant in cultural interpretation means not to be less objective, but to be more aware in a hermeneutic sense of one's own prejudices. Self-reflexivity about our research practices such as observation, interviewing, and searching digital spaces is crucial because these are, as Alvesson (2003) reminds us, modes of knowledge production, and not mere techniques. Always embedded in organizational commitments of various sorts, always acting within power and information networks connected to other networks of influence and articulation, netnographic researchers must engage in reflexive accounts as well as in acknowledging the presence and support of participants (Cunliffe, 2003).

This is the netnography we wish to present. It is an approach, a discipline, a set of guidelines that evolves with every project, through every article and with each chapter written—as it did with this one. Reflecting the times we inhabit, it is technological as well as social, observational as well as participatory, structured and improvisational, unstable and destabilizing. Above all, in its search for human voices, its wayfinding path, its insistence on ethics, and its quest for cultural understanding, we hope to have shown how, despite employing a toolset radically different from that of the traditional anthropologist, it remains profoundly ethnographic. Our complex times demand nothing less.

◼ REFERENCES

Aguilar Delgado, N. and Cruz, L.B. (2014). 'Multi-event ethnography: doing research in pluralistic settings', *Journal of Organizational Ethnography*, 3(1): 43–58.

Alvesson, M. (2003). 'Beyond neo-positivists, romantics, and localists: a reflexive approach to interviews in organizational research', *Academy of Management Review* 28(1): 13–33.

Belk, R. (2014). 'The labors of the Odysseans and the legacy of the Odyssey,' *Journal of Historical Research in Marketing*, 6(2): 379–404.

Bengry-Howell, A., Wiles, R., Nind, M., and Crow, G. (2011). 'A review of the academic impact of three methodological innovations: netnography, child-led research and creative research methods,' NCRM Hub, University of Southampton research paper.

Buchanan, D.A. and Bryman, A. (2007). 'Contextualizing methods choice in organizational research', *Organizational Research Methods*, 10(3): 483–501.

Buchanan, D., Boddy, D., and McCalman, J. (1998). 'Getting in, getting on, getting out and getting back.' In A. Bryman (ed.) *Doing Research in Organizations*. London: Routledge, pp.53–67.

Cayla, J. and Arnould, E. (2013). 'Ethnographic Stories for Market Learning', *Journal of Marketing*, 77(July): 1–16.

Coleman, E.G. (2010). 'Ethnographic approaches to digital media,' *Annual Review of Anthropology*, 39: 487–505.

Costello, L., McDermott, M-L., and Wallace, R. (2017). 'Netnography: range of practices, misperceptions, and missed opportunities', *International Journal of Qualitative Research Methods*, 16: 1–12.

Cunliffe, A.L. (2003). 'Reflexive inquiry in organizational research: questions and possibilities', *Human Relations* 56(8): 983–1003.

Ferdinand, J., Pearson, G., Rowe, M., and Worthington, F. (2007). 'A different kind of ethics', *Ethnography*, 8(4): 521–44.

Ford, H. (2014). 'Big data and small: collaborations between ethnographers and data scientists, *Big Data & Society*, 1(2): 1–3.

Fujita, M., Harrigan, P., and Soufar, G. (2017). 'A netnography of a university's social media brand community: exploring collaborative co-creation tactics', *Journal of Global Scholars of Marketing Science*, 27(2): 148–64.

Gherardi, S. (2009). 'Introduction: The critical power of the 'practice lens', *Management Learning*, 40(2): 115–28.

Guba, E.G. and Lincoln, Y.S. (1994). 'Competing paradigms in qualitative research.' In N.K. Denzin and Y.S. Lincoln (eds) *Handbook of Qualitative Research*. Thousand Oaks, CA: Sage.

Hemetsberger, A. and Reinhardt, C. (2009). 'Collective development in open-source communities: an activity theoretical perspective on successful online collaboration', *Organization Studies*, 30(9): 987–1008.

Heron, J. and Reason, P. (1997). 'A participatory inquiry paradigm', *Qualitative Inquiry*, 3(3): 274–94.

Hine, C. (2000). *Virtual Ethnography*. London/Thousand Oaks, CA/New Delhi: Sage.

Hsu, Sy, Dehuang, N., and Woodside, A.G. (2009). 'Storytelling research of consumers' self-reports of urban tourism experiences in China', *Journal of Business Research*, 62(12): 1223–54.

Huberman, A.M. and Miles, M.B. (1983). 'Drawing valid meaning from qualitative data: some techniques of data reduction and display', *Quality and Quantity*, 17: 281–339.

Ingold, T. (2000). *The Perception of the Environment: Essays on Livelihood, Dwelling and Skill*. London: Routledge.

Isaacs, E. (2012). 'The value of rapid ethnography: three cases studies. In Brigitte Jordan (ed.) *Advancing Ethnography in the Corporate Environment: Challenges and Emerging Opportunities*. Walnut Creek, CA: Left Coast Press, pp.92–107.

Kozinets, R.V. (1997). '"I want to believe": a netnography of The X-Philes' Subculture of Consumption'. In M. Brucks and D.J. MacInnis (eds) *Advances in Consumer Research, Volume 24*. Provo, UT: Association for Consumer Research, pp.470–5.

Kozinets, R.V. (1998). 'On netnography: initial reflections on consumer research investigations of cyberculture.' In J. Alba and W. Hutchinson (eds) *Advances in Consumer Research, Volume 25*. Provo, UT: Association for Consumer Research, pp.366–71.

Kozinets, R.V. (2001). 'Utopian enterprise: articulating the meanings of *Star Trek*'s culture of consumption', *Journal of Consumer Research*, 28(June): 67–88.

Kozinets, R.V. (2002). 'The field behind the screen: using netnography for marketing research in online communities,' *Journal of Marketing Research*, 39(February): 61–72.

Kozinets, R.V. (2010). *Netnography: Doing Ethnographic Research Online*. London: Sage.

Kozinets, R.V. (2015). *Netnography: Redefined*. Second edition. Thousand Oaks, CA: Sage.

Kozinets, R., Gretzel, U., and Dinhopl, A. (2017). 'Self in art/self as art: museum selfies as identity work', *Frontiers in Psychology*, 8(May): 1–12.

Kretz, G. and de Valck, K. (2010). '"Pixelize me!": digital storytelling and the creation of archetypal myths through explicit and implicit self-brand association in fashion and luxury blogs.' In Russell W. Belk (ed.), *Research in Consumer Behavior, Volume 12*. London: Emerald Group, pp.313–29.

Law, J. (2002). 'Objects and spaces', *Theory, Culture & Society*, 19(5/6): 91–105.

Madsen, V.T. (2016). 'Constructing organizational identity on internal social media: a case study of coworker communication in Jyske Bank', *International Journal of Business Communication*, 53(2): 200–23.

Marcus, G.E. (1995). 'Ethnography in/of the world system: the emergence of multi-sited ethnography, *Annual Review of Anthropology*, 24: 95–117.

Millen, D.R. (2000). 'Rapid ethnography: time deepening strategies for HCI field research.' *Proceedings from DIS '00: Conference on Designing Interactive Systems: Processes, Methods, and Tecniques*. New York, NY: ACM Press.

Miller, D. and Horst, H.A. (2012). 'The digital and the human: a prospectus for digital anthropology.' In H.A. Horst and D. Miller (eds.) *Digital anthropology*. London and New York: Berg, pp. 3–15.

Moreillon, J. (2015). '#schoollibrarians tweet for professional development: a netnographic case study of #txlchat', *School Libraries Worldwide*, 21(2): 127–37.

Muniz, A.M. and Schau, H.J. (2005). 'Religiosity in the abandoned Apple Newton brand community', *Journal of Consumer Research*, 31(4): 737–47.

Nelson, M. and Otnes, C. (2005). 'Exploring cross-cultural ambivalence: a netnography of intercultural wedding message boards', *Journal of Business Research*, 58 (January): 89–95.

Nocker, M. (2006). 'The contested object: on projects as emergent space.' In D. Hodgson and S. Cicmil (eds) *Making Projects Critical*. Basingstoke, UK and New York: Palgrave Macmillan.

Nocker, M. (2009). 'Struggling to "fit in": on belonging and the ethics of sharing in project teams.' Special Issue on Critical Project Studies, *Ephemera: Theory and Politics in Organisation*, 9(2): 149–67.

Nocker, M. (2017). 'On belonging and being professional: in pursuit of an ethics of sharing in project teams.' In W. Kuepers, S. Sonnenburg, and M. Zierold (eds) *ReThinking Management. Perspectives and impacts of cultural turns and beyond*. Management—Culture—Interpretation Series: Springer VS.

Nocker, M., Pearson, G., and Rowe, M. (2013). 'Letting go is hard to do: ethnographic selves in the face of endings.' Paper presented at the *The 8th Annual Ethnography Symposium*. VU, 28–30 August, Amsterdam.

Quinton, S. and Wilson, D. (2015). 'Tensions and ties in social media networks: towards a model of understanding business relationship development and business performance enhancement through the use of LinkedIn.' *Industrial Marketing Management*, 54: 15–24.

Sandlin, J.A. (2007). 'Netnography as a consumer education research tool', *International Journal of Consumer Studies*, 31(3): 288–94.

Schneier, B. (2015). *Data and Goliath: The Hidden Battles to Collect Your Data and Control Your World*. New York: W.W. Norton.

Turkle, S. (2012). *Alone Together: Why We Expect More from Technology and Less from Each Other*. New York: Basic.

Van Maanen, J. (1988). *Tales of the Field: On Writing Ethnography*. Chicago, IL: University of Chicago Press.

Zilber, T.B. (2014). 'Beyond a single organization: challenges and opportunities in doing field level ethnography', *Journal of Organizational Ethnography*, 3(1): 96–113.

8 Institutions under a microscope

Experimental methods in institutional theory

Alex Bitektine, Jeffrey W. Lucas, and Oliver Schilke

Introduction

Recent literature on institutional theory is replete with calls for greater use of experimental designs to explore the micro-foundations of institutions (Bitektine, 2011; Green, 2004; Kennedy and Fiss, 2009). Well-conceived and well-developed experiments can enable institutional theory scholars not only to scrutinize difficult-to-isolate relationships (David and Bitektine, 2009), but also to explore institutions as multilevel processes that form the foundation of organizational life (Thornton et al., 2012). Nevertheless, experimental methods have yet to occupy their due place in the toolkit of institutional researchers.

The purpose of this chapter is to draw researchers' attention to the potential of experiments to generate interesting and relevant insights for understanding institutions in organizational contexts, as well as to provide some guidance for scholars interested in using experimental studies in institutional theory research. In the following sections, we briefly elaborate on the importance of micro-level processes in institutional theory, discuss the advantages and challenges of experimental studies of institutional practices, and review examples of extant experimental research in institutional theory, with an emphasis on their methodological distinctions and the theoretical questions that they address. We close with practical recommendations for the design and implementation of experimental studies exploring micro-foundations of institutions, and a discussion of promising future directions for experimental research in institutional theory.

Microfoundations of institutions

Institutional theory has made tremendous progress in helping us understand how organizations navigate the environments in which they are embedded.

This navigating, of course, is done by people—individuals with their own cognitions and agency (Battilana, 2006; Hallett, 2010). Traditionally, institutional theory research has drawn attention to contextual, higher-order factors such as the society's culture, norms, and taken-for-granted beliefs (Schneiberg and Clemens, 2006). At the same time, nagging questions about the place of individual cognition and agency with respect to institutions have persisted throughout the history of new institutionalism—from interest to cognitive foundations of institutional persistence (George et al., 2006; Zucker, 1977), to exploring the role of individual and collective actors in changing institutional order (DiMaggio, 1988; Greenwood and Suddaby, 2006; Maguire et al., 2004), and to the recent and growing interest in micro-foundations of institutions (Haack et al., 2014; Powell and Colyvas, 2008; Tost, 2011).

Although institutional theory has long maintained a macro focus, the roots of institutional research are grounded in Berger and Luckmann's (1966) treatise on the social construction of reality, where the emergence of institutions is explored at the level of individuals ('organisms') and their everyday interactions. In this respect, the current interest in micro-foundations of institutions represents a return to micro-sociological and social-psychological roots of institutional theory (Barley, 2008; Zucker, 1991). In other words, institutional theorists' interest in how individual-level factors affect collective-level concepts (and vice versa; Felin et al., 2015) traces back to the conceptual foundations laid out by Berger and Luckmann (1966).

Although the interest in the micro level implies a multilevel conceptualization of institutional processes (Bitektine and Haack, 2015), the issue of levels and level interactions has only recently started to gain significant traction in institutional theory research. The micro-foundations research program in this respect holds great promise: it draws attention to lower-level and inter-level mechanisms that provide micro-foundations for macro outcomes (Felin et al., 2015). The challenge of this research agenda is that macro-level effects of these micro-mechanisms are not simply additive, but they 'can take on complex forms and lead to surprising aggregate and emergent outcomes that are hard to predict based on knowledge of the constituent parts' (Barney and Felin, 2013, p.141).

While *micro-to-macro* causation represents a particular interest for micro-foundations research (Bitektine and Haack, 2015; Felin et al., 2015), the scarcity of published papers (and abundance of research opportunities) on all types of causal relationships between institutional variables at different levels calls for further exploration of not only micro-to-macro causation, but also of *macro-to-micro* and *micro-to-micro* causation. Indeed, despite the well-developed literature in sociological social psychology (e.g., Walker et al., 1988; Walker et al., 1986; Zelditch and Walker, 1984), these types of causal relationships remain largely disconnected from mainstream institutional theory.

Extant micro-foundations research in institutional theory is characterized by substantial methodological diversity—from ethnomethodology (Barley, 2008) and discourse analysis (Alvesson and Kärreman, 2011; Phillips and Oswick, 2012) to time series studies segmenting monolithic 'audiences' of early institutional theory into smaller and smaller segments (Lamin and Zaheer, 2012) and experimental studies exploring interactions between individuals and institutions (Raaijmakers et al., 2015). We focus here on the promise of experimental methods for research in institutional theory—in part due to their relative novelty to most institutional scholars and in part due to their effectiveness in unpacking micro-foundations of institutions and organizations. Highly relevant—and so far largely unanswered—questions in institutional analysis amenable to experimental research include:

- How can macro-level consensus coexist with diversity at the individual level?
- How do individuals choose among different responses to institutional pressures?
- How do individuals determine which institutional logic is an appropriate foundation for judgments and actions in a given context?

This is just a small sample of the many possible questions.

The case for experiments

Experiments are an 'unconventional' research method only when it comes to employing them for macro-organization theory research. They have long been used in many other fields interested in the cognition and behaviour of actors (Webster and Sell, 2014), but only the increased interest in micro-foundations, along with rising concerns regarding endogeneity inherent to other research methods (Shaver, 1998), have put experiments on the agenda of institutionalists.

TWO LOGICS IN EXPERIMENTAL RESEARCH

In institutional theory, and in the social and behavioural sciences broadly, experiments can be characterized along one of two archetypical research logics that can be termed 'applied' and 'fundamental'. The particular logic dominating a research project affects not only the study design and selection of research subjects, but also the ways the findings of the study can be generalized.

In the *applied research logic*, researchers attempt to simplify the natural world in such a way as to be able to isolate meaningful independent variables and vary them across conditions. The goal is then to generalize results of these studies to specific natural settings. Examples of this research are marketing studies that have customers express preferences for products with different package designs (e.g. Reimann et al., 2010), or mock jury studies that vary instructions to jurors to determine how real jurors might respond (e.g. Kerwin and Shaffer, 1994). Another area of research that follows this approach concerns audit studies of employment discrimination (e.g. Pager, 2003). In these studies, researchers send fictitious applications to real job postings, randomly varying characteristics of candidates (such as a candidate's gender or race) in order to determine whether or not employers discriminate based on these characteristics. This kind of experimental research thus attempts to simplify the real world by producing data that generalizes directly to specific real-world settings from which the sample is drawn.

By contrast, in the *fundamental research logic*, rather than simplifying processes in the natural world, researchers attempt to create conditions that are relevant to some theory under test. In these studies, the goal is not to generalize results directly to natural settings. Rather, the goal is to demonstrate a theorized process—generalization happens through support of a theory that has relevance in the domain to which the theory applies (its scope). This type of generalization, often referred to as 'analytical' (Yin, 2010; Yin, 2003), entails two steps. The first involves a conceptual claim whereby investigators demonstrate the process or relationship between constructs as described by a particular theory. The second 'involves applying the same theory to implicate other, similar situations where analogous events also might occur' (Yin, 2010, p.21). An example of this type of experiment is Lynne Zucker's (1977) landmark study on institutional persistence, conducted in an artificial context in which participants assessed the movement of a stationary, small point of light (see below for more details). Although a clear departure from real-life organizational activity, Zucker's experiments played a pivotal role in providing support for core tenets of institutional theory and helped explain the transfer of norms from generation to generation (Heath and Sitkin, 2001).

Which of the two logics is invoked to guide one's research has important implications for both the design of a study and the types of conclusions a researcher can draw. Whereas features of experiments that mirror real-world processes are desirable for experiments driven by the applied research logic, the presence of elements that approximate real-world conditions in the fundamental type of experiments (i.e. experiments designed explicitly to test theory) can be a disadvantage. If the goal is to test a broad theory rather than to generalize to specific natural settings, elements of the design that approximate natural settings but aren't theoretically relevant may interfere with tests of the theory. In other words, researchers won't know if experimental participants respond to theoretically relevant features of the experiment or to features designed to mirror natural settings. The approximation to natural settings will create unnecessary variation in the experiment design.

The same applies to research subjects. If the goal is to generalize findings to specific natural settings, then subjects similar to those to whom the researcher wishes to generalize are desirable. For example, mock jury studies attempt to have participants as much like real jurors as possible, while market research studies attempt to have real consumers who frequently face the types of decisions included in the study. However, if the goal is to test a general theory, representative samples are at best unnecessary since the goal is to demonstrate a process—not to draw conclusions about how certain types of people will respond to particular conditions. Also, diverse samples will tend to increase random variations in behaviour, making it more likely that an experiment will find effects when none in fact exist (Lucas, 2003b).

The key differences between the two logics are summarized in Table 8.1.

Table 8.1 Applied and fundamental research logics

	Applied research logic	Fundamental research logic
Theory scope	**Limited to a specific natural setting** in which a certain process or a relationship between variables is expected (e.g. customers, executives, judges, etc.).	**A broad theory**, whose scope is not limited to a particular natural setting (e.g. prospect theory, institutional theory, agency theory, etc.)
Researchers' strategy	**Simplify the natural world** in such a way as to be able to isolate meaningful independent variables and vary them across conditions.	Rather than simplify processes in the natural world, researchers attempt to **create conditions that are only relevant to some theory under test.**
Objective	Generalize results to natural settings: • customers in the market • jury members at a trial • employer at hiring, etc.	Generalize to theory: to **demonstrate a theorized process**—generalization happens through support of a theory that has relevance in the domain to which the theory applies (its scope).
Examples	**Product choice** studies, where customers express preferences for products with different packaging. **Mock jury** studies that vary instructions to jurors in an effort to determine how real jurors might respond. **Employment discrimination** studies, fictitious applications sent in response to real job postings (e.g. varying gender or race) to determine whether employers discriminate.	**Autokinetic situation** to study institutional persistence (Zucker 1977). **Trust game** to explore cooperation in repeated interactions (Schilke et al., 2013) **Standardized experimental situation** to study the role of status characteristics in social influence (Berger et al., 1977). **Bargaining experiments** to study aspects of social exchange (Cook and Emerson, 1978).
Mirroring real-world settings	**Is desirable:** it increases our confidence that the findings will generalize to those settings. • e.g. using real managers; • approximating real work conditions in organizations;	**Is a disadvantage:** it creates unnecessary variation in the research setting. If the goal is to test general theory, representative samples are at best superfluous, since the goal is to demonstrate a process, not to directly draw conclusions about how managers will respond to particular conditions.
The issue of low external validity (a common critique of experiments)	If the goal of an experiment is to generalize to natural settings, then **it is appropriate to critique features of the setting that are unrealistic** or features of the sample that don't mirror those of the population to which results are to be generalized.	If the goal of an experiment is to test theory, a critique of the study as having low external validity is usually misguided, **it is not necessarily wrong, but it's irrelevant. It is critical to recreate only theoretically relevant elements of natural settings** to increase our understanding of social processes.

Experiments following both the applied and fundamental logic can make important theoretical contributions. For fundamental experiments, however, testing theory is the primary goal, and any generalization to natural settings happens through theory. For applied experiments, on the other hand, empirical generalization is the primary goal, although results of the studies may have relevant implications for theory.

THE QUESTION OF EXTERNAL VALIDITY

A common critique of experimental studies in organization studies is that they are low in external validity, that they are not generalizable to real-world settings (Aguinis and Bradley, 2014). This issue typically follows from either the artificiality of their settings or the idiosyncratic nature of their participant pools. However, whether external validity is a legitimate concern for researchers depends on the nature of the investigation. If the main goal of an experiment is to generalize to natural settings and to a specific population of actors (the applied research logic), then it is appropriate to critique features of the setting that are unrealistic or features of the sample that don't mirror those of the population to which results are to be generalized. For example, we could say that an audit study on employment discrimination is low in external validity if the sample for the study only included a narrow and idiosyncratic pool of undergraduate students.

On the other hand, if an experiment is designed with the primary purpose of testing a well-specified abstract theory (the fundamental research logic), whose application is not limited to a particular group of actors, such as board members, human resource managers or the jury, a critique of the study as having low external validity may be misguided. In other words, it's not so much that such a critique is wrong, but rather that it's irrelevant. Results from basic social science experiments that recreate only theoretically relevant elements of natural settings increase our understanding of fundamental social processes. They are not designed to directly generalize to a particular kind of natural setting (e.g. jury members or consumers); they generalize to theory, and then it is the theory that determines the scope of generalization (Kanazawa, 1999; Lucas, 2003b; Martin and Sell, 1979; Stolte et al., 2001; Zelditch, 1980). The primary advantage to testing theoretical explanations with experiments is precisely that they control for extraneous factors found in complex natural settings that may mask fundamental processes. Put differently, the goal of experiments following the fundamental research logic is to demonstrate a theorized process rather than to claim that a demonstrated relationship holds in some particular settings or populations. Once the process is demonstrated to operate in a manner consistent with what was theorized, then other types of research can investigate features of natural settings or types of people that exacerbate or mitigate the process that was demonstrated to operate in the artificial experimental setting.

It should be noted that the common demands from reviewers and editors for 'realism' of experimental settings can introduce a certain mismatch in experimental research in institutional theory by pushing researchers pursuing fundamental research objectives to adopt features of the applied research logic, to the detriment of (theoretical) generalizability of the findings. Below we review some notable studies in institutional theory and discuss compromises in logic the researchers faced in these studies.

Experimental research in institutional theory

Experimental research in institutional theory, although not yet mainstream, has already covered a number of important areas. The studies described below give us a glimpse into the types of contributions experiments can make to the institutional research agenda. They also serve as exemplars for possible experimental procedures that can be employed to study institutions in future investigations.

MICRO-LEVEL SOURCES OF INSTITUTIONAL PERSISTENCE

Zucker (1977) published a seminal piece on institutionalization and persistence of group norms. The study builds on Sherif's (1935) autokinetic situation, where participants assess the movement of a stationary point of light. In Zucker's study, participants joined a two-person group, and institutionalization was manipulated by either only telling them about the presence of the other group member, by additionally priming them with an organizational context, or by also introducing different organizational roles. Zucker (1977) investigated how increasing degrees of institutionalization elevate:

generational uniformity—the extent to which early responses are predictive of responses at later generations;

maintenance—the extent to which participants' responses in a follow-up experiment one week later resemble their responses in the first experiment, and;

resistance to change—the extent to which a confederate brought in at a later point would be able to alter participants' responses.

These experiments demonstrate that slight differences in the way the group situation was framed had significant effects on all three dependent variables: generational uniformity, maintenance, and resistance to change.

In another study of institutionalization that uses a fundamental research logic, Kurke (1988) looked at the adaptability of organizational strategy. Groups of three participants completed seven consecutive trial sets, with one group member leaving and one new member joining the group prior to each new set. Groups solved the common target game (Weick and Gilfillan, 1971), in which each subject contributed a number. The goal was that the sum of the three numbers equalled a target number announced by the experimenter. Participants were taught three strategies in this game: one generalist and two specialist strategies. As hypothesized, results showed that changes between strategies were less likely the less adaptation had occurred in the past and the more stable the environment was.

THE ROLE OF INSTITUTIONAL CONTEXT AND ITS CONSTITUTIVE ELEMENTS

Although experimental research methods are sometimes charged with ignoring the importance of social context (Tetlock, 1985), it is exactly experiments that best shed light on the role of contextual factors in social behaviour. Interestingly, a study of contextual factors does not necessarily entail the adoption of an applied research logic. For example, Lucas (2003a) used fundamental logic to study how institutionalization affects interactions in small group contexts. He sought to create a context in which a social group, in this case women, was institutionalized as leaders in a particular setting. A particular challenge was to create a belief among experimental participants, who were only in the lab for a short period of time, that a particular practice was institutionalized.

Lucas (2003a) manipulated institutionalization by using a 'training video' that participants (like new members of an organization) watched, ostensibly to familiarize themselves with the purpose of the organization. In the institutionalization condition, the narrator in the video discusses how female leaders are common and effective in many organizations these days. The video describes how companies have identified that women tend to possess just the sorts of skills necessary for leadership in modern organizations.

Lucas (2003a) also faced the task of determining how to measure the consequences of institutionalization. He did this by adopting a commonly used measure of social influence used in group processes research in sociology. After watching the video, participants were assigned a leader for their group (either female or male) and then responded to a set of ambiguous questions pertaining to various organizational scenarios. In each trial, participants made their initial choice first, then learned about the choices of their fellow group members, and ultimately indicated their final choice. Results showed that when female leadership was institutionalized, women in leadership positions were as influential as men in such positions.

Using fundamental logic, Hafenbrädl and Waeger (2017) primed participants with different institutionalized belief systems related to a fair market ideology. The manipulation was based on a sentence-unscrambling activity similar to the one used by Feinberg and Willer (2011). Following the manipulation, participants played a prediction game that captured participants' beliefs in the financial performance effects of corporate social responsibility (CSR). Results showed that participants who espouse a fair market ideology were more likely to believe in the business case for CSR, suggesting that actors closely tied to an institutionalized system will not look for and thus are unlikely to perceive alternatives to that system.

Sitkin et al. (1993) conducted a field experiment to explore how pharmacists resolve the dilemma of conflicting institutional logics. The experiment was performed using a mailed survey in which pharmacists were presented with a hypothetical scenario about a potentially serious drug interaction problem with a patient, and were asked to indicate what they would do, and to explain their decision. The explanations were coded as reflecting professional, managerial, or legal concerns. The study found that pharmacists provided professional accounts more frequently than managerial accounts, and that legal accounts were used least. Although the study was conducted using the applied research logic, its findings imply that individuals draw selectively on a variety of institutionalized norms to make their ambivalent actions appear more justifiable.

Using the fundamental logic approach, Glaser et al. (2017) provided experimental evidence that exposure to contextual cues associated with a particular institutional logic make people act upon that logic's implicit theory. Specifically, they used subliminal priming techniques to induce either a market or a family logic, and had participants write an essay about why they chose to attend college and to describe their future actions after college. Results revealed that a subject's exposure to a market (rather than a family) logic leads to a greater emphasis on material self-interest. In their second study, Glaser et al. (2017) had participants perform a word search task. Their findings showed that participants primed with a market logic put more effort into solving the task when facing a self-interest incentive (to earn money), whereas participants primed with a family logic invested more effort when facing an other-interest incentive (to help out).

ADOPTION AND DIFFUSION OF INSTITUTIONAL PRACTICES

To study the effects of institutional complexity on compliance to coercive pressures, Raaijmakers et al. (2015) employed an experimental vignette that describes a new law requiring 'digital walls' (a kind of web-connected play tool) to be introduced in all childcare centres. Participants were managers of childcare organizations in the Netherlands. Two independent variables were manipulated—support of a powerful constituent, and support of organization members for the mandated digital wall. The dependent variable captured the delay of intended compliance with the new law. The researchers found the shortest delay in the low complexity condition (high support from both powerful external constituents and organization members), and the longest delay in the high complexity condition (low support from both powerful external constituents and organization members). Although the study followed an applied logic in attempting to draw conclusions specifically about managers of childcare organizations, the research demonstrated an important social process with implications that might extend to other types of organizations.

In another experimental study, Lauer et al. (2008) used fundamental research logic to explore the effects of adoption of normative codes of conduct on cooperation. Subjects were presented with an option to contribute up to twenty tokens to a collective task that maximized the value for everyone. The framing of the task was manipulated in four out of five treatments. The baseline treatment provided no hints to a context. In the 'company treatment' the situation was framed as a firm context. The 'recruitment test treatment' additionally included a recruitment test as a typical tool used for personnel selection. In the 'code of conduct treatment' the firm context framing was augmented by the presentation of normative codes of conduct containing the explicit expectation to cooperate. The researchers found that the introduction of normative codes of conduct significantly boosted cooperation.

Contributing to knowledge of relevant micro-level predictors of responses to institutional pressures from the organizational environment, Schilke (2015) adopted a fundamental research logic and manipulated the extent to which decision makers identify with their organization (Doosje et al., 1995) to observe whether this manipulation affects the likelihood those individuals resist institutional pressures. Two mediators were investigated: the participants' level of situational confidence, and the attention they pay to environmental stimuli. Schilke (2015) also looked at the moderating influence of organizational status (Brewer et al., 1993) and identity type (using a novel manipulation of utilitarian versus normative identity).

Schilke (2015) defined three scope conditions that the experimental setup needed to satisfy. First, the experiment must establish a situation where participants would make ambiguous organizational decisions. Second, participants must be confronted with environmental pressures, with which they may choose to resist or comply. Finally, participants must be task-oriented and expect to be evaluated, increasing their motivation to perform the task well. To establish such a setting, Schilke's experiments were based on the standardized experimental situation that is commonly used in status characteristics research (Berger et al., 1977), slightly adapted to introduce an organizational decision-making setting. A key advantage of this approach is that it is amenable to computerization, which reduces experimenter effects, and provides greater control over timing (Molm, 2007).

To introduce relevant organizational features to the standardized experimental situation, the task required participants to complete twenty-five binary-choice trials in which they made decisions on behalf of a large flower shop. In each of the trials, they were first asked for their initial baseline response. Subsequently, they were shown the (ostensible) choice of another study participant, which was coded such that it created disagreement with the participant's initial response in the majority of the twenty-five trials, introducing mimetic pressures. Participants then had the option to either stick with their initial response (and resist mimetic pressures), or change their response to imitate the other study participant (and give in to mimetic pressures).

To avoid introducing potential confounding factors, organizational identification had to be manipulated without using interpersonal interactions between participants assigned to the same organization. To this end, Schilke (2015) followed Doosje et al. (1995) and Ellemers et al. (1997) by using a manipulation of organizational-identification that involved a series of steps, including similarity-based group assignment, voluntary group commitment, an intergroup reward allocation task, and feedback on a bogus group involvement score. While the mediator of 'confidence' was measured in the post-task questionnaire (based on items originally devised by Sniezek, 1992), the other mediator of 'attention to environmental stimuli' was captured behaviourally by measuring the time spent studying the information about the other participant's choice.

The population of the experiment comprised undergraduate students, who passed an attention screener and demonstrated sufficient comprehension. Results showed a positive link between organizational identification and resistance to environmental pressures. Mediation analyses revealed that both confidence and attention are key underlying processes explaining the identification-resistance effect. Follow-up experiments showed that the identification-resistance effect is particularly strong when organizational status is high (as opposed to low) and when the organizational identity is normative (as opposed to utilitarian). Furthermore, a final experiment suggested the findings not only apply to the context of mimetic pressures but to normative pressures as well.

LEGITIMACY ANTECEDENTS AND OUTCOMES

In institutional research, legitimacy can be defined as 'a generalized perception or assumption that the actions of an entity are desirable, proper, or appropriate within some socially constructed system of norms, values, beliefs, and definitions' (Suchman, 1995, p.574). The legitimacy construct is usually divided into two components: *propriety*, or 'an individual's own judgment of the extent to which an entity is appropriate for its social context' (Tost, 2011, p.689), and *validity*, or an apparent collective consensus about the appropriateness of an entity (Bitektine and Haack, 2015; Dornbusch and Scott, 1975). Validity has two sources—*authorization* by actors with power and authority, and *endorsement* by peers (Walker et al., 1986).

Legitimacy antecedents: Focusing on the propriety component of legitimacy, Elsbach (1994) conducted one of the few studies to identify antecedents to perceptions of organizational legitimacy. She used a vignette experiment, in which participants read a news story and press releases about a supermarket being boycotted because it sold beef raised with hormones. The 2 x 2 design manipulated the form of verbal accounts (acknowledgments or denials) and the content of the verbal accounts (references to institutional procedures or references to technical procedures). The dependent variable—perceived legitimacy of the supermarket—was captured with a twelve-item survey scale. The study found that legitimacy ratings were higher when acknowledgments (rather than denials) and references to institutional procedures (rather than technical procedures) were made. Moreover, there was a positive interaction between the two factors. Although the study used an applied research logic and introduced a number of specific contextual elements in the vignette, its findings are likely to generalize to other industrial contexts. However, as the author herself notes, the observations may be limited to moderately damaging events.

Legitimacy outcomes: In a series of experimental studies that used the fundamental research logic, Zelditch, Walker and colleagues (Walker et al., 1988; Walker et al., 1986; Zelditch and Walker, 1984) explored the effects of legitimacy on stability of authority. The researchers manipulated endorsement of an inequitable social structure (where one actor was given a substantial advantage to earn a monetary bonus in a task) by asking subjects before they performed ten trials of the task to rate the social structure, and then informing the subjects that others 'highly approve' of this structure. The bonus was designed to create pressure for the group members to seek changes to the task structure. The authors report that 38.4 per cent of structure change demands experienced in the unendorsed condition were prevented or delayed by endorsement. Thus, endorsement was shown to provide an important positive effect on stability of authority. Further investigations along these lines (Thomas et al., 1986; Walker et al., 1988) revealed that validity (authorization and endorsement) has a negative effect on mobilization for collective action.

HOW DO THOSE WHO 'OWN' LEGITIMACY BEHAVE?

Finally, it should be noted that legitimacy as property can be 'owned' not only by organizations and social structures, but also by individuals, positions, actions, and practices (Johnson, 2004; Zelditch, 2006). This opens up the possibility to explore the behaviour of (il)legitimate actors not only through observation of organizations and industries, but also using experimental methods. Thus, using the fundamental research logic, Lammers et al. (2008) demonstrated in four experiments that when subjects were primed to hold power illegitimately, they were less likely to act, had lower propensity to negotiate, and were more risk-averse. In other words, the effects of power on actors' propensity to act, negotiate, and take risks were all moderated by legitimacy.

Similarly, Haccoun and Klimoski (1975) manipulated legitimacy possessed by elected negotiators and observed that negotiators who were made to believe they were elected to their role due to their 'competence' perceived more latitude in their roles and felt more free to deviate from their team's position, but took longer to reach agreement. In contrast, negotiators that were made to believe that they were elected because of their 'amiability' (a less legitimate reason) seemed to adopt a compromising strategy—staying very loyal to their groups and not deviating.

Sitkin and George (2005) explored the behaviour of decision-makers using the applied logic. Graduate human resource (HR) management students were presented with a situation in which they had to make a decision that could threaten their legitimacy as HR managers—the issue of firing a well-performing employee due to his costly health condition. The researchers manipulated the nature of the employee's illness (associated or not associated with social stigma) to create a legitimacy-threatening condition. They found that when HR decision-makers perceive a potential threat to their legitimacy, they 'engage in behaviours that appear even-handed and above board' (p.324) by maintaining their reliance on formal decision criteria and at the same time relying less on informal criteria that could be seen as potentially less legitimate. The findings from these experimental studies provide micro-level evidence of an important effect of legitimacy on the behaviour of those who possess it, as well as the effect of a potential threat to an actor's legitimacy.

SUMMARY

This review of experimental studies addressing relationships and concepts at the heart of institutional theory shows a marked breadth of applicability of experimental methods. Experimental research has provided important insights into relevant micro-level sources of institutional persistence, the role of institutional context, adoption and diffusion of institutional practices, and legitimacy antecedents and outcomes, as well as the behaviour of those who 'own' legitimacy. Some of the studies described above have already become foundational works in institutional theory (e.g. Zucker, 1977; Elsbach, 1994), while others have yet to be fully integrated into the mainstream institutional tradition. The need to clarify causality and process in institutional research calls for further development of the experimental research agenda and the generation of more micro-level insights in order to support (or to challenge) prior macro-level theorizing.

Recommendations for experimental investigations in institutional theory

Designing sound experimental studies is not easy. In this section, we present some advice to institutional theory scholars who may have only limited experience in conducting experimental studies, but are interested in expanding their methodological toolbox in order to explore those elements of institutional theory that do not easily lend themselves to more traditional research methods.

CONSISTENCY IN RESEARCH LOGIC

We believe it is critical that researchers, along with editors and reviewers, strive for high consistency between study design and objective. That is, studies using an applied logic can only speak directly to a very confined setting, and any broader theoretical implications are necessarily speculative and in need of further investigation using a fundamental logic. On the other hand, studies using a fundamental logic have the potential to speak to institutional theory, but cannot provide direct recommendations and practical insight to a specific real-life setting. Notably, we do not mean to say that either the applied or the fundamental research logic is superior per se. Each logic has its distinct advantages and limitations, and it is critical that researchers are aware of these considerations and make an informed choice, given their objectives.

ONLINE VERSUS LABORATORY DATA COLLECTION

An important consideration when planning an experimental study is whether to collect data from participants in person (typically in an experimental laboratory or a classroom setting) or online. Web-based data collection platforms, such as Amazon's Mechanical Turk (MTurk), have become exceptionally popular for experiments in the social and behavioural sciences (Weinberg et al., 2014). Experimentalists will often design studies on platforms such as Qualtrics, recruit participants through MTurk, and then pay them each perhaps $3 for a study taking about 20 minutes. These platforms have made experimental data collection affordable, fast, and efficient. A researcher launching an experiment on MTurk requiring 200 or 300 participants can have data collection complete within a matter of hours, often at a fraction of the cost of running the experiment in a laboratory. Moreover, such data collection methods have become widely accepted in most major journals. Aguinis and Lawal (2012) discuss aspects related to sampling participants in online environments such as MTurk.

There are tradeoffs to the ease and efficiency of carrying out experimental studies online versus in a laboratory. The most significant of these is a loss of experimental control. Every experiment by definition involves random assignment to levels of an independent variable; this is referred to as manipulating the independent variable. The experimentalist's primary goal is to determine whether the manipulation of the independent variable has an effect, and so the stronger the manipulation the better. Experimentalists tend to favour manipulations that are powerful over ones that are cleverly subtle. Online experiments, with participants sitting at their computers at home, oftentimes just don't allow a researcher to construct manipulations with the power that can be possible in laboratory settings.

Notably, some designs that can be run in experimental laboratories simply cannot be carried out online. For example, it is difficult to have participants interact together in a group in an online experiment. In general, many types of deception are difficult to make believable in online studies. And, some common types of experimental manipulations and tasks (such as psychological priming and certain economic games) have become impossible to run effectively on MTurk because participants there have become so familiar with them. For all of these reasons, laboratory experiments are the gold standard for data quality, but as stated earlier, the efficiency and ease of online studies make them an attractive option for many experiments.

ATTENTION AND MANIPULATION CHECKS

A crucially important, but sometimes overlooked consideration for experiments is building checks into designs. Attention checks increase confidence that participants were actually paying attention and engaging with study materials (Berinsky et al., 2014). For example, if participants answer a long questionnaire, a question in the middle might say something like 'What is 2+2? Whatever the correct answer, please select 7.' Then, both 4 and 7 would be options in the question responses. If respondents answered 4, it would be an indication that they were not paying sufficient attention to study materials.

The most important checks tend to be manipulation checks. Many experiments include checks to ensure that manipulations of independent variables were indeed noticed by participants and manipulated what the researcher intended them to. For example, if a study had low and high legitimacy conditions, questionnaire items might ask participants to indicate their perceptions of legitimacy to see if their answers align with their assigned condition. Additionally, a question while debriefing might tell participants the conditions of the study and ask which one they received to ensure they were paying attention. Whatever types of checks a study includes, these checks increase confidence in reliability of findings.

We detailed here only a handful of the considerations that researchers face when designing experimental studies. Again, while we make an effort to lay out some of the most important considerations that researchers face when designing experimental studies, we refer the reader to several volumes dedicated to discussing the design of experiments for more details (for an excellent example, see Webster and Sell, 2014).

Conclusion

In this chapter, we have addressed some of the common concerns with respect to external validity of experimental studies and have drawn a distinction between *applied* experimental research, where external validity is an important concern, and *fundamental* studies, where experiments are used to test a theory, and thus other considerations, such as whether experimental operationalizations are effective and whether experimental variables faithfully reflect theoretical constructs, are of central concern. We have also discussed some notable examples of experimental studies in institutional theory, and provided recommendations on possible research designs that can enable institutional scholars to test many fundamental tenets of institutional theory.

Experiments hold the potential to generate interesting and relevant insights into processes driving institutions and organizations. Through their ability to isolate independent variables and determine causality, experiments have tremendous power to help us understand the social world. For this reason, the use of experimental studies is expanding in social and behavioural sciences, and new methods of data collection (such as online experiments; Aguinis and Lawal, 2012), as well as other approaches that take experiments out of the laboratory (such as natural experiments; Azoulay et al., 2010), have become more prevalent. Moving forward, we anticipate that this trend will increasingly spill over to institutional theory, and future experimental investigations will improve our understanding of micro- and cross-level processes—for instance, how and why individual actors behave under certain institutional conditions and how, in turn, their micro-level perceptions, judgments, and actions aggregate to produce a macro-level change. A related promising direction is the exploration of effects of shared cognitions, normative pressures and regulations on perceptions, judgments, and actions of individual actors. What factors contribute to micro-level diversity in perceptions, judgments, and actions? And what factors suppress this diversity, yielding the conformance and isomorphism commonly observed in highly institutionalized fields?

Experiments can also help us explore micro-level processes leading to macro-level institutional change. What prompts actors to form deviant judgments, to resist institutions, or engage in institutional work to change the norms and institutionalized practices in their field? How do these actors influence each other? How do their micro-level behaviours lead to the emergence of new institutions and the institutionalization of new practices? Such research can substantially advance our understanding of institutions and organizations, and can also shed light on the processes underlying institutional stability and change in organizational fields.

The implementation of this research agenda requires skill and expertise that is largely scattered across the community of management scholars. Given that experiments hold a great promise in exploring micro-level cognition and behaviour, we see great promise in cross-disciplinary collaborations, where the expertise of institutional scholars is complemented with hands-on experience of experimentalists from psychology, micro-sociology, and organizational behaviour. Such collaborations can help ensure reliable study designs while reinvigorating institutional theory research with high-quality and high-relevance empirical insight.

REFERENCES

Aguinis, H. and Bradley, K.J. (2014). 'Best practice recommendations for designing and implementing experimental vignette methodology studies', *Organizational Research Methods*, 17(4): 351–71.

Aguinis, H. and Lawal, S.O. (2012). 'Conducting field experiments using eLancing's natural environment', *Journal of Business Venturing*, 27(4): 493–505.

Alvesson, M. and Kärreman, D. (2011). 'Decolonializing discourse: critical reflections on organizational discourse analysis', *Human Relations*, 64(9): 1121–46.

Azoulay, P., Graff Zivin, J.S., and Wang, J. (2010). 'Superstar extinction', *Quarterly Journal of Economics*, 125(2): 549–89.

Barley, S.R. (2008). 'Coalface institutionalism.' In R. Greenwood, C. Oliver, and R. Suddaby (eds) *The Sage Handbook of Organizational Institutionalism*. Los Angeles, CA: Sage, pp.491–518.

Barney, J. and Felin, T. (2013). 'What are microfoundations?', *Academy of Management Perspectives*, 27(2): 138–55.

Battilana, J. (2006). 'Agency and institutions: the enabling role of individuals' social position', *Organization*, 13(5): 653–76.

Berger, J., Fisek, H.F., Norman, R.Z., and Zelditch, M. (1977). *Status Characteristics and Social Interaction: An Expectation-States Approach*. New York: Elsevier.

Berger, P.L. and Luckmann, T. (1966). *The Social Construction of Reality: A Treatise in the Sociology of Knowledge*. Garden City, NY: Doubleday.

Berinsky, A.J., Margolis, M.F., and Sances, M.W. (2014). 'Separating the shirkers from the workers? Making sure respondents pay attention on self-administered surveys', *American Journal of Political Science*, 58(3): 739–53.

Bitektine, A. (2011). 'Towards a theory of social judgments of organizations: the case of legitimacy, reputation, and status', *Academy of Management Review*, 36(1): 151–79.

Bitektine, A. and Haack, P. (2015). 'The macro and the micro of legitimacy: towards a multi-level theory of the legitimacy process', *Academy of Management Review*, 40(1): 49–75.

Brewer, M.B., Manzi, J.M., and Shaw, J.S. (1993). 'In-group identification as a function of depersonalization, distinctiveness, and status', *Psychological Science*, 4(2): 88–92.

Cook, K.S. and Emerson, R.M. (1978). 'Power, equity and commitment in exchange networks', *American Sociological Review*, 43(5): 721–39.

David, R. and Bitektine, A. (2009). 'The deinstitutionalization of institutional theory? Exploring divergent agendas in institutional research.' In D. Buchanan and A. Bryman (eds) *Handbook of Organizational Research Methods*. London: Sage, pp.160–75.

DiMaggio, P. (1988). 'Interest and agency in institutional theory.' In L.G. Zucker (ed.) *Institutional Patterns and Organizations: Culture and Environment*. Cambridge, MA: Ballinger, pp.3–22.

Doosje, B., Spears, R., and Koomen, W. (1995). 'When bad isn't all bad: strategic use of sample information in generalization and stereotyping', *Journal of Personality and Social Psychology*, 69(4): 642–55.

Dornbusch, S.M. and Scott, W.R. (1975). *Evaluation and the Exercise of Authority*. San Francisco, CA: Jossey-Bass Publishers.

Ellemers, N., Spears, R., and Doosje, B. (1997). 'Sticking together or falling apart: in-group identification as a psychological determinant of group commitment versus individual mobility', *Journal of Personality and Social Psychology*, 72(3): 617–26.

Elsbach, K.D. (1994). 'Managing organizational legitimacy in the California cattle industry: the construction and effectiveness of verbal accounts', *Administrative Science Quarterly*, 39(1): 57–88.

Feinberg, M. and Willer, R. (2011). 'Apocalypse soon?', *Psychological Science*, 22(1): 34–8.

Felin, T., Foss, N.J., and Ployhart, R.E. (2015). 'The Microfoundations Movement in Strategy and Organization Theory', *The Academy of Management Annals*, 9(1): 575–632.

George, E., Chattopadhyay, P., Sitkin, S.B., and Barden, J. (2006). 'Cognitive underpinnings of institutional persistence and change: a framing perspective', *Academy of Management Review*, 31(2): 347–65.

Glaser, V., Fast, N., Harmon, D. & Green, S. (2017). 'Institutional Frame-switching: Institutional Logics and Individual Action', *Research in the Sociology of Organizations*, 48A: 35–69.

Green, S.E. (2004). 'A rhetorical theory of diffusion', *Academy of Management Review*, 29(4): 653–69.

Greenwood, R. and Suddaby, R. (2006). 'Institutional entrepreneurship in mature fields: the big five accounting firms', *Academy of Management Journal*, 49(1): 27–48.

Haack, P., Pfarrer, M., and Scherer, A.G. (2014). 'Legitimacy-as-feeling: how affect leads to vertical legitimacy spillovers in transnational governance', *Journal of Management Studies*, 51(4): 634–66.

Haccoun, R.P. and Klimoski, R.J. (1975). 'Negotiator status and accountability source: a study of negotiator behaviour', *Organizational Behaviour and Human Performance*, 14(3): 342–59.

Hafenbrädl, S. and D. Waeger (2017). 'Ideology and the Microfoundations of CSR: Why Executives Believe in the Business Case for CSR and how this Affects their CSR Engagements', *Academy of Management Journal*, 60(4): 1582–606.

Hallett, T. (2010). 'The myth incarnate: recoupling processes, turmoil, and inhabited institutions in an urban elementary school', *American Sociological Review*, 75(1): 52–74.

Heath, C., and Sitkin, S.B. (2001). 'Big-B versus Big-O: what is organizational about organizational behaviour?', *Journal of Organizational Behaviour*, 22: 43–58.

Johnson, C. (2004). 'Introduction: legtimacy processes in organizations.' In C. Johnson (ed.) *Research in the Sociology of Organizations*, Vol. 22. Bingley, UK: Emerald Group, pp.1–24.

Kanazawa, S. (1999). 'Using laboratory experiments to test theories of corporate behaviour', *Rationality and Society*, 11(4): 443–61.

Kennedy, M.T. and Fiss, P.C. (2009). 'Institutionalization, framing, and diffusion: the logic of TQM adoption and implementation decisions among US hospitals', *Academy of Management Journal*, 52(5): 897–918.

Kerwin, J. and Shaffer, D.R. (1994). 'Mock jurors versus mock juries: the role of deliberations in reactions to inadmissible testimony', *Personality and Social Psychology Bulletin*, 20(2): 153–62.

Kurke, L.B. (1988). 'Does adaptation preclude adaptability? Strategy and performance.' In L.G. Zucker (ed.) *Institutional Patterns and Organizations: Culture and Environment*, Cambridge, MA: Ballinger, pp.199–222.

Lamin, A. and Zaheer, S. (2012). 'Wall Street vs. Main Street: firm strategies for defending legitimacy and their impact on different stakeholders', *Organization Science*, 23(1): 47–66.

Lammers, J., Galinsky, A.D., Gordijn, E.H., and Otten, S. (2008). 'Illegitimacy moderates the effects of power on approach', *Psychological Science*, 19(6): 558–64.

Lauer, T., Rockenbach, B., and Walgenbach, P. (2008). 'Not just hot air: normative codes of conduct induce cooperative behaviour', *Review of Managerial Science*, 2(3): 183–97.

Lucas, J.W. (2003a). 'Status processes and the institutionalization of women as leaders', *American Sociological Review*, 68(3): 464–80.

Lucas, J.W. (2003b). 'Theory testing, generalization, and the problem of external validity', *Sociological Theory*, 21: 236–53.

Maguire, S., Hardy, C., and Lawrence, T.B. (2004). 'Institutional entrepreneurship in emerging fields: HIV/AIDS treatment advocacy in Canada', *Academy of Management Journal*, 47(5): 657–79.

Martin, M.W. and Sell, J. (1979). 'The role of the experiment in the social sciences', *Sociological Quarterly*, 20(4): 581–90.

Molm, L.D. (2007). 'Experiments on exchange relations and exchange networks in sociology.' In M. Webster and J. Sell (eds) *Laboratory Experiments in the Social Sciences*. Amsterdam: Academic Press, pp.379–406.

Pager, D. (2003). 'The mark of a criminal record', *American Journal of Sociology*, 108(5): 937–75.

Phillips, N., and Oswick, C. (2012). 'Organizational discourse: domains, debates, and directions', *Academy of Management Annals*, 6(1): 435–81.

Powell, W.W. and Colyvas, J.A. (2008). 'Microfoundations of institutional theory.' In R. Greenwood, C. Oliver, K. Sahlin, and R. Suddaby (eds) *The Sage Handbook of Organizational Institutionalism*. London: Sage, pp.276–98.

Raaijmakers, A.G.M., Vermeulen, P.A.M., Meeus, M.T H., and Zietsma, C. (2015). 'I need time! Exploring pathways to compliance under institutional complexity', *Academy of Management Journal*, 58(1): 85–110.

Reimann, M., Zaichkowsky, J., Neuhaus, C., Bender, T., and Weber, B. (2010). 'Aesthetic package design: a behavioural, neural, and psychological investigation', *Journal of Consumer Psychology*, 20(4): 431–41.

Schilke, O. (2015). 'Organizational identity and resistance to environmental pressures', *Academy of Management Proceedings*, 2015(1): 1–6.

Schilke, O., Reimann, M., and Cook, K.S. (2013). 'Effect of relationship experience on trust recovery following a breach', *Proceedings of the National Academy of Sciences*, 110(38): 15236–41.

Schneiberg, M. and Clemens, E.S. (2006). 'The typical tools for the job: research strategies in institutional analysis', *Sociological Theory*, 24(3): 195–227.

Shaver, J.M. (1998). 'Accounting for endogeneity when assessing strategy performance: does entry mode choice affect FDI survival?', *Management Science*, 44(4): 571–85.

Sherif, M. (1935). 'A study of some social factors in perception', *Archives of Psychology*, 187: 1–60.

Sitkin, S. and George, E. (2005). 'Managerial trust-building through the use of legitimating formal and informal control mechanisms', *International Sociology*, 20(3): 307–38.

Sitkin, S.B., Sutcliffe, K.M., and Reed, G.L. (1993). 'Prescriptions for justice: using social accounts to legitimate the exercise of professional control', *Social Justice Research*, 6(1): 87–111.

Sniezek, J.A. (1992). 'Groups under uncertainty: an examination of confidence in group decision making', *Organizational Behaviour and Human Decision Processes*, 52(1): 124–55.

Stolte, J.F., Fine, G.A., and Cook, K.S. (2001). 'Sociological miniaturism: seeing the big through the small in social psychology', *Annual Review of Sociology*, 27: 387–413.

Suchman, M.C. (1995). 'Managing legitimacy: strategic and institutional approaches.' *Academy of Management Review*, 20(3): 571–610.

Tetlock, P.E. (1985). 'Accountability: the neglected social context of judgment and choice', *Research in Organizational Behaviour*, 7(1): 297–332.

Thomas, G.M., Walker, H.A., and Zelditch, M. (1986). 'Legitimacy and collective action', *Social Forces*, 65(2): 378–404.

Thornton, P.H., Ocasio, W., and Lounsbury, M. (2012). *The Institutional Logic Perspective: A New Approach to Culture, Structure and Process*. Oxford: Oxford University Press.

Tost, L.P. (2011). 'An integrative model of legitimacy judgments', *Academy of Management Review*, 36(4): 686–710.

Walker, H.A., Thomas, G.M., and Zelditch, M. (1986). 'Legitimation, endorsement, and stability', *Social Forces*, 64(3): 620–43.

Walker, H.A., Rogers, L., and Zelditch, M. (1988). 'Legitimacy and collective action: a research note', *Social Forces*, 67(1): 216–28.

Webster, M. and Sell, J. (2014). *Laboratory Experiments in the Social Sciences*. Second edition. London: Elsevier.

Weick, K.E. and Gilfillan, D.P. (1971). 'Fate of arbitrary traditions in a laboratory microculture', *Journal of Personality and Social Psychology*, 17(2): 179–91.

Weinberg, J.D., Freese, J., and McElhattan, D. (2014). 'Comparing data characteristics and results of an online factorial survey between a population-based and a crowdsource-recruited sample', *Sociological Science*, 1: 292–310.

Yin, R. (2003). *Case Study Research: Design and Methods*. Third edition. Thousand Oaks, CA: Sage.

Yin, R. (2010). 'Analytic generalization.' In A.J. Mills, G. Durepos, and E. Wiebe (eds) *Encyclopedia of Case Study Research*. Thousand Oaks, CA: Sage, pp.21–3.

Zelditch, M. (1980). 'Can you really study an army in a laboratory?' In A. Etzioni and E.W. Lehman (eds) *A Sociological Reader on Complex Organizations*. Third edition. New York: Holt, Rinehart, and Winston.

Zelditch, M. (2006). 'Legitimacy theory.' In P.J. Burke (ed.) *Contemporary Social Psychological Theories*. Stanford, CA: Stanford University Press, pp.324–52.

Zelditch, M. and Walker, H.A. (1984). 'Legitimacy and the stability of authority.' *Advances in Group Processes*, 1: 1–25.

Zucker, L.G. (1977). 'The role of institutionalization in cultural persistence', *American Sociological Review*, 42: 726–43.

Zucker, L.G. 1991. 'Postscript: microfoundations of institutional thought.' In W.W. Powell and P. DiMaggio (eds) *The New Institutionalism in Organizational Analysis*, pp.103–6. Chicago, IL: University of Chicago Press.

9 Beyond one voice

Co-constructed analytic auto-ethnography

Steve Kempster and Ken Parry

Auto-ethnography: so much more than 'confessional tales'

This chapter explores analytic auto-ethnography and how it can be used to examine organizational subjects that are difficult to access through traditional qualitative and quantitative approaches. Informed by a critical realist narrative, we outline how analytic auto-ethnography seeks to go beyond an individual's socially constructed experience by testing to see if the insights of experience resonate with the encounters of people who have been through similar experiences. Through examining the inter-related phenomena of emotional labour and authenticity in leadership practice, the chapter provides the detail of undertaking analytic auto-ethnographic research.

There are many topics in organization and management research that have been difficult to research. Examples include sexual harassment, bullying, socialized immoral practices, ethical dilemmas, and emotion management. The method of auto-ethnography that sits at the very margins of convention and acceptability provides a significant opportunity to develop social theory of these difficult to reach but important phenomena. However, the perceived limitations of auto-ethnography—most notably the 'n' of one—have severely limited its acceptability as a method (Delamont, 2007; Anderson and Austin, 2012). The purpose of this chapter is to address concerns and limitations through outlining an approach to analytic auto-ethnography (Anderson, 2006) that draws on a critical realist perspective and utilizes a co-constructed research partnership. Analytic co-constructed auto-ethnography goes beyond the individual's voice to develop a co-constructed explanation of causal influences that are suggested to have shaped phenomenon manifestation. Rooted in a realist tradition, the explanation needs to be tested for resonance in other contexts. To do this we draw upon Parry and Kempster's (2014) use of the graphic scale (Shamir and Kark, 2004) to measure such resonance. The approach is illustrated with a case example in which a hospital manager was faced with the challenging responsibility of closing a hospital ward.

Anderson's (2006) analytic auto-ethnography (AE) is similar and very dissimilar to aesthetic (also referred to as 'evocative') auto-ethnographic research in the sense that it seeks to illuminate personal experience in order to understand cultural experience by 'describ[ing] a story of experience—how it is used, understood, and responded to for and by us and others' (Ellis et al., 2011, p.282). It provides the opportunity to open up avenues of research that would otherwise have been overlooked or assumed as not meaningful knowledge as a result of the 'unorthodox' non-canonical approaches (ibid., p.273). It allows us to stand in the shoes of the respondent to understand what it is like to experience the phenomenon under consideration. And it offers the potential for social change (Ellis et al., 2011) through giving important emphasis to 'understanding subjective meanings as the basis of social action' (Rees and Gatenby, 2014, p.135). However, the dissimilarity is quite profound. Aesthetic auto-ethnography is rooted in post-structural assumptions and thus puts limitations on theory development. It does not seek to offer up the account as useful to explain phenomenon emergence in other contexts. In contrast, analytic auto-ethnography, which draws from a long ethnographic realist tradition, seeks to go beyond the boundary of insight and understanding with a central purpose 'directed toward theoretic development, refinement and extension' (Anderson, 2006, p.387). The realist orientation to analytic auto-ethnography seeks to explain as well as describe social phenomena (Rees and Gatenby, 2014, p.132). Questions that emerge from a realist perspective regarding external validity might reflect: How does the account describe social processes and structural conditions? Does the explanation seem plausible? Does it resonate with others by capturing something of social structures that are present and shaping lived experience of a particular phenomenon? How are these social processes and social structures occurring in other contexts?

For realist (and critical realist) auto-ethnographers the insights from one person's lived experience of a phenomenon is but the start of the research journey. Anderson (2006, p.386) gives voice to the necessity for auto-ethnographic work to engage with others, to triangulate, to test, to develop or to refine explanations of social processes. He helpfully suggests (p.387) the need for auto-ethnography to embrace a fundamental tenet of realist social science to 'use empirical data to gain insight into some broader set of social phenomena'. It is the insight into social phenomena that is why auto-ethnographic research is so very useful to social science and in particular to management studies. Insights from one autoethnography can open up rich avenues of discovery. The contribution this chapter seeks to offer is two-fold. First, it develops the potential of mixed methods in undertaking analytic auto-ethnography to examine organizational phenomena that have been hard to reach through traditional methods. Second, it moves auto-ethnography from the margins of acceptability, to become a useful and complementary addition to organization and management research.

The role of critical realism

The approach we outline is set within a critical realist frame. We are not suggesting that critical realism is the only frame through which analytic auto-ethnography can be undertaken. However, critical realism does provide a philosophical foundation for seeking external validity through testing emerging insights from an auto-ethnographic account, and embracing quantitative techniques to support this process alongside the qualitative. For critical realists, auto-ethnography is merely an approach, or even a technique, that can help us to understand and explain a social phenomenon. It assumes all social theory is subject to revision because social practice and social processes undergo continual emergence and development and their manifestation is situationally contingent. Causes shaping such manifestation are affected by a combination of transitive (aspects like meanings, or roles, or people's ambitions) and intransitive (aspects like patriarchy, or perhaps national or even organizational culture) causal influences (Sayer, 1992). Yet such causes can be difficult to observe (particularly intransitive), and their effects are difficult to predict. In essence, a critical realist orientation seeks contingent explanation of social processes which is offered up for testing.

Analytic auto-ethnography is complementary to a critical realist perspective in four ways. First, it allows exploration of phenomena which are difficult to reach. The *sine qua non* of auto-ethnography is a contextualized and reflexive in-depth examination of an individual's experience. This approach may give access to underlying structures and influences that previous approaches have had limited success in revealing as a consequence of not plumbing the depths of social experience offered in the interrogative approach of co-constructed autoethnographic research (more on co-construction shortly). Second, it overtly seeks a context-based explanation of social process manifestation. Third, it offers up a theoretical generalization to be tested in other contexts. Fourth, that such testing is for degree of plausibility and resonance; does the explanation of one context connect with others' experiences?

We begin by first suggesting how analytic auto-ethnography is enhanced through critical realism and the notion of co-construction. The importance is to provide the philosophical argument for a mixed methods approach. Second, we briefly describe the case phenomenon being used to illustrate the opportunity for a mixed method analytic auto-ethnography. Third, we provide a detailed approach outlining a set of steps that are applied to the case research from which themes are generated to form an explanation of the social processes of emotional labour and authenticity in leadership practice. Emotional labour reflects the management of emotions displayed which may not be the same as felt emotions. Fourth, we outline the testing phase. This seeks to measure the degree of resonance and identification of the suggested explanations with other practising managers' experiences of emotional labour and authenticity. Fifth, we critique the challenges and opportunities of undertaking analytic auto-ethnographic research in organization and management research through Delamont's (2007) six criticisms of auto-ethnography. Through addressing these criticisms, we suggest auto-ethnography can move from being prominently 'confessional tales' to becoming insightful, relevant, and rigorous as a research approach.

Critical realism and co-constructed analytic auto-ethnography

> What matters is the way in which the story enables the reader to enter the subjective world of the teller—to see the world from her or his point of view, even if this world does not 'match reality' (Plummer, 2001, p.401).

Here lies the separation between 'traditional' aesthetic (or evocative) auto-ethnography, and analytic auto-ethnography. Of importance is the ontological orientation to the notion of reality. Aesthetic and evocative based research are rooted in a constructionist frame—understanding the experience, to give felt insight, and perhaps a shared understanding and appreciation. External validity is problematic due to the assumption of multiple realities; one person's reality is just that—interesting and illuminating—and gives insight to other people's sense-making of their realities. In contrast, an analytic orientation assumes an independent reality to which sense experience provides an interpretation and hopefully understanding of reality. The purpose of analytic auto-ethnography is to offer up insights, explanations and theories of social reality (Anderson, 2006). One description of reality offers a perspective, but this is not sufficient; there is the necessity to pursue other perspectives, to test and triangulate, to develop and extend the explanation of the phenomenon. As Anderson asserts, this is not new, but rather is a reinstatement of ethnographic endeavour: 'The defining characteristic of analytic social science is to use empirical data to gain insight into some broader set of social phenomena than those provided by the data themselves' (2006, p.387). This characteristic captures a realist ethnographic project and has strong resonance with critical realism—the notion of going beyond empirical data in theoretical exposition. Critical realism has much to offer (auto-)ethnographers seeking to theorize (Rees and Gatenby, 2014). Barron (2013) usefully points to the opportunities critical realism offers to examining and theorizing on the causes shaping empirical experience.

A critical realist ontological perspective assumes a stratified reality (Bhaskar, 1978), reflected in sense experience, events and the notion of a deep reality (Fleetwood, 2004). There is a malleable interplay of the deep reality with events and sense experience. Archer's work (1995, 2000) explores the interplay of structure and agency: the role of the individual in sustaining structures (morphostasis) and also evolving structures (morphogenesis), while at the same time structures shape individual activity. As Searle (1995, p.190) comments, 'we do not "create" social structure, we reproduce and transform it', the consequence of which is that 'a socially constructed reality presupposes a *non*-socially constructed reality'. Auto-ethnographic accounts provide an explicit process for illuminating such structure–agency interplay. The deep reality is seen to reflect causal powers that may operate unnoticed to agents. Their impact in generating structures that shape agency activity may not always be in play as the influence is contingent on other causal powers present in a particular context. In this way, critical realists seek to give prominence to specifying causal powers (often described as mechanisms: Bhaskar, 1978), the context in which this occurs, and the consequential outcomes (Pawson and Tilley, 1997).

In the process of identifying causal powers, attention is given to the entities from which such powers emanate, including agents, the roles they occupy, and the historic social practices they draw from (Reed, 2005). Rees and Gatenby (2014, p.141) provide a useful set of categories that enable examination of agency-structure interaction. Examples include emails, computers, activities of work, buildings, away-days, routines and cycles, feelings, and symbols such as uniforms. Further in the chapter we will explore a case example where the social processes of leadership are being impacted by desires for authenticity from the leader and followers, and emotional labour expectations of followers, line managers and more broadly the organization. This case situation will be shown to be situated in a configuration of other causal powers that may or may not have impact dependent on the context.

Thus an emergent reality occurs generated from a configuration of causal powers drawn from entities (Fleetwood, 2004). So, critical realist analytic auto-ethnography would seek to develop an explanation of social processes occurring in a specific context. There would be an assumption that empirical observations of experience *may not* be able to recognize underlying causal influences impacting on the reality they have experienced (Bhaskar, 1978). We suggest that two consequences are significant. First, the need for assistance to explore the experience—co-construction of an auto-ethnographic account. Second, that any explanation is offered to others who may have had a similar experience of the phenomenon under examination—that is seeking external validity by testing whether the ideas resonate.

CO-CONSTRUCTED ANALYTIC AUTO-ETHNOGRAPHY

Both Anderson (2006) and Barron (2013) speak of the need for reflexivity in the research process, to plumb the depths of the everyday practices researchers are a part of. To be both practitioners and researchers is a rare thing. It is unsurprising that published auto-ethnographic accounts tend to be from academics examining such topics as a tool for reflexive learning (boyd, 2008), exploring the potential of the method to examine everyday organizational phenomena (Greiner, 2015), or even pastimes, such as the experience of skydiving (Anderson and Austin, 2012).

There are very few managers exploring their practice. The work of Kempster and Stewart (2010) is helpful and an instructive exception. As a partnership of an academic and a senior manager, together they explore the senior manager's three-month journey learning to develop a new identity, a chief operating officer. It is overtly an analytic auto-ethnography. It examines the theoretical concept of situated curriculum, and seeks to develop this theory with regard to understanding processes of leader becoming. The significance of this example is the notion of co-constructed auto-ethnography (Parry and Boyle, 2009). Kempster and Stewart highlight the 'interrogating' role undertaken by the academic partner—in this instance Steve. He pursued a research agenda to understand more about situated curriculum in management learning. Steve probed deeply into Stewart's activities, creating a hyper-reflexive sensitivity in his research partner. The reflexive nature allowed tacit awareness to be expressed and for the underlying assumptions to be exposed. Drawing on Cunliffe's (2002) notion of reflexive dialogue Kempster and Stewart (2010, p.217) assert, rightly in our judgement, that it would be deeply problematic for a practitioner alone to engage in such reflexive examination.

Anderson (2006) sees the necessity of analytic reflexivity as a fundamental dynamic; but he does not speak of how this might occur for management practitioners. The process of co-construction as reflexive dialogue enables an exploration of social reality that is difficult to reveal (Kempster and Parry, 2011). It is, we suggest, an important element for analytic auto-ethnography in order to become a method to be used on complex organizational topics that have been difficult to access and gain rich depth. Yet despite the co-constructed cross-examination, the tests and probes for respondent triangulation, and the emergence of a 'truthful' account, it remains but one account of social reality. We still have the need, as Anderson (2006, p.385) puts it, to have 'dialogue with informants beyond self', or beyond the co-constructed partnership.

TESTING OF IDEAS

The explanation or theoretical generalization that emerges from the co-constructed analytic auto-ethnography is more than an individual's sense of the experience. It has been questioned, probed, and tested for plausibility with the research partner. It seems highly unlikely that an explanation of the phenomenon under examination would be offered that seems implausible to the research partner. The probing and questioning of the reflexive dialogue is a form of testing that generates an explanation that has a sense of practical adequacy; an explanation 'about the world and about the results of our actions which are actually realized' (Sayer, 1992, p.69). However, from a critical realist perspective, the notion of a configuration of generative influences (common to many contexts) combines with context-based influences. Thus the explanation offered is contextual and contingent.

An emerging co-constructed auto-ethnographic explanation should be tested with others from different contexts; not for replication, as there is a given assumption of contingent contextual variation. What we suggest is a testing for resonance and plausibility; to test to see whether the generative influences appear to be present and having an effect, alongside the contextual influences. Research approaches could be further qualitative methods, or indeed quantitative. We emphasize that if a mixed methods approach is chosen this should not negate contextual sensitivity—appreciation for contextual variation is fundamental. So a quantitative survey (akin to the example used later) would provide opportunity for respondents to comment; seeking to allow respondents to explain the offered measure of resonance and plausibility of the co-constructed auto-ethnographic account.

The testing is not the final phase. Rather we suggest it should open up opportunity for further in-depth ethnographic research for theory development to be interpretively rich (Greiner, 2015, p.345). The quantitative testing provides a sense of reassurance that the orientation of emerging theory building does capture *something* of the reality that respondents are experiencing. However, it is only *something* of the reality. The stratified nature of reality and the underlying influences are difficult to reveal. If testing provides such reassurance of resonance then in-depth qualitative research would necessarily follow to understand and explain contextual variation, from which subsequent testing may follow. Auto-ethnography can be but a first step of a journey of research. This is a journey in which mixed methods is arguably a necessary approach. In this way, theory development building from co-constructed analytic auto-ethnography seeks to explain plausibly a specific outcome that has potential plausible reach in other contexts—not replication as generalization, but rather offering generative influences that may underlie a phenomenon's manifestation on a contingent basis.

To summarize, 'analytic auto-ethnography is grounded in self-experience but reaches beyond it as well' (Anderson, 2006, p.386). It seeks to 'reach beyond' and test whether the account evokes a sense of identification that 'the experience described is life-like, believable, and possible' (Ellis and Bochner, 2006, p.751). In the case example, we shall explore whether senior managers drawn from a similar context recognize, resonate and see plausible David's leadership experience of addressing emotional labour and authenticity.

The critical realist orientation thus seeks to develop explanations from one setting to be tested in other settings, the goal being to suggest a plausible explanation for phenomena emergence (Kempster and Parry, 2011). We now move to the case example, the closing of a hospital ward.

EMOTIONAL LABOUR AND AUTHENTICITY IN THE PRACTICE OF LEADERSHIP

The 'absence of auto-ethnography from practising managers' (Kempster and Stewart, 2010, p.206) reflects issues of confidentiality and ethical considerations; but it also arises because such research fundamentally relies on practitioners being able to take a hyper-reflexive stance and provide deep self-disclosure: 'a conscious experiencing of the self as both inquirer and respondent, as teacher and learner, [...] coming to know the self within the process of research' (Kempster and Stewart, 2010, p.210). The case research enables such respondent reflexivity through the use of co-constructed analytic auto-ethnography.

David (pseudonym) is a senior manager implementing the closure of a hospital ward. The phenomenon being examined in this experience is how emotional labour impacts on the manager's authenticity in the practice of leading. The scope of this chapter does not allow for a full discussion on extant understanding regarding the phenomenon of emotional labour. We limit this discussion to defining it, creating the connectivity to authenticity in leadership, and highlighting the limitations of research thus far being able to examine these related phenomena.

Emotional labour is broadly seen as a process by which employees (including managers: Humphrey et al., 2008) are expected to manage their feelings in line with organizational display rules (Hochschild, 1983). Two aspects of emotional labour are of significance: surface acting and emotional dissonance. Surface acting is seen as 'deliberate emotional displays that are intended to deceive other persons about what the actor actually feels' (Gardner et al., 2009, p.471) that can generate feelings of inauthenticity when 'faking in bad faith' (Humphrey, 2013, p.96). Emotional dissonance is connected to surface acting and becomes manifest when there is a pronounced disjuncture between felt and displayed emotion resulting in a diminished sense of self-worth (Ashforth and Humphrey, 1993).

Research has shown that professional roles can help to mitigate felt inauthenticity and limit emotional dissonance that emerges through surface acting (Brotheridge and Grandey, 2002)—a sense of 'faking in good faith' (Humphrey et al., 2015). However, what is not known is how this plays out at the level of leadership lived experience. For example, how does someone leading a challenging activity manage emotional demands of expected performativity when they are experiencing doubts of achieving the expected outcome?

Presently we know very little of the complex and paradoxical relationship between authentic leadership and emotion management from a leadership practitioner's perspective (Smollan and Parry, 2011).

There are four reasons for this paradoxical relationship. The first reason is that the predominant nomothetic research approaches to authentic leadership skew orientation away from contextualized qualitative research—therefore not allowing the lives and realities of management practitioners to inform management research (Watson, 2011; Van Maanen, 2011). Second, within mainstream authentic leadership research there are severe limitations of access to observe everyday practices of leadership. The third reason is the ethical dilemmas of revealing insights of practice. The fourth reason is the difficulty of enabling managers to comment on practices that they either wish to keep hidden from others; or that they are not aware of; or which are prominently tacit in nature and cannot be expressed to reveal the depth of practice. Speaking about emotional labour and research with practising managers, Turnbull (2013, p.153) comments that it 'is a phenomenon that few practicing managers feel able to discuss, and yet it continues to be of vital importance for our understanding of organizations'.

THE CASE EXAMPLE

The '*universal* can be found in the particular' (Van Maanen, 2011, p.229). The particular revealed in this auto-ethnographic account does not necessarily reflect other contexts; it is an insight into what may be occurring. Analytic auto-ethnography encourages going beyond the particular to see how this insight may speak to broader possible 'universal' social processes at play. David has been tasked with implementing the closure of a ward. The case examines his reflections of his emotional displays engaging with his colleagues over a period of two weeks. The context is explained up front.

The period that led up to the closure of the ward points to many workload staffing problems generated from high absences through sickness. However, bed capacities at this moment throughout the hospital were good, operational indicators suggested that pressures in the 'system' were not exceptional, and performance leading up to the ward closure was acceptable. Following a period of major investment through public–private funding initiatives, a change of government and government policy had moved to seeking efficiencies by shifting resources into community-based services. This configuration of influences on the hospital provides a context that was exercising senior management's strategic thinking—in particular, how to address the crisis in the hospital budget. How could they reduce expenditure consumed by inpatient care, notably hospital wards? How should they respond to the policy movement away from the hospital and towards outpatient community services, that was having such an impact on hospital income? These questions in response to the operational details at a particular moment led to the difficult strategic decision to close a ward.

Co-constructed analytic auto-ethnography and mixed methods research

THE RESEARCH PROCESS

There is the difficulty of exploring underlying influences that may not be readily apparent to individuals undertaking auto-ethnography. There are the associated challenges of expressing tacit awareness. There are also the challenges of authenticity and self-censorship, in particular in undertaking emotion research (Sturdy, 2003) associated with such topics as bullying, harassment, and in this case faking emotions. There is a sense of what Ellis and Bochner (2006, p.40) describe as the 'vulnerable author', which can become manifest in issues of balancing self-protection and protecting the organization (Wall, 2008). There is also the issue of modesty or alternatively of self-aggrandizement.

The role of the partner in the co-constructed auto-ethnography is to be supportive of these issues, yet also seeking to pursue exploration more deeply into the social practices and structures shaping experiences and activity. In this way, the research partner enables a construction of the experience that addresses self-censorship in a supportive and ethical manner. Through the co-construction process the endeavour is to establish an account of the experience that is truthful and authentic; but also provides a glimpse of the social reality that David has been part of. The aim is to describe enough of the *'particular'* that it may grasp something of the *'universal'* (Van Maanen, 2011). The endeavour is also to construct an explanation of emotional labour and authenticity drawn from David's experience. The second stage of the research is the testing of this 'particular' explanation with other managers. To ask the questions: Does this account and its explanation seem plausible? Does it resonate with the experience of other managers?

FROM 'CO-CONSTRUCTED' TO 'ANALYTIC'

Anderson's (2006) helpful exposition of analytic auto-ethnography provides a useful foundation to engage in undertaking such research. However, there is little detail contained therein, or indeed elsewhere, on how to implement analytic auto-ethnography. Accordingly, we outline the steps we have developed and used in our case study research. In major part we draw on Kempster and Stewart's (2010) guidance. The steps are outlined in Table 9.1.

With this chapter being an examination of methods, and not emotional labour, we do not lay out here the full account of David (interrogated by Steve). Rather we summarize the emerging three themes prominent in the explanation of David's experience of addressing emotional labour and authenticity in his leadership practice. We give illustrations of his emotional journey over the two-week period after the closure of the ward.

Table 9.1 Analytic auto-ethnography

process	activity	commentary
1 empirical grounding	Scrutiny of empirical data, specifically: emails, minutes, meeting notes documents, and diary reflections.	David, the 'ethno' and the 'graphy' as the spatial and temporal aspects associated with closing Ward X.
2 sensemaking as dialogue with the data	Continuous and iterative critical reflection of the data through applying extant theory of emotional labour and authentic leadership to reveal themes of social processes of the experience.	Going beyond individual reflections on experience through dialogue (Anderson, 2006, p.386) with [first author] to probe into taken-for-granted assumptions through applying extant theory. Through much iterative back-and-forth examination of empirical data an emergent set of themes, a draft auto-ethnographic account, and a social process was developed.
3 validating	Independent scrutiny to test emergent themes in order to reach beyond self-experience.	Prior to theorizing [third author] examined the emerging themes from perspective of being most conversant with emotional labour in the context of leadership.
4 crafting an account of the social experience	A combination of an aesthetic narrative alongside a theoretical interpretation.	The continual dynamic of writes and rewrites of the account achieved a two-fold need for: first, an aesthetic narrative that truthfully captures the social process of what occurred; second, a theoretical interpretation of the social process.
5 testing the resonance of the auto-ethnographic account with other managers	Middle managers from a similar context read the account and indicated the degree of resonance using Shamir and Kark's (2004) graphic rating scale against three aspects: activities undertaken; emotions expressed; and mitigation of felt inauthenticity.	Seeking to understand whether the suggested theorizing has reach to contexts beyond the auto-ethnographic account.In this context to see whether leadership experiences of other managers resonate with David's account. Not to (dis)prove but rather to measure perceptions of identification and resonance.

CLOSING WARD: IMPACT OF EMOTIONAL LABOUR ON AUTHENTIC LEADERSHIP PRACTICE

David's biggest single revelation was that emotional labour and reconciling emotional dissonance was a 'way of life for him' as a leader. It underpinned almost all of the interactions with colleagues at work, in one way or another (see also Lewis, 2008; Gardner et al., 2009; Bryant and Wolfram Cox, 2014) almost regardless of the events of the day. In the context of closing Ward X emotional labour was certainly ever-present. Drawing from the examination of David's experience we suggest an explanation of the phenomenon of emotional labour and authenticity occurring within leadership practice as follows:

For David, the emotional labour is generated through a combination of organizational display rules and professional display rules, within which there are learned expectations from himself and from followers of appropriate emotions. Thus the emotional labour generated is a continual process of seeking to present authentic emotions, yet being susceptible to inauthenticity through surface acting (e.g. arising from uncertainty as to whether the ward will reopen). The consequence of the emergent surface acting leads to emotional dissonance, and to the exhaustion that David reports. Importantly though, David's experience also points to this dissonance being mitigated by three aspects. First, an authentic commitment to the organizational purpose. Second, and aligned with the first, the necessity for the closure of the ward. Third, that managing his emotional performance is simply part of the role as a manager/leader.

Considering emotional labour and authenticity in ongoing leadership practice, David's account highlights an important issue. Purpose (organizational and task) and alignment with his role as a leader help to mitigate felt inauthenticity emerging from the seemingly inevitable requirement to perform surface acting. So, how plausible is this emerging explanation drawn from a single account? To what extent does David's narrative of closing Ward X resonate with other managers? It is to these questions we turn next.

TESTING FOR THEORY RESONANCE

Here we summarize the approach to testing resonance using the Single Item Graphic Scale (Shamir and Kark, 2004)—step 5 in Table 9.1. This seeks to measure perception of separateness through a visual representation of simi-larity between constructs while simultaneously quantifying them (Parry and Kempster, 2014, p.28). The sample is constituted from a cohort of fifty middle managers from an acute hospital on a leadership development programme. The process we undertook followed a series of stages. First, the managers were asked to read David's auto-ethnographic account prior to arrival at the workshop. Second, at the workshop the managers were introduced to the notion of emotional labour. Third, using Shamir and Kirk's instrument, we asked the managers to compare their own experiences against that of David closing the ward. The three questions enabled us to understand which aspects resonated and the degree of such resonance. For example, someone might identify with the activity and not the emotions expressed or the need for mitigating emotional dissonance. The results of the graphic rating scales are shown in Table 9.2 and Figure 9.1.

The sample results indicate a perception of strong resonance with David's experience in terms of emotions expressed and the three causes that helped him to mitigate felt inauthenticity—commitment to purpose, commitment to task, and alignment to his role as a manager/leader. This was most noticeable with regard to questions 2 and 3. There is a degree of resonance with question 1, but this is weaker. Qualitative comments suggest that such strategic change activity as closing a ward was much less prevalent in the sample.

Table 9.2 Degree of perceptual identification with the auto-ethnographic account*

perception of resonance with David's account	n	mode	mean: scale 1 to 7	standard deviation	skewness	kurtosis
task	47	7	4.60	1.77	−0.35	−1.14
emotions	50	5	5.23	1.47	−0.37	−0.69
explanation of mitigating emotional dissonance	49	6	5.42	1.25	−0.28	−0.87

* All figures are distributed normally, with neither significant skewness nor kurtosis.

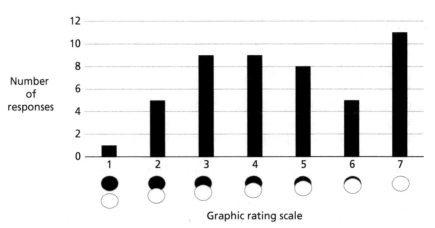

Que 1: To lead the implementation of necessary change.
Please select the number that reflects your identification with the type of task David undertook compared to your own experience

Graphic rating scale

Figure 9.1 Data from graphic rating scales

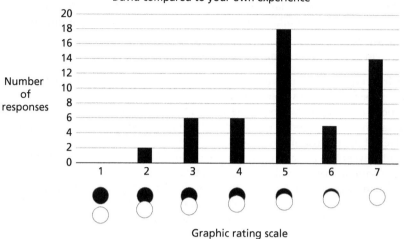

Que 2: Emotions displayed when undertaking this activity. Please select the number that reflects your identification with the emotions experienced by David compared to your own experience

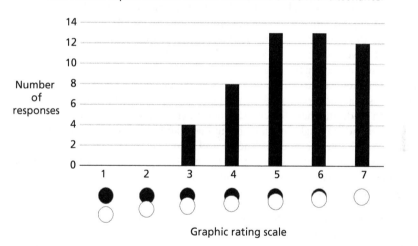

Que 3: Limiting emotional inauthenticity by aligning with purpose and role in undertaking the task. Please select the number that reflects your identification with David's explanation of how he limited his emotional dissonance.

Figure 9.1 Continued

An important critical realist aspect here is that we are not exploring a population; rather we are exploring a phenomenon. The testing has shown that the explanation of the phenomenon of authenticity and emotional labour in leadership practice through David's account is perceived as resonating with managers from a similar context: that is, it seems plausible because it connects in some way to the experiences of those managers. We are not seeking to suggest the testing can assure inferential generalization of the explanation. It is a given that configurations of influences on the manifestation of emotional labour and its effect on authenticity in leadership in specific contexts would vary. There were numerous comments from respondents to the graphic rating scale that spoke of such variations. Here are George's comments on question 3:

My lived experience equates to a 5 [graphic rating scale]. In such a situation, decisions have to be taken about who will depart from the organization. The robustness of that rationale is usually not without some doubt. I have mitigated that by also interrogating the rationale for why other people are not being selected—there are typically identifiable, substantive reasons *why not*.

It is never ok to mislead, or worse, to lie. I do believe (and practise) that it is OK to take a position that will reduce short-term uncertainty, based on work yet to be done or determinations that have yet to be made. That may mean stopping short of providing all info that one knows at a given moment. That is not being inauthentic, or disingenuous. It is necessary to help lead individuals or a group through significant change.

If a person asks directly about their position, when others who may also be impacted do not know equivalent info regarding their situation, then it is not OK to share definitive information that others don't have. It is OK—desirable even—to signal what people should be ready for, directionally. That may mean speculating, in order to offer helpful perspectives and resulting implications for people.

During the most recent, similar situation that I was part of, we (my leadership team and I) were working to a set of principles that included saving as many jobs as possible, while meeting the targets that [have] been placed upon our function. To do that, we did not execute and communicate as fast as some other groups, the result of which was that some of our team thought we were simply not moving fast enough. That's an understandable reaction, when other colleagues were finding certainty (good and bad) through decisions being made and communicated. It simply reaffirmed that the perspectives of leaders and those following may be at odds, even when the intentions of leaders are for the greater good. One course of mitigation would be [to] update followers/those following, as far as is practical, so that intentions are better understood.

George's account resonates with David's explanation, but also offers up differences as a result of his unique lived experience of the phenomenon. This variation is surely inevitable; but does not necessarily undermine the explanation. Rather it is a prompt to return to qualitative contextual depth to understand more about the causes of variation. However, confidence of resonance indicated by quantitative measurement encourages further exploration in other contexts due to the strength of its resonance and sense of plausibility of the explanation. The next stage of the research is to examine in depth the variation. This is not about proving or disproving. Law-like regularities are not the goal of critical realism. At a fine-grain level of contextual analysis, research will illuminate immense subtle variation through the countless social interactions that generate ongoing emergence within particular settings. How could it be otherwise? The purpose of the research endeavour is to suggest the presence of generative causal influences that have a tendency to impact on the emergence of phenomena. At best, repeated exploring, explaining, and testing will give confidence in suggesting tendencies for similar outcomes, as well as giving insight on how local variation occurs. At high levels of abstraction, statistical analysis through quantitative research can greatly help in confidence building. But we must not fall into (the positivists') trap of deluding ourselves that we can predict in a 'law-like' manner.

Auto-ethnography repositioned

The argument we have sought to explicate is that management research would be well served by the possibilities that co-constructed analytic auto-ethnography can bring. The much-voiced criticisms of post-structural versions of the auto-ethnographic genre are of substance. Most notable perhaps is Delamont's (2007, p.2) 'arguments against auto-ethnography'. In broad sweep she asserts, rightly in our opinion, that evocative and aesthetic auto-ethnography 'violates the two basic tasks of social science': to study the social world through collecting data; and to 'move [the] discipline forward'. Her examination of these critical points is through six criticisms. We use these to structure our contribution.

CRITICISM #1—AUTO-ETHNOGRAPHY CANNOT FIGHT FAMILIARITY

The notion that the auto-ethnographer cannot escape the familiar may not be such a problem seen through a critical realist lens. Familiarity provides an opportunity to access social process and social reality. But the familiarity of the auto does paradoxically limit access. Lone auto-ethnographers are limited in exploring and questioning taken-for-granted assumptions of which they are part—or in the lexicon of the critical realist, limited in pointing to possible generative causal powers shaping the social processes which they sustain as agents (Rees and Gatenby, 2014). Our suggestion for analytic auto-ethnography to embrace the notion of co-construction addresses this paradox directly. It provides for the familiar to be examined through reflexive dialogue (Cunliffe, 2002). The partner can help to make the familiar seem very different. The partner's purpose is not about recalling the story but rather revealing social process, through interrogation—helping to construct an explanation of what is occurring.

CRITICISM #2—AUTO-ETHNOGRAPHY IS ALMOST IMPOSSIBLE TO WRITE AND PUBLISH ETHICALLY

The ethical aspect is related to the auto-ethnographer being a complete member researcher, and as such this is applicable to all ethnographic research (Bryman and Bell, 2007). The example we have offered of the closure of Ward X provides a clear illustration of ethical concerns, notably ethics of representation (Allen-Collinson and Hockey, 2008). None of David's colleagues were aware that he was keeping a diary of events and reflections. Although anonymity is in part provided through omitting names and any unnecessary facts about those mentioned in the research, there is the need to describe David's reactions and feelings in his relationships and interactions with particular key participants. Consent has subsequently been granted for use of the data. However, obtaining data without consent upfront is questionable.

Wall (2008, p.49) brings useful attention to the ethical question of how should we use another person's life to tell auto-ethnographic narratives. Similarly Wall (2008) highlights the ethical issue of risks to the auto-ethnographer; the 'outing' of oneself on an issue that was otherwise unknown to others. Risks associated with being in employment and revealing aspects of the context, and risks to the individual 'when revealing the highly personal and vulnerable self' (Doloriert and Sambrook, 2009, p.41: see Vickers, 2007, for a discussion on bullying in the workplace seen through an auto-ethnographic account). Similarly, there are ethical risks in inviting managers to read David's account and compare this to their lived experience. For example, this can open up ethical considerations of the effect of recalling episodes and incidents that may at the time have been impactful or even harmful to them. In small part, the co-constructed process with the partner provides a sounding board for discussion of these ethical aspects, and creates the potential for reflexive dialogue to surface and explore these aspects (Cunliffe, 2002; Allen-Collinson and Hockey, 2008).

Doloriert and Sambrook (2012) suggest the possible use of fictionalizing as a method for addressing these ethical issues. We fear though that this rather creates a cul-de-sac for the progression of moving forward on the key principle of ethnographic research to understand and explain the social world (Delamont, 2007). In essence ethnography has no easy answers on this criticism other than keeping this issue highly salient throughout the research process.

CRITICISM #3—RESEARCH IS SUPPOSED TO BE ANALYTIC NOT MERELY EXPERIENTIAL

We have centred our argument on the principles of analytic auto-ethnography (drawing on Anderson, 2006). For us, the argument for an analytic approach that builds towards explanation is central to the critical realist agenda. But the experiential is such an important aspect of the research process. It provides essential insight to everyday milieu of practices, identities, meanings, and aspects that are obscured as well as those privileged (more on this shortly). Too many approaches to research cannot access this experiential depth that is organizational life. Auto-ethnography is such a useful approach for engaging researchers to 'get right down and dirty' in this milieu. However, this is only through partnership, through co-construction. It is the co-construction that illuminates the experiential and also provides the analytic. The analytic is the probing and testing of what the experiential reveals of the social practices being examined. The analytic is seeking to develop an explanation for testing in other contexts. Through co-construction, researchers gain access to organizations to develop theory and move respective disciplines forward.

CRITICISM #4—AUTO-ETHNOGRAPHY FOCUSES ON THE POWERFUL NOT THE POWERLESS TO WHOM WE SHOULD BE DIRECTING OUR SOCIOLOGICAL GAZE

Delamont (2007) is hinting that the present focus is on researchers that are most able to communicate and use publishing platforms to profess their experiences. We have highlighted earlier that the voice of managers has been mostly limited. Steve's recent work (Kempster and Gregory, 2015) using co-constructed analytic auto-ethnography offers a rare opportunity for the manager's voice. They worked with a middle manager to explore an ethical dilemma he was placed within. The contribution they offer is to problematize 'that normative ethical theorizing that has been unable to cater for the complexity of middle manager work' (Kempster and Gregory, 2015, p.3). In part their case gives attention to a voice that is less powerful, perhaps self-censored from being heard, or institutionally overlooked—for example, middle managers coping with organizational and personal pressures impacting on ethical conduct. It also speaks to how previous research methods have not had either a desire to move away from prominent nomothetic approaches that generate 'normative ethical theorizing' as is being suggested, or have not had access to less powerful and prominent voices.

CRITICISM #5—IT ABROGATES OUR DUTY TO GO OUT AND COLLECT DATA

The two aspects we have given emphasis to, namely co-construction and analytic, necessitate the process of 'going out' and collecting data; this occurs immediately in terms of co-construction. The analytic process similarly stimulates the desire for an outgoing perspective to build explanation. Moreover, our intent to show how mixed methods can be a necessary part of the analytic auto-ethnographic project firmly addresses this criticism. We welcome the notion of duty. Reflecting on Steve's work in Kempster and Gregory (2015), they did not seek to go beyond the experience; they did not speak of testing their insights and illumination of identified social processes in other contexts. Our argument here, informed through a critical realist perspective, is to assert the necessity of any account to test for plausibility and resonance.

CRITICISM #6—ACADEMICS ARE NOT INTERESTING ENOUGH TO WRITE ABOUT IN JOURNALS

The answers to the criticisms thus far have suggested that it would be a potential misuse of the auto-ethnographic method to persist in examining academics' experiences. Bracketing out any author self-absorption (Anderson, 2006), a number of factors explain why it is understandable that such auto-ethnographic accounts have been prevalent in published work. First has been the overt commitment to a post-structural position that may limit a desire to investigate others' experiences. Second is a limited desire to overcome access issues into organizations. Third, the lack of method, encouragement, and confidence to use a co-constructed approach. Fourth, and linked to the third, a limited number of people that embrace the analytic orientation to auto-ethnography. We hope that our explanation of co-constructed analytic auto-ethnography using mixed methods opens up the movement away from the academic context to the managerial and organizational context.

Conclusion

The development of co-constructed analytic auto-ethnography provides scope for organization studies to explore subjects that are difficult to access in terms of getting close to everyday practice. We have argued that there is the necessity for auto-ethnographic research to reach beyond the experience and test whether the insights of one context connect to other contexts. The mixed methods approach we have shown that seeks to test perceived resonance with managers in similar (or dissimilar) contexts provides a novel and rigorous way of developing theory of the social world—a fundamental contribution of realist research. By addressing rigour and relevance through the approach we have outlined, auto-ethnography may become accepted as a useful method for advancing understanding of organizations; and in particular enabling research to engage with topics that have thus far been difficult to reach through mainstream methods.

Focusing on a realist and analytic grounding and making plausibility of explanations the priority allows for auto-ethnography to move from the margins of mainstream acceptability to become much more accepted as a useful approach to management and organizational studies. Perhaps convincing researchers is not the biggest challenge; with much respect, it is perhaps reviewers and editors from both positivist and structuralist orientations that require convincing.

■ REFERENCES

Allen-Collinson, J. and Hockey, J. (2008). 'Auto-ethnography as "valid" methodology? A study of disrupted identity narratives', *The International Journal of Interdisciplinary Social Sciences*, 3(6): 209–17.

Anderson, L. (2006). 'Analytic auto-ethnography', *Journal of Contemporary Ethnography*, 35(4): 373–95.

Anderson, L. and Austin, M. (2012). 'Auto-ethnography in leisure studies', *Leisure Studies*, 31(2): 131–46.

Archer, M. (1995). *Realist Social Theory: The Morphogenetic Approach*. Cambridge: Cambridge University Press.

Archer, M. (2000). *Being Human: The Problem of Agency*. Cambridge: Cambridge University Press.

Ashforth, B.E. and Humphrey, R.H. (1993). 'Emotional labor in service roles: the influence of identity', *The Academy of Management Review*, 18(1): 88–115.

Barron, I. (2013). 'The potential and challenges of critical realist ethnography', *International Journal of Research and Method in Education*, 36(2): 117–30.

Bhaskar, R. (1978). *A Realist Theory of Science*. New York: Harvester Press.

Bhaskar, R. (1998). 'Philosophy and scientific realism.' In M. Archer, R. Bhaskar, A. Collier, T. Lawson, and A. Norrie (eds.), *Critical Realism: Essential Readings*. New York: Routledge, pp.16–47.

boyd, d. (2008). 'Autoethnogaphy as a tool for transformative learning about white privilege', *Journal of Transformative Education*, 6(3): 212–25.

Brotheridge, C.M. and Grandey, A.A. (2002). 'Emotional labor and burnout: comparing two perspectives of "people work"', *Journal of Vocational Behavior*, 60: 17–39.

Bryant, M. and Wolfram Cox, J. (2014). 'Beyond authenticity? Humanism, posthumanism and new organization development', *British Journal of Management*, 25: 706–23.

Bryman, A. and Bell, E. (2007). *Business Research Methods*. Oxford: Oxford University Press.

Cunliffe, A. (2002). 'Reflexive dialogical practice in management learning', *Management Learning*, 33(1): 35–61.

Delamont, S. (2007). 'Arguments against auto-ethnography', *Qualitative Researcher*, 4: 2–4.

Doloriert, C. and Sambrook, S. (2009). 'Ethical confessions of the "I" of auto-ethnography: the student's dilemma', *Qualitative Research in Organizations and Management*, 4(1): 27–45.

Doloriert, C. and Sambrook, S. (2012). 'Organisational autoethnography', *Journal of Organizational Ethnography*, 1: 83–95.

Ellis, C.S. and Bochner, A.P. (2006). 'Analyzing analytic auto-ethnography: an autopsy', *Journal of Contemporary Ethnography*, 35(4): 429–49.

Ellis, C.S., Adams, T.E., and Bochner, A.P. (2011). 'Auto-ethnography: an overview', *Historical Social Research*, 36(4): 273–90.

Fleetwood, S. (2004). 'The ontology of organization and management studies.' In S. Fleetwood and S. Ackroyd (eds.), *Realism in Action in Management and Organization Studies*. London: Routledge, pp.27–53.

Gardner, W.L., Fischer, D., and J.G. Hunt (2009). 'Emotional labor and leadership: a threat to authenticity?', *The Leadership Quarterly*, 20(3): 466–82.

Greiner, R.S. (2015). 'Autoethnography as a legitimate appraoch to HRD Research: a methodological conversation at 30,000 feet', *Human Resource Development Review*, 14(3): 332–50.

Hochschild, A.R. (1983). *The Managed Heart: Commercialization of Human Feeling*. Berkeley, CA: University of California Press.

Humphrey, R.H. (2013). 'How leading with emotional labour creates common identities.' In M. Iszatt-White (ed.) *Leadership as Emotional Labour: Management and the 'Managed Heart'*. Abingdon, UK: Taylor and Francis, pp.56–79.

Humphrey, R.H., Pollack, J.M., and Hawver, T. (2008). 'Leading with emotional labor', *Journal of Managerial Psychology*, 23(2): 151–68.

Humphrey, R.H., Ashforth, B.E., and Diefendorff, J.M. (2015). 'The bright side of emotional labour', *Journal of Organizational Behavior*, 36(6): 749–69.

Kempster, S. and Gregory, S. (2015). 'Should I stay or should I go?' Exploring leadership-as-practice in the middle management role. *Leadership*, 13(4): 496–515.

Kempster, S. and Parry, K.W. (2011). 'Grounded theory and leadership research: a critical realist perspective', *Leadership Quarterly* 22(1): 106–20.

Kempster, S. and Stewart, J. (2010). 'Becoming a leader: a co-produced auto-ethnographic exploration of situated learning of leadership practice', *Management Learning*, 41(2): 205–19.

Lewis, P. (2008). 'Emotion work and emotion space: using a spatial perspective to explore the challenging of masculine emotion management practices', *British Journal of Management*, 19:S130–40.

Parry, K.W. and Boyle, M. (2009). 'Organizational auto-ethnography.' In D. Buchanan and A. Bryman (eds) *The Sage Handbook of Organizational Research Methods*. London: Sage, pp.690–702.

Parry, K.W. and Kempster, S. (2014). 'Love and leadership: constructing follower narrative identities of charismatic leadership', *Management Learning*, 45: 21–38.

Pawson, R. and Tilley, N. (1997). *Realistic Evaluation*. London: Sage.

Plummer, K. (2001). 'The call of life stories in ethnographic research.' In P. Atkinson, A. Coffey, S. Delamont, J. Lofland, and L. Lofland (eds) *Handbook of ethnography*. Thousand Oaks, CA: Sage, pp.395–406.

Reed, M. (2005). 'Reflections on the "realist turn" in organization and management studies', *Journal of Management Studies*, 42: 1621–44.

Rees, C. and Gatenby, M. (2014). 'Critical realism and ethnography.' In P.K. Edwards, J. O'Mahoney, and S. Vincent (eds) *Studying Organizations Using Critical Realism: A Practical Guide*. Oxford: Oxford University Press, pp. 132–47.

Sayer, A. (1992). *Method in Social Science; A Realist Approach*. London: Routledge.

Searle, J. (1995). *The Construction of Social Reality*. New York: Free Press.

Shamir, B. and R. Kark (2004). 'A single-item graphic scale for the measurement of organizational identification', *Journal of Occupational Psychology*, 77: 115–23.

Smollan, R.K. and Parry, K.W. (2011). 'Follower perceptions of the emotional intelligence of change leaders: a qualitative study', *Leadership*, 7(4): 435–62.

Sturdy, A. (2003). 'Knowing the unknowable?: a discussion of methodological and theoretical issues in emotion research and organizational studies', *Organization*, 10(1): 81–105.

Turnbull, S. (2013). '"Middle managers" emotional labour in disseminating culture change: a case study in the requirement for changing values.' In M. Iszatt-White (ed.) *Leadership as Emotional Labour: Management and the 'Managed Heart'*. Abingdon, UK: Taylor and Francis, pp.153–72.

Van Maanen, J. (2011). 'Ethnography as work: some rules of engagement', *Journal of Management Studies*, 48(1): 218–34.

Vickers, M.H. (2007). 'Auto-ethnography and sensemaking: a story of bullying in the workplace', *Culture and Organization*, 13(3): 223–37.

Wall, S. (2008). 'Easier said than done: writing an auto-ethnography', *International Journal of Qualitative Methods*, 7(1): 38–53.

Watson, T.J. (2011). 'Ethnography, reality and truth: the vital need for studies of "how things work" in organizations and management', *Journal of Management Studies*, 48(1): 201–17.

10 Participant-led video diaries

Rebecca Whiting, Helen Roby, Gillian Symon,
and Petros Chamakiotis

Introduction

In this chapter, we introduce the unconventional methodology of participant-led video diaries which, combined with narrative interviews, involves collecting and analysing multi-modal (audio, visual, and textual) data, adopting a qualitative perspective and a social constructionist epistemology (Knoblauch, 2012). Our study was part of a multi-disciplinary research council-funded project, which sought to explore how digital technologies affect our ability to manage switches across work-life boundaries. The 'For Interested Readers' box at the end of this chapter provides links to further information on this project. Our analysis of our participants' video diaries, and their discussion of these, illustrates the theoretical and reflexive insights to be gained from this method. However, our main aim here is to encourage use of this methodology by presenting a description, including participants' feedback, to encourage an informed choice for video researchers. In so doing, we consider some of the more pragmatic problems and pitfalls we encountered, so that future video researchers are prepared to confront these.

The use of video as research methodology in organization and management studies is not widespread, although Christianson (2016) argues that it is growing, with six times as many studies in top-tier organization and management journals for the period 2010–2015 compared to 1990–1994. However, her review still only amounts to fifty-six articles between 1990 and 2015. Currently then, video research is 'unconventional' for this field. However, video research methodology has been used in other disciplines (e.g. psychology, human-computer interaction, sociology), many of which overlap with organization and management, including studies of specific occupations (e.g. Heath et al., 2007).

A recent increase in video-based research (see the special issue of *Organizational Research Methods*, 2018) may reflect growing interest in the visual elements of organization and management (e.g. Meyer et al., 2013). This recognizes the importance of capturing not just the *extent* of experience through quantitative measures, or the *meaning* of experience through textual data, but also the *symbolic and tacit* aspects of experience through visual framing (i.e. how visual representation may present a particular construction of reality that is difficult to verbalize). It may also reflect widespread general use of digital technologies, such as the increasing use of videos for training and other purposes (Jarrett and Liu, 2016). While not seeking to equate detailed empirical enquiry with, say, YouTube content, the potential relevance and impact of video-based research to wider audiences is clear. Indeed, Jewitt (2012, p.4) celebrates the 'share-ability' of the video method.

Researchers incorporate video into their research designs in many ways depending on their research objectives (Jewitt, 2012): analysing existing videos; creating their own; recording specific events as they unfold; or, less often, asking participants to make their own video recordings. In general, however, supporters of the methodology highlight its ability to capture naturally occurring, real-time events and activities, micro-interactions, including non-verbal aspects of communication, and tacit or unacknowledged actions and knowledge which would not be recalled in surveys or interviews. Additionally, videos can be considered a uniquely multi-modal method of research, capturing both sound and vision (Toraldo et al., 2016). In this chapter, we review some of the range of relevant video research studies to give an idea of the versatility of the method and to attract others to consider how video research might develop their own area of interest.

The main part of the chapter describes our own methodology, which is unconventional for a video study because we asked research participants to keep their own video diaries. These were then sent to the research team for analysis, later forming the focus for in-depth narrative interviews. It is far more common for researchers to video some event or activity themselves (e.g. through a static camera or as a form of video ethnography) than put the camcorder in the participants' hands (Hindmarsh and Llewellyn, 2016). Doing so raises new issues around ethics, research participation, and power. Our approach prompted reflection on the nature of participant involvement, emphasizing that it is not only the content of the videos which is of research interest but also the taking of the videos themselves (i.e. how and why particular images were captured). Methodological reflexivity (Johnson and Duberley, 2003) encouraged us to consider how the conduct of our research affects findings; our study encouraged not only reflection on our adoption of video as methodology, but also how participants shaped the design and outcomes of the study (see also Whiting et al., 2016). Additionally, we draw attention to how the videos encouraged the participants to reflect on their actions in relation to the management of work-life boundaries, an effect referred to by Toraldo et al. (2016, p.10) as 'video as reflective artefact'.

We begin the chapter with a review of current visual/video research, and then describe our own study, including the motivation and rationale for adopting this particular video methodology. We recount the method as it unfolded and provide some detail on our own data analysis strategy so far. Our intention is to revisit the data with other foci and strategies in mind, thus illustrating the potential malleability of the video method (Jewitt, 2012). We highlight the theoretical and practical implications of our video study for our research field of work-life boundary management, and finish with a reflexive section on our experience of the method, both empirically and pragmatically.

Visual research methods: a brief review

Visual research methods have been used in the humanities for many years (Crary, 1990), spreading to medicine, cognitive science, and classroom studies (Erickson, 2011), as well as social sciences such as anthropology and sociology (Bell and Davison, 2013). However, those in organization and management studies have been slower to adopt visual methods (Bell and Davison, 2013; Ray and Smith, 2012). Among the first were Lucy Suchman's work at Xerox in the 1980s and Christian Heath's work on the London Underground in the 1990s (Erickson, 2011). Since then, video recordings have been used to make detailed studies of specific occupations such as surgeons and auctioneers (e.g. Heath et al., 2007), and more recently to capture the unfolding of strategic decisions in meetings (Gylfe et al., 2016). Video enables the study of interactions in these occupational and organizational settings; not just talk, but gesture, tone, use of artefacts and spatial interactions.

The late adoption of visual methods in organizational settings facilitates learning from other disciplines, 'borrow[ing] from arts disciplines and the social sciences' (Bell and Davison, 2013, p.171), and consolidating learning rather than 'reinventing knowledge about the visual and its workings' (Meyer et al., 2013, p.491). Frameworks or typologies of visual methods within organization studies are embryonic. Ray and Smith (2012) classify research by who (participant, researcher, archive, or hybrid) produces the visual material. Bell and Davison (2013) categorize by whether visual research is empirically or theoretically driven. Meyer et al. (2013) identify five approaches to visual data based on research designs: archaeological, practice, strategic, dialogic, and documenting. In our own research, user participation was critical to the research design, execution, and interpretation. Participatory video research embraces a range of different methods, including: participant-generated video; video diaries; auto-videography; distributed video studies; and community videos. Images created by research participants can be used in 'photo/video elicitation interviews' to better understand social and cultural phenomena (Erickson, 2011). Non-participatory methods which use researcher-produced visual images include video interaction analysis, workplace studies, focused ethnography, video ethnography, and video shadowing. Here video extends and supplements more traditional methods such as ethnography (Meyer et al.,

2013; Rose, 2007). Third party pre-existing video material can also be analysed as data.

Visual images are becoming increasingly important in organization and management research, reflecting the changing nature of organizations and society. Visual communication provides an 'immediate, multisensory impact that comes from viewing an image' (Bell et al., 2014, p.2), which gives 'an accuracy and plenitude of description that the verbal language cannot match' (Meyer et al., 2013, p.496). This multisensory impact aids cognitive processing, improving memory and communication of complex messages. From the researcher's perspective, visual images benefit over notes or transcripts in allowing the researcher to view the video repeatedly, effectively 'revisiting the field' (Gylfe et al., 2016). Visual methods have an important role as a way of observing organizational practices and behaviours, and learning from these observations in a reflexive manner.

Video diaries potentially benefit both researcher and participant, producing a real-time record of people's behaviours and thoughts. They capture rich visual and audio data portraying 'emotions and complexity' (Roberts, 2011, p.679), affording participants the ability to record non-linear and disjointed trains of thought in less structured ways than in text (Noyes, 2004). For example, Alonzo and Kim (2015, p.5) describe how the use of videos allowed them to 'preserve some of the messiness and complexity of classroom studies', while Christianson (2016) considers capturing non-verbal behaviours useful in the study of emotion.

One important claim is for participants' self-expression and 'voice' in the research process, affording them the ability to 'frame and represent their own lives' (Jones et al., 2014, p.396), to 'talk more freely about their unseen day-to-day experiences' (Noyes, 2004, p.196), and encouraging self-examination and reflection (Jones et al., 2014). Participant voice and self-expression are claimed to support participant empowerment, through their ability to talk freely without interference from the researcher. However, these claims of empowerment are contested. Participants are unlikely to have total freedom or control over what they film, as the content will have been conceptually framed by the researcher and therefore the researcher is not totally absent from the filming (Jones et al., 2014). This does not mean, however, that participants totally lack empowerment; they remain experts of their context, even when making choices in response to researcher prompts (Tribe, 2006). A further criticism is that providing prompts to participants may lead to 'ventriloquization' (Jones et al., 2014, p.399), where the researcher influences their thoughts and words. Others suggest that this influence by the researcher on the participant lends itself to a more collaborative form of image production, overcoming some of the ethical concerns in such work (Bell and Davison, 2013). Nevertheless, the questions of whose voice is actually being heard in a video diary and to what extent claims of equalizing the power relationship between researcher and participant are justified need to be considered (Pauwels, 2004).

Whether these issues are relevant will largely depend on the empirical question and epistemology of the research. However, there are practical and methodological challenges associated with visual research methods, including video diaries, which will be relevant whatever the design. One major challenge is the potentially large dataset, and its storage, sharing, and analysis. There are also ethical and legal challenges for the publication of visual materials in terms of confidentiality and copyright (Bell and Davison, 2013). Some of these challenges can be overcome through the use of video diaries, where research participants choose the content and therefore have control over the data collected and through the use of adaptive consent forms, discussed below. We now turn to our own use of video methodology, addressing many of the issues just raised.

The Digital Brain Switch project: capturing and understanding boundary transition in the digital age

Here, we introduce our research project to provide context and to explain our rationale for adopting a video methodology. Our research sought to explore how digital technologies affect our ability to manage switches across physical, temporal, and psychological boundaries (Ashforth et al., 2000; Clark, 2000). Switches were theoretically defined as rapid (almost instantaneous) transitions between different activities or areas of our lives; for example, switching from reading personal emails to work emails on a mobile phone. We sought to develop previous research that has examined the nature of work-life boundaries (e.g. Clark, 2000), work-life boundary management (Ashforth et al., 2000; Cohen et al., 2009), and the impact of digital technologies on working lives (Mazmanian et al., 2013). We were interested in bringing these literatures together and developing them further. We observed the immediacy of using personal, mobile, handheld devices and the plethora of social media available relating to both working and personal lives. We noted how individuals can move fairly seamlessly between professional and personal social media platforms, by using devices that support both personal and working lives. As such, we wondered whether the idea of 'microtransitions' (Ashforth et al., 2000)— for example, commuting or going to a movie after work—were quite 'micro' enough in the digital age. We felt that such digitally supported transitions could be considered fairly immediate 'switches', and wondered what the implications of these might be for boundary management and identity transitions (Ollier-Malaterre et al., 2013). We wanted to capture some of these digitally supported switches, observe their context and understand how individuals manage these switches in real-time.

Our two major issues at the outset were: whom to observe, and how to capture these switches. First, we adopted a purposive sampling approach by deciding to focus on three 'extreme' case examples (Saunders, 2012). This involved selecting participants whose data would enable us to find out the most (Patton, 2002). Here, their selection was driven by boundary theory (Ashforth et al., 2000). A total of forty-five participants were drawn from three UK-based groups: (1) social entrepreneurs (SEs), whose challenges might include financial insecurity, commitment to create social value, and lack of a defined workplace; (2) office workers (OWs), whose challenges might include having less control over work processes and use of technologies and a variety of more closely defined role identities; and (3) university students (USs) aged 18–25, whose challenges might include ill-defined work-life boundaries and identity permeability. Our recruitment literature made it clear that participation involved a video diary study, and we did not observe any differences between the groups in terms of receptivity or approaches to this method. We found examples of creativity and reflexivity in respect of filming in each group. We did note that, compared to the other groups, some office workers found it difficult to film in their offices (though some filmed themselves working at home).

Second, we wanted participants to capture what was meaningful to them so we could understand their interpretations and experiences. This was also a potent reason for wanting the data collection to be in the hands of the participants. We left it to participants to decide what constituted a switch, what technologies mattered, and what boundaries were salient to them. As highlighted earlier, this is one element of our study which makes it unconventional in relation to previous video-based methodologies. Coming from a social constructionist perspective, we understood that boundaries and transitions are not existing 'out there' as objective, observable, generalizable entities, but would be named and positioned as such by individuals in interaction with others (Cohen et al., 2009); we were interested in capturing this process itself. Similarly, we did not want to make temporal or conceptual assumptions about when 'work' ends and 'life' begins or what these concepts constituted for our participants. Not having pre-determined categories would allow new meanings and constructions to emerge, thus potentially challenging assumptions in the work-life boundary literature, which is rather restricted by a focus on family, 9–5 employment schedules, and concepts of work rooted in the pre-digital 1950s (Davies and Frink, 2014).

Participants could have kept written diaries (Bolger et al., 2003) or audio recordings (Crozier and Cassell, 2016) to capture such material. However, written diaries rely too much on reported behaviour, and audio recordings would not fully capture the role of the technology in the switch (or other kind of materiality; Hindmarsh and Llewellyn, 2016). Additionally, we wanted to capture the more tacit elements of switching—the potential messiness, complexity and disjointed nature of its construction—as well as the physical and social contexts of switching. Retaining a sense of the participants' understanding and interpretation of, and reflections on, these switches was also important. Participants were encouraged to narrate their filming where relevant, providing a valuable commentary on their own experience of the method as well as adding interpretation to the videos themselves (see next section).

Once the week of videoing was completed, we conducted narrative interviews (Holloway and Jefferson, 2000), partly to ensure that we fully captured individual interpretation and reflection. Our study also used 'video elicitation' (Henry and Fetters, 2012), asking our participants to review and comment on a small selection of the video clips *they* had taken, which was important in situating the video clips in a narrative account of the participants' lives. Video diaries can capture the minutiae of moment-to-moment events and activities, but may neglect an in-depth understanding of an individual's life history (Musson, 2004). We wanted to understand the specific switching moments captured in the videos in the context of the individuals' backgrounds, personal and work roles, and general experience of boundaries and transitions. By conducting the interviews post-filming, we could discuss the videos themselves and avoid participants' videoing being affected by detailed pre-discussion of their circumstances.

Clearly, asking participants to keep video diaries raises important issues concerning informed consent and confidentiality (Whiting and Pritchard, 2018). This was addressed at the design stage. We took steps to ensure the study did not overstep ethical boundaries or place others in difficult positions. This required careful planning, input from institutional ethical committees, and negotiation with participants themselves. It meant recognizing that obtaining informed consent is not a one-off 'tick box' exercise nor a 'one size fits all' arrangement (Mok et al., 2015). As it was a relatively unconventional method for the institutions involved, there was some prolonged consultation and iterative ethical planning.

To ensure that participants knew what they were committing to, we produced detailed information sheets and conducted individual briefings, assuring them they could contact us at any time during the study if any issues arose or if they wanted to withdraw. We were also aware that the 'share-ability' of videos (Jewitt, 2012, p.6) might raise issues of confidentiality. With videos forming a major part of our dataset, we knew we would want to show them at various events and online. Consequently, we advised participants not to film: anything of a confidential, sensitive or highly personal nature; children (unless their own children and both parents gave their consent); other people (unless in a public place where they might reasonably expect to be observed); in shopping centres or areas with high security status; or when cycling or driving. We were careful to obtain informed consent and give participants options regarding their identifiability and our use of their video data. For example, participants had the option to refuse our use of any data in presentations or academic publications if they were potentially identifiable from those video clips.

This was our plan. We now set out what actually happened once we were confronted by the participants' lived context.

Methodology

Table 10.1 summarizes the key methodological stages of our planned research. We have published further detail of this elsewhere, with our commentary on the issues that we encountered in carrying this out (Whiting et al., 2016). Here we want to highlight issues that the participants confronted in performing this methodology, drawn from their feedback, comments and actions captured in the videos, debrief, and interviews.

We undertook a pilot study using members of the research team and a few university colleagues to help refine the detail and work out the practicalities of the methodology. This meant that we could offer practical guidance to participants about the filming. In wording our recruitment literature in the main study, we struggled to find the right balance between making it sound interesting and worthwhile, and being realistic about the time, energy, and commitment involved. So we applied our learning from the pilot to foreshadow issues in recruitment and provide solutions. For example, we (rightly) anticipated that some would find it hard to maintain recording for seven consecutive days. We suggested taking a short break if it became too onerous, so long as they ultimately filmed footage across a mix of weekdays and weekends. We knew that asking participants to take part in the video study required considerable commitment; so, unsurprisingly, recruitment took longer than anticipated.

Table 10.1 Key methodological stages

Stage 0	Pilot study with researchers (and colleagues) as participants
Stage 1	Initial briefing, mostly over Skype, after camcorder (Toshiba S40 Camileo) and project documents (instructions, information sheet, consent form) posted to participants; briefing includes outline ethical guidance on 'what not to film'
Stage 2	Participants carry out a 7-day period of filming; researchers remain in contact
Stage 3	Short post-filming debriefing of participant by telephone; researcher views videos to assess quality, quantity, and scope of footage
Stage 4	Researcher conducts in-depth interviews with participants (face-to-face or via Skype) which includes reviewing video excerpts
Stage 5	Researcher analysis of video and interview data including: thematic analysis across data sources; individual case study analysis; discourse analysis
Stage 6	Webinar with participants to exchange feedback and discuss future joint steps

We used the share screen function of Skype to brief participants via a short presentation including guidance on what to film, ethical considerations, and camcorder features such as its tripod, flip-out rotatable screen, and review function. Our instructions asked them to focus on their different roles in their work and private lives, and to record how they switched, tried to switch, or were externally prompted/forced to switch between them. Ideally, we wanted them to capture what they saw in front of them rather than narrating switches retrospectively, though the latter was useful for switches too difficult to capture in the moment. Copies of participant documentation are available from our project website (see 'For Interested Readers' box). Sending the camcorder and instructions in advance allowed participants to practise filming and to identify issues to discuss at the briefing. A few struggled with set-up issues, such as not realizing that we had pre-loaded the camcorder with a memory card. The camcorder itself was generally seen as appealing in terms of its size and design; one participant described it to his colleagues as 'quite cool' (Adam, OW, video). Even those who initially worried that they might struggle to use it, later commented on its ease of use ('rather marvellous', Cressida, SE, video). Of course, we could have asked them to make videos on their own devices with which they were already familiar. However, this would have meant collecting a variety of different formats and qualities of video material, which also may have been incompatible with our analysis software and, crucially, would have made it more difficult to capture switches involving their own devices. We were in the fortunate position of having research funding which covered the equipment costs. However, providing the camcorders brought its own difficulties in terms of ensuring delivery and return of the devices with the data. We resolved this by using a courier service to collect the camcorder with the data from each participant from a location and at a time of their choosing.

We debriefed participants shortly after they completed their video recording, asking them to reflect on their experience of taking part in the video study. This was when many mentioned the effect of the camcorder—and taking part in the study more generally—on their behaviour. We took notes of these phone conversations, later typed up. This was followed a couple of weeks later by an in-depth narrative interview (mostly face-to-face, but a few via Skype) lasting around one hour. The aim was to discuss excerpts from the video data and to embed these discussions in a deeper understanding of participants' work-life narratives. Using a set of open-ended questions concerning general career narrative, technology use, meaning and experience of work-life balance, and switching, we explored their own constructions of these concepts through the reflexivity afforded by the video methodology. Meanwhile, we also viewed the videos and selected excerpts to discuss in the interviews as 'critical incidents', in that selected videos might include 'moments of success, failure or puzzlement' but also other 'instances worthy of comment' (Fry and Ketteridge, 2009, p.477). We had intended participants to select these, but most said they did not have the time, so the choice was usually made by us. We selected videos that either appeared particularly representative or contradictory, required some explanation, or raised a seemingly critical issue for the participant. Three or four videos per interview were all that we could accommodate without overburdening the rest of the interview. These were watched together by participant and researcher, with the participant prompted to reflect on the bigger picture in terms of what had been happening at the time of the recording.

Our instructions assured participants that there was no one right way to approach the filming and to be creative. Comments by participants about taking part, often made in passing whilst engaged in their daily activities, showed the video study as a lived experience. Some related to the mechanics of recording the video data, but we also observed how participants performed two sometimes competing roles: that of being a 'good participant' versus being their 'authentic selves'.

For example, in the following extract, Simon is attempting to bring a very large model into a school prior to use in a street parade. These attempts feature the participant (mainly voice only) and school staff, as between them they seek a doorway tall enough to accommodate the model.

> *Participant*   I'm doing a video diary of my day for the Open University.
> *Staff member*   Oh sorry [puts hand over her mouth].
> *Participant*   No, it's not a problem. But I keep forgetting to turn [the camcorder] on and do things, so that little bit at reception where they were trying to... would have been really good. (Simon, SE, video)

The idea of a university-sponsored video study initially silences the school staff member who perhaps fears her utterance will be out of place. However, we also hear the participant's wistful reflection on material that could have been used as video footage but which was missed, an example that indicates responsibility to the project to show us 'good' or 'useful' data. In some videos the potential for a disappointed reaction from the researchers is anticipated:

I feel like I shouldn't waste your time by showing you lots of boring things.

(Xanthe, US, video)

This quote is typical of participants' apprehension that we would find their data 'boring' and regretting that their week had not been more eventful. In debriefings and interviews, we sought to reassure participants of the value of everyday ordinary routines. One participant shared his delight with us over a particularly satisfying moment he captured:

There was one stellar moment when I was filming something and my dad got in touch with me via iChat and his video came up on my screen.   (Stephen, SE, debrief)

This represented a rare instance of an unplanned perceived switch caught live on video, since the research design made it easier to capture planned transitions (as opposed to unexpected ones such as interruptions). Having been advised by us about ethical considerations, acting these out also became part of being the 'good participant'; participants devised ways of informing those in their lives what was going on (one student posting a notice on Facebook warning fellow students she would be on campus with a camcorder). Others recorded themselves negotiating access, providing a visual/audio record of others consenting to be filmed.

The creativity of being a 'good participant' extended to adapting and developing the methodology. They recorded sometimes quite lengthy pieces to camera, addressing us with their reflections. Several created innovative ways of filming: in a shared quiet work space, one participant typed and filmed messages to us which appeared on his computer monitor (see Figure 10.1). Another filmed a restaurant setting at waist height to avoid showing colleagues' faces (see Figure 10.2).

Others supplemented their own reflections with interviews with family members, colleagues, and flatmates. Participants were also keen for us to

Figure 10.1 Example of participant creativity: the 'silent movie' approach

Figure 10.2 Example of participant creativity: avoiding filming colleagues' faces

know that their videos did not fully represent their lives and to explain this lack of authenticity or completeness. A few commented on how hard they had found the filming, because it was difficult to remember to take the camcorder with them; their work involved confidential meetings; they worked with children; or shared offices with colleagues who objected to being filmed. Participants also reported being too exhausted to film, editing what they were prepared to show us (house too untidy), and explaining the absence of family and friends in the footage (family members not wanting to be filmed, or being too tired to negotiate consent from others). These adaptive methods and reflections show how participants became researchers into their own lives as they reflected not just on their switches but on the wider context of their lives. They also prompted insight into our empirical investigation by demonstrating the extent to which we can only partially control how we conduct our lives, given the degree of intertwining with the demands and expectations of others.

Although we anticipated the camcorder's role as an audience or observer, we realized that this was two-fold as participants filmed both themselves and others. For some, the camcorder had a discomfiting effect, causing them to reflect on the effects on themselves, and on the others that they filmed, of watching and of being watched. At its most straightforward, the discomfort related to self-consciousness when filming out and about:

When I was in the street I felt that people probably thought what I was doing was a bit odd so after a while I pretended that the camcorder was a mobile phone.

(Charles, OW, debrief)

One participant sought to explain his reluctance to film due to its effects on others:

I think what I found difficult was that I work in an open plan office, so when I say that it was intrusive, it would be intrusive to other people if I had video recorded in that space. (Alastair, OW, debrief)

In the end, the only videos from this participant were pieces he recorded to camera at home at the beginning and end of each day, though this was an exception in our study. The effects of using video technology extended to a more disciplinary effect, with one participant likening the camcorder to an invisible line manager:

It kind of made me try to be more coherent in what I was doing in demonstrating levels of efficiency that I might not have bothered about before, because it was like you have an audience, so you want to be able to do it well, and this is like an invisible line manager. (Michael, SE, interview)

Here the camcorder role leads to self-monitoring and impression management as the participant reflects on how filming changed his work behaviour during the study, needing to demonstrate efficiency. But in performing his authenticity, the participant reflects on and reports this to us as well.

Analysis and findings

Our data were multi-modal: visual, audio, and textual. Analysis is widely acknowledged as the most complex aspect of the methodology (e.g. Gylfe et al., 2016). There are various strategies to choose from, ranging from content analysis to more in-depth analytic techniques such as discourse analysis and visual semiotics, though many adopt a broad thematic analysis.

Initially, the video and interview data with accompanying transcripts plus debrief notes were all uploaded to NVivo10 for analysis. This is one of a range of software options for data storage, management, and analysis. We required an analysis package that could handle multi-modal data including video clips with accompanying transcripts, and which could be stored on a secure server to enable shared access by the research team.

As qualitative researchers, we focused on the meaning and interpretation of the visual images, spoken commentary, and interview narratives. One challenge in analysing participant video diaries is that, unlike interviews or shadowing (Gill, 2011), the researcher is not physically present when the data are constructed. So the contents can surprise the researcher. Participatory methods offer the opportunity to analyse both data and methodological process. We had not anticipated the creativity of our participants, the extent to which the videos would yield methodological as well as empirical insights, or how the former could inform the latter (Whiting et al., 2016). A second challenge is that videos are time-consuming to view and analyse. Interviews, once converted into a transcript, can be scanned for key words or themes; the researcher is already familiar with the contents having been present when the interview data were constructed. Video's dual modalities require viewing in real time.

We analyzed both video and interview data initially using thematic analysis (Braun and Clarke, 2006). A thematic approach is often the starting point for qualitative analysis, can be used with visual and textual data, is adaptive to different epistemologies (compared with content analysis), and was familiar to the research team working on the data. It provided an initial overview of the dataset enabling identification of areas for greater attention and was compatible with supplemental and more specialized forms of analysis as mentioned below. The same umbrella themes (work-life balance, identity, boundaries, switching, technology, and methodology) were used across the video and interview datasets for coherence of analysis. These themes were both 'top-down' and 'bottom-up' in that they drew from academic theory and literature but also from our pilot data. Detailed sub-themes were developed as emergent from the analysis of each umbrella theme. Following this initial thematic analysis, further analysis was carried out; for example, individual case study analysis and discourse analysis, in relation to specific research questions. Though analysis is still ongoing, our innovative method revealed new conceptual issues in the field of work-life boundary management. The 'For Interested Readers' box below provides links to our dissemination videos and metadata statement.

One area that emerged from the analysis relates to the changing nature of boundaries and the dynamic nature of how these are managed. By inviting participants to determine what constituted a switch for them (see Figure 10.3), we were able to see their use of technology in how boundaries were maintained, eroded, and reinforced, often in ways they did not articulate verbally (Chamakiotis et al., 2015). Video and interview data offered a more nuanced approach that goes beyond simply describing people as 'integrators' (those who blend boundaries) or 'segmenters' (those who keep them separate) (Sayah, 2013). Our analysis included the emergence of new 'domains'; for example, where participants drew boundaries between being online and offline. The 'online domain' was constructed as a space that participants switched to and from and in which both personal and work-related activities took place (Whiting et al., 2015a).

Other empirical findings could also only have come from video data. For example, one emergent finding relates to what we have termed 'digi housekeeping' (Whiting et al., 2015b). This refers to the range of tasks that participants undertook daily to support and maintain the 'online domain'; for example,

Figure 10.3 Ailsa (US) and her digital switch

Figure 10.4 Simon (SE) undertakes some 'digi-housekeeping'

charging devices, deleting junk emails, and setting up laptops in different locations, to name but a few (Figure 10.4). This was not a concept we had foreseen or asked participants to consider. Its emergence was solely based on what we observed participants doing, sometimes without any specific accompanying commentary.

Reflections: the pros and cons of video diaries

Having outlined our methodology and some of our findings, we now reflect on what we and our participants have learnt. We start by drawing together some key advantages and disadvantages as set out in Table 10.2.

Our study successfully captured the mundane and everyday aspects of our participants' lives. It allowed us to see places and behaviours to which we would not otherwise have had access; for example, the early morning routine of one participant as he switched between firing up his laptop, eating breakfast, playing solitaire on his notebook, listening to the radio, checking work emails, and feeding the chickens. As discussed, however, it was also seen by some as intrusive (of themselves, families, or colleagues). Participants told us how they had edited out some of the 'messiness and complexity' of everyday lives, prompting us to undertake a more reflexive approach to the data. Specifically, we sought to understand rather than resolve the tension within a method which some claim produces naturalistic data yet also involves participant behaviours prompted by the recording device itself, a phenomenon referred

Table 10.2 Key methodological pros and cons of video diaries

advantages	disadvantages
capture mundane and everyday in the moment	intrusive technology
participants' definitions of boundaries and transitions	disciplining effects
capture the context of transitions as they occur, including the presence of others and the physical surroundings	analytic challenge
allow participants to 'see' themselves for reflexive learning	persuading participants to take part
echoes the visual nature of new digital technologies and digital media culture	technical difficulties with camcorders

to as the 'observer's paradox' (Labov, 1972). Recognizing this paradox as inevitable (Gordon, 2012), our constructionist approach meant we saw this as an opportunity to investigate what this involved in our own study (Whiting et al., 2016).

The camcorders allowed participants not only to film themselves but to capture a narrative to accompany whatever they filmed. The methodological combination of visuals and narrative is not unique to video, as photo-narrative studies such as Woodley-Baker (2009) show, but it does offer the unique combination of participant decisions over what to film and narrate simultaneously rather than as a two-stage process. This resulted in data which captured 'in the moment' actions together with explanations for such filming. Physical switches offered time for reflection by participants, as they narrated their transition, often from one role to another. Camcorders thus allowed us to become a virtual shadow to our participants. They allowed us to capture both visio-spatial information and the context of the micro-transition as it unfolded, enabling us to explore boundary management in a much more detailed way than has previously been attempted in this research area.

We also reflected on the extent to which the video study was participant-led. Although the study enabled participants to become 'researchers' into their own lives, we were also an absent presence. The camcorder was a physical proxy for us, a reminder of the additional role that we had asked them to undertake, and itself an additional piece of digital technology with which they had to engage. Further, in keeping with the view that 'the researcher, whether physically present or not, is inevitably part of the research world being studied' (Gibson, 2005, p.3), we also left a trace in the data through our research agenda and language. One-way conversations and comments like 'Hopefully this has been of some help to you and no doubt we'll talk about it' (Stephen, SE, video) reaffirmed not only our presence in the data through our research objectives, but also the research team as an audience who would later watch the footage.

Less obvious instances of our presence included participants adopting the language of the research study in their video narratives, using terms from our briefing material, an act of 'ventriloquizing' (Jones et al., 2014). For example, one participant filmed his usual commuter train and simply narrated 'transitioning tool—most days' by way of description. On the face of it, this is slightly at odds with claims that video diaries allow participants 'to use their own voices, language and expression to narrate their lives' (Brown et al., 2010, p.423). Adopting our terms closes down rather than opens up the narration, using our language as the end point, not the starting point for their own commentary. We found that this kind of interaction revealed insights into the methodology, challenging us to explore our data more reflexively.

Our own participation in the pilot study alerted us to the importance of the video diary as a reflective tool, particularly when the video data were reviewed and considered, including in the follow-up interview. It enabled us to consider both empirical and methodological aspects of the study from the participant perspective. Videos also prompted reflection, learning, and some reported behaviour change on the part of participants. This reflexivity led to the objectification of self (allowing participants a new perspective on their daily lives); affirmation (of valued activities and experiences); realization and learning about themselves; and recognition of the need for change (which led to making plans for different behaviours).

To summarize, the visual nature of the video data made it more graphic and memorable; this creates the potential for simultaneous data gathering and impact, on other researchers, and on participants themselves. The video data allow participants to 'see' themselves over time, achieving the benefits of the cumulative nature of longitudinal reflection. Participants did not need specific expert intervention (in the form of our analysis) in order to recognize issues in their lives and to consider changes. Unlike, say, a questionnaire, videos capture 'what actually happened' and participants themselves noted how this differed from what they thought happened and how they would have reported it if simply asked. Arguably, reflecting on this makes participants more likely to implement and own these changes. Our research design has not allowed us to investigate this empirically, but where participants engage in sense-making in their own terms they may be more able to relate to it.

In terms of research dissemination, the videos make for striking and memorable components to presentations at academic conferences and practitioner-focused events. Audiences always comment on how struck they are by the video excerpts we show (a picture may be worth a thousand words, a video even more). This prompted us to seek follow-on funding to produce two research dissemination videos, including participant footage, to capitalize on this feature (see links in 'For Interested Readers' box below). However, presenting videos was often fraught with technological difficulty (despite our efforts to ensure software compatibility on unfamiliar computers). On occasion we have had to show videos without sound and without a red filter which turned our video clips pond green. Neither of these are ideal scenarios, but adding subtitles to the video excerpts in our presentations turned out to be a really good decision. As videos grow in popularity, we anticipate presentation venues becoming more sophisticated in providing the necessary supportive technology.

Conclusion

Our aim here has been to present our unconventional methodology, participant-led video diaries combined with narrative interviews, to encourage others in its use. We have been open about the problems encountered, and taken a reflexive approach to the methodology which appreciates the inevitability of research and researcher effects in any research design, providing some orientation for budding video researchers. Overall, our conclusion is that the insights provided by the method far outweigh the problems, as we find ourselves still fascinated by the data and keen to share them with others. Our hope is that others will incorporate participant-led video methodology in their own research areas and that this methodology will become accepted practice rather than unconventional in the organization and management field.

■ **ACKNOWLEDGEMENTS**

The Digital Brain Switch project was funded by the EPSRC (EP/K025201/1). We thank all the participants who generously gave up their time and made this research possible.

■ **REFERENCES**

Alonzo, A. and Kim, J. (2016). 'Declarative and dynamic pedagogical content knowledge as elicited through two video-based interview methods', *Journal of Research in Science Teaching*, 53(8): 1259–86.

Ashforth, B., Kreiner, G.E., and Fugate, M. (2000). 'All in a day's work: boundaries and micro role transitions', *Academy of Management Review*, 25(3): 472–91.

Bell, E. and Davison, J. (2013). 'Visual management studies: empirical and theoretical approaches', *International Journal of Management Reviews*, 15(2): 167–84.

Bell, E., Warren, S., and Schroeder, J. (2014). 'Introduction: the visual organization.' In E. Bell, S. Warren, and J. Schroeder (eds) *The Routledge Companion to Visual Organization*. New York: Routledge, pp. 1–16.

Bolger, N., Davis, A., and Rafaeli, E. (2003). 'Diary methods: capturing life as it is lived', *Annual Review of Psychology*, 54(1): 579–616.

Braun, V. and Clarke, V. (2006). 'Using thematic analysis in psychology', *Qualitative Research in Psychology*, 3(2): 77–101.

Brown, C., Costley, C., Friend, L., and Varey, R. (2010). 'Capturing their dream: video diaries and minority consumers', *Consumption Markets and Culture*, 13(4): 419–36.

Chamakiotis, P., Symon, G., Whiting, R., and Roby, H. (2015). 'Exploring boundaries in the hybrid environment.' Presented at *WORK 2015: New Meanings of Work, Stream: Sites and Places of Work*, Turku, Finland.

Christianson, M. (2016). 'Mapping the terrain: the use of video-based research in top-tier organizational journals', *Organizational Research Methods*. <http://doi.org/10.1177/1094428116663636>

Clark, S.C. (2000). 'Work/family border theory: a new theory of work/family balance', *Human Relations*, 53(6): 747–70.

Cohen, L., Duberley, J., and Musson, G. (2009). 'Work-life balance? An autoethnographic exploration of everyday home-work dynamics', *Journal of Management Inquiry*, 18(3): 229–41.

Crary, J. (1990). *Techniques of the Observer: On Vision and Modernity in the Nineteenth Century*. Cambridge, MA: MIT Press.

Crozier, S.E. and Cassell, C. (2016). 'Methodological considerations in the use of audio diaries in work psychology: adding to the qualitative toolkit', *Journal of Occupational and Organizational Psychology*, 89(2): 396–419.

Davies, A.R. and Frink, B.D. (2014). 'The origins of the ideal worker: the separation of work and home in the United States from the market revolution to 1950', *Work and Occupations*, 41(1): 18–39.

Erickson, F. (2011). 'Uses of video in social research: a brief history', *International Journal of Social Research Methodology*, Special Issue, 14(3): 179–89.

Fry, H. and Ketteridge, S. (2009). 'Enhancing personal practice: establishing teaching and learning credentials.' In H. Fry, S. Ketteridge, and S. Marshall (eds) *A Handbook for Teaching and Learning in Higher Education: Enhancing Academic Practice*. London, Routledge, pp.469–97.

Gibson, B.E. (2005). 'Co-producing video diaries: the presence of the "absent" researcher', *International Journal of Qualitative Methods*, 4(4): 34–43.

Gill, R. (2011). 'The shadow in organizational ethnography: moving beyond shadowing to spect-acting', *Qualitative Research in Organizations and Management: An International Journal*, 6(2): 115–33.

Gordon, C. (2012). 'Beyond the observer's paradox: the audio-recorder as a resource for the display of identity', *Qualitative Research*, 13(3): 299–317.

Gylfe, P., Franck, H., Lebaron, C., and Mantere, S. (2016). 'Video methods in strategy research: focusing on embodied cognition.' *Strategic Management Journal*, 37(1): 133–48.

Heath, C., Luff, P., and Sanchez Svensson, M. (2007). 'Video and qualitative research: analysing medical practice and interaction', *Medical Education*, 41(1): 109–16.

Henry, S.G. and Fetters, M.D. (2012). 'Video elicitation interviews: a qualitative research method for investigating physician-patient interactions', *The Annals of Family Medicine*, 10(2): 118–25.

Hindmarsh, J. and Llewellyn, N. (2016). 'Video in sociomaterial investigations: a solution to the problem of relevance for organizational research', *Organizational Research Methods*. <http://doi.org/10.1177/1094428116657595>

Holloway, W. and Jefferson, T. (2000). *Doing Qualitative Research Differently: Free Association, Narrative and the Interview Method*. London: Sage.

Jarrett, M. and Liu, F. (2016). ' "Zooming With": a participatory approach to the use of video ethnography in organizational studies', *Organizational Research Methods*. <http://doi.org/10.1177/1094428116656238>

Jewitt, C. (2012). *National Centre for Research Methods Working Paper: An Introduction to Using Video for Research* (Working Paper). London: National Centre for Research Methods.

Johnson, P. and Duberley, J. (2003). 'Reflexivity in management research', *Journal of Management Studies*, 40(5): 1279–303.

Jones, R., Fonseca, J., Silva, L.D.M., Davies, G., Morgan, K., and Mesquita, I. (2014). 'The promise and problems of video diaries: building on current research', *Qualitative Research in Sport, Exercise and Health*, 7(3): 395–410.

Knoblauch, H. (2012). 'Introduction to the special issue of Qualitative Research: video-analysis and videography', *Qualitative Research*, 12(3): 251–4.

Labov, W. (1972). 'Some principles of linguistic methodology', *Language in Society*, 1(1): 97–120.

Mazmanian, M., Orlikowski, W.J., and Yates, J. (2013). 'The Autonomy Paradox: the implications of mobile email devices for knowledge professionals', *Organization Science*, 24(5): 1337–57.

Meyer, R.E., Höllerer, M.A., Jancsary, D., and van Leeuwen, T. (2013). 'The visual dimension in organizing, organization, and organization research: core ideas, current developments, and promising avenues', *Academy of Management Annals*, 7(1): 489–555.

Mok, T.M., Cornish, F., and Tarr, J. (2015). 'Too much information: visual research ethics in the age of wearable cameras', *Integrative Psychological and Behavioral Science*, 49(2): 309–22.

Musson, G. (2004). 'Life histories.' In C. Cassell and G. Symon (eds) *Essential Guide to Qualitative Methods in Organizational Research*. London: Sage, pp.34–44.

Noyes, A. (2004). 'Video diary: a method for exploring learning dispositions.' *Cambridge Journal of Education*, 34(2): 193–209.

Ollier-Malaterre, A., Rothbard, N.P., and Berg, J.M. (2013). 'When worlds collide in cyberspace: how boundary work in online social networks impacts professional relationships', *Academy of Management Review*, 38(4): 645–69.

Patton, M.Q. (2002). *Qualitative Research and Evaluation Methods*. London: Sage.

Pauwels, L. (2004). 'Filmed science in search of a form', *New Cinemas: Journal of Contemporary Film*, 2(1): 41–60.

Ray, J.L. and Smith, A. D. (2012). 'Using photographs to research organizations: evidence, considerations, and application in a field study', *Organizational Research Methods*, 15(2): 288–315.

Roberts, J. (2011). 'Video diaries: a tool to investigate sustainability-related learning in threshold spaces', *Environmental Education Research*, 17(5): 675–88.

Rose, G. (2007). *Visual Methodologies: An Introduction to the Interpretation of Visual Methods*. London: Sage.

Saunders, M. (2012). 'Choosing research participants.' In G. Symon and C. Cassell (eds) *Qualitative Organizational Research*. London: Sage, pp.37–55.

Sayah, S. (2013). 'Managing work-life boundaries with information and communication technologies', *New Technology, Work and Employment*, 28(3): 179–96.

Toraldo, M.L., Islam, G., and Mangia, G. (2016). 'Modes of knowing: video research and the problem of elusive knowledges.' *Organizational Research Methods*. <http://doi.org/10.1177/1094428116657394>

Tribe, J. (2006). 'The truth about tourism', *Annals of Tourism Research*, 33(2): 360–81.

Whiting, R. and Pritchard, K. (2018). 'Digital ethics.' In C. Cassell, A. Cunliffe, and G. Grandy (eds) *Sage Handbook of Qualitative Business and Management Research Methods*. London: Sage (Vol. 1, pp. 562–579).

Whiting, R., Roby, H., Symon, G., and Chamakiotis, P. (2015a). 'Beyond work and life: constructing new domains in the digital age.' In *EGOS 2015 COLLOQUIUM: Organizations and the Examined Life: Reason, Reflexivity and Responsibility, Subtheme 56: 'Reflections on New Worlds of Work.'* July. Athens, Greece.

Whiting, R., Roby, H., Symon, G., and Chamakiotis, P. (2015b). 'Digi-housekeeping: a new form of digital labour?' Presented at the *WORK 2015: New Meanings of Work, Stream: 'Reconceptualizing Work.'* Turku, Finland.

Whiting, R., Symon, G., Roby, H., and Chamakiotis, P. (2016). 'Who's behind the lens? A reflexive analysis of roles in participatory video research', *Organizational Research Methods*. <http://doi.org/10.1177/1094428116669818>

Woodley-Baker, R. (2009). 'Private and public experience captured: young women capture their everyday lives and dreams through photo-narratives', *Visual Studies*, 24(1): 19–35.

FOR INTERESTED READERS

Digital Brain Switch project website

The project website includes a section with copies of the participant documentation i.e. information sheets, instructions for videoing and consent forms
http://digitalbrainswitch.org.uk

Dissemination videos on YouTube of Digital Brain Switch project findings

Work-life boundaries in the digital age
https://www.youtube.com/watch?v=Ima1HsT8QYA

Three implications of our digi lives
https://www.youtube.com/watch?v=7w-huJ4Z544

The project metadata statement is available here: http://oro.open.ac.uk/46687/

11 Inter-organizational ethnography

Promises and problems

Olivier Berthod, Michael Grothe-Hammer, and Jörg Sydow

Introduction

Currently, ethnography is experiencing a revival in the study of organizations, work, and management. Organizational ethnography sets out to understand the processes that underlie the construction of the social context in which organizing takes place, thereby acknowledging organizational complexity and the difficulty of generalizing findings across contexts. Therefore, ethnographies are often associated with specific writing conventions and with thinking about organizations, in ways that aim to immerse the researcher and the reader into the field and show 'how things work' (Watson, 2011, p.202).

Because of the richness of the data it produces, ethnography is regularly pushed to the fore as one of the most revered approaches to qualitative research in organizations (Miettinen et al., 2009; Ybema et al., 2009). In fact, fieldwork and anthropology in organizations has contributed some of the seminal work in organization theory (e.g. Blau, 1963; Selznick, 1957). Van Maanen (1979) in particular popularized ethnography in the late 1970s, and the more recent practice-turn in organization studies (Feldman and Orlikowski, 2011; Nicolini, 2012) relies on this methodology to unpack the practices that explain how social structures are performed into organizational existence.

Recent discussion has called for more ethnography about inter-organizational phenomena (Van Maanen, 2010; Zilber, 2014; Berthod et al., 2017a). The nature of new work arrangements, globalization, the seemingly unlimited flow of knowledge, and other forces at play on organizations drive the need for more studies of organizing as a process that crosses organizational boundaries to other stakeholders. Quite often, however, the problem of site multiplicity challenges the presence of ethnographers, prompting them to make decisions about where to begin, whom to shadow and why—which tends to explain the paucity of research on inter-organizational settings so far.

In this chapter, we discuss potential avenues for more ethnography of inter-organizational relations (IORs), looking at market, hierarchy, and networks as three ideal types of governance. Our goal is less to develop guidelines for inter-organizational ethnography that will fit them all. Rather, we wish to highlight promising opportunities for conducting ethnography among multiple sites no matter how they are coordinated, to show how researchers could deal with the challenges of doing fieldwork at multiple sites, and identify problems one might want to consider in the research process. We introduce briefly the notions of organizational ethnography and IORs. Then, we reflect about the ethnographies of such relations in markets, hierarchies, and networks. We conclude with a discussion on the promises and pitfalls of conducting ethnography in and about IORs.

From organizational to inter-organizational ethnography

Ethnography 'is about understanding human experience—how a particular community lives—by studying events, language, rituals, institutions, behaviors, artifacts, and interactions' (Cunliffe, 2010, p. 227). The interested reader will find countless articles and books elsewhere on how to conduct and write ethnography (Emerson et al., 2011; Gobo, 2008; Golden-Biddle and Locke, 1993; Hammersley, 1992; Van Maanen, 1988; Watson, 2011). So let us begin, and restrict ourselves, by repeating that ethnography, classically speaking, implies lengthy stays in a clearly defined social setting, the prominent usage of observation techniques oriented towards proximity, and the absence of filters between informants and researchers—all allowing the production of highly descriptive, subjective, and evocative reports, literally describing (graphy) people (ethno), and often including vivid reflections about the ethnographer's immersion in the field (e.g. Jarzabkowski et al., 2014; Van Maanen, 1979, 2010; Watson, 2011). Seen as a methodology for scientific inquiry, ethnography is 'at least as old as the work of Herodotus [...] that ancient Greek ethnographer (who) recorded the infinite variety and strangeness he saw in other cultures' (Sanday, 1979, p.527).

John Van Maanen (1979), most notably, contributed to reviving ethnography as a methodology for organizational studies at a time when statistical analysis dominated the field (Van Maanen, 1995; Ybema et al., 2009). Organizational ethnography, he proposed (Van Maanen, 1979, 2006), is the approach of anthropology: understanding the cultural context in which organizing takes place, thereby acknowledging the complexity and dynamics of organizations, the contextuality of practices, and the difficulty of generalizing findings across contexts. Organizational ethnographers often stay in the field over the course of one year or two, which is less time taken than for the traditional ethnography of, say, a whole society (Eberle and Maeder, 2011; Jeffrey and Troman, 2004; Rosen, 1991), but more than is required using other qualitative methodologies of organizational research. Ethnographers supplement their observations with interviews, audio-visual recordings of work situations (Neyland, 2008), and documents, usually produced by the organization under scrutiny (Pratt, 2000; Yanow, 2009). Because of the richness of the data it produces, ethnography is usually seen as one of the most promising approaches to qualitative research in organizations (Miettinen et al., 2009; Ybema et al., 2009; see also the special issue on qualitative methods in *Administrative Science Quarterly*, 1979, and *Journal of Management Studies*, 2011, with a point and counterpoint on why we need more of it). Ethnography now has a dedicated journal: *Journal of Organizational Ethnography*. However, Bate (1997) reminds us that ethnography should not be mistaken for a method alone; it necessitates specific writing conventions and thinking about organizations that aim at immersing the researcher as well as the reader into the field in order to show 'how things work' (Watson 2011, p.202).

Over the last decade or so, a resurgence of fieldwork and direct observations has been related to the study of practices in organizational settings and practices of organizing more specifically. The practice-driven approaches of scholars to strategy (e.g. Jarzabkowski, 2008) and institutional complexity (e.g. Smets et al., 2015), to sociomateriality (e.g. Kellogg et al., 2006), or to routines (e.g. Feldman, 2000) have been particularly influential in this respect. 'Practice', as a term, is now widely used to imply the idea that social structures are best expressed and studied via socially embedded and recurrent activities that constitute a bridge between agency and structures (e.g. Giddens, 1984; Simpson, 2009; Nicolini, 2009, 2012; Feldman and Orlikowski, 2011). In most research pertaining to this stream, ethnographic techniques are used to observe exactly what it is that people do in organizations instead of relying on statements from interviews. It must be noted, however, that much contemporary work (including that of one of the authors of this chapter) increasingly faces the difficult task of highlighting what useful concepts or important issues their fieldwork entails (thereby departing from the richness of details; see Barley, 2016, for a critique of this development).

Ethnography can be applied to inter-organizational settings too (Eberle and Maeder, 2011; Yanow, 2009). Several new forms of organizational ethnography recommend dealing with pluralistic settings in general and moving beyond organizational boundaries (Delgado and Cruz, 2014; Desmond, 2014; Hannerz, 2003; Howard, 2002; Marcus, 1995; Nicolini, 2007; Van Maanen, 2010; Zilber, 2014). As noted earlier, however, the problem of site multiplicity challenges the presence of the ethnographer. However, ethnographies that evolve beyond organizational boundaries are urgently required.

As Van Maanen notes (2010, p.244), 'with the rise and expansion of vast human migrations, vanishing natives, market globalization, enhanced information, communication and transportation technologies, the anthropologizing of the West, ethnography has become rather deterritorialized'. Consider, for example, ethnographies of communities of practice (Orr, 1996), virtual work environments (Nicolini, 2007), professions (Smart, 1998), infrastructures (Star, 1999), or even of large-scale, inter-organizational operations (Berthod et al., 2017b). In such settings, as Green (1999) puts it, it often is the connections, and the meaning ascribed to them, that become the object of study, thereby opening new dimensions to the study of organizing, organizational forms, and organized orders.

Defining and distinguishing inter-organizational relations

IORs as a topic have found applications in disciplines as diverse as strategic management (Jarillo, 1988), organization studies (Cropper et al., 2008), public administration (Provan and Milward, 1995), and criminal studies (Raab and Milward, 2003). In the face of such variety, IORs are equally diverse in form, content, and level (Sydow et al., 2016), making their analysis particularly challenging.

To give contours to our discussion, we structure this chapter using three *ideal types of governance* of IORs. Williamson (1991) famously distinguished between hierarchy, market, and hybrids, the latter being also conceived as cooperative IORs (Ring and Van de Ven, 1994) or, in the case of more complex constellations, inter-organizational networks (Sydow and Windeler, 1998). (Note: although we focus on three ideal types of governance, the methodological implications that we outline can be applied to other theoretical viewpoints, such as the perspective of meta-organizations (Ahrne and Brunsson, 2008)). These three forms are ideal types in the sense that they never materialize in their perfect, theoretical form: markets, hierarchies, and networks always include traces of the other two ideal types in their structures and functioning (Powell, 1990). Nevertheless, this typology is useful to distinguish between dominant modes of governance among IORs.

IORs emerge with each transaction. *Markets* imply IORs that are predominantly coordinated via price and other market-based mechanisms. The emerging relations are in consequence considered as loose and fleeting, allowing only for a limited amount of knowledge exchange. By contrast, IORs come to resemble inter-organizational *networks* when repetition, collaboration, reciprocity, loyalty and/or trust feed swifter and richer exchange (Powell, 1990). Finally, IORs can also take place in the shadow of *hierarchy*, when multiple firms are part of, and dependent upon, a company or business group (Colpan, 2010), or when local agencies carry the delivery of public services under the control of a central administration (Provan and Kenis, 2008). In this ideal type, hierarchical fiat, rather than price or cooperation, dominates inter-organizational coordination.

In addition to diversity in modes of governance, IORs also differ in their *content*. IORs can include organizations operating on similar levels of a same value chain (horizontal IOR), organizations operating at various stages of the same chain (vertical IOR), or organizations operating in different, yet potentially related value chains (lateral IOR). Similarly, IORs can be formally mandated and governed, but they can also be the result of informal processes with little visibility for researchers. Finally, beginning with three organizations (Provan et al., 2007), IORs can also differ in their topological structure (i.e. the structural arrangement of their elements). Two organizations pursuing a common goal form a dyad; three or more form an inter-organizational network.

The study of IORs necessarily implies issues of multiple analytical *levels*. Organizations are represented by individuals such as professionals, managers, or executives who operate in boundary-spanning roles (Langan-Fox and Cooper, 2014) with some responsibilities, formal or informal, in the management of specific relations. Needless to say, interests can collide across levels. How does coherence emerge nonetheless? Researching IORs, therefore, should embrace at least the neighbouring levels of the relation (Sydow et al., 2016, pp.15–17), for example the field or industry on the one hand, and the organization or an organizational sub-system on the other. Opening the scope to multilevel thinking brings us one step closer to institutional and spatial embeddedness on the one hand (Sydow and Staber, 2002), and cognitive distance and the reduction thereof on the other (Beckert, 2007, 2010; Stark, 2009).

Against this background, ethnographies of IORs are necessary if we want to understand more readily *how* such relations come to be in terms of governance, content, and level of analysis, i.e. how relations are enacted, nurtured, or controlled, and how they become the object of change and purposeful management. In contrast with single organizations, IORs may be less visible. Nonetheless, even less formal IORs can end up with a dedicated administrative organization (Provan and Kenis, 2008) and a common name over the door (see, for example, the case of Star Alliance in the aviation industry). Some networks even chose to work on dress code and logos to give a sense of unity to temporary collaborations (Stadtler and van Wassenhove, 2016). The use of ethnography can provide access to such practices and to the members' tacit knowledge about the enactment, reproduction and transformation of IORs, their history, and their meaning. For example, we know a lot about *why* such relations emerge, but much less about how (Kenis and Knoke, 2002; Krueathep et al., 2010; Ring and Van de Ven, 1994; Van de Ven, 1976).

Similarly, there remains a lot to learn about how such IORs evolve as they become the object of structuration (Sydow and Windeler, 1998), and how agents leverage IORs to pursue specific goals (Walker et al., 1997; Maurer and Ebers, 2006).

Inquiring into inter-organizational relations

More often than not the three different forms of governance—hierarchy, market, and network—can only be distinguished by inquiring into exactly how the coordinative mechanisms influence inter-organizational practices and how these practices, in turn, reproduce or transform the particular form of governance. In this case, inter-organizational ethnography is not only helpful, but may be even necessary, in particular to identify boundary cases. What is more, ethnography, in contrast to other qualitative techniques, is more likely to unearth tensions and contradictions in such processes.

We have recently proposed (Berthod et al., 2017a) a research design that mixes quantitative social network analyses with ethnography, toward what we call 'network ethnography', for application in inter-organizational networks. Social network analysis helps to investigate even complex inter-organizational arrangements. Complementary ethnographic techniques have the potential to unearth unacknowledged practices and the members' tacit knowledge about the enactment, reproduction, and transformation of IORs and their structures. Specifically, we highlight four such techniques for fieldwork in inter-organizational settings: (1) following boundary objects; (2) capturing network enactments; (3) multiplying investigators; and (4) interviewing repeatedly. But We argue that these techniques, with some adaptations, could be applied to ethnography in most IOR settings—networks and markets as well as hierarchies.

The technique of following boundary objects stands at the centre of fieldwork in IORs. The main idea is to apply a multi-site approach, by which the ethnographer does not stay permanently in one department or organization but follows 'something' throughout the field of praxis. This tracing process can involve individuals, artefacts, metaphors, conflicts, research themes, or practices (Hannerz, 2003; Marcus, 1995; Nicolini, 2009). The method involves following IOR-enacting 'objects' that, as boundary spanners, connect several organizations and the emerging governance form.

The following of boundary objects should be supplemented with attention to instances of IORs and their enactments. Many IORs are enacted via planned meetings or events, as well as more spontaneous occasions to see how these relations function when they materialize (e.g. by staying in the vicinity of its most important operative actors or by observing crossing points, such as in production facilities, where just-in-time deliveries take place).

It is often necessary and valuable to multiply investigators, even if an additional observer cannot replace the socialization of the first ethnographer, to maximize field observations. For example, teaming up to observe two firms within one company group, or having an observer at strategy meetings and another observing the operative level of IORs.

Finally, interviewing the same people several times is an effective approach to reviewing events involving important actors, and increasing knowledge and understanding of what the events meant for them. By doing so, one is still not able to capture the whole picture. But several accounts of how the different parts of an inter-organizational constellation are intertwined while focusing on the same object can provide substantial material to capture the essence of what it means to work in such an environment and to cope with a specific form of governance and related instruments of control.

In the following sections we discuss the potential and problems for ethnography in each of the three governance forms in turn. We rely on a study which we conducted in the field of emergency management in the city of Düsseldorf, Germany. This exemplary study is particularly relevant for our purpose because the IORs we observed portrayed predominantly the form of a network, but also included market-based and more hierarchical forms of IORs.

Specifically, to cope with emergencies and larger crises, the city of Düsseldorf relies on an inter-organizational network comprising over eighty organizations, managed more or less formally by its municipal fire and emergency department (FED), and carrying out well over 100,000 operations annually, of which only 2 per cent relate to fire. During emergencies, the operation relies on ad hoc collaboration under the formal leadership of the FED. Between crises, however, managing this network proves more complex, as cooperation relies on more informal planning and meetings that are not mandated (for more details, see Berthod et al., 2015; Berthod et al., 2017b). Network management between crises thus relies on recent experience, and influences future operations in return, in a constellation of IORs that are hierarchical (the FED and the environmental agency both report to the Mayor as head of the city administration), market-based (Emergency medical service—EMS—organizations provide personnel for the FED's own EMS), and cooperative (the FED prepares an emergency action plan with the local airport authorities, federal police, and other participants).

HIERARCHY

Hierarchy is an important coordinating device not only within but also among organizations. Instances of organizational hierarchy, as an instrument to coordinate IORs, can be found in groups of companies under the command and control of a parent organization (Sydow et al., 2016) or in the case of public agencies and their hierarchical relation to local or state authorities. Organizational hierarchy as a form of governance for IORs, in particular in the case of holding companies, can be seen as a boundary case, since the coordination via hierarchy itself constitutes an organization, the company group, or municipal and state administrations. The company group has subsidiaries as member organizations, but these subsidiaries lack autonomy because they are under direct control of the parent organization. Nevertheless, each individual organization within the group has its own offices, legal existence and work processes, not least because of their embeddedness in local institutions and relations.

Company groups, as the prototypical example for coordinating IORs via hierarchy, are usually very large, often with dozens or even hundreds of organizations and tens of thousands of individuals working for them. The sheer size and spatial distribution of such groups makes it impossible to study them as a whole (Eberle and Maeder, 2011). The above-mentioned approach via multi-site ethnography can help to cope with this difficulty. Following people, strategies, products, raw materials, themes, decisions, life histories, or even visual identities across the boundaries of the members of a holding company, for instance, illuminates not only how organizations in such groups differ with regard to structures, cultures, and processes. Rather, it enables us to study how communication or other types of interaction are organized across organizational boundaries. Against this background, it is important to capture top-down as well as bottom-up perspectives.

In the case of our project, we quickly had to face, and understand, hierarchical IORs. Generally speaking, the FED coordinates emergency management in the city of Düsseldorf, which includes significant efforts between crises to animate the relations they build with recurring partners. During operations, however, the FED officers are omnipotent and hold a mandate that gives them the right to command and require other organizations' full cooperation. We made such observations possible by having an ethnographer stay long periods of time in an accommodation close to the FED. He wanted to make sure that he would not miss an opportunity of observing the FED as it imposes decisions and sends orders to other partners. This decision implies an important aspect in such a research design: rarity of the phenomenon and access. The strategy of staying longer periods of time implies a substantial increase in the probability to observe rare or non-schedulable phenomena.

This strategy was only possible because our ethnographer had built a reliable relationship with a set of key people in the FED who would inform him in due time. Hence, between crises and emergencies, he used his time in situ to interview these informants and others repeatedly, in order to 'go native' and be accepted by others when an operation emerged. Similarly, we used the case of a more complex crisis to observe hierarchical IORs between FED and the city's leadership. We needed to observe the FED officer during his work to coordinate other agencies. In major crises, the leadership is not in the FED's hands, but in those of the mayor. This relation could be observed best in inter-organizational meetings as typical instances of IOR enactment. Sitting in the same room with all participating organizations, we took notes on the FED officer's role and rhetoric while planning with other agencies, the reactions and roles of these agencies, and then the role and rhetoric of the FED officer when he was reporting to the deputy mayor who was present on this day. Here again, this opportunity could only be seized because of the quality of the relation with officers at the FED and the necessity to become an informal part of the team of this central organization, at least in the eyes of the other participants. An advantage in this case, however, is that participants in such meetings do not possess the same knowledge of who is who than employees do when their own organization is concerned. Hence we experienced it as much easier to blend into the landscape in such large meetings or instances of IOR enactment while observing exercises or planning activities.

Ethnography has also been used to study company groups, especially multi-national corporations, although not necessarily reflecting explicitly on IORs and their relation to hierarchy (Fayard and Van Maanen, 2015; Jordan and Lambert, 2009). For example, Moore (2006) followed expatriate managers in a German multinational bank and concluded that, although the head office regarded expatriates as a resource to maintain control, these expatriates actually facilitated dynamic negotiation between the groups. Lauring and Klitmøller (2015) followed another object—interactions—and traced the theme of 'corporate language-based communication avoidance' through eleven subsidiaries of three multinational corporations. In the end they identified several contextual factors affecting the avoidance of verbal communication in English, the cor-porate language within the company groups. Particularly impressive, Sedgwick (2011) draws on a two decade-long multi-sited ethnography in a Japanese multinational corporation, tracing the life histories of several informants. Growing older along with his informants allowed him to comprehensively investigate the different levels of 'age hierarchies' among the Japanese.

MARKETS

A study of IORs dominated by the market as the main mode of governance is more likely to be concerned with rather fleeting relations, with what these transactions are about, with the notion of worth, or with explaining why the participants keep each other at arms' length instead of evolving towards more cooperative interactions. Ethnographies of markets are more convenient to design when focusing on individuals in particular localities—visits to local flea markets or stadiums betray a great deal (Sherry, 1990; Holt, 1995). Markets, in the more abstract sense, are the object of discursive and material constructions that stretch over time and space (Araujo et al., 2008; Beckert, 2007; Callon, 1998; Giddens, 1984). Ethnographies of market-coordinated IORs are interested in the way agents shape such transaction-based relations, often with unintended consequences, along three main types of practices (see Kjellberg and Helgesson, 2006, for a discussion): exchange; normalization (activities that form normative expectations about markets); and representation (activities that produce images and evaluation of markets).

A first approach is concerned with the notion of price as a coordination mechanism. Prices are often considered as objectively 'a given fact'. We seldom get to experience how practitioners set prices and make sense of prices and pricing, or negotiations, for example. Similarly, how does meaning emerge out of the process of pricing and defining the tasks to be performed, and how does this collective work contribute to building an economic relation? The latter point highlights a second avenue. Market-based relations are often distinguished from other forms of exchange by highlighting their loose and fleeting nature, comparable to discrete transactions. However, as real transactions typically have a history as well as a future, the limitations to forming a cooperative relation are, most likely, more elusive and could well become clearer with the help of fieldwork. Finally and relatedly, ethnographic fieldwork could shed light on the process of terminating market-based IORs (including its antecedents, its genesis, and consequences), or how the prospect of terminating relations is leveraged.

Observing market relationships, we found out, is more complicated than hierarchical and network-based IORs for one specific reason: much happens in the participants' heads and is not immediately accessible via direct observation. In this case, we realized that it would be more productive to rely on ex-post or ex-ante interviews to go through the process of setting up bids and prices and to reconstruct how the FED or other organizations would handle transactions among each other. For example, we used interviewing to decipher the process of finding the appropriate supplier for the pumping out of silos on the verge of explosion. In sharp contrast, we found that direct observations would tell plenty about dynamics of coopetition. Our ethnographer spent time with EMS organizations and learned that, on many occasions, these organizations were addressed as one group, although his observations had revealed that they were indeed competitors for contracts with the FED as well as for many other contracts, such as medical service contracts with private business entities. However, due to the high degree of uncertainty about the form and scope of incidents, the EMS organizations pooled their resources to face unexpected demands better. Eventually, interviews with our informants revealed that the bids of the EMS organizations often relied on the resources of all the others as additional backups. Strictly speaking, this case did not reflect idealized forms of market coordination but, as often, contained elements of networked IORs.

Extant ethnographies of markets seldom look at IORs governed by market mechanisms. Some contributions, nonetheless, show the potential of such an approach far beyond the specific setting of our project. For example, Cayla et al. (2013) reported on the importance of business parties and sponsored events for creating and maintaining commercial relations. Executives dropped their customary jargon and management codes of conduct and discussed matters on a more personal basis. The parties are filled with games and rituals and leave, in fact, little room for business, for they offer an ideal opportunity to build bonds between business partners that will reach beyond mere economic interests and form a sense of community. On a similar note, Darr (2003) shows how gifting and counter-gifting practices take part in the constitution of business relationships in the exchange of electronic components. Free products and samples helped to identify new relations and constitute an obligation to buy in the future. And the reactivation of older ties came together with private gifts directly from the individual salesperson to the individual buyer to blur the lines between business and a personal bond. Finally, Marion et al. (2015) highlight how emerging ventures made their business relations migrate from market transactions to alliances as a means to gain stability in their operations. They also show, however, that the socio-emotional bonds that were formed in these relationships overshadowed the business outcomes in many ventures, thereby harming the companies.

NETWORKS

A study of collaborative IORs, including whole inter-organizational networks, implies considering this form of governance (and its many variants, see Provan and Kenis, 2008) as a distinct form of a goal-directed system instead of a mere context, or means to acquire resources. IORs are assembled purposefully and aim to grant more agentic autonomy to their participants while increasing degrees of connectedness (Provan et al., 2007). Here also, a common understanding of shared goals is constituted over time, not least as a function of the structuration of the network (Sydow and Windeler, 1998), and contributes to the emergence of a diversity of tensions that need to be addressed via managerial practices (Sydow et al., 2016; Provan and Kenis, 2008). From this point of view, agents engage in a diversity of efforts to shape collaborative IORs, often with unintended consequences, along four main types of inter-organizational practices: selection, regulation, evaluation, and allocation (Sydow et al., 2016).

Ethnographies of networks and collaborative ties, as in market and company groups, are difficult to conduct because of the problem of site multiplicity. Against this background, an ethnography of networks should help us understand better how the rules and resources that underlie the structuration of networks are negotiated in the first place, how they shape action and how they are applied—and thereby eventually modified or even transformed—in practice (Giddens, 1984). Similarly, we need to understand better how participants in collaborative IORs design, hybridize, and practice the governance of their relations, and relating to markets: how participants in collaborative IORs terminate relations, or cope with the possibility of that happening in the course of their work.

In the course of our project, network-informed IORs were our primary focus. We experimented with all four techniques, depending on the opportunities that arose. Combining social network analysis with ethnographic fieldwork, we tried to make sense of the shape of the whole network, and identify the most central actors. This exercise, however, prompts many questions. Social network analysis (SNA) relies heavily on documents to identify evidence for, or traces of, IORs (e.g. patents, co-authorship of articles, newspaper and industry reports). Doing the same, we realized that the images that we obtained from SNA applications were sometimes difficult to make fit with our field observations. The difficulty for the researcher, then, becomes a matter of identifying what research questions might be unpacked below such tensions. For example, SNA results based on standard operating procedures would reveal an equally strong role for the police and FED due to their mandates in this field. Our observations helped us to understand how these central agencies supported this cohabitation. Our fieldwork revealed how the FED and the police nurtured a very close relationship with each other, which helped officers decipher responsibilities and jurisdictions on a case-by-case basis. Observing cooperation, we realized, was easier than market transactions, especially when creativity and problem-solving were involved, because it implicated lengthy, open meetings, much prototyping, and many iterations until a general solution could be agreed upon. Here again, however, the importance of having a strong gatekeeper on our side was unavoidable.

Ethnographic work on network-informed IORs has proven particularly promising, especially due to the domination of structural explanations of networks (Berthod et al., 2017a). For example, Paquin and Howard-Grenville (2013) highlight the role of 'orchestrators' in the process of setting up an industrial symbiosis network (i.e. the physical exchange of by-products to geographically proximate facilities). Orchestrators are those actors who develop and lead networks and, importantly, determine the recruitment of their members and their interactions. The fieldwork of Lorenzoni and Baden-Fuller (1995) puts tensions to the fore. Orchestrators, they show, face two dilemmas. First, they need to build interest in the network and its activities in face of multiple, intra-organizational interests. Second, they need to balance two types of orchestration: blind dates (helping the emergence of new, serendipitous connections), and arranged marriages (supporting the connections that were once brokered by the orchestrator). Their ethnography shows how these dilemmas evolve over time and how shifts in the network development are both outcomes of past actions and mediums for new ones. Similarly, Saz-Carranza and Ospina (2011) highlight the need for networks to balance unity (the state of being in accord) and diversity (the state of having variety) among participants, and show how the framing of collective work contributes to aligning the IORs along the same goals (e.g. via distributed decision-making structures, or efforts in establishing a network culture). Expanding the findings of Paquin and Howard-Grenville (2013), the Network Administrative Organization was instrumental in recruiting participants, but also in building their capacities when it was deemed necessary, which contributed towards balancing tensions in the network. Finally, the mismanagement of such tensions has revealed the limitation of notions of collaborative IORs based on the idea of loyalty alone. In the study by Marion et al. (2015), the socioemotional bonds that developed between those who were involved clouded the judgements of their partner's abilities, thus threatening the survival of the collaboration.

Conclusion

The aim of this chapter was to highlight promising opportunities for conducting ethnographic research on IORs, irrespective of how they are predominantly coordinated—be it by a market, hierarchy, or network mode of governance. At the same time, we wanted to show how researchers could deal with the challenges of doing fieldwork at multiple sites, a necessity in such inter-organizational settings. We introduced briefly the notions of organizational ethnography and IORs and explained the three forms of governance and their relationship to practice. Then, we reflected about ethnographies of IORs in markets, hierarchies, and networks, each in turn.

We conclude by shedding light on a few pitfalls that might be important to consider for ethnographic research on IORs. We argued that understanding how such relationships are cultivated into existence implies specific methodological challenges, and contrasted these challenges with the promises of such studies. Around each of the three governance forms, research questions abound, not to mention their possible combination into what is commonly called 'plural forms' (Bradach, 1997; Sydow et al., 2016). But ethnographies are not only interesting for the sake of understanding IORs. They also open the door to additional insight into the nature of managerial work in contemporary settings which are increasingly interconnected, global, and ubiquitous, with little geographic stability in careers. Against this background, how do managers and employees create meaning out of increasingly complex organizational arrangements? How do they cope with questions of identity when their work crosses organizational boundaries? Ethnographers interested in IORs need to immerse themselves and the reader into what it means for the individuals to experience such organizational forms. Sociologists interested in relational ethnography propose to consider individual actors in their social context by taking their positions in the field into account (Desmond, 2014). When looking at organizations, this question is equally relevant for the collective and the individual level and raises the question of the consequences of IORs for the field, the organizations, and their members.

Most studies using ethnography or related techniques as a starting point investigate either the governance form (e.g. how marketers shape markets), or the point of view of one focal organization instead of the relation as such. As highlighted by the research questions discussed throughout the chapter, vast avenues of future research remain unexplored when it comes to IORs and how these relationships are practised beyond the three ideal types identified in theory. In particular, research needs to focus on the tensions and contradictions that emerge at the interplay of these ideal types. These forms are useful heuristics to apprehend practices of IORs. But as for any ideal type, deviations in practice are not surprising findings as such. Instead, the strength of fieldwork is to show how practice copes with the contradictions and complexity that, inevitably, emerge out of such situations.

Finally, we wish to shed light on the implications and limitations of ethnography as it becomes a buzzword in management and organization research methods. As Bate (1997) points out, there is a danger of ethnography turning into a pastiche. For some, ethnography is more of a *Weltanschauung* than a method. Review processes and related expectations of rigour (and the demonstration thereof) tend to push qualitative research towards more 'ethnography' than ever. Obsession with richness in data, however, should not be the reason for conducting ethnography, especially if we take the definitions introduced above seriously. And yet, there is a tendency to regard the length of a stay in a field, or the number of hours of observation as being a threshold for quality. This, we argue, represents a problem. First, normative standards in methods do not make up for ethnographic quality, because they say little about the richness of scholars' experience in the field and the quality of their reports. Second, this evolution pushes other qualitative methods out to the fringe of qualitative scholarship. Not every question needs ethnography (or, more generally, direct observation) to be addressed properly. Interviews, historical analysis, qualitative comparative analyses, will often suffice. Similarly, not every institution and school can afford to send its staff out into the field for months at a time. Direct observation, taken more generally (and herewith out of the norms of ethnography), is one of the oldest instruments for data collection in social research. Ethnography should not, however, become home for an elite in the community of qualitative scholarship.

▇ REFERENCES

Ahrne, G. and Brunsson, N. (2008). *Meta-organizations*. Cheltenham, UK: Edward Elgar.

Araujo, L., Kjellberg, H., and Spencer, R. (2008). 'Market practices and forms: Introduction to the special issue', *Marketing Theory*, 8(1): 5–14.

Barley, S.R. (2016). '60th anniversary essay: ruminations on how we became a mystery house and how we might get out', *Administrative Science Quarterly*, 61(1): 1–8.

Bate, S.P. (1997). 'Whatever happened to organizational anthropology? A review of the field of organizational ethnography and anthropological studies', *Human Relations*, 50(9): 1147–75.

Beckert, J. (2007). 'The social order of markets', *Theory and Society*, 38(3): 245–69.

Beckert, J. (2010). 'How do fields change? The interrelations of institutions, networks, and cognition in the dynamics of markets', *Organization Studies*, 31(5): 605–27.

Berthod, O., Grothe-Hammer, M., and Sydow, J. (2015). 'Some characteristics of high-reliability networks', *Journal of Contingencies and Crisis Management*, 23(1): 24–8.

Berthod, O., Grothe-Hammer, M., and Sydow, J. (2017a). 'Network ethnography? A mixed-method approach for the study of practices in interorganizational settings', *Organizational Research Methods*, 20(2): 299–323.

Berthod, O., Grothe-Hammer, M., Müller-Seitz, G., Raab, J., and Sydow, J. (2017b). 'From high-reliability organizations to high-reliability networks: the dynamics of governance in the face of emergency', *Journal of Public Administration Research and Theory*, 27(2): 352–71.

Blau, P.M. (1963). *The Dynamics of Bureaucracy: A Study of interpersonal relations in Two Government Agencies*. Chicago, IL: University of Chicago Press.

Bradach, J.L. (1997). 'Using the plural form in the management of restaurant chains', *Administrative Science Quarterly*, 42(2): 276–303.

Callon, M. (1998). *The Laws of the Markets*. Oxford: Blackwell.

Cayla, J., Cova, B., and Maltese, L. (2013). 'Party time: recreation rituals in the world of B2B', *Journal of Marketing Management*, 29(11): 1394–421.

Colpan, A.M. (2010) (ed.). *The Oxford Handbook of Business Groups*. Oxford: Oxford University Press.

Cropper, S., Ebers, M., Huxham, C., and Ring, P.S. (2008) (eds). *Oxford Handbook of Inter-Organizational Relations*. Oxford: Oxford University Press.

Cunliffe, A.L. (2010). 'Retelling tales of the field: in search of organizational ethnography 20 years on', *Organizational Research Methods*, 13(2): 224–39.

Darr, A. (2003). 'Gifting practices and interorganizational relations: constructing obligation networks in the electronics sector', *Sociological Forum*, 18(1): 31–51.

Delgado, N.A. and Cruz, L.C. (2014). 'Multi-event ethnography: doing research in pluralistic settings', *Journal of Organizational Ethnography*, 3(1): 43–58.

Desmond, M. (2014). 'Relational ethnography', *Theory and Society*, 43(5): 547–79.

Eberle, T.S. and Maeder, C. (2011). 'Organizational ethnography.' In Silverman, D. (ed.) *Qualitative Research. Issues of Theory, Method, and Practice*. Third edition. Los Angeles, CA: Sage, pp.53–73.

Emerson, R.M., Fretz, R.I., and Shaw, L.L. (2011). *Writing Ethnographic Fieldnotes*. Chicago, IL: University of Chicago Press.

Fayard, A.-L. and van Maanen, J. (2015). 'Making culture visible: reflections on corporate ethnography', *Journal of Organizational Ethnography*, 4(1): 4–27.

Feldman, M.S. (2000). 'Organizational routines as a source of continuous change', *Organization Science*, 11(6): 611–29.

Feldman, M.S. and Orlikowski, W. (2011). 'Theorizing practice and practicing theory', *Organization Science*, 22(5): 1240–53.

Giddens, A. (1984). *The Constitution of Society—Outline of the Theory of Structuration*. Cambridge: Polity Press.

Gobo, G. (2008). *Doing Ethnography*. Los Angeles, CA: Sage.

Golden-Biddle, K. and Locke, K. (1993). 'Appealing work: an investigation of how ethnographic texts convince', *Organization Science*, 4(4): 595–616.

Green, N. (1999). 'Disrupting the field: virtual reality technologies and "multisited" ethnographic methods', *American Behavioral Scientist*, 43(3): 409–21.

Hammersley, M. (1992). *What's Wrong with Ethnography? Methodological Explorations*. London: Routledge.

Hannerz, U. (2003). 'Being there...and there...and there!: Reflections on multi-site ethnography', *Ethnography*, 4(2): 201–16.

Holt, D.B. (1995). 'How consumers consume: a typology of consumption practices', *Journal of Consumer Research*, 22(1): 1–16.

Howard, P. (2002). 'Network ethnography and the hypermedia organization: new media, new organizations, new methods,' *New Media and Society*, 4(4): 550–74.

Jarillo, J.C. (1988). 'On strategic networks', *Strategic Management Journal*, 9(1): 31–41.

Jarzabkowski, P. (2008). 'Shaping strategy as a structuration process', *Academy of Management Journal*, 51(4): 621–50.

Jarzabkowski, P.A., Bednarek, R., and Lê, J.K. (2014). 'Producing persuasive findings: demystifying ethnographic textwork in strategy and organization research', *Strategic Organization*, 12(4): 274–87.

Jeffrey, B. and Troman, G. (2004). 'Time for ethnography', *British Educational Research Journal*, 30(4): 535–48.

Jordan, B. and Lambert, M. (2009). 'Working in corporate jungles: reflections on ethnographic praxis in industry.' In M. Cefkin (ed.) *Ethnography and the Corporate Encounter. Reflections on Research in and of Corporations*. New York: Berghahn Books, pp.95–133.

Kellogg, K.C., Orlikowski, W.J., and Yates, J. (2006). 'Life in the trading zone: structuring coordination across boundaries in postbureaucratic organizations', *Organization Science*, 17(1): 22–44.

Kenis, P. and Knoke, D. (2002). 'How organizational field networks shape interorganizational tie-formation rates', *Academy of Management Review*, 27(2): 275–93.

Kjellberg, H. and Helgesson, C.-F., (2006). 'Multiple versions of markets: multiplicity and performativity in market practice', *Industrial Marketing Management*, 35(7): 839–55.

Krueathep, W., Riccucci, N.R., and Suwanmala, C. (2010). 'Why do agencies work together? The determinants of network formation at the subnational level of government in Thailand', *Journal of Public Administration Research and Theory*, 20(1): 157–85.

Langan-Fox, J. and Cooper, G. (2014) (eds). *Boundary Spanning in Organizations: Network, Influence, and Conflict*. London: Routledge.

Lauring, J. and Klitmøller, A. (2015). 'Corporate language-based communication avoidance in MNCs: a multi-sited ethnography approach', *Journal of World Business*, 50(1): 46–55.

Lorenzoni, G. and Baden-Fuller, C. (1995). 'Creating a strategic center to manage a web of partners', *California Management Review*, 37(3): 146–63.

Marcus, G.E. (1995). 'Ethnography in/of the world system: the emergence of multi-sited ethnography', *Annual Review of Anthropology*, 24(1): 95–117.

Marion, T.J., Eddleston, K.A., Friar, J.H., and Deeds, D. (2015). 'The evolution of interorganizational relationships in emerging ventures: an ethnographic study within the new product development process', *Journal of Business Venturing*, 30(1): 167–84.

Maurer, I. and Ebers, M. (2006). 'Dynamics of social capital and their performance implications: lessons from biotechnology start-ups', *Administrative Science Quarterly*, 51(2): 262–92.

Miettinen, R., Samra-Fredericks, D., and Yanow, D. (2009). 'Re-turn to practice: an introductory essay', *Organization Studies*, 30(12): 1309–27.

Moore, F. (2006). 'Strategy, power and negotiation: social control and expatriate managers in a German multinational corporation', *The International Journal of Human Resource Management*, 17(3): 399–413.

Neyland, D. (2008). *Organizational Ethnography*. Los Angeles, CA: Sage.

Nicolini, D. (2007). 'Stretching out and expanding work practices in time and space: the case of telemedicine' *Human Relations*, 60(6): 889–920.

Nicolini, D. (2009). 'Zooming in and out: studying practices by switching theoretical lenses and trailing connections', *Organization Studies*, 30(12): 1391–418.

Nicolini, D. (2012). *Practice Theory, Work, and Organization: An Introduction*. Oxford: Oxford University Press.

Orr, J.E. (1996). *Talking About Machines: An Ethnography of a Modern Job*. Ithaca, NY: ILR Press.

Paquin, R.L. and Howard-Grenville, J. (2013). 'Blind dates and arranged marriages: longitudinal processes of network orchestration. *Organization Studies*, 34(11): 1623–53.

Powell, W.W. (1990). 'Neither market nor hierarchy: network forms of organization', *Research in Organizational Behavior*, 12: 295–336.

Pratt, M.G. (2000). 'The good, the bad, and the ambivalent: managing identification among Amway distributors', *Administrative Science Quarterly*, 45(3): 456–93.

Provan, K.G. and Kenis, P.N. (2008). 'Modes of network governance: structure, management, and effectiveness', *Journal of Public Administration Research and Theory*, 18(2): 229–52.

Provan, K.G. and Milward, H.B. (1995). 'A preliminary theory of interorganizational network effectiveness: a comparative study of four community mental health systems', *Administrative Science Quarterly*, 40(1): 1–33.

Provan, K.G., Fish, A., and Sydow, J. (2007). 'Interorganizational networks at the network level: a review of empirical literature on whole networks', *Journal of Management*, 33(3): 479–516.

Raab, J. and Milward, H.B. (2003). 'Dark networks as problems', *Journal of Public Administration Research and Theory*, 13(4): 413–39.

Ring, P.S. and Van de Ven, A.H. (1994). 'Developmental processes of cooperative interorganizational relationships', *Academy of Management Review*, 19(1): 90–118.

Rosen, M. (1991). 'Coming to terms with the field: understanding and doing organizational ethnography', *Journal of Management Studies*, 28(1): 1–24.

Sanday, P.R. (1979). 'The ethnographic paradigm(s)', *Administrative Science Quarterly*, 24(4): 527–38.

Saz-Carranza, A. and Ospina, S. (2011). 'The behavioral dimension of governing interorganizational goal-directed networks—managing the unity-diversity tension', *Journal of Public Administration Research and Theory*, 21(2): 327–65.

Sedgwick, M.W. (2011). 'At a tangent to belonging: "Career progression" and networks of knowing Japanese multinational corporations', *Anthropology and Humanism*, 36(1): 55–65.

Selznick, P. (1957). *TVA and the Grass Roots*. New York: Harper and Row.

Sherry, J.F. (1990). 'Dealers and dealing in a periodic market: informal retailing in ethnographic perspective', *Journal of Retailing*, 66(2): 174–200.

Simpson, B. (2009). 'Pragmatism, Mead and the practice-turn', *Organization Studies*, 30(12): 1329–47.

Smart, G. (1998). 'Mapping conceptual worlds: using interpretive ethnography to explore knowledge-making in a professional community', *International Journal of Business Communication*, 35(1): 111–27.

Smets, M., Jarzabkowski, P., Burke, G.T., and Spee, P. (2015). 'Reinsurance trading in Lloyd's of London: balancing conflicting-yet-complementary logics in practice', *Academy of Management Journal*, 58(3): 932–70.

Stadtler, L. and van Wassenhove, L.N. (2016). 'Coopetition as a paradox: integrative approaches in a multi-company, cross sector partnership', *Organization Studies*, 37(5): 655–85.

Star, S. (1999). 'The ethnography of infrastructure', *American Behavioral Scientist*, 43(3): 377–91.

Stark, D. (2009). *The Sense of Dissonance: Accounts of Worth in Economic Life*. Princeton, NJ: Princeton University Press.

Sydow, J. and Staber, U. (2002). 'The institutional embeddedness of project networks: the case of content production in German television', *Regional Studies*, 36(3): 215–27.

Sydow, J. and Windeler, A. (1998). 'Organizing and evaluating interfirm networks: a structurationist perspective on network processes and effectiveness', *Organization Science*, 9(3): 265–84.

Sydow, J., Schüßler, E., and Müller-Seitz, G. (2016). *Managing Inter-organizational Relations. Debates and Cases*. London: Palgrave Macmillan.

Van de Ven, A.H. (1976). 'On the nature, formation and maintenance of relations among organizations', *Academy of Management Review*, 1(4): 24–36.

Van Maanen, J. (1979). 'Reclaiming qualitative methods for organizational research: a preface', *Administrative Science Quarterly*, 24(4): 520–26.

Van Maanen, J. (1988). *Tales of the Field: On Writing Ethnography*. Chicago, IL: University of Chicago Press.

Van Maanen, J. (1995). 'Fear and loathing in organization studies', *Organization Science*, 6(6): 687–92.

Van Maanen, J. (2006). 'Ethnography then and now', *Qualitative Research in Organizations and Management: An International Journal*, 1(1): 13–21.

Van Maanen, J. (2010). 'A song for my supper: more tales of the field', *Organizational Research Methods*, 13(2): 240–55.

Walker, G., Kogut, B., and Shan, W. (1997). 'Social capital, structural holes and the formation of an industry network', *Organization Science*, 8(2): 109–25.

Watson, T. J. (2011). 'Ethnography, reality, and truth: the vital need for studies of "how things work" in organizations and management', *Journal of Management Studies*, 48(1): 202–17.

Williamson, O.E. (1991). 'Comparative economic organization: the analysis of discrete structural alternatives', *Administrative Science Quarterly*, 36(2): 269–96.

Yanow, D. (2009). 'Organizational ethnography and methodological angst: myths and challenges in the field', *Qualitative Research in Organizations and Management: An International Journal*, 4(2): 186–99.

Ybema, S., Yanow, D., Wels, H., and Kamsteeg, F. (2009) (eds). *Organizational Ethnography: Studying the Complexities of Everyday Life*. Thousand Oaks, CA: Sage.

Zilber, T.B. (2014). 'Beyond a single organization: challenges and opportunities in doing field level ethnography', *Journal of Organizational Ethnography*, 3(1): 96–113.

Part 3

Unconventional Analytic Approaches

12 Unconventional yet consequential

Using a sociomaterial approach to drive impact in organization studies research

Paul R. Carlile and Karl-Emanuel Dionne

Introduction

In this chapter, we take a sociomateriality approach to provide guidance in how unconventional research can have greater impact in organization studies. To do this, we take seriously the challenge embedded in our title, 'unconventional yet consequential.' This acknowledges that what doesn't conform to what has been done in the past has a liability of newness that can render it of little consequence. Magnifying this novelty challenge, prominent scholars such as Steve Barley (2015, 2006) and Michael Tushman (Benner and Tushman, 2015) have cautioned organization studies researchers. They suggest that the proliferation of novel approaches over the last two decades to explain organizational phenomena has generated variety, but also a lack of comparability that hinders collective learning from our empirical efforts.

Our goal is to examine empirical research as a sociomaterial practice that produces a variety of artefacts (i.e. recorded observation, data, charts, presentations, articles, etc.) that can function as boundary objects in the collective process of developing and transforming our understanding of organizations. To increase the impact of what we produce, we revisit key concepts and distinctions—such as process and outcome, and unit and level of analysis—that we use as we observe, collect and analyse data, to recognize there is often more that we can do to produce unconventional research has lasting impact.

As Carlile (2015, p.22) argued, 'The wonderful thing about focusing on materiality is that it allows us to revisit current approaches to how we think about organizations to make them more useful for ourselves and useable by others.' It is our hope that when we recognize the sociomaterial dimensions of our methodological efforts, it will help us to identify commonality that will make collective progress easier (Christensen and Carlile, 2009) as we pursue the diverse empirical and conceptual approaches that make up unconventional research.

A sociomaterial perspective

Sociomateriality is built on the idea that social practices are material, that material practices are social (Leonardi and Barley, 2010), and that the social and the material are constructed relationally (Orlikowski, 1992; Carlile et al., 2003). This link between the social and the material culminates in the assertion that: 'Without the material stuff of our everyday lives, human action would not be possible. That is, practice necessarily entails materiality. And just as materiality is integral to practice, so is it integral to the knowing enacted in practice. Put more simply, knowing is material' (Orlikowski, 2006, p.3).

A sociomaterial approach recognizes that actions are activated and constrained by structures, and that structures are the result of accumulations of previous actions shaped by material consequences. Structures include rules, standards, and human and material resources that agents mobilize in their daily interactions. These structures mediate human action, while being reaffirmed in their daily use (Orlikowski, 1992, 2010; Black et al., 2004). This approach shifts the attention of analysts to the processes that bind structures and daily action. Depending on the archaeological depth of structures, it becomes more or less difficult to distinguish the social from the material given the nature of their entanglement (Barad, 2003; Leonardi, 2012) and their accumulation over time (Carlile, 2015).

The early seeds of sociomateriality in organization studies can be seen in the structuration approach to technology (Orlikowski, 1992; DeSanctis and Poole, 1994), object or artefact use and design (Carlile, 2002; Leonardi, 2012), or in the understanding of organizational structures in relation to new technologies (Orlikowski, 2010; Mazmanian et al., 2013). However, the sociomaterial approach also suggests that organizing action is always material, as well as social, that materiality is not circumstantial but integral to it (Howard-Grenville and Carlile, 2006; Orlikowski, 2007), and that organizations are built on sociomaterial arrangements that generate consequences. A sociomaterial lens allows researchers to improve their understanding of organizational processes by considering how materiality is activated in organizational structures and how it constrains these structures.

Recognizing that there is always a sociomaterial entanglement in both what we study and how we study it, we focus on materiality as a shared door we go through as we consider how to create more impact from the unconventional methods that can be used. To accomplish this, we first outline the five dimensions that change how we think about the social and the material and how this can help us better imagine how we use our methods as both conceptual and empirical tools. The first dimension we explore is *outcomes and not just process*. The second is *accumulations and not just activities*. The third and fourth respectively concern *layers of analysis and not just levels of analysis*, and *relative durability and not just dynamics*. The fifth dimension is *consequences and not just change*.

Following the conceptualization of each dimension, we use Stephen Barley's 1986 article in *Administrative Science Quarterly*, 'Technology as an occasion for structuring: evidence from observations of CT scanners and the social order of radiology departments', to demonstrate each dimension. Barley's work is particularly useful since it used an unconventional approach that was recognized twenty years later as one of the most impactful articles in the field of organizations studies (Bartunek et al., 2006). We also use the research of Black et al. (2004) that builds directly upon Barley's study using the unconventional approach of 'system dynamics' to demonstrate additional empirical dimensions that allow unconventional research to have greater impact.

Five guides from a sociomaterial approach to research

It should not come as a surprise that, as an empirical science, organizational studies is and needs to be grounded in materiality. What do we mean by that? Materiality refers to the settings that we study, the people that we interview, the words that they utter in reference to things they and we observe, the words that we write down in our journal or record in the transcript, the summary notes that we record at the end of each day, the tables that we build to create order across sources of data, the figures that we design and the dimensions that we define to give the direction, the paragraphs that we write and the headings that we change. It is therefore hard to get away from the materiality of our work and the potential consequences that this generates in what we see as empiricists, what we conclude in what we write, and how we theorize. So, however you define your epistemological bookends, from realism to idealism, a focus on materiality encourages you to live curiously in between the extremes.

Here we focus on five key dimensions concerning how we think about the world as we adopt a specific methodological approach. Paying attention to the materiality of these dimensions allows us to see them not just as abstractions, but *as questions we can raise as we do our work. Each dimension is described and then applied to Barley's (1986) research on CT scanning.

OUTCOMES AND NOT JUST PROCESSES

Outcome versus process approaches, sometimes described as variance versus process models of research (Mohr 1982), represents one of the most basic juxtapositions in methodological and empirical conversations in organization studies besides quantitative and qualitative. Unconventional methodologies often emphasize process over outcome approaches.

Taking a sociomaterial approach means that we have to focus on both process and outcome. This was easier to see before quantitative methods became developed by Paul Lazersfeld and others in the 1930s. Up until this point, there wasn't a distinction between theory and methods classes in PhD programs in Europe and the United States. Phenomena were treated holistically since they were full of processes that produced a variety of outcomes; whether those were outcomes observed in society or in singular instances. One of the unintended consequences of modern statistical approaches is that they allow for aggregations of data and the comparisons of those aggregations as outcomes. So, these new quantitative tools and the increasing specialization required to use these approaches inadvertently created the modern-day separation of outcome and process approaches in the social sciences.

As outcome approaches became more popular and began to dominate, process perspectives were declared as unique and separate. We see this building in the 1960s in anthropology with Geertz (1973) and in sociology with Garfinkel's (1967) work. In organization studies, we see the formal specialization of process theory in Langley's (1999) work that has now become a distinctive methodological approach with accompanying special issues and conventions.

As this specialization was solidified, unconventional approaches were usually associated with process rather than outcome approaches. This separation became an ideological rift in the form of anti-positivism and postmodernism which eschewed a desire to be comparative and therefore 'practical'. This discomfort with comparing outcomes in the qualitative sciences often resulted in the baby being thrown out with the bath water. Outcomes were only pointed to as a justification for why things are unique in a given context, and making comparisons across contexts was frowned upon as breaking some unspoken rule of process-oriented research.

From a sociomateriality approach there is a sense of humility when it comes to making comparisons of outcomes across different processes. However, that humility is accompanied by a deeper curiosity about how to potentially make such comparisons with greater empirical specificity and concreteness (Carlile, 2015). So instead of stopping with the process, materiality invites us to look at both outcomes and process, and what accumulates through them both as a potential basis of comparison.

Using Barley

In Barley's ethnography of the implementation of CT scanning technology in two hospitals, we see a powerful combination of process and outcomes orientations toward data and phenomena. It is not surprising that Barley's work has become an exemplar in qualitative organization studies. Not only did he pursue big conceptual themes around structure and structuring, but more importantly the ethnographic closeness he achieved surrounding the implementation of this new technology and its use by radiologists and technicians brought a unique rigor. Ultimately, his thorough ethnographic approach allowed him to describe the interaction of radiologists and technologists in terms of patterns of behaviour emerging and changing over time. He compared these patterns in one hospital, then compared how those interactions differed between Suburban and Urban Hospitals.

Making comparisons of processes and outcomes allowed him to identify deeper questions about why particular patterns of interaction emerged and how they changed over time. For example, in the case of Suburban, he identified two distinct phases: *Negotiation of discretion* and *Usurping autonomy* (see Table 12.1). Barley identified what he called 'scripts' of action that were different across the two phases at Suburban. In phase 1, he described the

Table 12.1 Summary of Barley's observations of patterns of interaction at two hospitals*

	Suburban	
	phase 1 negotiation of discretion	phase 2 usurping autonomy
staffing change		CT-inexperienced radiologists added
scripts	unsought validation anticipatory questioning preference stating	clandestine teaching role reversals blaming the technologist
pattern of interaction	collaboration	occupational separation

	Urban		
	phase 1 negotiating dependence	phases 2 and 3 constructing and ensuring ineptitude	phase 4 toward independence
staffing change		radiologists stay in office to encourage technologists to make decisions on their own	CT-inexperienced radiologists added, and least competent technologists transferred
scripts	direction giving countermands usurping the controls direction seeking	unexpected criticisms accusatory questions	technical consultation mutual execution
pattern of interaction	professional dominance	professional dominance	collaboration

* Based on Black et al. (2004, p.581).

sequence of interaction scripts: 'unsought validation, anticipatory questioning, and preference stating.' In phase 2, he described the sequence: 'clandestine teaching, role reversals, and blaming the technologist.'

Combining these concrete process and outcome data allowed Barley to describe the details of how the phases and patterns of interaction were different. Ultimately this led him to explain the difference in the pattern of phase 1 as being structured through centralized decision making, while phase 2 was shaped by decentralized decision making. He emphasized the powerful position that radiologists had in relation to technologists in either allowing for a centralized or decentralized approach to occur.

ACCUMULATIONS AND NOT JUST ACTIVITIES

Accounting for outcomes within process suggests an accumulation of outcomes and the patterns that such accumulations establish in a given context. This is why materiality shares so many similarities with theories of practice and in particular Bourdieu's practice approach (Bourdieu and Wacquant, 1992) that emphasizes how accumulations through practices helps explain the reproduction of social structures through processes of education (Bourdieu and Passeron, 1970/1990). If we think about a practice only as an activity then we lose sight of what is being accumulated or not.

Examining the materiality of a practice provides a window on actors' efforts to produce or consume knowledge and resources. Since the knowledge that people develop is essential for past actions it is naturally at stake and so of consequence when moving into future action that requires change (Carlile, 2002). This is another reminder that much is shared among sociomateriality and practice approaches since, if there were nothing of consequence, then there would be very little that would draw the attention of actors to engage in a social context. That there is something 'of consequence' to be accumulated suggests a relationality among actors and things; a relational ontology lies at the heart of a sociomaterial approach. Outcomes, capital, resources, experience, skills, knowledge, or status can only be created and consumed through an activity, through a practice. But only paying attention to an activity, not as a means of accumulation, is to miss the opportunity to use a method to account for what is of consequence as a relational and comparative tool.

Seeing both allows for a deeper set of questions: what is being accumulated, who is accumulating it, and how are they accumulating it? And further, what outcomes do they lead to, and what observed patterns can be explained by those accumulations? And how do some actors' accumulations relative to other actors help explain a set of outcomes across larger processes observed?

Using Barley

Barley's insight proved deeper when he moved beyond comparing the differences between the processes and outcomes at the two hospitals, to the changing patterns of decision-making across their CT scanning activities. At Urban, he identified four different phases of interaction. Phase 1 was 'Negotiating dependence'. Phases 2 and 3, he labelled 'Constructing and ensuring ineptitude', and phase 4 he called 'Toward independence'. Similar to Suburban, he described the big shift from phases 1–3 to phase 4 in terms of moving from centralized to decentralized decision making. Barley identified a comparable event in this shift in both hospitals concerning a similar staffing change where inexperienced radiologists and experienced technologists were now participating in the CT scanning activity. It was this change in relative accumulations of experience from the previous staff that led to this overall dominant shift in a pattern from centralized to decentralized, for now the technologists had more accumulated experience in operating the CT machines than radiologists.

Not only did the rotation of inexperienced radiologists mean a significant change of accumulated experience from the previous radiologists, but also for the technologists who stayed on at Suburban and who had accumulated a lot of experience given the positive pattern of scripts of interaction that had taken place (i.e. anticipatory questioning and preference stating). Thus the accumulation of experience in the activity of scanning led to what Barley felt as an adequate explanation in terms of a shift from centralized to decentralized decision making on behalf of the radiologists. However, Barley left an anomaly unexplained: a similar staffing change in terms of accumulated expertise of radiologists and technologists led Suburban to complete occupational separation, while at Urban there was a highly collaborative learning context for the new technology.

Anomalies are important to consider when working between theory building and empirical work (Christensen and Carlile, 2009). To address this anomaly, we must look into the sociomateriality of this setting, and not just examine the activity and accumulation of scanning expertise, but how other types of accumulations impact the scanning activity and the outcomes observed. Focusing on both accumulations and activities allows for a deeper understanding of why and how relational differences among actors arise, and so are consequential. So the relational ontology inherent in a sociomaterial approach, and a focus on accumulations/outcomes in a given process/activity, is a natural connection between ontology and epistemology that must be carried out. But we have to think about the context of these accumulations, not just in terms of a place, but also the layers of accumulation generated from other places are critical. For that we turn to the third dimension and to Black et al.'s (2004) extension of Barley's 1986 data through the unconventional method of system dynamics.

LAYERS OF ANALYSIS AND NOT JUST LEVELS

Materiality focuses on the practical where consequences arise and where accumulations take place. It is therefore important to see why the unit of analysis when taking a sociomaterial approach focuses on day-to-day practices where consequences play out and where accumulations potentially occur.

Practice is itself a sociomaterial process that provides integrative conduit among what we refer to as micro and macro levels. Here what is of consequence at the individual or micro level plays out within a given practice. What proves of consequence at the social or macro level can only be created and consumed through a practice. Even markets, one of the most abstract macro level concepts, are still enacted in concrete practices where goods can be bought and sold. Focusing on practice grabs individuals' motivations and actions in a social activity as they create or consume social resources that they need to accumulate to carry out subsequent actions. Further, practice as a unit of analysis is not just another level called meso. Rather, it is a space where individuals accumulate resources of social consequence. This is consistent with other perspectives that focus on material consequences such as actor network theory. The practical orientation of a sociomaterial approach means that it doesn't see the world through levels of analysis, and so avoids the whole micro/macro split and the significant efforts made to link them (Alexander, 1987).

An extension to unit of analysis is what we call layers of analysis, or more accurately how accumulations form layers that have consequences for other practices. So resources or expertise accumulated in one practice can impact another. We see this in how financial resources accumulated in one practice can be taken to another to improve the status of the actor in getting access to other kinds of resources. We see this at play in institutional theories' attention to imitation and legitimacy.

For example, in Barley's study there is more than just the accumulation of experience in operating the machines and the power that affords, but also the accumulations that occur given that all technologists were women and nearly all the radiologists were men. Further, technologists' education consisted of technical training and typically an associates degree, whereas radiologists had extensive educational certifications that included undergraduate, MD, PhD, residency and fellowships that can often take 15 years to acquire. The value and power of these educational accumulations for the radiologist are brought to bear on the activity of CT scanning which accounts for the significant power difference between themselves and technologists. So we must recognize that there are sociomaterial layers that are accumulated that form a kind socio-archaeological layering of accumulations that constrain and enable actions in the focal practice (Carlile, 2015).

Any practices where actors are trying to drive innovation are nested among and so constrained by a larger set of practices, and innovative outcomes require transforming the accumulated knowledge from across these inter-dependent practice or routines through new methods and technologies (Carlile, 2002; Deken et al., 2016).

Using Barley

Barley made two main observations. First was the accumulated experience in operating the CT machines. Second was how those accumulations differed between technologists and radiologists, especially in terms of the rotation of new technologists and radiologists at Urban and Suburban. He explained the consequences for observed behaviour in terms of the centralization and decentralization of decision-making among radiologists and technicians.

As alluded to in the previous section, this did not explain the anomaly of why a similar rotation of experience levels of technicians and radiologists resulted in such different collaborative outcomes (e.g. collaboration at Urban, and occupational separation at Suburban). By appealing to centralization and decentralization of decision-making, Barley left unexplored the diagnostic expertise that for inexperienced radiologists was only accumulated in practices outside of the activity of CT scanning. Although Barley acknowledged the importance of diagnosis, he didn't separate it from operating knowledge. Black et al. (2004) built on Barley's work by separating accumulations of operating knowledge from diagnostic knowledge and then formally oper-ationalizing both.

Diagnostic expertise refers to a type of knowledge that for the most part only radiologists have and they accumulate across a variety of medical prac-tices over many years. Operating expertise is only accumulated by operating the CT machine and as you accumulate it, you also accumulate diagnostic expertise that is unique to the new method of CT scanning. What is unique to the new practice of CT scanning is that it blurs the relationship between these two types of expertise. If you were a radiologist with no experience using the CT machine, it is almost certain that you would not be able to use this machine to diagnose effectively, since you would have no experience in interpreting the scans. However, if you were an experienced technologist, you have some expertise interpreting scans to diagnose a disease (so, diagnostic knowledge). For example, an experience technologist would be able to distinguish between blood and water on the kidney, whereas a radiologist who lacked experience in using the new technology could not.

In the case of phase 2 at Suburban, the relationship between these layers of accumulated expertise (or lack thereof) led to such strange patterns as clan-destine teaching and role reversals, which eventually led to the pattern of occupational separation. By contrast, a similar rotation at Urban in phase 4 led to technical consultation and mutual execution that eventually produced a pattern of collaboration and learning that maximized the benefits of CT machines as a new diagnostic capability. Separating out the different types of expertise, and how the layer of diagnostic expertise is accumulated in a whole host of activities outside CT scanning, explains the anomaly that Barley could not.

For Barley these highly varying patterns of behaviour led him to state that the success or relative failure of the implementation of the new CT technologies depended on complex features embedded in all social contexts. This broad statement was accepted, since it was criticizing the technological imperative assumptions that dominated most of the social sciences at the time. However, in the conclusion of his article, Barley (1986, p.106) called attention to the 'relative distribution of expertise' as a future, more nuanced, avenue to develop a fuller explanation of the structuring process around new technology implementation. Black et al. used the unconventional method of system dynamics to tease out the potential consequences of these different layers of accumulated expertise to better explain the processes and outcomes that Barley described.

RELATIVE DURABILITY AND NOT JUST DYNAMICS

Many unconventional methods seek to explain phenomena that are dynamic and complex. A dynamic system examines the interfaces across layers of accumulations produced by other units of analysis and how these impact accumulations in the focal practice. This dimension focuses on the temporal consequences that arise from the previous dimension. Dynamics concern the passage of time, and also relations across people, activities and accumulations that occur over time. But once we entertain dynamics and time, it is also about the relative durability of one process in relation to another; one layer of accumulation in relation to another. Since temporal dynamics are always at work, to render them practical we must consider the relative stability or durability of some layers of accumulation in relation to another. Black et al. outlined the importance of doing this as they operationalized the relationship between operating expertise and diagnostic expertise to account for the anomaly of why the same rotation of radiologist and technicians created such contrasting outcomes.

As we elongate the temporal horizon, we naturally get at bigger concepts such as structure and environments and not just practices and contexts. So questions such as, what is structure (so what is stable), and what is structuring (what is dynamic), are powerfully relevant, but also hard to address. In the case of operating and diagnostic knowledge, we have to consider the relative durability of one layer in relation to another. If we maximize the time scale of examination out to a million years, then nearly all that we study as organization scholars becomes irrelevant. So what is key is recognizing that we must choose a time scale that is most consequential to the phenomena we are trying to understand. What makes the implementation of a new technology or a new routine empirically valuable is that it potentially creates changes in spatial and temporal relations in a given context. So there becomes much to observe and account for in terms of the patterns of potential change that result.

This allows us to ask more specific and deeper questions about the nature of dynamics. Not only does this allow us to see dynamics differently, but to consider change itself in a new light; that change itself is not a convenient abstraction but an outcome that requires more empirical questions and specificity about the origins and time scale of the relative durability of the layers of accumulations observed.

Using Barley

The system dynamic treatment to which Black et al. (2004) subjected Barley's CT scanning study directly assessed the dynamics of the structure and the structuring by recognizing that some structures change at faster rates than others; some accumulations are more stable than others. The argument being that radiologists' diagnostic knowledge in general is changing at a much slower rate (more stable) than diagnostic knowledge accumulated from operating the new CT scanning machine. In the title of Barley's 1986 article, he refers to 'Technology [the new CT scanning machines] as an occasion for structuring', but what he didn't account for is that there were two layers of accumulations of knowledge that differed in their relative durability.

Modelling this allowed Black et al. to go beyond the decentralization of decision-making argument to explain the phases and patterns that Barley observed, and also explain the anomalies he didn't see. It was the relative stability or durability of diagnostic knowledge in relation to operating knowledge that provided the fuller explanation of what was observed in the two Suburban and Urban hospitals. Much like process, dynamics also grow into outcomes and accumulations; and then further temporally representing the relational consequences of layers of accumulation in the focal unit of analysis (in this case CT scanning). System dynamics may be seen as an unconventional methodology, but this approach exposed the consequences of the actions taken by the radiologists and technicians involved in terms of the relative stability and duration of different accumulations.

CONSEQUENCES AND NOT JUST CHANGE

Methods that embrace process and emphasize dynamics naturally focus on change. There is a natural bias toward looking for change; for if there isn't change there isn't much of an empirical story to tell. Unconventional methods also naturally focus on change as a meaningful empirical window into social phenomena since change puts what we currently know about the world in contrast to what is a novel discovery or contribution. But the concept of change is much harder to pin down than we realize because it potentially impacts everyone. It is hard to know what change to account for and make meaningful consequences other than retrospectively.

Change only becomes meaningful as we invoke the pragmatics of the question that each of us faces daily: what do I change and what do I keep the same? And how do I understand what is consequential to help me determine what to change and what not to change? Once change becomes specific and not abstract, questions become about a given actor determining what to change: how do they determine what is consequential, and then what is worthy of inclination and ability to change?

These questions and the deeper issues behind them come from the pragmatist tradition in philosophy. Peirce (1902/1974) gave this a unique focus as he wrestled with the age-old question of what has meaning. His answer related to what has 'practical bearing' which became known as the pragmatic maxim. William James (1907) developed the pragmatic method to suggest that what has meaning is what is of consequence to us. This focus on consequences has a way of pushing aside our tendency toward abstraction for explanations to look closer at what arises in our day-to-day activities. This also influenced Wittgenstein's theory of language as embedded in the consequences of human practices, and Bourdieu's focus on practical consequences, what is at stake, as a way to 'ground' social analysis.

The origins of change are tracked and originated through the consequences that arise for actors in a given social practice. Change is an outcome of a social process that generates accumulations that are consequential for the actors involved and so shapes their future actions. Understanding the sources of these consequences is made easier by accounting for the first four sociomaterial dimensions: both processes and outcomes; activities and accumulations; relationships among layers accumulations; and the relative durability of some accumulations in relation to others.

Using Barley

As an occasion of structuring, the new CT scanning technology created a lot of unintended consequences that diminished the capability of this new technology to more effectively improve patient diagnosis at both hospitals. Barley explained this in terms of centralized or decentralized decision-making. However, he didn't identify the underlying consequences for radiologists and technicians because he didn't separate and measure the accumulations of both operating and diagnostic expertise.

If consequences drive the pragmatics of action, then we must account for the sources of these consequences. These five sociomaterial dimensions add to our ability to account for where the consequences of action arise and how

Table 12.2 Total practical CT knowledge among doctors and technologists after nine months*

	Technologists' initial CT knowledge		
Doctors' initial CT knowledge	low CT expertise *operating 10%* *diagnostic 10%*	medium CT expertise *operating 50%* *diagnostic 18%*	high CT expertise *operating 90%* *diagnostic 35%*
Low CT expertise *operating 10%* *diagnostic 20%*	99%	55%	75%
Medium CT expertise *operating 50%* *diagnostic 60%*	56%	98%	85%
High CT expertise *operating 90%* *diagnostic 90%*	55%	81%	96%

* Based on Black et al. (2004, p.598).

they shape patterns of action. Black et al. used Barley's substantive analysis and applied system dynamics to build a formal approach. In this way, they followed the movement of Glaser and Strauss (1967) from substantive to formal theory. The formal model could then account for how activities (processes), accumulations (outcomes), and recursive dynamics could specify how the relative distribution and accumulation of two types of expertise and their interaction could account for the behaviours observed. They then used this formal model to identify what relational constructions among technicians and radiologists would induce the most collaborative patterns leading to the most rapid development of the knowledge necessary to best leverage the new technology for improving patient outcomes in both hospitals.

Table 12.2 summarizes the findings of the formal model. What is revealed is that the best outcomes are reached when the relative amount of operating expertise is matched or balanced between technologists and radiologists. The high percentages running across the diagonal of the table reveal that when operating knowledge is balanced then collaboration and learning are maximized. The mistake made in both hospitals was to pick either an experienced technician or an experienced radiologist which created an unbalanced relationship and produced much lower accumulations of the necessary knowledge to perform and interpret scans.

Identifying change by itself was not sufficient; accounting for the underlying consequences provided a specific, grounded prescription of what needed to change to address those underlying consequences. What proves hard in any methodological effort is accounting fully for all the potential factors that can generate consequences on the patterns of observed action. Each of the five sociomaterial dimensions increase a researcher's capacity to account for the consequences that impact human action.

The challenge of novelty in unconventional research

There are two related challenges that researchers must address to create impact with unconventional methodologies. First, explaining their novel approach, and second, addressing the gap between that approach and established methodology. Addressing this gap is a challenge since researchers come from varied conceptual and methodological domains that are constructed with different languages, interpretations, and interests. We offer five empirical dimensions to put the material nature of the phenomena of interest at center stage by providing a shared language to address the methodological and contextual issues of an unconventional approach. One needs to present research findings so that members of the organization studies community (editors, reviewers, researchers, practitioners) may understand and value it and subsequent researchers can build on it to better understand the phenomena they themselves analyse. As Barley (2006, p.19) stated, 'papers that break too many substantive, methodological, or theoretical rules are more likely to be called flaky or wrongheaded than interesting.' Each of our five dimensions provides a means of constructing concepts and representations of data as boundary objects to address the knowledge boundaries that exist across researchers (Carlile 2002, 2004).

Our approach is rooted in the importance of phenomena and data as the materiality that allow for meaningful conceptual and empirical contributions, whether taking a conventional or an unconventional approach. When you think about it, there is a great deal of materiality observed and created as we engage in research practices. The materiality of what we include as data, the words we use to describe our research setting, the literature we read and articles we reference, the surveys we create, the people we interview and the notes that we record and then analyse. These have a social dimension that involves co-authorship, the research communities we seek to contribute to, the authors we cite, and those that review our work.

Below we offer some methodological suggestions for each of the five dimensions, and an additional application to a current field work project. We are studying the development of a movement called Hacking Health (HH) that supports the creation of digital health solutions. HH adopts open source software techniques and activities to take ideas to implementation. A HH hackathon is a 48-hour competition where interdisciplinary teams solve a specific health challenge through the development of digital solutions. We followed four projects that produced working prototypes in distinct hackathons, to identify what would lead to a successful implementation of a digital health solution. Ultimately, only two of the four projects moved to the development and implementation stages. The successful projects were able to move beyond just seeing the challenge as technical, but also a scientific, user, organizational, and regulatory challenge. By tracking actors' interactions and project development related to intellectual property (IP) issues, we were able to track the who, when, and why of how teams transformed and expanded their approach of developing a solution or did not, allowing us to consider the complex picture of innovation in the digital health field.

OUTCOMES AND PROCESSES

The impact of this dimension of doing research as a sociomaterial practice is twofold. First, identifying outcomes occurring inside a process is a way to increase the variance in a study, allowing greater comparison inside single case studies and across multiple cases and therefore increasing the validity of the research. This increase of variance can then respond to reviewers' concerns regarding, for example, the internal validity of an argument. Second, and foremost, by focusing on in-depth reporting, describing and analysing of outcomes accumulating in a process instead of looking more broadly at such processes, researchers increase their capability to connect with past research and scholars as well as making it easier for future researchers to connect to their work. As discussed earlier, quantitative methods have long relied on outcomes analysis, where qualitative approaches have generally turned their backs on comparing outcomes. Analysing outcomes of a process is but one way of intersecting historically separated approaches to better construct a shared understanding of organizational phenomena.

In our fieldwork, we look at the processes of shaping digital health solutions in an open innovation environment involving multiple practices. To understand the potential of open innovation in healthcare, we did not focus on the hackathon as a process in itself, but as an opportunity to observe a series of outcomes inside a larger innovation process. The hackathon results were but an outcome on which teams would build to continue their innovation process. Focusing on the hackathon as an outcome of a bigger process allowed us to consider the iterative complexity of developing digital solutions in healthcare. Indeed, the hackathon was a good enough tool to support ideation and prototyping—activities central to technological development—but did not allow the management of issues related to the complexities of healthcare. Healthcare is an evidence-based sector that demands research validation before implementation. However, changing lines of code in a hackathon went faster than validating these changes through rigorous experimentation.

ACCUMULATIONS AND ACTIVITIES

In addition, we suggest looking for the accumulations of these outcomes to better understand organizational phenomena. Outcomes can accumulate in various ways depending on the process that you are observing. This highlights a potential for comparison between phenomena that may appear similar at first sight, but that may be hiding fundamental differences. For example, in the CT scanning case, examining accumulations of knowledge revealed additional and deeper social and material organizational layers that were driving the patterns of behaviour. One of the strengths of focusing on artefacts is that they provide a relatively stable empirical window to account for accumulations in a given process or activity.

To understand the complexities of digital health innovation, we tracked the accumulations occurring around IP management such as accumulations of activities, participating actors, and their interactions. Developing this complex artefact demands the involvement, at the right timing, of multiple actors with a variety of types of knowledge. We then looked for whose expertise was needed and why, and for each actor's vision with regard to how IP should be managed. Project teams that did not tolerate the ambiguity around IP did not succeed in managing the complex interactions that needed to be accumulated in the artefact so that the project would move out of this stage of the innovation process. For example, in one of the unsuccessful projects, the healthcare professionals did not want to build a startup but the developers wanted to be rewarded for their work and knowledge. However, based on the partner hospital IP policies, it was unclear who would own the IP and in what proportions. They ended up not being able to agree on the way IP should be managed. But why was that the case?

UNITS AND LAYERS OF ANALYSIS

By emphasizing practice as the unit of analysis, we avoid the problematic abstractions we call levels of analysis. Levels of analysis are helpful categories to make sense of the complex social world we try to research (micro/individual; meso/group; macro/society). However, these distinctions have grown into subfields in organization studies with their own academic outlets, conferences, virtual community websites and evaluation criteria. In that sense, each of these subfields is built on distinct sociomaterial practices. By avoiding the well-intended constructs of levels of analysis by focusing on practice, scholars will be more capable of opening these invisible iron cages. Practice is a unifying conduit that bridges the inclinations behind each level of analysis. All of the phenomena that are analysed by these traditions are occurring within a practice, that is, day-to-day human and non-human interactions where knowledge and resources are generated and accumulated over time.

To analyse key interactions at the level of practice, we observed different and comparable cases by tracking interactions around IP. Clashes between project members' visions often led to breakdowns that were interesting sites of struggles to be analysed to better understand the collaboration processes across institutional and knowledge boundaries, without having to rely on predetermined and stereotyped boundaries. The ambiguities related to digital health innovation discussed in the previous dimension were managed in different ways by the four projects. These differences could be explained by the project members' entrepreneurial experience, experience in managing the healthcare system, and familiarity with IT innovation in healthcare. The successful projects involved individuals who had a mix of backgrounds or were willing to interact with other backgrounds in developing new knowledge and evolving their healthcare solution.

RELATIVE DURABILITY AND DYNAMICS

This dimension calls attention to differences in temporal dynamics. Often, temporal dynamics (i.e. recursiveness) can be left abstract and so lack practical meaning. As we account for the outcomes of processes, the accumulation of resources within a practice and different layers of accumulations, we are left with the relative durability of these different layers of accumulations to determine what is of consequence and what drives the patterns of behaviour observed. By looking at temporal dynamics and relative durability, researchers examine multiple outcomes and accumulations, which allows for additional comparisons of empirical phenomena, and contributes to the analytical generalization of findings (Yin, 2013). In addition, the distinctions between levels of analysis presented earlier are nothing else than the outcome of accumulations that occur over increasingly longer periods of time. In that sense, empirical research can be related by spatial categories such as the team, the organization, and the environment (as it is done now), but additionally through differences in their temporal or developmental time scales (Howard-Grenville and Carlile, 2006).

In our research, we are following the innovation processes of comparable digital solutions from idea creation to implementation. We can thus observe the temporality of the construction of such projects, and the relative temporality between intervening actors and the practices they rely on. For example, healthcare scientists have to prove the efficiency of a solution before it gets translated into practice. This evidence-based process of conducting research, getting it published and accepted by practitioners can take several months, and even years, and has been dominant for decades. However, the software development process of digital solutions can move at a faster pace, and the entrepreneurial processes evolve at a much faster pace so that projects can maintain their competitive advantage. Actors from these four domains (scientists, healthcare practitioners, developers, and entrepreneurs) had different time scales to develop their knowledge.

We then looked at these relational differences across comparable sub-cases to understand how they were managed. The two projects that were successful aligned their research-validation process to the coding process by dividing the former into multiple stages, with the first research stages focusing on a smaller sample that could provide a first analytical glance and a sufficient validation of the project in regard to the entrepreneurial and coding processes. The other projects did not succeed because of their inability to compromise between different experiential backgrounds and to manage the relative temporal differences between the timing of coding and health research.

CONSEQUENCES AND CHANGE

The first four dimensions increasingly locate sociomaterial processes that play out over a larger spatial and temporal expanse. Given this expanding scope, change across places and times proves easy to spot because change in itself becomes a comparative outcome. What is harder as we expand out is to identify consequences that shape people's behaviour and larger patterns of action. The movement from description to prescription is both controversial and a challenge in management research (Christensen and Carlile, 2009). This suggests that a prescribed change needs to address the consequences faced by different parties of interest. Corley and Gioia (2011) have pointed out that organizational research in the context of a business school faces these challenges since it often connects scholars with practitioners along with the increasing need to reduce the growing division between practitioners and researchers in (Carlile et al., 2016). Researchers then have to ask themselves, 'for whom am I doing this research?', 'why am I doing this research?', and 'what will be the consequences of this research?' Research can and should be consequential for practitioners and organizations in providing guidelines for change. Our sociomaterial approach via all five dimensions allows us to answer the question of what to change as seen through the relational construction that is sociomateriality. So, desired change happens in system where understanding what is of consequence, what is at stake, for the actors involved needs to be a constant question.

In our fieldwork, we look for the mobilization of new types of activities and behaviours and how these new activities impacted the outcomes of the overall process, from ideation to implementation. For example, the evolution of the structure of the IP agreement in one of the successful projects resulted in transforming the knowledge (Carlile, 2004) of the healthcare practitioner leading the project. She gained entrepreneurial experience, allowing her to understand the benefits of building a start-up out of the project, and then impacted her way of interpreting the type of IP agreement needed for the project. This knowledge transformation process demanded a lot of work and took more than a year. Her partner in the project (a developer, with entrepreneurial and health IT experience) continued to develop the mobile application without a clarified IP solution while continuously sharing new ideas related to both the technology and business model that helped shape the eventual IP agreement. These extended observations of process and outcome, and of the accumulation of transformation of different kinds of knowledge, informed not only what was of consequence across all cases, but what proved of consequence in successful cases that reshaped ideas all the way to implementation.

Conclusion

We have used a sociomaterial approach to show how unconventional research can have greater impact in organization studies. Our aim is to provide guidance to scholars to 'think empirically' in a way that is more grounded in the accumulations and consequences of the contexts they study. Our argument isn't that they need to adopt a formal sociomaterial lens or that they should apply all five dimensions, but rather that scholars should consider choosing the dimensions that are most useful to their inquiry as they address the novelty challenge that comes when taking an unconventional approach.

Other impactful work also demonstrates some of the dimensions outlined in this chapter. For example Orlikowski's (1992) work outlining the duality of structure (technology and human action) looks at both process and outcomes and the temporal accumulations that shape this duality. Kaplan (2011) focuses on the elementary activities related to the development of Powerpoint presentations and how this sheds light on who shapes the strategizing process and its outcome. By doing so, she was able to highlight two core discursive practices and how these impact strategy development across knowledge and institutional boundaries over time.

At its core, sociomateriality is a relational construction; what is real, what has meaning, what has consequence is only in relation to other people and things. Accepting a relational construction necessarily combines ontology and epistemology. Our five dimensions invite a way of thinking about the world and ways of accounting for it. For example, our foundational dimension of outcome and process is more than a duality (light is both particle and wave), as these are in relation with each other. This leads us to see accumulations as both outcome and process. Expanding our methodological horizon, we see accumulations relationally in both the spatial and temporal sense. Then, recursive dynamics follow with the relative and relational durability of layers of accumulations to consider. Finally, questions of change bring us back to the bedrock of relationality: what is of consequence, to whom, when, and how? So, the relational construction embedded in a sociomaterial approach is both expansive and specific at the same time. It is this purposeful tension that proves both imaginative and unconventional, but also consequential. Overall, the approach we have taken in this chapter is to offer guidance in how unconventional research can become conventional in an impactful way.

■ REFERENCES

Alexander, J.C. (ed.). (1987). *The Micro-macro Link*. Los Angeles, CA: University of California Press.

Barad, K. (2003). 'Posthumanist performativity: toward an understanding of how matter comes to matter', *Signs: Journal of Women in Culture and Society*, 28(3): 801–31.

Barley, S.R. (1986). 'Technology as an occasion for structuring: evidence from observations of CT scanners and the social order of radiology departments', *Administrative Science Quarterly*, 31(1): 78–108.

Barley, S.R. (2006). 'When I write my masterpiece: thoughts on what makes a paper interesting', *Academy of Management Journal*, 49(1): 16–20.

Barley, S.R. (2015). '60th anniversary essay: ruminations on how we became a mystery house and how we might get out', *Administrative Science Quarterly*, 61(1): 1–8.

Bartunek, J.M., Rynes, S.L., and Ireland, R.D. (2006). 'What makes management research interesting, and why does it matter?', *Academy of Management Journal*, 49(1): 9–15.

Benner, M.J. and Tushman, M.L. (2015). 'Reflections on the 2013 decade award— "exploitation, exploration, and process management: the productivity dilemma revisited" ten years later', *Academy of Management Review*, 40(4): 497–514.

Black, L.J., Carlile, P.R., and Repenning, N.P. (2004). 'A dynamic theory of expertise and occupational boundaries in new technology implementation: building on Barley's study of CT scanning', *Administrative Science Quarterly*, 49(4): 572–607.

Bourdieu, P. and Passeron, J.C. (1970/1990). *Reproduction in Education, Society and Culture* (Vol. 4). Sage.

Bourdieu, P. and Wacquant, L.J. (1992). *An Invitation to Reflexive Sociology*. Chicago, IL: University of Chicago Press.

Carlile, P.R. (2002). 'A pragmatic view of knowledge and boundaries: boundary objects in new product development', *Organization Science*, 13(4): 442–55.

Carlile, P.R. (2004). 'Transferring, translating, and transforming: an integrative framework for managing knowledge across boundaries', *Organization Science*, 15(5): 555–68.

Carlile, P.R. (2015). 'The irony of making materiality of consequence', *British Journal of Management*, 26(S1): S22–S25.

Carlile, P.R., Nicolini, D., Langley, A., and Tsoukas, H. (eds). (2013). *How Matter Matters: Objects, Artefacts, and Materiality in Organization Studies*. Oxford: Oxford University Press.

Carlile, P.R., Davidson, S.H., Freeman, K.W., Thomas, H., and Venkatraman, N. (eds). (2016). *Reimagining Business Education: Insights and Actions from the Business Education Jam*. Bingley, UK: Emerald Group.

Christensen, C.M. and Carlile, P.R. (2009). 'Course research: using the case method to build and teach management theory', *Academy of Management Learning & Education*, 8(2): 240–51.

Corley, K.G. and Gioia, D.A. (2011). 'Building theory about theory building: what constitutes a theoretical contribution?' *Academy of Management Review*, 36(1): 12–32.

Deken, F., Carlile, P.R., Berends, H., and Lauche, K. (2016). 'Generating novelty through interdependent routines: a process model of routine work', *Organization Science*, 27(3): 659–77.

DeSanctis, G. and Poole, M.S. (1994). 'Capturing the complexity in advanced technology use: adaptive structuration theory', *Organization Science*, 5(2): 121–47.

Garfinkel, H. (1967). *Studies in Ethnomethodology*. New Jersey: Prentice Hall.

Geertz, C. (1973). *The Interpretation of Culture: Selected Essays*. New York: Basic Books.

Glaser, B. and Strauss, A. (1967). *The Discovery of Grounded Theory*. London: Weidenfield & Nicolson.

Howard-Grenville, J.A. and Carlile, P.R. (2006). 'The incompatibility of knowledge regimes: consequences of the material world for cross-domain work', *European Journal of Information Systems*, 15(5): 473–85.

James, W. (1907). *Pragmatism: A New Name for Some Old Philosophy, Old Ways of Thinking*. Popular Lectures on Philosophy. New York: Longmans, Green.

Kaplan, S. (2011). 'Strategy and PowerPoint: an inquiry into the epistemic culture and machinery of strategy making', *Organization Science*, 22(2): 320–46.

Langley, A. (1999). 'Strategies for theorizing from process data', *Academy of Management Review*, 24(4): 691–710.

Leonardi, P.M. (2012). 'Materiality, sociomateriality, and socio-technical systems: what do these terms mean? How are they related? Do we need them?' In P.M. Leonardi, B.A. Nardi, and J. Kallinikos (eds) *Materiality and Organizing: Social Interaction in a Technological World*. Oxford: Oxford University Press, pp.25–48.

Leonardi, P.M. and Barley, S.R. (2010). 'What's under construction here?: social action, materiality, and power in constructivist studies of technology and organizing', *Academy of Management Annals*, 4(1): 1–51.

Mazmanian, M., Orlikowski, W.J., and Yates, J. (2013). 'The autonomy paradox: the implications of mobile email devices for knowledge professionals', *Organization Science*, 24(5): 1337–57.

Mohr, L.B. (1982). *Explaining Organizational Behaviour: The Limits and Possibilities of Theory and Research*. San Francisco, CA: Jossey-Bass Publishers.

Orlikowski, W.J. (1992). 'The duality of technology: rethinking the concept of technology in organizations', *Organization Science*, 3(3): 398–427.

Orlikowski, W.J. (2006). 'Material knowing: the scaffolding of human knowledgeability', *European Journal of Information Systems*, 15(5): 460.

Orlikowski, W.J. (2007). 'Sociomaterial practices: exploring technology at work', *Organization Studies*, 28(9): 1435–48.

Orlikowski, W.J. (2010). 'The sociomateriality of organisational life: considering technology in management research', *Cambridge Journal of Economics*, 34(1): 124–41.

Peirce, C.S. (1902/1974). *Collected papers of Charles Sanders Pierce* (Vol. 2). Cambridge, MA: Harvard University Press.

Yin, R.K. (2013). *Case Study Research: Design and Methods*. Fifth edition. Thousand Oaks, CA: Sage.

13 Path constitution analysis

A methodology for understanding path dependence and path creation

Jörg Sydow, Arnold Windeler, Gordon Müller-Seitz, and Knut Lange

Introduction

An increasing number of studies in the fields of technology and innovation management, strategic management and organization, and, most recently, project management, international management and business logistics are informed by path concepts (<www.wiwiss.fu-berlin.de/forschung/pfadkolleg/downloads/Current-Interests-in-the-Theory-of-Path-Dependence.pdf>). This kind of research can be traced back to David's (1985) and Arthur's (1989) famous studies of the QWERTY keyboard in which they developed their theoretical understanding of path dependence. These studies emphasize the importance of self-reinforcing processes that are triggered by (small) events leading to a (potential) lock-in and occurring mainly behind the backs of agents. In contrast, Garud and Karnøe (2001) call for a more explicit conceptualization of (multiple) actor(s) in the creation of paths. Even if previous studies have tried to integrate these different views of path development (Sydow et al., 2009, 2012), there are few studies devoted to the question of how such paths can be analysed empirically (but see Schubert and Windeler, 2007; Vergne and Durand, 2010; Koch, 2011).

In this chapter, *path constitution* refers to the concepts of path dependence and path creation, embedding these two perspectives into the idea of social constitution (Giddens, 1984; Windeler, 2003; Sydow et al., 2012; Jing and Benner, 2016). We also propose a multi-level process analysis of paths which integrates an institutional with a strategic analysis. While the former concentrates on the reproduction of structural properties by individual or collective agents, the latter focuses 'upon modes in which agents draw upon structural properties in the constitution of social relations' (Giddens, 1984, p.88).

Against this background and consistent with calls to pay attention to qualitative methodological approaches (Aguinis et al., 2009), we develop an unconventional, fine-grained, processual methodology that is informed by structuration theory and tailored to the specific phenomenon under scrutiny—the field of technology and innovation management in which organizations, inter-organizational arrangements, and other institutions matter.

This chapter has two objectives. First, we *introduce a novel and comprehensive methodology*, path constitution analysis (PCA), building on prior work on path dependence and path creation. PCA provides an interpretative, social constructivist methodology that sticks neither to methodological individualism nor to simply applying an institutional or structural analysis. Second, we *offer a detailed processual procedure* that serves as a guiding template for other researchers. Following the exposition of this methodology, we present PCA in action, by describing a longitudinal case study using processual data. We examine our own empirical work in the semiconductor manufacturing industry with regard to the development of a technological path by multiple organizations, and critically reflect on the adequacy of PCA (Sydow et al., 2012; Schubert et al., 2013).

PCA as a methodology

PCA methodology is a generic framework that complements epistemology and ontology and helps to detect, analyse, interpret, and systemize processes of social praxis (see Giddens, 1984).

PATH DEPENDENCE

The analysis of technological—and later institutional—path dependence began with a critique of neoclassical economics that was grounded in evolutionary and institutional economics (Arthur, 1989; David, 1985; North, 1990). Whereas orthodox economics assumes the primacy of optimal solutions in terms of efficiency, the theory of path dependence pays attention to the impact of past events, often captured in the phrase 'history matters'. However, the concept of path dependence goes beyond mere 'past-dependence' (Antonelli, 1999). It acknowledges the importance of self-reinforcing processes that are triggered by one or more often 'small' events and drive the development of a path (Arthur, 1994; David, 2007). Although the primary conditions of any path-dependent process are contingent, the respective events represent initial conditions that, by triggering a self-reinforcing process, have an enduring impact upon the course of the path's future trajectory. However, the impact is anything but clear at the start of the process; paths are *non-ergodic*, meaning that they do not converge automatically to a fixed outcome (David, 1985).

Studies of path dependence use a range of methodological approaches. This is not surprising, given the broad field of application of path dependence and creation thinking, covering technologies and increasingly organizations as well as institutions. The case-study design (Yin, 2013) is nevertheless the most prominent approach utilized in studies of path dependence, almost always using a combination of historical data, qualitative and/or quantitative. Examples include the seminal study by David (1985) of the technological path dependence of the QWERTY keyboard, and the study of organizational path dependence by Koch (2011), who analysed the strategic development of media corporations producing high-quality newspapers in Germany. Another example is the study of behavioural lock-ins in the US health industry and beer market by Barnes et al. (2004). Other methodological approaches are utilized, too. Koch et al. (2009), for example, use an experimental design to investigate the relationship between environmental complexity and path dependence in sequential decision-making processes.

The debate about appropriate methodology gained momentum when Vergne and Durand (2010) not only called for more robust research designs, but questioned the value of real-time data collection and process-oriented case studies. They advocated computer-based simulations, counterfactual investigations, and experimental designs to 'test' path dependence and causal relationships. In response, Garud et al. (2010) argued for more case-study research, using more qualitative and fine-grained ethnographic methods of data gathering and analysis. Dobusch and Kapeller (2013) continued this debate by asking for methodological openness and a combination of research methods, quantitative as well as qualitative.

PCA, while open to a quantitative, qualitative, or multi-method approach (Creswell and Clark, 2007), is closer to the position of these latter authors. It is also important to note that PCA is distinct from grounded theory (Glaser and Strauss, 1967) because it builds on explicit theorizing, in this case about path constitution, integrating path dependence and creation research with the help of a structurationist framework. Consequently, the constitutive features and potential indicators of paths are derived from theory, not from empirical data.

PATH CREATION

Garud and Karnøe (2001) complement the notion of path dependence with the concept of path creation. In contrast to path dependence, path creation emphasizes agency, and the roles of multiple, competent individual and organizational actors, who coordinate their activities. Therefore, not only external shocks—as conceived by David (2001) and other path researchers— lead to deviations from existing technological, institutional, or organizational paths, but also mindful deviations by the collective intervention of actors, who may not be proficient enough to initiate or control the deviation entirely.

To date, methodological approaches studying path creation predominantly use case studies. Almost all of the cases that Garud and Karnøe (2001) collected for their edited volume on path creation use case approaches, but not confined to qualitative data. Binz et al. (2016) apply this approach to study the formation of an on-site water recycling industry in Beijing.

PATH CONSTITUTION

The concept of path constitution integrates the concepts of path dependence and creation. Instead of 'mixing ontologies' (Garud et al., 2010), this concept offers a constructivist understanding in which path dependence and path creation are only two possible ways to build and transform a path in time and space; others are intentional path *defense* or *extension*, unintended path *dissolution*, path *renewal* or *breaking* a path without creating a new one (Meyer and Schubert, 2007; Sydow et al., 2012; Isaksen, 2015; Jing and Benner, 2016). In line with received path dependence theory, the constitutive understanding of techno-logical, institutional or organizational paths *always implies a certain degree of path dependence* in the sense that path processes, even if they are intentionally created, show a kind of irreversibility, momentum, and potential lock-in.

The concept of path constitution calls for a theoretical understanding which acknowledges the constructivist turn in path research (Garud and Karnøe, 2001; Windeler, 2003; Sydow et al., 2009, 2010, 2012) and applies recent path concepts without losing the ability to explain path-*dependent* processes. Structuration theory (Giddens, 1984) underpins the following definition and conceptualization, calls for an integration of institutional and strategic analyses, and provides a sophisticated theoretical lens for data analysis and interpretation.

DEFINITION AND CONSTITUTIVE FEATURES OF A PATH

Bearing the concept of path constitution in mind, we define a *path* as being a course of events interrelated on different levels of analysis, such as a single organization or an organizational or technological field, and in which one of the available technological, institutional, or organizational options gains momentum in time-space, but cannot automatically be determined from the onset. This development is triggered by certain actions or events, and driven by specific self-reinforcing mechanisms that not only cause the momentum, but might lead the whole process into a lock-in that is, at least from a strategic perspective, inefficient (Sydow et al., 2009).

It remains an empirical question as to whether the path is predominantly constituted by processes beyond the reach and awareness of knowledgeable actors ('behind their backs') or by reflexive processes designed or at least

Table 13.1 Constitutive features and potential indicators of paths

Constitutive features	Description	Indicators
level interrelatedness	conceptualize focal level of analysis in relation to surrounding micro and macro levels of analysis	actors relate their activities to the focal level of analysis and also to micro and macro levels
triggering event	incident that potentially induces the current and potential future trajectory of a path	actors see an incident as decisive, initiating self-reinforcing processes making one particular option more likely in the future
non-ergodic process	sequence of events leading to an outcome that is neither arbitrary, nor automatically determined from the start	options of equal potential are progressively narrowed down to a final outcome
self-reinforcing processes	sequence of events that are progressively aligned, creating momentum, and pushing a path in a particular direction	creation of institutions that pursue joint objectives; design of complementary management systems; learning effects which reinforce the dominant path
lock-in	path trajectory is confined to a single outcome—even if that is not efficient	investment in prevailing option is stable or increasing, investment in alternatives reduced
multiple actors	constellations of individual or collective agents	more than two actors bound together by sets of relationships

shaped by powerful collective interventions of actors through path creation (Garud and Karnøe, 2001). It makes sense to speak of a path only where competing options exist, and the later 'solution' is not foreseeable at the beginning—and where the development culminates in a process of narrowing down to one option.

Given this definition of a path (see Table 13.1), PCA requires a precise understanding of (a) *level interrelatedness*, (b) *triggering events*, (c) *non-ergodic processes*, (d) *self-reinforcing processes*, (e) *lock-in*, and (f) *multiple actors* who intentionally or unintentionally (re-)produce the path in time-space. In what follows, we set out our detailed understanding of these constitutive features, with the potential indicators that need to be sampled purposefully:

(a) *Level interrelatedness* refers to the fact that a certain path can only be observed when it is put into perspective with regard to the surrounding (contextual) levels of analysis. Level interrelatedness, however, is produced and reproduced by knowledgeable and powerful agents who refer in their activities recursively, but not necessarily reflexively, to contextual or institutional features in their strategic behaviour (Windeler, 2003). This so-called 'focal level' of analysis relates to the level on which the path under scrutiny develops, whether this is of a technological, institutional or organizational nature, or—as in the case of technology-intensive firms (Valorinta et al., 2011) or regional clusters (Sydow et al., 2010)—a mixture of these. In contrast, the surrounding levels of analysis are those that are relevant for understanding the development of the focal path because of possible interference from processes from above ('upper boundary level') as well as from below ('lower boundary level') the focal level of analysis.

The identification of potential indicators for level interrelatedness relies on the researcher's empirical or conceptual interest. It is advisable to start with the focal level of analysis, but the lower and upper boundary levels of analysis should also be considered. In the case of regional clusters or strategic alliances and networks, this would be the field and the organizational levels respectively (see Windeler and Sydow, 2001, for an example in the media industry).

(b) *Triggering events* are incidents, or series of incidents which, for relevant actors or observers, initiate a path process. Even though such path-triggering events are often 'small' (David, 1985), in retrospect they can turn out to be neither small nor innocent in relation to their long-term implications. Consider, for example, the strategic move of JVC and other video player manufacturers to sign a contract with leading Hollywood studios to secure content in the VHS format consistent with their products (Cusumano et al., 1992).

Indicators for triggering events must be seen as decisive for initiating the respective path at what is often called a 'critical juncture' (Collier and Collier, 1991). The assessment of the relevance of the particular event stems either from actors who are engaged with the path or from observers. The latter are important, because triggering events may emerge 'behind the backs of the actors'. Observers (consultants, market analysts, researchers) can thus add valuable insight and shed fresh light on the ex-post reconstruction of the respective paths. Associated with this observation is the assumption that causality, between the event and the trajectory of the path, can be established.

(c) *Non-ergodicity* is a process characteristic that implies a sequence of events culminating in an outcome that is not automatically determined from the start, but not arbitrarily either (Arthur, 1994; David, 1985, 2001, 2007). While different outcomes are possible at the beginning, the range of options narrows over time. Consider again the case of VHS versus Beta versus Video 2000 in some European countries.

Indicators for non-ergodic processes can either be gathered retrospectively or in real-time. The process can be captured by first identifying options that have more or less equal potential at the beginning. If a path process is at work, one would expect the number of options to fall over time (in the case of video recorders, from 2 or 3 to 1). However, if a few options cease to exist but the overall number of options remains high, this is not sufficient. In the final phase of a path process, a single final solution prevails (VHS). Although other options might still be available, they represent at best niche solutions.

(d) *Self-reinforcing processes* are characterized by positive feedback mechanisms which continue to drive the course of a path in an established direction (Arthur, 1989). These mechanisms are at the heart of path dependence theory. They comprise coordination and complementarity as well as learning effects and adaptive expectations (Sydow et al., 2009), and are embedded in the specific multi-level context with which they interact (Koch, 2011). These mechanisms generate an overall direction, supported by actions that are progressively aligned, thus giving the process momentum, while accompanied by an increasing degree of rigidity, which can culminate in lock-in.

Indicators of self-reinforcing processes relate to the dimensions of social (re)production: signification, domination, and legitimation (Giddens, 1984). The indicators must be set against the background of both the shared cognitive and normative assumptions of the actors and their ways of dealing with the material and immaterial facilities that lead to rigidity once a path has been established (Windeler, 2003; Schubert and Windeler, 2007; Sydow et al., 2012). Shared assumptions can contribute to the coordination and complementarity effects mentioned earlier. Indicators for coordination effects include the establishment of institutions that formulate and pursue joint objectives. Complementarity effects relate to synergies based on a *bundle* of resources, rules or practices, rather than using each element of the bundle independently. Indicators for such effects include the use of complementary technologies (VHS cassettes and Hollywood movies) and organizational management systems. These effects are also responsible for building momentum for some alternatives while reducing momentum in others (Page, 2006; Vergne and Durand, 2010).

(e) *Lock-in* occurs when the trajectory of a path becomes confined to a single outcome that, even in the face of more efficient alternatives, agents have to follow. Such a lock-in may be of a predominantly cognitive, normative or resource-based nature. Being locked-in implies that subsequent developments become predictable, or predetermined as long as the lock-in exists. Lock-in is not an inevitable consequence from the onset, but only a *likely* result of the self-reinforcing processes at work. Moreover, given the principal ability of agents to 'act otherwise' (Giddens, 1984), we assume from a constructivist perspective that a lock-in is never final, particularly not in the institutional and organizational realm. Even in the case of technology, the dominance of the QWERTY keyboard may be challenged by voice recognition (as VHS was replaced by DVD which is now being overtaken by Blu-ray).

One indicator for a lock-in is when relevant actors or observers take for granted the assumption that no alternative option appears to be available for some period of time and assess alternative and formerly competing options increasingly as being of minor importance or as niches.

(f) *Multiple types of actors* need to be identified, along with their positions, and roles in the path constitution process, and the influence they have on each other as well as on the development of the path. Their roles may depend on different forms of markets, such as those for consumer or industry goods. For PCA, an actor can comprise any individual or any collectivity such as an organization or an inter-organizational network.

A potential indicator for multiple actors is the number of relevant actors or actor constellations, often usefully qualified by the type and size of organization or other attributes. Indicators for the positions and roles of actors can be found in relation to the authority assigned to them by others in path processes. At least two actors must have an interest in a certain path in order to allow for a kind of 'comparative process analysis', as was the case in our study of the next generation of lithography technology for manufacturing semiconductors.

Research setting and methods

Our study is set in the semiconductor manufacturing industry and focuses on the creation of a technological path by multiple organizations through mindful deviation from an established path (Sydow et al., 2012; Schubert et al., 2013). However, as we will show, the innovation aimed at by the organizational actors will, at least if they are successful, constitute a new technological path, involving path dependence. We selected the semiconductor manufacturing industry, as the dominant optical lithography reflects a path-dependent technology that is vital for all highly developed market economies.

The research focused on two inter-organizational networks. SEMATECH, based in Texas, is a global consortium of leading semiconductor manufacturers and tool suppliers. Extreme Ultraviolet Lithography Limited Liability Company (LLC) is a consortium established by Intel in the mid-1990s to promote ultraviolet lithography. The selection, development and introduction of a completely new procedure to manufacture computer chips—which remains a key issue in this industry—provides an excellent opportunity for demonstrating PCA 'in action'. This manufacturing process has long been plagued by path dependence. It is currently regarded by the actors themselves as a case for possible path creation; the actors are convinced that they have to choose only one new technology from a range of options, because the promotion of more than one would be too costly. And if the selected technology is finally introduced, actors will have to stick to it for at least 15 years, but probably longer (Linden et al., 2000).

DATA COLLECTION

We opted for PCA as a qualitative approach for several reasons. First, the inter-organizational creation of a technological path is still uncharted territory (for an exception: Garud and Karnøe, 2001) and studies of path creation have used such an approach so far. Second, in the analysis of path constitution processes, 'how' and 'why' questions are predominant. In such circumstances, qualitative case studies are appropriate. However, in line with recent calls (Aguinis et al., 2009), our approach differs from classic case study research. We include, for example, historical and real-time analyses that are theoretically informed, tailoring our approach to the specific characteristics of path concepts. Third, in order to investigate processes of path constitution, a longitudinal explorative inquiry is necessary. Fourth, qualitative methods such as in-depth case studies, using semi-structured interviews and archival data, allow us to uncover how actors and incidents on different levels are related to each other. As a path cannot be measured objectively, we disclose respondents' personal viewpoints, in the interests of data 'richness'.

We studied how complex system technologies are extended and created in the semiconductor industry, focusing on a novel manufacturing technology— next-generation lithography. Data were collected retrospectively for the years prior to the project work, and in real time from 2003 to 2015. Data were initially only drawn from secondary sources. The following five sources were then utilized for triangulation purposes, to heighten construct validity, and to prevent post-hoc rationalization and potential bias.

First, we analyzed a range of documents including online materials (brochures, company periodicals, video footage of the organizations involved), archival databases (e.g. LexisNexis), and other industry documents such as annual reports. These documents provide secondary data, but are useful in reconstructing path processes at different levels of analysis over a prolonged period.

Second, 119 semi-structured interviews were conducted with semiconductor industry experts, company engineers and senior executives. We identified interviewees by 'snowball sampling', and initial contacts were asked to identify other potential respondents involved in coordinating industry activities. The interviewees originated from the 'organizational field' (DiMaggio and Powell, 1983), whereby the focal level of analysis was the network of organizational actors involved in the process of path creation and extension. With regard to the micro level, we opted for the level of the organization. Our decision for the organizational field as the macro level and the organization as the micro level is based on the fact that our interviewees referred to these levels in their explanations of the technology development.

Third, an annual panel was established each spring from 2007 to 2010. Each of the panel interviews was held after a major industry conference to allow for first-hand, up-to-date industry insights. Five senior experts, with different organizational and professional backgrounds and deep insights into the technology development process, were interviewed, covering the same issue as the semi-structured interviews, and also addressing generic future technological trends.

Fourth, we drew from participant observation during on-site visits and at major industry conferences, also analysing conference presentations, slides and public announcements.

Finally, we conducted follow-up interviews and e-mail correspondence with key respondents, as well as scholarly discussions with five US and three European colleagues from the fields of strategic management, research methods and organizational sociology. Industry respondents were asked to comment on prior drafts of this study and their insights were integrated into two seminars in order to enhance internal validity. This process helped us to avoid misinterpreting the data, as triangulating by means of multiple sources and our prolonged engagement in the field between 2003 and 2015 is in line with previous research informed by structuration theory (Sydow and Windeler, 1998; Berends et al., 2011) and enhances the trustworthiness of the data.

DATA ANALYSIS

First, we compiled a comprehensive case study database to heighten reliability, including 150 pages of field notes, 1,493 pages of interview transcripts, a significant volume of archival information (media coverage, by online journals and trade periodicals, LexisNexis database) and conference materials. The data also included written comments and reports on the organizations involved and the practices pursued in the field to coordinate the competing technological paths.

Second, we developed brief descriptions of how the different organizations and inter-organizational networks interacted to pursue joint technological options.

Third, we condensed our empirical data and strengthened the interpretation from a structurationist perspective, referring to aspects of structures (rules and resources), and also to the knowledge and reflexivity of agents and their potential to intervene in the face of the dialectic of control.

PCA in action

We applied PCA to the constitution of a new technological path for the manufacturing tools of semiconductors. As summarized in Table 13.2, this path displays six constitutive features.

Table 13.2 Empirical evidence for potential indicators of paths

constitutive feature	indicators	illustrative evidence
level interrelatedness	actors relate their activities to a focal level of analysis and to more micro and macro levels	R&D consortia relate their activities to the (lower) organizational and (upper) organizational field levels
triggering event	actors assess an incident as decisive in initiating self-reinforcing processes promoting a likely future option	proof of concept of EUVL by the LLC consortium in 2001; delivery of the first EUVL alpha tool in 2006
non-ergodic process	options of equal potential are narrowed down to a final solution	initially, five 'next-generation lithography' options; support first focused on EPL, but EUVL was eventually supported
self-reinforcing processes	creation of institutions that pursue joint objectives; design of complementary management systems; learning effects which reinforce the dominant path	observable global coordination of actors involved in EUVL development; visible interplay between commitment and performance of EUVL
lock-in	investment in prevailing option stable or increasing, investment in alternatives reduced	stable or increasing investments in EUVL; disappearance of support for other options
multiple actors	more than two actors bound together by sets of relationships	R&D consortia are critical; intense ongoing communication between chip and tool manufacturers and suppliers

* EUVL = extreme ultraviolet lithography.
* EPL = electron projection lithography.

LEVEL INTERRELATEDNESS

Our interest lies with the creation of a new technological path, extreme ultraviolet lithography (EUVL), from an existing one by mindful deviation and building momentum. For the creation (and subsequent maintenance and possible extension) of this technological path, inter-organizational R&D networks are extremely important (Browning and Shetler, 2000; Carayannis and Alexander, 2004; Sydow et al., 2012; Kapoor and McGrath, 2014). For EUVL, SEMATECH is the leading global consortium for organizing pre-competitive R&D in semiconductor manufacturing by, for example, organizing field-wide events:

SEMATECH and its subsidiaries sponsor, host, and participate in a variety of public semiconductor industry meetings and events worldwide to enhance global cooperation and provide important forums for fostering dialogue and creating industry consensus. Experts at SEMATECH's public conferences share data and methodologies, rank critical issues required to bring R&D concepts to commercial production [and] guide the industry in seeking effective solutions for future technology generations.

(SEMATECH, 2010)

The network level thus constitutes the focal level of analysis. Typical network events include the Litho Forum, focusing on competing next-generation lithography technologies, where EUVL is a leading candidate.

Other key events include the International Technology Roadmap for Semi-conductors (ITRS) workshops (the company of the same name, ITRS, is a subsidiary of SEMATECH). These workshops are regarded as *the* field-wide events where actors develop a joint understanding of future technological milestones, offering guidance to the sector.

As a level *above* the network level of analysis, we selected the organizational field in which the technological path is constituted. First, while the field concept seems similar to that of the industry, it is more open and emphasizes the importance not only of organizations, but also of technologies in use and institutionalized practices (Leblebici et al., 1991). Second, the field concept is not restricted geographically. This helps our analysis, because this industry is highly international and clarification of the regional agglomeration of activities is one of the first research tasks (see, Martin et al., 2010). Third, an organizational field may cut across the boundaries of a single industry and include additional actors such as regulatory agencies and capital providers. This suits our analysis of the EUVL path constitution process, because tool suppliers are crucial in this respect, along with the semiconductor industry.

As a level *below* the network, we selected the organization, because companies like Intel, Samsung or ASML do not outsource all their R&D activities:

[I]mportant parts of the technological development take place at SEMATECH, that's tremendously important and, apart from that, every company has their own interests with regard to what they intend to pursue. Only to a limited extent, everybody [SEMATECH members] is able and willing to collaborate.   (I-05)

This happens for various reasons. First, companies want to maintain their core competencies. Second, in consortia they do not have complete control over the financial resources provided, but—based upon their own resources—have to negotiate with other members about their joint use. Third, when technological development reaches a stage where the products are close to market and companies want to have sole responsibility or bilateral development partnerships, they integrate the project into their organization.

The evidence shows that these levels of analysis are strongly interrelated. Interviewees frequently referred to the 'industry' and to the 'organization' level when explaining processes and events related to the development of EUVL. Many recurrent activities on the network level, for instance, are also oriented towards the organizational field and the organizational level (e.g. the activities of ITRS outlined above). One example was the set-up of field-wide EUVL programs by R&D consortia to spread the message that this technology will be supported by government funding:

SEMATECH tries to set up and identify what are the critical issues within [EUVL] technology, try to build the right projects behind it, and so you try and build projects around that within the lithography technology division, which try to deliver value to our member companies.   (I-31)

TRIGGERING EVENTS

With regard to the constitution of the EUVL path, there were several candidates for triggering events. One was the decision by the SEMATECH consortium to organize the first conferences in 1998 and 2000. These events initiated the discussion about next-generation lithography, and at subsequent conferences in 2000 and 2002, EUVL emerged as the most likely candidate:

At LLC there was a point in time...this was the SEMATECH workshop...when in 2002 EUVL emerged as the next-generation lithography option. The [research results] that came out of this workshop and the data that LLC shared with the broader industry community have finally persuaded [other participants in the field] that EUV is the technology. (I-21)

The fact that EUVL was ranked highest by the global technological community gave this option significant legitimacy across the field. The event with the greatest impact on the creation of a new technological path, however, was LLC's proof-of-concept of EUVL:

LLC also initiated EUV...and then they said 'Well, take a look, it works!' Now there are several steps to say 'it works'. What they have shown is that, indeed, with this technology, with those mirrors they developed, it can be made. That was a critical step. (I-13)

This event triggered the creation of a large EUVL program at SEMATECH and of programs by national governments, as well as EUV-related R&D by companies such as Zeiss, for example.

Other triggering events were the investments by Intel and its corporate venture-capital arm Intel Capital in crucial component suppliers for EUVL. These investments increased the probability that the technological challenges of EUVL could eventually be solved, and they demonstrated the overwhelming interest of the market leader in this technology, thus sending a powerful message to the semiconductor industry, triggering further investments by others. EUVL was also promoted in 2005 by the South Korean chip manufacturer Samsung, which is now the second largest company in this industry. Samsung joined SEMATECH to benefit from the consortium's EUVL program. This strengthened the belief in the ultimate success of EUVL, which was important because the technology had run into serious problems:

Other companies became very aggressive and very interested in EUV lithography in the same timeframe. For example, SEMATECH actually picked up a member, Samsung, roughly during that period [to head the development for the consortium]. (I-37)

Since the proof-of-concept of EUVL in 2001, the focus has shifted to the question of whether this technology could eventually be used for mass manufacturing. In this respect, the delivery of the first EUVL alpha tools (prototypes) in 2006 was important, because this allowed actors to test and improve the technology. With the delivery of these alpha tools, tool producers such as ASML were able to generate a return on investment, which could then be reinvested into the development of beta tools. In sum, the occurrence of several events, large and small, some of them occurring in sequence, triggered the creation of EUVL—and potentially a new technological path.

NON-ERGODIC PROCESSES

Non-ergodic processes could be observed in the global semiconductor industry in the late 1990s when actors attempted to enhance the established optical lithography and extend its reach, but were giving top priority to the quest for a radical alternative. The view prevailed that optical lithography could not print patterns below 45 nanometers half pitch. In order to print smaller patterns, industry respondents considered a novel kind of lithography imperative. For this reason, in 2004 experts were still working on four other different options of so-called next-generation lithography: Electron Projection Lithography (EPL), Ion Projection Lithography (IPL), Proximity X-Ray Lithography (PXL), and Projection Electron Lithography (PEL).

Characteristic of a non-ergodic process, it was not at first clear which candidate would succeed. At the start, EUVL was not even regarded as the most likely candidate. The SEMATECH consortium organizes an annual global conference on this matter. At the first conference in 1998, EPL (supported by the EPL consortium PREVAIL) was the winner, measured by a ranking of lithography scientists at the end of the conference. Consequently, Intel established EUV LLC in order to support this technology. This consortium included several chip manufacturers and three national laboratories from the United States. At the second conference, EUVL became the first-ranked option, even though EPL was only narrowly beaten:

As from 1995 there were biannual workshops organized in which these champion groups were promoting data and results on their technology of choice and I think in the late 1990s, in fact, EUVL came out of that technology as the clear winner as the technology that has the largest potential to take over from optical lithography in the future. But still, there were companies like the ones focused on EPL that continued to work on their preferred option and, like, for example, Nikon together with IBM, have been running a joint program on EPL for a number of years.   (I-15)

LLC gained further momentum when the semiconductor firms Infineon and Micron joined the consortium in 2000, and IBM followed in 2001. The latter was particularly important, because until then IBM had exclusively promoted EPL. LLC's technological proof of concept in 2001 eventually turned the balance in favor of EUVL. The successful members of the LLC consortium, with other industry members, then transferred further EUVL research and development to SEMATECH as the accepted, neutral locale for collaborative technology development. The EPL consortium PREVAIL was dissolved shortly after the success of its rival. To date, EUVL is the only remaining candidate with potential to be *the* next-generation lithography, although it is still unclear if this technology will be used for mass manufacturing because many problems remain to be solved (Shilov, 2016). Surprisingly, the only competing option to EUVL is not a new alternative, but immersion lithography, which represents only an extension of the current technological path of optical lithography (Sydow et al., 2012).

SELF-REINFORCING PROCESSES

Coordination effects pertaining to the development of EUVL are already discernible. The coordination between different consortia in the field, from different regions, and incorporating new actors, has been much improved. There are several semiconductor consortia which focus on EUVL. To cover all critical aspects of EUVL and to avoid excessive duplication of R&D efforts, actors created the International EUV Initiative (IEUVI). This loose network of consortia serves as a global forum of exchange with regard to EUVL and, as it provides the structures needed for more effective coordination, is of tremendous importance for tackling the worldwide challenges of EUVL with limited resources by setting technological standards that help to coordinate the various activities. Over time, the field-wide coordination has significantly improved, even though it is by no means a process without friction.

Complementarity effects are also observable, with regard to the activities of SEMATECH. This highly influential consortium comprises thirteen organizations that represent half of the worldwide semiconductor market, and which have worked together over many years. In addition, it provides joint resources, for instance in the form of testing facilities, on which all SEMATECH members can draw. These financial and strategic commitments are indicators for complementarity effects.

Thus, as in most cases of path dependence, several self-reinforcing mechanisms are at work in the field of semiconductor manufacturing technology. These mechanisms can be identified not only for the established optical but also post-optical lithography.

LOCK-IN

We must concede that, despite an ongoing development process which began more than 15 years ago, there is still no real lock-in for EUVL, as nobody knows whether this technology will ever be introduced into mass manufacturing. Nevertheless, as the website of the 2016 International Symposium of Extreme Ultraviolet Lithography claims:

There is a general consensus that the EUVL technology will definitely be applied for 7nm logic technology nodes in the coming years. EUVL technology for the sub-7nm logic technology nodes is regarded as the most promising way for High Volume Manufacturing production of devices. However, many obstacles remain to be overcome. (<http://eidec.co.jp/EUVL2016/>; see Bakshi, 2016)

Another competing option that has not yet been foreseen as relevant may surface, such as enhanced optical lithography (Singer, 2014). However, several indicators suggest that a 'soft' lock-in for EUVL has already occurred, as the pursuit of alternative technological paths already appears to be unlikely. Indeed, indicators suggest that investments have increased with regard to EUVL:

You can find many people that simply say 'We have no choice anymore', and if EUVL is not going to succeed this would have hefty consequences. (I-74)

This holds true whether we focus on consortia, companies or regions. As mentioned above, SEMATECH set up a large EUVL program in 2002 after LLC's proof-of-concept. The EUVL program which was set up in 2008 exceeded the earlier one, as the State of New York subsidized it to create new jobs. This manifests in conference series that are geared towards EUVL and which we attended for data collection purposes. In contrast, there are no other conference series of comparable size and prestige, which serves as a further indicator of the increasing dominance of EUVL as next-generation lithography.

Additionally, key companies such as Intel announced that 'significant strides have been made in EUV lithography over the past year taking the technology from a question of *if* to a question of *when*' (Golda, 2016). This optimism is shared by the world's largest producer of semiconductor manufacturing tools, ASML (2016), which assumes that 'EUVL is at the cusp of being introduced in volume chip production'. Furthermore, huge EUVL initiatives have started in Japan, which had long been skeptical with regard to the technology.

In contrast, investments in alternative options have been sharply reduced. Whereas at the beginning of the process five options received support, investments soon focused on two options, EUVL and EPL. However, due to the dominant assumption that EUVL ought to be followed because of an increasing engagement of powerful actors by means of coordinating joint efforts, the EPL consortium PREVAIL was dissolved and the Japanese EPL program was replaced by an EUVL program. To date, actors in all five world regions support EUVL as a next-generation lithography option.

Nano-imprint lithography is the only remaining viable option that is being promoted by SEMATECH. However, this is considered a niche option due to low throughput, i.e. the amount of chips produced in a certain period of time. Therefore, even though the ultimate success of EUVL is still questionable, indicators suggest a 'soft' lock-in at time.

MULTIPLE ACTORS

Many strongly interlinked actors are important for the constitution of the EUVL path, including several R&D consortia such as SEMATECH, which includes the largest global semiconductor firms as equal partners. However, this role might change in future as Intel and Samsung left SEMATECH in 2015 (Diana, 2015).

Besides SEMATECH, consortia-like network organizations like ASET (dissolved in 2013) and SELETE, along with the Evolving Nano-Process Infrastructure Development Center in Japan, IMEC, MEDEA and LETI in Europe are crucial to the constitution of the EUVL path. IEUVI is the platform where all these consortia coordinate their activities. LLC stopped its R&D activities after the proof-of-concept. A recent consortium solely related to EUVL is INVENT at the University at Albany, SUNY, which includes chip manufacturers and suppliers.

On the organizational level, chip manufacturers and producers of semiconductor manufacturing tools are relevant, as well as their suppliers. The chip manufacturers most interested in EUVL are Intel, AMD and IBM from the United States, and Samsung from South Korea; apart now from Intel and Samsung, all of these are members of SEMATECH. There are only three major tool manufacturers or system integrators: the market leader ASML from the Netherlands, and Nikon and Canon from Japan. There are many suppliers of EUVL, but there are only one to three global suppliers for many critical components. Chip manufacturers and tool suppliers are locked into supply chains, engaged in an intense communication process. Because failure to develop a critical component could threaten the constitution of the entire EUVL path, these actors are strongly interrelated.

Several public organizations and investors are also of importance to EUVL. National and supranational governments in Japan and Germany, as well as the European Union, cannot easily stop EUVL programs. In the United States, the Department of Defense and several states also promote the development of EUVL. Finally, venture capitalists are relevant for some of the EUVL suppliers. They sometimes invest in cooperation with corporate venture capital entities of semiconductor firms, most notably Intel Capital. However, due to the time-consuming development process, independent venture capitalists are reluctant to invest in this technology.

Conclusion and limitations

We began this chapter by observing that the rising interest in path concepts, including dependence and creation, relates mainly to theoretical debates, but has little reflected methodological implications. Our aim is to complement this discourse by developing PCA as theoretically informed methodology for predominantly qualitative analyses in a post-positivist manner, offering a valuable platform for further analyses of these processes. Our contribution, therefore, is to offer a first step towards a detailed approach informed by the concepts of path dependence and path creation, integrating these into a comprehensive understanding of path constitution informed by structuration theory. This approach contrasts sharply with the earlier intentions of propon-ents of path creation (Garud and Karnøe, 2001). In addition, we identify six constitutive features of paths: level interrelatedness; triggering events; non-ergodic processes; self-reinforcing processes; lock-ins; and multiple actors. We also provide indicators for analysing these features in order to encourage diffusion of these ideas on a common basis.

We demonstrated PCA in action by applying it to a longitudinal, multilevel analysis in the field of semiconductor manufacturing. We were able to enrich our understanding of indicators with concrete examples from our field research. Hence, we offer a pragmatic and yet theoretically informed guide for other researchers interested in the analysis of paths, not necessarily just technological ones.

Our approach has three limitations.

First, when applying PCA, investigation at multiple levels of analysis could encounter conflicting perspectives, not least due to the post-positivistic nature of our research design. For instance, we interviewed members of different corporations with different backgrounds. When asked about the same phe-nomena, sometimes differing opinions were aired, with regard to the economic importance and/or impact of a path. The triangulation of perspectives—seen as an advantage of qualitative inquiries (Seale, 1999)—can lead to contradictions, and it remains an open question as to how to deal with them.

Second, in our application of the methodology we referred solely to quali-tative data. The lack of quantitative data may be a shortcoming as we are not able to relate to other, quantitatively oriented discourses. This, however, should be possible if relevant data are available.

Third, we relied upon an understanding of path constitution informed by Giddens' overarching idea of social constitution processes (Windeler, 2003).

Future research comparing different types of paths may well deliver intriguing results. For example, what kinds of organizational practices should be considered (human resource, personal leadership, strategic planning) when exploring organizational path dependencies? What do organizational, technological and/or institutional paths have in common? How do they interact in producing an outcome that has been considered a technological lock-in, even if multiple technological paths are investigated in one industry (Bergek and Onufrey, 2014)? The empirical scope of analyses can be widened to include non-corporate settings, e.g. paths of political regulation. Incorporating quantitative analyses should increase the validity and significance of the conclusions. PCA, after all, is a comprehensive methodology, embracing where appropriate quantitative and qualitative approaches to organization and management research.

▣ ACKNOWLEDGEMENTS

We thank the Volkswagen Foundation, Germany, for funding this research under grant AZ II/80308; the German Research Foundation (DFG) for additional funding from grant MU 3070/1-1; and our interviewees for their time and patience. A previous version of this chapter was presented at the 2009 Annual Meeting of the European Academy of Management in Liverpool and first published in *Business Research* (2010), 5(2):155–76.

▣ REFERENCES

Aguinis, H., Pierce, C.A., Bosco, F.A., and Muslin, I.S. (2009). 'First decade of organizational research methods. Trends in design, measurement, and data-analysis topics', *Organizational Research Methods*, 12(1): 69–112.

Antonelli, C. (1999). 'The economics of path-dependence in industrial organization', *International Journal of Industrial Organization*, 15: 643–75.

Arthur, W.B. (1989). 'Competing technologies, increasing returns, and lock-in by historical events', *The Economic Journal*, 99: 116–31.

Arthur, W.B. (1994). *Increasing Returns and Path Dependency in the Economy*. Ann Arbor, MI: University of Michigan Press.

ASML (2016). 'EUV production insertion: factors to watch', <www.asml.com/euv-is-at-the-cusp-of-being-introduced-in-volume-chip-production-the-industrialization-metrics-of-euv-most-importantly-productivity-and-availability-will-drive-the-decision-/en/s41905?rid=41906> (last accessed 18 September 2016).

Barnes, W., Gartland, M.P., and Stack, M. (2004). 'Old habits die hard: path dependency and behavioral lock-in', *Journal of Economic Issues*, 38(2): 371–7.

Bakshi, V. (2016). 'Update from EUVL workshop in Berkeley. <http://electroiq.com/euvl-focus/2016/07/22/update-from-euvl-workshop-in-berkeley/> (last accessed 18 September 2016). San Francisco, CA: Extension Media.

Bergek, A. and Onufrey, K. (2014). 'Is one path enough? Multiple paths and path interaction as an extension of path dependency theory', *Industrial and Corporate Change*, 23(5): 1261–97.

Berends, H., van Burg, E., and van Raaij, E.M. (2011). 'Contacts and contracts: cross-level network dynamics in the development of an aircraft material', *Organization Science*, 22(4): 940–60.

Binz, C., Bernhard, T., and Coenen, L. (2016). 'Path creation as a process of resource alignment and anchoring: industry formation for on-site water recycling in Beijing', *Economic Geography*, 92(2): 172–200.

Browning, L.D. and Shelter, J.C. (2000). *Sematech: Saving the US Semiconductor Industry*. College Station, Texas: A&M University Press.

Carayannis, E.G. and Alexander, J.M. (2004). 'Strategy, structure and performance issues of pre-competitive R&D consortia: insights and lessons learned from SEMATECH', *IEEE Transactions on Engineering Management*, 51(2): 226–32.

Collier, R.B. and Collier, D. (1991). *Shaping the Political Arena: Critical Junctures, the Labor Movement, and Regime Dynamics in Latin America*. Princeton, NJ: Princeton University Press.

Creswell, J.W. and Plano Clark, V.L. (2007). *Designing and Conducting. Mixed Methods Research*. Thousand Oaks, CA: Sage.

Cusumano, M.A., Mylonadis, Y., and Rosenbloom, R.S. (1992). 'Strategic maneuvering and mass-market dynamics: the triumph of VHS over Beta', *Business History Review*, 66: 51–94.

David, P.A. (1985). 'Clio and the economics of QWERTY', *American Economic Review*, 75(2): 332–7.

David, P.A. (2001). 'Path dependence, its critiques, and the quest for historical economics.' In P. Garrouste, and S. Ioannides (eds) *Evolution and Path Dependence in Economic Ideas*. Cheltenham: Edward Elgar, pp.15–40.

David, P.A. (2007). 'Path dependence: a foundational concept for historical social science', *Cliometrica, Journal of Historical Economics and Econometric History*, 1(2): 91–114.

Diana, C. (2015). 'Intel, Samsung leave Albany semiconductor consortium', <www.bizjournals.com/albany/news/2015/04/06/intel-samsung-leave-albany-semiconductor.html> (last accessed 18 September 2016).

DiMaggio, P.J. and Powell, W.W. (1983). 'The iron cage revisited: institutional isomorphism and collective rationality in organizational fields', *American Sociological Review*, 48(2): 147–60.

Dobusch, L. and Kapeller, J. (2013). 'Striking new paths: theory and method in path dependence research', *Schmalenbach Business Review*, 65: 288–311.

Garud, R. and Karnøe, P. (2001). 'Path creation as a process of mindful deviation.' In R. Garud and P. Karnøe (eds) *Path Dependence and Creation*. Mahwah, NJ: Earlbaum, pp.1–38.

Garud, R., Kumaraswamy, A., and Karnøe, P. (2010). 'Path dependence or path creation?', *Journal of Management Studies*, 47(4): 760–74.

Giddens, A. (1984). *The Constitution of Society: Outline of the Theory of Structuration*. Polity Press: Cambridge.

Glaser, B.G. and Strauss, A.L. (1967). *The Discovery of Grounded Theory. Strategies for Qualitative Research*. Chicago, IL: Aldine.

Golda, J.M. (2016). 'EUV Lithography—Progress on the journey to manufacturing magic.' <http://blogs.intel.com/technology/2016/02/euv-progress/> (last accessed 18 September 2016).

Isaksen, A. (2015). 'Industrial development in thin regions: trapped in path extension?', *Journal of Economic Geography*, 15(3): 585–600.

Jing, R. and Benner, M. (2016). 'Institutional regime, opportunity space and organizational path constitution: case studies of the conversion of military firms in China', *Journal of Management Studies*, 53(4): 552–79.

Kapoor, R. and McGrath, P.J. (2014). 'Unmasking the interplay between technology evolution and R&D collaboration: evidence from the global semiconductor manufacturing industry, 1990–2010', *Research Policy*, 43: 555–69.

Koch, J. (2011). 'Inscribed strategies: exploring the organizational nature of strategic lock-in', *Organization Studies*, 32(3): 337–63.

Koch, J., Eisend, M., and Petermann, A. (2009). Path dependence in decision-making processes: exploring the impact of complexity under increasing returns', *Business Research*, 2(1): 67–84.

Leblebici, H., Salancik, G.R., Copay, A., and King, T. (1991). 'Institutional change and the transformation of interorganizational fields: an organizational history of the US radio broadcasting industry', *Administrative Science Quarterly*, 36: 333–63.

Linden, G., Mowery, D.C., and Ziedonis, R.H. (2000). 'National technology policy in global markets: developing next-generation lithography in the semiconductor industry', *Business and Politics*, 2(2): 93–113.

Martin, X., Salomon, R.M., and Wu, Z. (2010). 'The institutional determinants of agglomeration: a study of the global semiconductor industry', *Industrial and Corporate Change*, 19(6): 1769–800.

Meyer, U. and Schubert, C. (2007). 'Integrating path dependency and path creation in a general understanding of path constitution: the role of agency and institutions in the shaping of technological innovations', *Science, Technology & Innovation Studies*, 3(1): 23–44.

North, D.C. (1990). *Institutions, Institutional Change, and Economic Performance*. Cambridge: Cambridge University Press.

Page, S.E. (2006). 'Path dependence', *Quarterly Journal of Political Science*, 1: 87–115.

Schubert, C. and Windeler. A. (2007). 'Pfadkreationsnetzwerke aus methodischer Sicht. In H. Hof and U. Wengenroth (eds) *Innovationsforschung. Ansätze, Methoden, Grenzen und Perspektiven*. Hamburg: Lit Verlag, pp.117–26.

Schubert, C., Sydow, J., and Windeler, A. (2013). 'The means of managing momentum: bridging technological paths and organisational fields', *Research Policy*, 42(8): 1389–405.

Seale, C. (1999). *The Quality of Qualitative Research*. London: Sage.

SEMATECH (2010). Conferences and Events. <www.sematech.org/meetings/events.htm> (last accessed 16 January 2010).

Shilov, A. (2016). 'EUV lithography makes good progress, still not ready for prime time', <www.anandtech.com/show/10097/euv-lithography-makes-good-progress-still-not-ready-for-prime-time> (last accessed 8 September).

Singer, P. (2014). 'Lithography: what are the alternatives to EUV?', <http://semimd.com/blog/2014/08/28/lithography-what-are-the-alternatives-to-euv/> (last accessed 18 September 2016).

Sydow, J. and Windeler, A. (1998). 'Organizing and evaluating interfirm networks— a structurationist perspective on network processes and effectiveness', *Organization Science*, 9(3): 265–84.

Sydow, J., Lerch, F., and Staber, U. (2010). 'Planning for path dependence? The case of a network in the Berlin-Brandenburg optics cluster', *Economic Geography*, 86(2): 173–95.

Sydow, J., Schreyögg, G., and Koch, J. (2009). Organizational path dependence: opening the black box', *Academy of Management Review*, 34(4): 689–709.

Sydow, J., Windeler, A., Schubert, C., and Möllering, G. (2012). 'Organizing R&D consortia for path creation and extension: the case of semiconductor manufacturing technologies', *Organization Studies*, 33(7): 907–36.

Valorinta, M., Schildt, H., and Lamberg, J-A. (2011). 'Path dependence of power relations, path-breaking change and technological adaptation', *Industry and Innovation*, 18(8): 765–90.

Vergne, J-P. and Durand, R. (2010). 'The missing link between the theory and empirics of path dependence: conceptual clarification, testability issue, and methodological implications', *Journal of Management Studies*, 47(4): 736–59.

Windeler, A. (2003). 'Kreation technologischer Pfade: ein strukturationstheoretischer Analyseansatz', *Managementforschung*, 13: 295–328.

Windeler, A. and Sydow, J. (2001). 'Project networks and changing industry practices—collaborative content production in the German television industry', *Organization Studies*, 22(6): 1035–61.

Yin, R.K. (2013). *Case Study Research*. Fifth edition. Thousand Oaks, CA: Sage.

14 Methodology matters

David A. Buchanan

Scaffolding and hygiene?

Methodology matters: that is one of the main arguments of this book. Methodology affects what you see, how you see it, and what you do not see. Methodology is not just the scaffolding on which the real research work is carried out. Methodology shapes your interpretation of the information that you gather, influencing ways of thinking and reasoning, along with your styles of theorizing and reporting. Methodology is not just a 'hygiene factor'. The value in developing unconventional approaches to methodology lies with reshaping what we see and how we see it, and in developing novel ways of reasoning, reporting, and theorizing. As we noted in Chapter 1, however, this is not an argument for abandoning traditional methods. On the contrary, we referred to McGrath's (1981) argument that, because all research strategies are seriously flawed, it is important to use an array of methods, in order to compensate for the inherent weakness of each of them. Staw (2016, p.11; internal citations omitted) restates McGrath's call for methodological diversity:

Established wisdom on research methodology teaches us that different methods possess distinctive strengths and weaknesses in terms of internal and external validity. Moreover, a quick survey of the social sciences would lead us to conclude that particular methods tend to be disproportionately associated with certain academic disciplines (e.g. lab experimentation with psychology, archival research with economics and sociology, qualitative methods with anthropology and sociology). Therefore, given that all research is flawed in some fundamental way, the only route to achieving a better understanding of a phenomenon is through the use of multiple methodologies. [T]ypically, topics are explored almost exclusively by a particular methodology, and this is especially the case when most of the researchers addressing the topic have come from a common disciplinary background. Thus, my plea to young scholars is to try some alternative methodologies, even if they are only a means to enrich the methods on which one normally depends.

Unconventional methods are not superior to traditional approaches. Significant breakthroughs continue to be made with conventional methods. But unconventional methods extend the available array, either used on their own or, as we have seen in many of the chapters in this volume, in creative combinations with traditional methods. *Unconventional methodology matters.*

This chapter has three aims. First, we offer our editorial reflections on the methodological developments explained in this book. What does this collection tell us about the nature and status of unconventional methodologies in organization and management research? Second, we confront the views of those who argue that the pursuit of novelty in research is damaging and undesirable. We face an awkward contradiction here, because the main objective in breaking with methodological convention is precisely to generate novel perspectives and ideas. Finally, based on the survey of journal editors introduced in Chapter 1, we will feed back the advice from those editors. How should researchers considering the development of unconventional approaches proceed?

Looking at this collection as a whole, we can identify a number of emerging views:

- dissatisfaction with what conventional interviews and surveys can capture;
- frustration with the limitations that traditional methods can place on the research questions that we can ask, and how we can approach them;
- an appetite for innovation with regard to new sources of information or data;
- a desire to break new ground, to push the boundaries, to explore the as yet unexplored and difficult to explore;
- exploiting the range of opportunities that have been opened up by new technologies; and
- reviewing the purpose of research and what it can achieve, as ethical considerations with respect to informed consent, right to withdraw, and ownership of information are challenged by technology developments that put personal information into the public domain.

Looking at specific contributions, we can identify four developments which follow and extend the structure of the book. These concern the use of unconventional data sources, novel research designs which explore new domains, the development of new analytic approaches, and the exploitation of developments in technology.

UNCONVENTIONAL DATA SOURCES

The use of unconventional sources is illustrated in several chapters. For their study of celebrity careers, Laurie Cohen and Joanne Duberley (Chapter 2) make creative use of a radio programme, which is available to the public in the broadcaster's archives. The BBC Radio 4 programme, *Desert Island Discs*, uses a consistent structured interview format with its 'castaways', and also asks them to select music which is in some way special to them, thus revealing aspects of their careers and life experiences not easily covered by traditional questioning. The BBC archives hold many other materials of potential interest to organization and management researchers. Holt and Zundel (Chapter 3) analyse a fictional television crime drama series, *The Wire*, as a social and organizational ethnographic case study. The use of fictional sources, such as novels and feature films, is not new in organization and management research (e.g. Phillips and Zyglidopoulos, 1999; Buchanan and Huczynski, 2004). However, this approach is far from being regarded as 'mainstream', although Penfold-Mounce et al. (2011) argue that *The Wire*, in its exploration of the challenges of urban life and inequality, could be seen as 'better sociology' than sociologists produce.

Andrew Knight (Chapter 4) is interested in the unobtrusive measures of human behaviour that can now be captured using digital trace data from smartphones and tablets, online access to public and personal archives, and a range of wearable sensors. The use of unobtrusive measurement has a long history in social and organizational research methods, but they have probably been under-utilized in the past as cumbersome and unreliable. Developments in technology have fundamentally altered this situation by allowing real-time access to 'big data' concerning behaviour, complemented by systems which can automatically code text, and audio and video recordings. David A. Buchanan and David Denyer (Chapter 5) argue that research concerning extreme (risky, dangerous) contexts is not as challenging as the label indicates. They show how extreme context research has been made possible with the use of a range of non-traditional sources of information, with embedded researchers, and with the use of fictional accounts from film and television. These approaches cast the researcher in the unconventional roles of historian and detective, sifting and weighing sources of evidence to produce a coherent account.

These examples invite the question—what other unconventional sources of data, information, and evidence are still waiting to be identified and exploited? It is unlikely that the chapters in this section have exhausted the possibilities, and we hope that they provide inspiration to other researchers.

NOVEL RESEARCH DESIGNS

The development of unconventional research designs is also illustrated in a number of chapters. Alex Bitektine, Jeffrey W. Lucas, and Oliver Schilke (Chapter 8) advocate the novel use of experimental research designs to develop understanding of institutions in organizational contexts, focusing in particular on the micro-foundations of institutions in individual cognition and agency. This approach shifts attention away from the traditional focus of insti-tutional research which has tended to focus on contextual, higher-order factors such as culture, norms, and beliefs. Steve Kempster and Ken Parry (Chapter 9) explain co-constructed analytic auto-ethnography—an unconventional approach to research design and data collection, informed by a critical realist ontology.

This design involves a collaborative partnership between researcher and participant. The collaboration begins with an in-depth exploration of the participant's socially constructed experience, which is then tested to see if those insights resonate with others who have had similar experiences. It is not difficult to see how this collaborative approach complemented by subsequent testing can access issues which conventional methods cannot.

Video methods also have a long history of use in the social sciences, but these approaches are still rare in organization and management research. Where video is used, it is more often produced by the researcher. In contrast, Rebecca Whiting, Helen Roby, Gillian Symon, and Petros Chamakiotis (Chapter 10) report an unconventional research design based on participant-led video diaries, a process which is complemented by follow-up narrative interviews. This research design generates multi-modal data: audio, visual, and textual. Capturing naturally occurring, real-time events and activities, and micro-interactions including non-verbal behaviours, issues that are not often recalled or captured in surveys or interviews can be investigated in depth. This research design is also appealing to participants, a factor that is significant in relation to the 'survey fatigue' reported in Chapter 1. Olivier Berthod, Michael Grothe-Hammer, and Jörg Sydow (Chapter 11) describe an unconventional research design based on multi-site ethnography to explore intra-organizational relationships. These relationships are not well understood. More important, they are not effectively addressed by traditional single-site ethnography, and new data collection methods are required: following boundary objects, capturing network enactments, using several investigators, and repeat interviews.

The first of these examples has adapted a research design commonly used elsewhere, in order to focus on new questions in another field, concerning the micro-foundations of institutions. The second example is a significant development of a fairly common design—auto-ethnography—which again opens up new areas of investigation. The third takes a technology—video—that is used in other subject areas, and combines this with a participant-led approach which uses other methods such as video elicitation and narrative interviews. Our final example, concerning multi-site ethnography, is another extension of an existing method, introducing novel data collection techniques. In other words, here we see the creative adaptation and extension of the traditional, in order to develop unconventional approaches that address new domains of interest and new research questions.

As with our examples of unconventional data sources, the scope for innovation in research design appears to be limited only by the ingenuity of the researcher.

NEW ANALYTIC APPROACHES

We have examples of two unconventional analytic approaches. Paul Carlile and Karl-Emanuel Dionne explain the novel analytic perspective of sociomateriality.

Research itself is a sociomaterial practice which generates a variety of artefacts; recorded observations, data, charts, presentations, and journal articles, for example. These artefacts function as boundary objects in the process of developing our understanding—a perspective that can generate fresh insights and produce unconventional research with lasting impact. A sociomaterial approach recognizes that actions are activated and constrained by structures, and that structures are the result of accumulations of previous actions shaped by material consequences. Structures include rules, standards, and human and material resources that agents mobilize in their daily interactions. This approach shifts the attention of analysts to the processes that bind structures and daily action. Using a systems dynamics perspective, a fresh analysis of Barley's (1986) influential study of CT scanners in radiology departments is explained to illustrate the power of a sociomaterial approach.

Jörg Sydow, Arnold Windeler, Gordon Müller-Seitz, and Knut Lange (Chapter 13) develop an unconventional analytic approach called path con-stitution analysis (PCA). This integrates the concepts of path dependence and path creation, ideas which have attracted limited methodological attention although they are widely applied for explanatory purposes. Path dependence describes the role of small triggering events and self-reinforcing processes, leading to unintentional lock-in as one outcome gains increasing support. Path dependence emphasizes the role of history and context in shaping outcomes, while path creation emphasizes the proactive role of agency. PCA is a comprehensive methodology for understanding outcomes through exploring constellations of multiple actors, on multiple levels of analysis, with a process perspective. In addition to dependence and creation, PCA explores path defence, extension, dissolution, renewal, and breaking. For the guidance of other researchers, the chapter presents a methodological template based on a longitu-dinal case study of a novel technological path in the semiconductors sector.

These unconventional approaches to analysis give us new lenses with which to view both known and less well understood phenomena. They also open up fresh research questions, with regard to the mutual relationships between actions and structures, and the constitution and outcomes of different kinds of organizational and technological paths, respectively. In researching possible content for this volume, we encountered many examples of new procedures for the statistical analysis of quantitative data. In spite of its title, most of the articles published in the journal *Organizational Research Methods* fall into this category. But novel stats procedures are not, in our definition, unconventional research methodologies, and were not included here. The scope for innovation in analytical perspectives thus appears to be wide.

EXPLOITATION OF TECHNOLOGY DEVELOPMENTS

We discussed Andrew Knight's work with new technology-enabled unobtru-sive measures earlier in this chapter. This is one of three examples of the opportunities which new technologies in general, and the Internet in particular, are creating for researchers. Christopher J. Schneider (Chapter 6) explains the use of Qualitative Media Analysis, which involves the unconventional use of the information that can be captured from YouTube and Twitter feeds, to study police-public relationships. For this study, Schneider captured over 100,000 tweets from around 120 Twitter accounts, and collated these for analysis in a searchable file that was around 7,500 pages long. Searches in that file for terms such as 'crime', 'safety', or 'prevention' each returned thousands of instances. Technology-based research such as this can generate considerable volumes of data. Similarly, Robert Kozinets and Manuela Nocker (Chapter 7) describe an early netnography which captured cultural data from online forums, fan web pages and corporate pages, to create a *Star Trek* Research website. The website invited fans of the programme to get involved in the research, and those contacts led to email correspondence with sixty-five community members from twelve different countries. Netnography (online ethnography) is not confined, as is traditional ethnography, to a single site or location of interest.

Internet research methods have traditionally been dominated by online surveys. This will change radically, and probably rapidly, with the advent of 'big data' (very large databases) and 'data analytics' (the ability to analyse that information quickly in sophisticated ways). With big data, Starbuck (2016) observes that researchers could be dealing with sample sizes in the hundreds of thousands, or millions. 'Sampling' at this level may cover complete or large segments of populations. Nevertheless, Starbuck points to some of the problems in using big data in research: restricted access, cost of data storage, data validity, accuracy and errors, definitional challenges, and generalizability.

Stephens-Davidowitz (2017) argues that big data, accessible through the Internet, will revolutionize the social sciences, in four ways, and not just by increasing the sample size of a typical traditional survey. First, by opening up new sources of information, giving researchers and others access to the information that we put online, for example. He sees the billions of Google searches that we make as a revolutionary resource, revealing hidden motives and highlighting social changes in real time. Second, big data captures what people actually do and think, rather than what they tell researchers. Third, researchers can focus on specific demographic or geographic groups. Fourth, randomized control trials, exploring causality, can be arranged and carried out quickly. The scale on which social—and organizational—research can be conducted will consequently grow, significantly. He also points to the risks involved, in basing judgements and decisions exclusively on quantitative data, and extrapolating to individuals findings that have been derived from studies of large groups.

The ways in which technology developments can be used to capture and analyse data are thus likely to expand in number, deployed either alone or in combination with more traditional methods. This is one area, therefore, where we will see further methodological experimentation and innovation. Unconventional today perhaps, these approaches are likely to become mainstream in the near future.

In our search for unconventional methodology in organization and management research, it did not prove difficult to bring together the examples and contributors for this volume. However, we wanted to include an illustration of unconventional research reporting, and were unable to do this. Perhaps journal norms are seen as being too rigid to challenge. But one article nominated as unconventional by a journal editor in our survey illustrates the possibilities. Writing in a constructivist epistemology, Parker (2011) reports a study of the circus as a mobile, temporary organization involved in 'the production of mystery'. He describes his reporting style as 'speculative exploration' rather than as a traditionally structured empirical research paper; indeed, this could be regarded as methodologically unconventional by having adopted *no* methodology for this particular study. The journals of the Academy of Management are now challenging the norms. The 'dynamic edition' of *Academy of Management Journal* invites authors to add audio, video, and slide presentations to their online articles, to summarize and highlight the contributions of their work. The online version of *Academy of Management Discoveries* encourages researchers to provide more of their data, and in other media such as photography, video, and author interviews, stating explicitly that, 'insightful qualitative studies that fall outside so-called "established templates" are welcome' (Arino et al., 2016, p.112).

Can novelty be dangerous?

A number of commentators challenge the aims of our volume by arguing that novelty in research is damaging and unwelcome. For example, Barley (2006) argues that there are limits on how far one is allowed to depart from established norms. Research papers which 'break too many rules' are unlikely to be accepted, as it is necessary to conform to 'genre constraints' and 'accepted canons' (p.17). However, he identifies three features which in his judgement make papers interesting. One is subject matter that departs from the mainstream. Another concerns theoretical perspectives that are different from what has gone before. And the third feature is research methods which are different from the norm, or are used in different combinations. It seems that, in Barley's (2006) view, one is allowed to overlook the constraints and break at least some rules, but he does not identify what those rules are.

Davis (2015) sets out a more uncompromising position, claiming that the pursuit of novelty by journals (instead of truth) is damaging. Novelty, he argues, may look good and be interesting, but still serve no useful purpose. Researchers are rewarded for being interesting rather than for being right, and a system that rewards novelty is therefore dysfunctional. Davis also argues that the availability of 'big data' will make this situation worse. The core of Davis' argument lies in his observation that: 'If the advancement of knowledge were the goal of science, then individual articles would be recognized as a means, not an end in themselves. In most cases, individual articles count only as part of a totality of evidence: they are one tile in a mosaic' (Davis, 2015, p.181). This argument is only valid in a positivist epistemology, where social science, as with natural science, is seen as an accretion of knowledge, as new findings replace the old (Davis discusses publication bias in medical journals). But knowledge across the social sciences is not cumulative in this manner, particularly when viewed through a constructivist lens, where conceptual development is regarded as more significant.

In a response to Davis' argument, Barley (2016, p.4) notes that papers are often rejected by journals because, 'the paper's contribution was not sufficiently novel.' Yes, journals value the novel and the interesting and the counterintuitive over the steady accumulation of knowledge. Academic incentives and rewards emphasize novelty and impact, 'rather than our plodding towards an accumulation of knowledge' (p.2). He then claims that:

> If being interesting requires a paper to be different, before long the field would be a mess. Every paper would take on a new topic, devise a new method or offer a new way of seeing things. With all of us so busily striving for the next interesting paper, no subjects would be studied more than once, no methods would be refined and no ideas would be worked though. The development of knowledge, at least in any scientific sense, would all but cease. Worse yet, because there would be no status quo to provide a measure of which new papers were interesting, the field would implode into humdrum. At that point only by taking the risk of sticking doggedly to a topic, a method, or a theory could scholars rescue us from the quicksand of being interesting.
>
> (Barley, 2016, pp.5–6)

This is criticism of novelty for the sake of novelty—quite different from the case for breaking with methodological convention in order to develop fresh insights and understanding. The claims of Davis and Barley also sit uncomfortably alongside the observations of those who argue that research work and publications are becoming more formulaic (Alvesson and Gabriel, 2013; Corbett et al., 2014; Cornelissen and Durand, 2014; Harley, 2015). Would our field be a mess if every paper addressed a new topic with a new method and a new perspective? Is a research domain (such as organizational behaviour) demonstrating its immaturity by offering a number of different theories for the same phenomenon (culture, leadership, motivation, power)? On the contrary, Anderson (2007) argues that different theories are valuable because they help us to fill our 'conceptual toolbox'. We live in a complex world, and we need a variety of tools and perspectives to deal with the many, and changing, issues and problems that we face. One theory could be valuable in one context, but a different perspective could be useful in another setting. An idea that appears to be of limited value today may help us to deal with tomorrow's challenges. From this viewpoint, there are no 'right or wrong' theories, or 'one best way', or 'absolute truth'. There are, however, theories that are more or less useful in helping us to deal with different issues in different settings at different times. We benefit from theoretical and conceptual novelty, and from having 'too many theories'. This is not a problem.

Criticisms of the pursuit of novelty in organizational and management research direct their arguments at *novel contributions to theory*. This emphasis certainly discourages replication studies, the comparability of research work, and the accumulation of evidence in specific areas. But those criticisms are not aimed directly at methodological innovation. Journal editors are broadly supportive of attempts to break methodological rules, as long as these departures from convention are adequately explained and justified. Reviewers, too, are generally open to persuasion in this regard. We will detail the advice from journal editors shortly.

How are researchers to navigate between these demands, to be innovative and surprising while conforming to the conventions of research conduct and reporting? Examining how research papers are 'crafted' for publication, Patriotta (2017, p.752) illustrates the use of 'text-building strategies', defined as, 'how authors construct meaning along a line of argument, and how this line of argument might lead to a contribution.' He advises researchers to address the tension between novelty and correctness through *optimal distinctiveness*. This involves using text-building strategies that balance innovation and tradition: 'As a result of optimal distinctiveness, journal articles contain elements of novelty and convention, deviation and reproduction, and surprise and predictability to varying degrees' (Patriotta, 2017, p.753).

Patriotta's advice relates to writing the journal article, and not directly to designing the research in the first place. But does his argument, by implication, involve accepting the existing rules, and either bending them 'optimally', or breaking them just a little bit, in the interests of appearing to be novel and inventive? The advice offered by the journal editors who responded to our survey presents a more radical approach to developing unconventional methodologies.

Unconventional methodology matters

As part of our survey of journal editors, introduced in Chapter 1, we asked what advice they would give to researchers who were considering the use of unorthodox methods in work that they planned to submit to their journals. It is helpful to remember that most editors believe that most researchers are too conservative. And although the institutional pressures in this direction are strong and are understood, most editors also want to see more papers that break with convention, that deviate from established norms, that address new and different questions in new ways, and that generate fresh understanding. Most editors thus welcome unconventional submissions. Indeed, some observed that, despite specific attempts to encourage non-traditional work, they have been disappointed by the lack of response in this regard from researchers. From the findings of our survey, it appears that the problem lies not with journal editors and reviewers, but with researchers who believe that they will be punished for adopting non-traditional approaches by having their submissions rejected.

Editors offered the following advice.

First, choose with care the journals to which you submit your papers. Some journals appear to prefer to publish more conventional work, while others have 'non-traditional research' sections and positively encourage 'deviant' submissions. A useful approach is to study recent editorials, to gain insights into editors' preferences and expectations. However, one editor advised researchers to 'avoid mainstream journals that say they encourage novelty, because often they do not'. A review of the articles published in recent issues should also reveal how welcoming a particular journal is to non-traditional articles.

Second, explain your unconventional approach clearly, justifying why this is superior to traditional options. If possible, give other examples of where the approach has been used, perhaps in a different field or topic area; some methodological approaches considered unconventional in organization and management studies have been imported, with appropriate adaptations, from other subject areas. Give an assessment of the circumstances in which this non-traditional approach would be appropriate, and where it would not. Remember that you are persuading someone who is potentially sympathetic to your approach, but who is also trained (and expected) to be sceptical.

Third, link your overall approach—research questions, methodology, and findings—to emerging and topical issues and problems (see Ashford, 2013). Editors are not immune to the institutional pressures facing researchers. They are also interested in article citations and journal impact factors. Current debates and research assessment regimes revolve around issues of the 'relevance' and the 'impact' of research outputs on organization and management practice. Establishing those links in your research offers no guarantees, but can increase the probability of publication.

Finally, remember that theoretical contribution remains central to the journal article review process. This book has focused on methodology, in the belief—evidently not shared by all editors—that this is an integral component of the research process (and not merely a 'hygiene factor'). However, the first and most significant question that reviewers always have to answer is, 'what is the contribution of this work?' In other words, the justification of an unconventional methodology has to be balanced with an explanation of the theoretical contribution of the study. (In some instances, of course, the main contribution may be methodological, as in a small number of the articles nominated by editors in this project.) Does this final piece of advice move methodology to the margins of our concern? On the contrary, conventional approaches are more likely to generate conventional conclusions (although it is fair to admit that conventional methodologies can still produce important work). We agree with those editors who argue that methodological innovation is more likely to generate fresh insights, to enable us to address new issues, and to strengthen the contributions of our research.

From our survey, therefore, and from the examples in this volume, the main advice for researchers considering adopting and developing unconventional methodology in their work and in the articles that they plan to submit for publication is—'go for it'.

■ REFERENCES

Alvesson, M. and Gabriel, Y. (2013). 'Beyond formulaic research: in praise of greater diversity in organizational research and publications', *Academy of Management Learning and Education*, 12(2): 245–63.

Anderson, M.H. (2007). 'Why are there so many theories?', *Journal of Management Education*, 31(6): 757–76.

Arino, A., LeBaron, C., and Milliken, F.J. (2016). 'Publishing qualitative research in *Academy of Management Discoveries*', *Academy of Management Discoveries*, 2(2): 109–13.

Ashford, S.J. (2013). 'Having scholarly impact: the art of hitting academic home runs', *Academy of Management Learning & Education*, 12(4): 623–33.

Barley, S.R. (1986). 'Technology as an occasion for structuring: evidence from observations of CT scanners and the social order of radiology departments', *Administrative Science Quarterly*, 31(1): 78–108.

Barley, S.R. (2006). 'When I write my masterpiece: thoughts on what makes a paper interesting', *Academy of Management Journal*, 49(1): 16–20.

Barley, S.R. (2016). '60th anniversary essay: ruminations on how we became a mystery house and how we might get out', *Administrative Science Quarterly*, 61(1): 1–8.

Buchanan, D.A. and Huczynski, A. (2004). 'Images of influence: Twelve Angry Men and Thirteen Days', *Journal of Management Inquiry*, 13(4): 312–23.

Corbett, A., Cornelissen, J., Delios, A., and Harley, B. (2014). 'Variety, novelty, and perceptions of scholarship in research on management and organizations: an appeal for ambidextrous scholarship', *Journal of Management Studies*, 51(1): 4–18.

Cornelissen, J. and Durand, R. (2014). 'Moving forward: developing theoretical contributions in management studies', *Journal of Management Studies*, 51(6): 995–1022.

Davis, G.F. (2015). 'Editorial essay: what is organizational research for?', *Administrative Science Quarterly*, 60(2): 179–88.

Harley, B. (2015). 'The one best way? "Scientific" research on HRM and the threat to critical scholarship', *Human Resource Management Journal*, 25(4): 399–407.

McGrath, J.E. (1981). 'Dilemmatics: the study of research choices and dilemmas', *American Behavioral Scientist*, 25(2): 179–210.

Parker, M. (2011). 'Organizing the circus: the engineering of miracles', *Organization Studies*, 32(4): 555–69.

Patriotta, G. (2017). 'Crafting papers for publication: novelty and convention in academic writing', *Journal of Management Studies*, 54(5): 747–59.

Penfold-Mounce, R., Beer, D., and Burrows, R. (2011). '*The Wire* as social-science fiction?', *Sociology*, 45(1): 152–67.

Phillips, N. and Zyglidopoulos, S.C. (1999). 'Learning from *Foundation*: Asimov's psychohistory and the limits of organization theory', *Organization*, 6(4): 591–608.

Starbuck, W.H. (2016). '60th anniversary essay: how journals could improve research practices in social science', *Administrative Science Quarterly*, 61(2): 165–83.

Staw, B.M. (2016). 'Stumbling towards a social psychology of organizations: an autobiographical look at the direction of organizational research', *Annual Review of Organizational Psychology and Organizational Behavior*, 3: 1–19.

Stephens-Davidowitz, S. (2017). *Everybody Lies: Big Data, New Data, and What the Internet Can Tell Us About Who We Really Are*. London: Bloomsbury.

■ INDEX

Tables and figures are indicated by an italic *t* or *f* following the page number.

Aalbers, M.B. 7
academic journals *see* journals
academics, and auto-ethnography 173, 186
access
  extreme contexts 83, 88–90, 91, 95–100
  and netnography 133–4, 136
  private archives 72–3
  public archives 71
  social media 111, 115, 118, 282
  and standardization 67–8
  and unobtrusive methods 66–8, 80, 279
accommodation, and netnography 136–7
accumulations of outcomes, and a
    sociomaterial approach 238–9,
    241–2, 248
actions, and a sociomaterial approach 238–9
actors, multiple types for PCA 262, 271
aesthetic auto-ethnography 169, 171, 183
Afghanistan 90–1
alteration, and netnography 133
Altheide D.L. 105–10
Alvesson, M. 9, 13–14, 40
American Journal of Sociology 5–6
analysis *see also* path constitution analysis
    (PCA); Qualitative Media Analysis
    (QMA)
  and netnography 135–6
  and a sociomaterial approach 240–2, 248–9
  and unconventional methodology 20
analytical refinement 88
analytic auto-ethnography
  co-constructed 171–7, 186–7
  and experiential research 184–5
  and mixed methods research 177–83
  as novel research design 279–80
  role of critical realism 170–2
  use 168–9, 178*t*
Anderson, L. 169, 171, 172–3
Anderson, M.H. 284–5
Anglo-American hegemony, and
    methodological conservatism 7
anthropology, digital 129
applied research logic
  consistency 160
  in experimental research 149–52, 151*t*

external validity 152
  use 155, 158
Archer, Mary 37
archives see also *Desert Island Discs*
    (radio programme)
  BBC 278–9
  and netnography 134
  private data 69*t*, 72–3
  public data 69*t*, 71–2
  radio 42
Askey, Arthur 27
Association of Business Schools 8
Attenborough, Sir David 27, 32
attention checks in experimental
    research 161–2
audio recordings 75
authenticity, leadership 175–7, 179–83
autobiography, and *Desert Island Discs* 42
auto-ethnography
  and academics 173, 186
  aesthetic 169, 171, 183
  analytic and experiential 178*t*, 184–5
  co-constructed analytic 168–9, 171–7,
    186–7
  data collection 185–6
  ethical issues 184
  familiarity 183
  and the less powerful 185
  and mixed methods research 177–83
  as novel research design 279–80
  repositioned 183–6
  role of criticial realism 170–2
  theory resonance 179–83, 180–1*f*, 180*t*
axiology, and netnography 131, 141–2

baby names research 71
Baer, M. 74–5
Barley, S.R. 235, 236–8, 237*t*, 239, 240–2, 243,
    244–6, 283–4
Barnaby Rudge (Dickens) 58–9
Barsade, S.G. 75–6
Battlestar Galactica (television series) 93
BBC archives 278–9 see also *Desert Island
    Discs* (radio programme)
Bengry-Howell, A. 11, 13

Bianchi, E.C. 71–2, 79
big data 107, 142–3, 282, 284
Black, I.J. 235, 242–3, 245
Black Hawk friendly fire incident 86
Black Lives Matter 105
Blackmore, Colin 38
Bleak House (Dickens) 59
Blumberg, Baruch 37
Blundell, Tom 37
brain switches *see* Digital Brain Switch project
Bryman, A. 5
Bublé, Michael 29, 35
Buchanan, D.A. 91–2, 95
Bucheli M. 30–1
Buffy the Vampire Slayer (television series) 92
Burnell, Dame Jocelyn Bell 31
business networks 140–1

Cameron, R. 7
career research 27–32, 38, 39–42, 278
case studies
    analytic auto-ethnography 175–83
    extreme contexts 85–8, 93–8, 94*t*
    generalization of single 87–8
Centrica Storage 94*t*, 96
Chaffin, D. 78–9
change
    measuring through unobtrusive methods
        65–6
    and a sociomaterial approach 243–6, 250–1
checks, experimental research 161–2
childcare centres 155–6
child-led research 13
citations 8, 11, 12*f*, 13, 110
Clark, Petula 27
codes of conduct 156
Coffey, A. 11–12
Cohen, L. 28, 31–2, 37
company groups, and ethnography 220
competition, and collective intelligence 76
computational resources for large datasets 68
computer-assisted coding 75–6
computer-driven devices, miniaturization in
    66–7
computer networks 67
confidentiality issues and video diaries 196–7
connected devices 64, 67–8
consequences, and a sociomaterial approach
    243–6, 250–1
conservatism, methodological 3, 6–10
consistency
    experimental research 160
    research logic 160

'Constructing careers through narrative and
    music: an analysis of *Desert Island
    Discs*' 28
contrived observation 69*t*, 75–7
Cooper, W.H. 90
Corbett, A. 9–10
Cornelissen, J. 14–15, 18, 87, 88
Cox, Brian 38
creative research methods 13
criminal gangs 88–9
critical incident interviews 2
critical realism, role in analytic
    auto-ethnography 170–2
cultural insight, and netnography 131

Dai, H. 70–1
data
    access *see* access
    analysis 5, 264, 282
    expansion of scale 66
data collection
    and auto-ethnography 185–6
    experimental research 160–1
    and netnography 135–6
    online versus laboratory 160–1
    for PCA 263–4
    from Twitter 114–17
    and unconventional methodology 20
    from YouTube 119–21
data science, and netnography 142–3
datasets
    big data 107, 142–3, 282, 284
    computational resources 68
    contrived observation 69*t*, 75–7
    and ethnography 142–3
    private archives 69*t*, 72–3
    public archives 69*t*, 71–2
    simple observation 69*t*, 74–5
    trace data 69–71, 69*t*, 279
data sources
    extreme contexts 85–8
    fiction 51–2, 57–8
    unconventional 278–9
    and unconventional methodology
        5, 19
    and unobtrusive methods 66–8
Davies, Kay 37
Davis, G.F. 283–4
Davis, M.S. 10
Dawkins, Richard 34
decision makers 156–7
DeNora, T. 37
de Rond, M. 90–1

Desert Island Discs (radio programme)
  benefits and limitations 39–42
  format 27
  music 36–9
  in organization and management research
    28–32
  public performance 32–6, 40–1
  reasons 28
  unconventional data source 278
Dickens, Charles 58–9
digital anthropology 129
Digital Brain Switch project
  analysis and findings 202–4, 203*f*, 204*f*
  boundary transition in the digital age
    194–7
  further details 210–11
  methodology 197–202, 197*t*, 200*f*
  reflections 204–7
digital health, and a sociomaterial
    approach 246–51
digital trace data *see* trace data
doctors, occupational research 29, 39
documents, social media 106–11
durability, and a sociomaterial
    approach 242–3, 249–50
Durand, R. 14–15, 18
Düsseldorf, Germany, emergency
    management 218–20
dynamics
  measuring using unobtrusive methods
    65–6
  and a sociomaterial approach 242–3,
    249–50

economy, and individualism 71
Elsbach, K.D. 158
embedded researchers 88–91
emergency management network 218–20
emojis, and netnography 131
emotional contagion 75–6
emotional labour, and leadership 175–7,
    179–83
epistemology, and netnography 132
ethical issues
  auto-ethnography 184
  netnography 130, 143
  social media 110–11
  unobtrusive methods 79–80
  video diaries 196
ethnography
  and company groups 220
  datasets 142–3
  difference to netnography 132–7

  and digital anthropologies 129
  inter-organizational *see* inter-
    organizational relations (IORs)
  and marketing 141
  as a methodology 213
  and netnography 127–9
  organizational to inter-
    organizational 213–15
  revival 212
  virtual 129
evocative auto-ethnography *see* aesthetic
    auto-ethnography
experiential research 184–5
experimental research
  checks 161–2
  consistency 160
  data collection 160–1
  in institutional theory 149–53, 153–60,
    162–3
  as novel research design 279
  recommendations 160–2
expertise, unobtrusive methods 77
extreme contexts *see also* settings
  access 83, 88–90, 91, 95–100
  advice for researchers 100–1
  case studies 85–8, 93–8, 94*t*
  data sources 85–8
  drawbacks and limitations 99–100
  embedded researchers 88–91
  ignoring convention 100
  possibilities and benefits 99
  research 84–5, 98–101
  and researchers 85–8
  social science fiction 91–3
  unconventional data source 279
extreme ultraviolet lithography
    (EUVL) 265–71, 265*t*
Extreme Ultraviolet Lithography Limited
    Liability Company (LLC) 262

Facebook
  ethical issues 79
  and netnography 131
  user behaviour 76, 79
fact, distinction from fiction 45–8
fair market ideology, effect of
    institutionalization 155
familiarity, and auto-ethnography 183
female leadership 154
fiction
  beginning as factual accounts 45–6
  benefits and drawbacks 55–60
  data source 51–2, 57–8

fiction (*cont.*)
distinction from fact 45–8
as inspiration 50–1, 56–7, 92–3
reasons for using 45–8
as research 52–5, 58–60, 91–2
social science 91–3
unconventional data source 279
use 48–55, 60–1
fictional research 49–50, 55–6
film narratives 91–2
Financial Times 8–9, 15
fitness behaviour 70
Forbes, I. 11
frames, and QMA analysis 108–9
frameworks, and visual research
methods 192
fundamental research logic
category of experimental research 150–2,
151*t*
consistency 160
external validity 152–3
use 154, 155, 156, 158, 159

Gabriel, Y. 13–14
'gap-spotting' 9, 14–15
Gardner, W.L. 7
Garmin 68
George, E. 159
Gilbert, N. 11–12
Glaser, V. 155
Goffman, E. 33–5, 40, 89–90
Gregory, S. 185–6
group creativity behaviour 74–5

Haccoun, R.P. 159
hackathon 246–7
Hacking Health (HH) 246–7
Hafenbrädl, S. 155
handwashing behaviour 70
Hanks, Tom 37, 41
Harley, B. 9, 15
healthcare, digital 246–51
Herzberg, F. 2
hierarchy, and inter-organizational relations
215–16, 218–20
history 30–2
hospitals research
and analytic auto-ethnography 175–83
handwashing behaviour 70
and a sociomaterial approach 235,
236–8, 237*t*, 239, 240–2, 243,
244–6, 245*t*
hygiene factors 2

identification-resistance effect 157
identity
analysis 47
music and constructing 38–9
negotiation 33–4
IKIWISI concept 4
incentive schemes, and fictional
research 49–50, 55
individualism
and song lyrics 71–2
and the state of the economy 71
information sources, extreme contexts case
studies 94*t*
Ingram, P. 74
innovation
methodological 3, 11–13, 12*f*
unobtrusive methods 64–5, 80
inspiration, fiction as 50–1, 56–7, 92–3
institutionalization, and interactions in small
group contexts 154
institutional persistence, micro-level
sources 153–4
institutional practices, adoption and
diffusion 155–7
institutional theory
case for experiments 149–53
experimental research 147, 153–60
microfoundations 147–9
recommendations 160–2
research 147–8, 162–3
role of contexts 154–5
Internet 64, 67, 282
inter-organizational relations (IORs)
defining and distinguishing 215–17
ethnography 212–13, 224–5, 280
hierarchy 215–16, 218–20
inquiring into 217–24
markets 215, 220–2
networks 215, 222–4
from organizational ethnography 213–15
interviews
critical incident 2
existing categories and concepts 61
fiction 61
performance 32
isomorphic learning 88
Israel 90

Jeffreys, Sir Alec 31
journal editors
advice 286–7
survey 283, 285–7
views on methodology 15–19

Journal of Management Studies 9–10
journals
impact factors 8
ranking lists 7–10, 15

Kaplan, S. 251
Kempster, S. 173, 175, 185–6
King, Rodney 118
Klimoski, R.J. 159
Knight, A.P. 74–5
knowledge
role of changing media 48
and sociomateriality 238, 241–3, 245, 245t, 250–1
Knox, D. 38
Kosinski, M. 76
Kozinets, R.V. 127–8, 133
Kramer, A.D.I. 79
Kroto, Harry 38
Kurke, L.B. 154

Laboratory Life (Latour and Woolgar) 46
Lammers, J. 159
language, in peer review process 7
Latour, B. 46, 55
Lauer, T. 156
Lawley, Sue 34
leadership
emotional labour and authenticity 175–7, 179–83
female 154
and fictional research 55–6
Leadership Quarterly, The 7
legitimacy 157–9
Les Mots et Les Choses (The Order of Things) (Foucault) 61
level interrelatedness, and PCA 259–60, 265–6
Levine, C. 59, 60
LexisNexis 118–19
lock-in, and PCA 261, 269–71
Lok, J. 90–1
Lucas, J.W. 154

MacDonald, R. 38, 39
Maclean, N. 50–1, 86
Magee, S. 35, 36
Magill Hospital 94t, 95–6, 98
mainstream methodology, and unconventional methodology 4–6, 15–19
management studies, use of netnography 129–30

manipulation checks in experimental research 161–2
marketing, and ethnography 141
markets, and inter-organizational relations 215, 220–2
materiality
definition 235
dimensions 235–46
importance 246
social practices 234
May, Lord 38
Mayakovsky, V. 56–7
McDonald, R. 29–30, 39
McGrath, J.E. 3, 277
measurement validity 78–9
Mechanical Turk (MTurk) (data collection platform) 160–1
media
and police studies 111–13
role of changing 48
meetings, video recordings 2
memory, role of music in evoking 36–7
Menezes, Jean Charles de 87
'metaphor' studies 56
method-bound results 2
methodological conservatism 3, 6–10
methodological innovation 3, 11–13, 12f
microfoundations 147–9
micro-level sources 153–4
Mingers, J. 7–9
miniaturization
computer-driven devices 66–7
sensors 67
mixed methods research 5, 7, 177–83
moderatum generalization 87
Molina-Azorin, J.F. 7
Montebello Summit 119–20
Moore, Gordon 66–7
'Moore's Law' 66–7
Morris, M.W. 74
motivator factors 2
music
and constructing identity 38–9
and Desert Island Discs 36–9, 40–1
and memory 36–7
for reflection 37–9
use 27

national research quality assessment panels, and journal ranking lists 8
naturalistic generalization 87
negotiation
and *Desert Island Discs* 40

negotiation (*cont.*)
  of identity in *Desert Island Discs* 33–4
  and legitimacy 159
netnography
  basis 129–32
  data collection 135–6
  difference to ethnography 132–7
  evolved from ethnography 127–9
  innovation 13, 282
  issue of time 128–9, 140–1
  liquidity of sites 128, 137–9
  open-endedness of participation 128, 139–40
  responsibilities and horizons 141–4
  and virtual ethnography 129
'network ethnography' 217
networks
  behaviour 74
  computers 67
  extreme contexts 98
  inter-organizational relations 215, 222–4
  social media 140–1
  1984 (Orwell) 45, 51
non-ergodicity for PCA 260, 268–9
novelty
  and analytic auto-ethnography 279–80
  challenge 246–51
  danger 283–5
  research design 279–80

observation
  contrived 69t, 75–7
  non-participant 2
  simple 69t, 74–5
  virtual 32
occupational research *see* career research
organizational ethnography, to inter-
    organizational ethnography 213–15
organizational resilience, and fiction as
    inspiration 50–1
Orwell, George 45, 51
outcomes approach versus process approach
    235–8

Park, G. 76–7
participation
  access *see* access
  netnography 139–40
  unconventional methodology 5
  video diaries 190–2, 193, 280
path, definition and features 258–62, 259t,
    265t
path constitution analysis (PCA)
  in action 264–71

concepts 255–6
conclusion and limitations 272–3
methodology 256–62
new analytic approach 281
research setting and methods 262–4
path creation 255, 257–8
path dependence 255, 256–7
PCA *see* path constitution analysis (PCA)
peer review process 7, 18
Pennington, Hugh 37
performance, public 32–6, 40–1
performance measures 7–10
Perrow, C. 86, 88
pharmacists, effect of institutionalization 155
Phillips, N. 91
photography 5–6
Pillinger, Colin 37, 38
Plomley, Roy 27, 30, 34, 35
police
  authority and legitimacy 112
  mandate 111–12
  and media 111–13
  and QMA analysis of social media 108
  use of social media 105–6, 112, 113–17,
    121, 282
  and YouTube 117–21
polymorphic research 13–14
positivist research 4
power, and auto-ethnography 185
practice, and a sociomaterial approach 240
Prasad, A. 90
Presentation of Self in Everyday Life, The
    (Goffman) 33
private archives 69t, 72–3
process approaches
  versus outcomes 235–8
  and a sociomaterial approach
    236–8, 247
propriety, and legitimacy 158
public archives 69t, 71–2
public performance, and *Desert Island
    Discs* 32–6, 40–1

qualitative information 2, 5, 7
Qualitative Media Analysis (QMA) 105–6,
    106–11, 113, 121, 282
quantitative information 2, 5, 7
questionnaires 7
QWERTY keyboard 255, 261

Raaijmakers, A.G.M. 155
radio archives 42 *see also Desert Island Discs*
    (radio programme)

rapport, for access in extreme contexts 97–8
reactance effects, avoidance 65
realism *see* critical realism
reciprocity, for access in extreme contexts 98
recording devices 75 *see also* video recordings
reflection
   through music 37–9
   through video diaries 206
relationships in extreme contexts 95–8
restaurant workers' behaviour 73
Richley Fire and Rescue 94*t*, 96–7
Roberts, K.H. 88
Rotblatt, Joseph 38

Saavedra, S. 72–3
Samsung Galaxy smartphone 67
Sandberg, J. 9, 14
scale of research 66
Scherer, K.R. 36–7
Schilke, O. 156–7
Schneider, C.J. 105–10, 116
Schwarzkopf, Elizabeth 35
scientific methods
   and fictional research 55–6
   limitations 47–8
scientists
   and fiction/fact distinction 46
   and music and identity 38
   and music and memory 37
   occupational research 30
   and radio archives 42
secondary sources, to study extreme contexts 85
security establishment, and fiction for inspiration 92–3
self-reinforcing processes, for PCA 261, 269
SEMATECH 262, 265–71
semiconductor manufacturing industry 262–71
sensors 67, 74–5
settings *see also* extreme contexts
   of *Desert Island Discs* 34–6
   and unconventional methodology 5, 19
simple observation 69*t*, 74–5
sites, and netnography 128, 137–9
Sitkin, S.B. 155, 159
small group contexts 154
smartphones 64, 67
Smith, Ali 35
Snook, S.A. 86, 88
'socially desired' versions of research 33, 40

social media
   big data 107
   citation style 110
   conceptual issues 106–11
   definition 106
   ethical issues 110–11
   and netnography 133, 136, 138–9, 140–1
   and police studies 111–13
   police use of 113–21
   and QMA 106–11
   qualitative approach 105–6, 121
   ratings behaviour 76
social movements, and social media 105
social practices, and materiality 234
social science fiction 91–3
social science methods, limitations 47–8
sociomaterial approach
   challenge of novelty 246–51
   dimensions 235–46
   as a new analytic approach 280–1
   perspective 234–5
   and unconventional research 233, 251–2
song lyrics, and individualism 71–2
Staats, B.R. 70–1
standardization
   of methodology 6, 10, 14
   of protocols and data access 67–8
Star Trek communities ethnographic study 127
statistical generalization 87
Steinbeck, John 51
Stewart, J. 173, 175
stock trading behaviour 72–3
'Stockwell Shooting, The' 87
structuration theory 258
'survey fatigue' 3
switches, individual management of digital brain 194–7

Taylor, C. 11–12
Taylor, F.W. 49–50, 55–6
technology *see also* sensors
   expertise for unobtrusive methods 77
   exploitation of developments 281–3
   and unobtrusive methods 66–8, 75–6
television
   extreme contexts 92–3
   potential resource 42
   unconventional data source 279
text-building strategies 285
thematic analysis 108–9, 202–3
Thirteen Days (film) 92
THORP Sellafield 94*t*, 96, 98

Three Mile Island nuclear power plant 86
time, netnography and 140–1
trace data 69–71, 69t, 279
Travers, M. 11–12
triggering events, for PCA 260, 267–8
Trump, Donald 45
Twitter 114–17
'two factor theory of work motivation' 2

unconventional methodology
  analysis 5, 20
  challenge of novelty 246–51
  data collection 20
  data sources 5, 19, 278–9
  definition 4–6
  developments 278
  gap with established methodology 246
  importance 1–2, 277, 285–7
  invitations 13–15
  and mainstream methodology 4–6, 15–19
  in organization and management research
    2–4
  research design 20
  and a sociomaterial approach 233
unemployment rates 71
United States, public archives 71
Unobtrusive Measures (Webb) 64–5
unobtrusive methods
  caveats in using 77–80
  data sources 66–8
  ethical issues 79–80
  innovations 64–5, 80
  measurement validity 78–9
  new 68–77, 69t
  propitious time for 66–8
  reasons for using 65–6
  requisite expertise 77
  unconventional data source 279, 281–2
  value of new 65–6

validity
  experimental research external 152–3
  and legitimacy 158
Van Maanen, J. 56, 90, 213

variance approach *see* outcomes approach
    versus process approach
Venkatesh, S.A. 88–9
video diaries
  advantages and disadvantages 204–7, 205t
  benefits and challenges 193–4
  Digital Brain Switch project 194–204
  participant-led 190–2, 207
  pros and cons 204–7, 205t
  for reflection 206
  visual research methods 192–4, 280
video recordings 2, 75, 117–21, 190–4, 280
virtual ethnography 129
visual research methods 190–4

Wadhwani, R.D. 30–1
Waeger, D. 155
Walker, H.A. 158
Walking Dead, The (television series) 93
Webb, E.J. 64–5, 66, 68, 69t, 71, 72,
    74, 75
Weick, K.E. 50–1, 56, 86, 88
Wharton, Edith 51
Whiteman, G. 90
Wiles, R. 11–12
Willmott, H. 7–9
Wire, The (television series) 52–5, 57–8, 59,
    92, 279
Wogan, Terry 27
Wolpert, Louis 37
Woman's Hour 42
women, effect of institutionalization 154
Woolf, Virginia 46
Woolgar, S. 46, 55
Woolley, A.W. 76

Xenitidou, M. 11–12

Young, Kirsty 27, 30, 36
YouTube 117–21

Zelditch, M. 158
Zentner, M.R. 36–7
Zucker, L.G. 150, 153